AMERICANS INTERPRET
THEIR CIVIL WAR

A great literature will yet arise out of the era of those four [Civil War] years, those scenes—era compressing centuries of native passion, first-class pictures, tempests of life and death—an inexhaustible mine for the histories, drama, romance, and even philosophy, of peoples to come—indeed the verteber of poetry and art (of personal character too) for all future America—far more grand, in my opinion, to the hands capable of it, than Homer's siege of Troy, or the French wars to Shakspere.

Walt Whitman, 1879

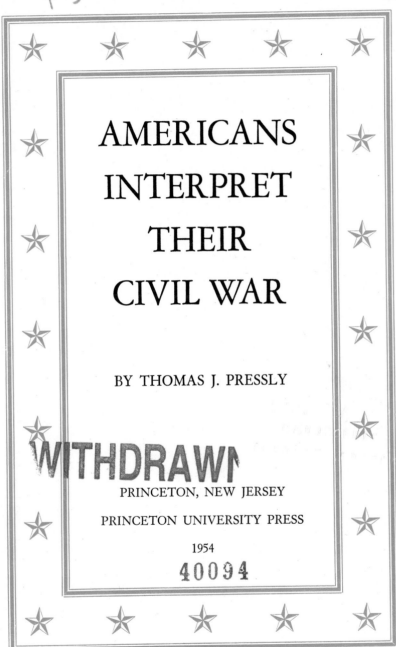

AMERICANS INTERPRET THEIR CIVIL WAR

BY THOMAS J. PRESSLY

PRINCETON, NEW JERSEY

PRINCETON UNIVERSITY PRESS

1954

Printed in the United States of America by
Princeton University Press, Princeton, New Jersey

For: L.C.P.
T.J.P. II
S.C.P.
B.B.P.

And the Memory of:
J.W.P.

★ PREFACE ★

Works of art, one observer has declared, change their nature as the times change, and he has cited the *Mona Lisa* as an example.[1] Leonardo's painting was praised by the artist Vasari in the sixteenth century for its realism in faithfully depicting a natural object to such a degree that the observer could almost believe that he saw the beating pulses and the living eyes of the subject. Three centuries later, in the golden glow of romanticism, Walter Pater saw in the painting not realism but practically the reverse—mystery and symbolism, an "unfathomable smile," a face on which was deposited "strange thoughts and fantastic reveries and exquisite passions." At a yet later date, Sigmund Freud perceived something different still, perceived in *Mona Lisa* a revelation of the intimate subjective life not only of the artist but also of the artist's mother. Freud explained that since the mother of Leonardo was not married to his father, she was forced to "compensate herself for not having a husband"; like "all ungratified mothers she thus took her little son in place of her husband, and robbed him of his virility by the too early maturing of his eroticism." On this basis, Freud wrote that the well-known smile of the painting was a reproduction by Leonardo of the "blissful and ecstatic smile" which "had once encircled his mother's mouth in caressing." After surveying such divergent appreciations of the *Mona Lisa* over a period of five centuries, the observer in question concluded that while the painting may not have changed in name or in physical characteristics, its content or nature did vary over the years as the interests or preconceptions of its observers varied.

Although an analogy between the appreciation of works of art and the understanding of history may not be an exact one in every respect, historians can nevertheless recognize in the varying critical estimates of the *Mona Lisa* a phenomenon familiar in their own studies. Historical events, just as Leonardo's famous painting, have not had a fixed, unchanging meaning to onlookers over the centuries, but have frequently appeared in different lights to successive individuals and eras. Thus, historical understanding has been "rel-

[1] George Boas, "The Mona Lisa in the History of Taste," *Journal of the History of Ideas*, I, 207-224 (April 1940). All quotations in this paragraph are taken from this article.

ative," in this sense of the word, rather than "absolute" or completely "objective" to the particular individual in question. The "relativism" of historical understanding is especially noticeable when historians are concerned, as they generally are most of the time, with the problem of "causation" in history—the problem of determining what forces and factors were responsible for, or led to, or caused a certain historical situation or action. When an individual states that a certain group of factors caused an historical event (as, for example, when Mark Twain wrote that Sir Walter Scott was in large measure responsible for the Civil War in the United States), he has selected certain facts from the many available and has arranged them into a particular pattern. The writings of most historians demonstrate that they, like laymen, regard this process of selecting and arranging facts into a cause and effect relationship as a fundamental feature of historical understanding. And yet it is precisely these arrangements of facts, these interpretations of history, which frequently vary most from one age to the next and which are thus most "relative."

These related problems of "relativism" and "causation" in the understanding of history provide one focus for this study of changing attitudes toward the causes and character of the American Civil War. That conflict is the classic example of a major event in the history of the United States which has been explained and interpreted in a wide variety of quite different ways. The changing attitudes toward the Civil War serve as a specific case history which illuminates to some extent the problems of relativism and causation. This case history reveals the change in historical interpretation from one individual writer of history or group of individuals to another; it reveals, in my opinion, that since the writer of history is himself a part of the historical process, his own personal background is a factor in his understanding of history. Likewise, the attitudes toward the Civil War of historians writing in a particular chronological era seem to have reflected in some fashion the interests and the outlook of that period; as these interests and that outlook changed, so have interpretations of the causes of the Civil War. Changing interpretations may not exactly have followed the election returns, but one can at least discover certain correlations between the changing interpretations and the social, intellectual, and economic developments of an historical era.

At the same time, it seems to me that this study demonstrates that "relativism" in the understanding of history operates within certain limits—the limits imposed by the facts of history-as-actuality (it is this, of course, which distinguishes historical understanding from historical fiction, which knows no such limits). To reduce it to absurdity, no one has suggested or can rationally suggest that the Civil War was caused, entirely or in part, by the development of monastic reforms in medieval Europe or by the perfection of the atomic bomb. Instead, one is impressed by certain continuities in explanations of the Civil War from 1861 to the present. For example, the institution of slavery has consistently occupied a place in many (although not all) interpretations of the causes of the Civil War; the nature of the institution of slavery in the Old South and its precise role as a cause of conflict and war have been defined and described in various ways, but, nonetheless, many writers of history have demonstrated their belief that one cannot explain the coming of the Civil War without taking some notice of this institution. (Even the interpretation of the painting *Mona Lisa*, it has been suggested, is limited by the fact that it depicts a woman, and can thus be given only those attributes which can be ascribed to a woman.) Historical understanding, it would seem, reflecting the complexity of history itself, is characterized both by "relativism" and also by "objectivity" and continuity.

This study has in addition a second focus, more closely related to the mainstream of the historical experience of the United States —the focus upon the meaning of the Civil War to successive generations of Americans. From its outbreak in 1861 down to the present, the Civil War has consistently held the attention of many Americans. The continued appeal of Civil War themes in literature, in the theater, and in historical writing can be explained in part by the opportunity such themes have afforded, from the 1880's on, for escape from present reality into a past that was appealingly pictured as colorful and idyllic. But at least a part of the sustained interest in that era would seem to be due to the fact that the Civil War has appeared to later generations as one of the pivotal events in the nation's history, comparable to the Revolution of 1789 in

the history of France or the seventeenth century Civil War in the history of England. It has seemed to involve questions which go to the very heart of the national life: the relationship between the national government and the states or the geographical sections; the question of "majority rule" in a constitutional democracy, expressed through regular elections, as opposed to the "minority rights" of those who are dissatisfied with the decisions of the majority; the role of the Negro in American life; the question of what economic policies the national government should adopt.

Since the Civil War has seemed to involve vital issues of lasting significance, it has enlisted not only the interest of successive generations but also their loyalties and their emotions. The emotional and intellectual impact of the war upon the generation which fought it was summed up in 1884 by Oliver Wendell Holmes, Jr., (a veteran of the Union Army, three times wounded in combat) in the well-known observation that his generation had been

set apart by its experience. Through our great good fortune, in our youth our hearts were touched with fire. It was given to us to learn at the outset that life is a profound and passionate thing.[2]

A glance at the language of some historians of our own day who have sought to interpret the conflict of the 1860's will suffice to show how persistent are the emotions and loyalties touched with fire.

In 1939, for example, we find historian Frank L. Owsley criticizing the view of his fellow historian Dwight L. Dumond and relegating him to the "Holy Band" of pre-Civil-War abolitionists. A year later, historian E. Merton Coulter ascribed to Dumond "abolition doctrines polished up with modern American scholarship." In a similar vein, historian Robert H. Woody suggested in 1948 that historian Allan Nevins had "too long been under the spell of Horace Greeley and . . . [had] imbibed the spirit of the antislavery crusaders of the 1850's." On the other side of the controversy, historian Richard Hofstadter declared in 1944 that the writings of historian Ulrich B. Phillips represented "a latter-day phase of the pro-slavery argument."[3]

[2] *Speeches by Oliver Wendell Holmes* (Boston, 1918) 11.
[3] Frank L. Owsley, review of Dwight L. Dumond, ed., *Letters of James Gillespie Birney, 1831-1857*, in *The Journal of Southern History*, v, 263 (May 1939); E. Merton

This persistence of sharp controversy in interpreting Civil War issues would seem in itself to indicate that the war involved questions of enduring significance in the history of the United States. That these controversies were not simply feuds among intellectuals was suggested by the fact that, at the time when twentieth century historians were describing one another as abolitionists or defenders of slavery, the nation at large was divided over the status of the Negro in American life, and sectional and ideological minorities once more, as in the 1850's and 1860's, were splitting away from national political parties.

A final word concerning the study of changing interpretations of the causes of the Civil War: it has been a subject of speculation for many historians, and a few have investigated it systematically and in some detail. Three pioneering descriptions are noteworthy: D.W. Brogan, "Historical Revisions LIII—The Origins of the American Civil War," *History* (London), new series, xv, 47-51 (April 1930); Charles W. Ramsdell, "The Changing Interpretations of the Civil War," *The Journal of Southern History*, iii, 3-27 (February 1937); and Howard K. Beale, "What Historians Have Said about the Causes of the Civil War," Social Science Research Council Bulletin 54, *Theory and Practice in Historical Study* (New York, 1946) 53-102. I have derived profit from these three accounts, even when I have disagreed with some of the conclusions reached in them; I have not thought that these essays precluded the sort of investigation which I have undertaken.

This study, like other inquiries into the history of ideas, cannot and does not claim to be based upon research in literally all the possible sources, for changing attitudes toward the Civil War, as it is hardly necessary to state, are reflected in a multitude of sources. There are writings not mentioned in this study which might well be included, and there are individuals omitted who might well be discussed; if the topic is to be covered in one volume of this size, selection must be made from the copious available materials bearing on the subject. No such selection, presumably, will seem rea-

Coulter, review of Dwight L. Dumond, *Antislavery Origins of the Civil War in the United States*, in *The Journal of Southern History*, vi, 271 (May 1940); Robert H. Woody, "Ordeal of the Union," *The South Atlantic Quarterly*, xlvii, 389 (July 1948); Richard Hofstadter, "U.B. Phillips and the Plantation Legend," *The Journal of Negro History*, xxix, 122 (April 1944).

sonable and proper in all respects to all observers, and the reader is due an explanation of the particular selections which have been made here.

As the table of contents indicates, I have sought to portray the varying historical images of the causes and character of the Civil War which, in my opinion, have been most important in the United States from 1861 to the present. My research has emphasized primarily, although not completely, the writings of historians, since such writings seem in general to constitute the most direct, most complete, and most accessible statements of attitudes toward the past. This volume is limited to the United States (and to the writings of a few Americans published elsewhere), because I think that the study of changing interpretations of the American Civil War outside the United States is a separate and in many respects a different subject, despite some interrelations and similarities, from the one investigated here. Throughout, I have attempted to understand the ideas of individuals and the reasons for their appeal rather than to evaluate these ideas in terms of present-day knowledge. Because an idea seems demonstrably false today does not mean that it was not influential in 1861 or later.

Wherever possible, I have tried to indicate what seems to me pertinent information about the personal backgrounds of the individuals discussed in this book. In doing this, I do not wish to suggest, even by implication, that interpretations of history are "determined" by geographical, social, or other influences in the backgrounds of the persons in question; in some cases, to cite only one example, individuals with quite disssimilar geographical backgrounds have held similar ideas on the causes of the Civil War, and vice versa. The formulation of ideas and attitudes concerning history is, in my opinion, too complex a process and one subject to too many variables to be summed up in any simple deterministic formula or pattern. I do think, however, that a knowledge of the personal background of an individual is frequently of great value in understanding his interpretations of history, and this is the reason for my attempt to supply such information.

It would seem only fair, in turn, that I should furnish the reader with information concerning my own background. I was born in the western section of Tennessee, of a family whose members had supported the Confederacy, and I lived in both the western (Confederate and, later, Democratic) and eastern (Unionist and, later, Republican) sections of Tennessee until my college days. My undergraduate and graduate study was at Harvard, and since attending college I have lived in the South only for relatively short periods. I presume that my own interpretation of the causes and character of the Civil War is obvious throughout the book, although I have tried to keep it from obtruding into the narrative, and I have attempted also, most difficult of all tasks, to understand points of view with which I disagree. In the gradual formulation of my own outlook, I owe much to the influence of Professor Paul H. Buck in my years of undergraduate and graduate study. Professor Buck suggested the topic of this book, and his help, particularly in the earlier stages of my study of the subject, was of great value; I am deeply indebted to him for counsel and encouragement over a number of years.

I should like also to express my gratitude to several other individuals who have aided in the preparation of this volume. Professors Wesley F. Craven, Pieter Geyl, Eric F. Goldman, and W. Stull Holt each read all or most of the manuscript and advised me on many matters; because of their suggestions, the book is much better than it would otherwise have been. In the composition of my ideas on such broad topics as the nature of history, I have drawn upon conversations with Professor Gaudens Megaro extending over more than a decade; Professor Megaro has been, in addition, a constant source of aid from the inception of this study until its completion, and practically every page has been improved by his thorough and incisive criticism. Needless to say, the author alone is solely responsible for the views expressed in the following pages.

In preparing this book for the press, I was given substantial aid from the Agnes H. Anderson Research Fund of the University of Washington.

Finally, my wife, Lillian Cameron Pressly, and my mother, Belle Bittick Pressly, have contributed to the writing of this book in ways too numerous to mention, and for their help I am grateful.

THOMAS J. PRESSLY

University of Washington
Seattle, Washington
January 1953

☆ CONTENTS ☆

CONTENTS

CHAPTER ONE

"THE WAR OF THE REBELLION"

On Behalf of the Union
1861 to 1865

THE Confederate attack upon Fort Sumter on April 12, 1861, produced a swift and dramatic reaction in the nonslaveholding states.
A surge of patriotic feeling swept over those states, so widespread
and so intense that observers were astonished and somewhat awed.
In Boston, the scholar George Ticknor observed that the

heather is on fire. I never knew [he wrote on April 21, 1861] what a
popular excitement can be. Holiday enthusiasm I have seen often
enough, and anxious crowds I remember during the war of 1812-1815,
but never anything like this. Indeed, here at the North, at least, there
never was anything like it. . . . Business is substantially suspended. Men
think, wisely or unwisely, of the state of affairs, and not of much else.
The whole population, men, women, and children, seem to be in the
streets with Union favors and flags.[1]

The response in Boston was matched throughout the North. Immediately after the firing on Fort Sumter, the well-known German
immigrant Carl Schurz traveled by train from his Wisconsin
home to Washington, D.C., and then on to New York City. Everywhere along the route he saw the same tremendous uprising—
huge excited crowds, emotional speakers, and martial music.[2] Even
in the Midwest, where in some areas sympathy for the South had
been strong (and was to continue throughout the war), the same
type of enthusiasm could be found. Typical of many towns in that
section were the scenes at Galena, Illinois, where the citizens
locked up their stores and surged into the street; at a tumultuous
mass meeting in the courthouse, it was unanimously resolved "that
we will support the government . . . and having lived under the

---

[1] *Life, Letters, and Journals of George Ticknor* (2v., Boston, 1876) II, 433-434.
[2] Carl Schurz, *The Reminiscences of Carl Schurz* (3v., New York, 1909) II, 223-232.
A description of the upheaval in New York City, drawn from contemporary accounts,
can be found in Philip S. Foner, *Business & Slavery: the New York Merchants and the
Irrepressible Conflict* (Chapel Hill, N.C., 1941) chap. 16.

Stars and Stripes by the blessing of God, we propose to die under them!"[3]

Public opinion in the North, divided, confused, and uncertain since the election of Lincoln in November 1860 and the secession of the Southern states, was now changing in a spectacular fashion. The long period of drift and of hesitation was ended. The President issued a call for troops, and volunteers responded in numbers which taxed available facilities. Republicans, Democrats, and men of all factions were now to be seen shaking hands, and party differences seemed to be almost obliterated in the widespread agreement that the Union must be maintained.

Leading advocates of compromise with the Confederacy now became, overnight, champions of war; critics of Lincoln as different as former President James Buchanan (who had previously insisted that the federal government possessed no authority to coerce sovereign states) and the abolitionist leader Wendell Phillips (who had previously urged letting the slaveholding states secede in peace) now united behind the administration. The rush to defend the Union seemed to the historian George Bancroft the "sublimest spectacle" he had ever known.[4] There were undoubtedly persons in the nonslaveholding states who were hostile to the Lincoln administration, but, as Carl Schurz noted, they either kept silent in the spring and early summer of 1861 or were hardly audible in the midst of the "patriotic storm."[5]

It was during this initial drive to uphold the flag that supporters of the federal government first formulated and gave expression to their opinions on the nature and the causes of the struggle which now engulfed them. The attack upon Fort Sumter had reduced all the many and diverse questions in dispute between North and South to the narrow, specific issue of upholding either the government headed by Lincoln or that led by Jefferson Davis. Upon this

[3] Lloyd Lewis, *Captain Sam Grant* (Boston, 1950) 398. For additional evidence of sentiment in the Midwest, see: Theodore C. Pease and James G. Randall, eds., *The Diary of Orville Hickman Browning* (2v., Springfield, Ill., 1927-1933) I, 462-464; Jesse Grant Cramer, ed., *Letters of Ulysses S. Grant to his Father and his Youngest Sister, 1857-1879* (New York, 1912) 25; Wood Gray, *The Hidden Civil War: the Story of the Copperheads* (New York, 1942) 51ff.; David Donald, *Lincoln's Herndon* (New York, 1948) 149.

[4] Bancroft to Dean Milman, August 15, 1861, in M.A. DeWolfe Howe, *The Life and Letters of George Bancroft* (2v., New York, 1908) II, 138.

[5] Schurz, *Reminiscences*, II, 231-232.

question individuals were now forced by events to take a stand, and in this process certain attitudes toward the war rapidly crystallized among Unionists.

In taking their stand, few individuals acted in a more significant fashion than did two important political figures in the North, Senator Stephen A. Douglas of Illinois and Edward Everett of Massachusetts. Senator Douglas furnished one of the most important demonstrations of bipartisan support of Lincoln in the nonslaveholding states at the beginning of the war. The most popular leader of the "opposition" (Democrat) political party, Douglas had long been an opponent of Lincoln and of the Republicans; as Presidential candidate of the Northern wing of his party in the election of 1860, he had been Lincoln's chief rival in the popular vote. After the Fort Sumter assault, however, he became one of the most enthusiastic defenders of the administration; soon, with Lincoln's approval, he was on his way from Washington to the Midwestern states to insure aid from the Democrats of that region for the war policy of the Republicans.[6]

Speaking before wildly enthusiastic audiences in Ohio, Indiana, and Illinois, Douglas appealed for unity behind the administration on the ground that the Confederacy was waging a "war of aggression" against the "Government established by our fathers."[7] He blamed the conflict directly upon Southern leaders who had plotted together to break up the Union and had used the slavery question and the election of Lincoln as pretexts to that end. "The present secession movement," he told an audience of ten thousand persons at Chicago, "is the result of an enormous conspiracy formed . . . by leaders in the Southern Confederacy more than twelve months ago."[8] In this crisis Douglas called upon Democrats and Republicans to put aside partisanship, for there were now "only two sides to the question. Every man must be for the United States or against it. There can be no neutrals in this war; *only patriots—or traitors.*"[9] (How effective Douglas's words could be may be

[6] Gray, *Hidden Civil War*, 58-59; George Fort Milton, *The Eve of Conflict: Stephen A. Douglas and the Needless War* (Boston, 1934) 545-546.

[7] See in particular Douglas's speech before the Illinois Legislature on April 25, 1861 (printed in the *New York Daily Tribune*, May 1, 1861), and his speech at Chicago on the night of May 1, 1861 (printed in the same newspaper, June 13, 1861).

[8] *New York Daily Tribune*, June 13, 1861.   [9] *ibid.*

judged from the actions of members of the Illinois Legislature. After Douglas's speech before that body, the legislators stopped their squabbling over a militia bill, and, after passing the measure, enlisted themselves as a company in the state militia.)[10]

The position of Douglas was paralleled by that of Edward Everett. In contrast to Douglas, the Democrat and the champion of the Midwest, Everett had always been identified with Massachusetts and with the conservative wing of the old Whig Party.[11] His career had been distinguished: Congressman, Senator, Governor of Massachusetts, President of Harvard, Minister to Great Britain, and Secretary of State. In the late 1850's, he had emerged as a spokesman for cautious, conservative men in all sections of the country who had sought to abate the conflict between North and South by ignoring it (and to his brother-in-law, Charles Francis Adams, he had seemed overly solicitous of Southern feelings). Such cautious men had opposed Lincoln and the Republican Party, and Everett, as Vice-presidential candidate of the Constitutional Union Party in the election of 1860, had been one of their leaders. But the firing on Fort Sumter galvanized him into immediate and active support of the President. From Portland, Maine, to Dubuque, Iowa, Everett, the mid-nineteenth-century oratorical spellbinder *par excellence*, carried on a crusade for the Union in long flowery addresses; early in the war he delivered one of his famous orations, "The Causes and Conduct of the Civil War," sixty times, in fourteen states, within eight months.

In most respects Everett agreed with Douglas. Southerners, particularly "Southern disunionist leaders," he told a throng which packed the Academy of Music in New York City on the Fourth of July, 1861, had forced this war upon the country. By contrast, the Union adherents were fighting for "the great inheritance of constitutional freedom transmitted from our revolutionary fathers"; their cause was that of republican institutions everywhere.[12] Unlike Douglas, however, Everett insisted that Southern grievances

[10] Gray, *Hidden Civil War*, 59.

[11] Paul Revere Frothingham, *Edward Everett, Orator and Statesman* (Boston, 1925) *passim*.

[12] This Fourth of July address was reprinted in numerous places and was widely circulated in pamphlet form. It can be found in Frank Moore, ed., *The Rebellion Record* (12v., New York, 1861-1871) I, Doc. Pages 5-46.

centered on issues related to the institution of slavery. On this question, above all, Southerners seemed to him the aggressors, because they had deserted the antislavery views of the Revolutionary generation and now defended the institution as a positive good. But, other than the emphasis upon slavery, Everett's views were fundamentally quite similar to those of Douglas, and they led him to the same conclusion: he urged that all men, whatever their past differences, should now come "to the rescue of the country."

While representative political leaders such as Douglas and Everett were so energetically defining their position in the spring and early summer of 1861, so also were other prominent individuals in the Union states.[13] The North's eminent historians, John Lothrop Motley, George Bancroft, and Francis Parkman, all made known in the early months of the war their views on the nation's crisis. Experienced in chronicling the wars of other lands or eras in their volumes, these men were faced in 1861 with a contemporary conflict which involved their own country and which had burst into flame before their own eyes. Their initial impressions of the origin and nature of the war, expressed in public and private letters, reveal sentiments strikingly similar to those which were being pronounced on the platform to cheering throngs by Douglas and Everett.

John Lothrop Motley was in England when the war began; there, just as in the United States, his *Rise of the Dutch Republic*, published in 1856, had won him a wide following among both scholars and the reading public. Immediately becoming an ardent advocate of the Union cause, he was disturbed over what seemed to him a lack of understanding in England regarding the true nature of the American conflict. In a long letter to the London *Times*, published late in May 1861, he sought in particular to combat the idea popular in England that the secession movement was

[13] Politicians representing many shades of opinion passed in July 1861, by an overwhelming vote, a joint resolution by the two houses of Congress declaring "That the present deplorable civil war has been forced upon the country by the disunionists of the Southern States now in revolt against the constitutional Government. . . ." This resolution was introduced in the House of Representatives by John J. Crittenden of Kentucky, longstanding champion of compromise between North and South, and in the Senate by Andrew Johnson of Tennessee—both of whom had remained loyal to the Washington government. Only two members voted against the resolution in the House and five in the Senate (*The Congressional Globe*, 37th Congress, 1st Session, 222-223, 257-265).

similar in nature to the American Revolution of 1776.[14] Motley specifically reaffirmed the principle under which the American colonists of 1776 had acted—the inalienable right of revolution. But the Confederate States, he contended, had claimed, not this eternal right, but rather that of constitutional secession. Motley found no justification for secession either in the Constitution of 1787 or in the history of the United States. The action of the Southern states was rebellion, pure and simple. These states had not revolted against the acts of a tyrannical government; nor had they raised a humanitarian standard in a declaration of independence; instead, they had rebelled because of a perfectly constitutional election, and they had based their new confederacy upon the institution of human slavery.

Shortly after Motley's communication to the *Times*, George Bancroft, in the eyes of his contemporaries the country's most distinguished historian, discussed the causes of the war in a long letter to an English friend.[15] Good republican that he was, Bancroft sought to make clear to his friend in monarchical England that the American conflict had come about through no defect in republican principles. According to him, slavery, an antirepublican institution, was the basic cause of the war. The desire to obtain land in and around the Caribbean for a "slave empire" had prompted certain leading Southern politicians to engage for over a quarter-century in a conspiracy to disrupt the government which they could no longer control. The doctrine of secession had been advocated in order to aid this purpose, and Bancroft held that secession was a principle which would have dissolved the country and society itself. He was confident that there were many Southern men (even in August 1861) who were Unionists and who disapproved of secession; the whole secession movement he thus

[14] *The Times* (London), May 23 and May 24, 1861. This letter was reprinted in pamphlet form in both England and the United States and was also published in Moore, *Rebellion Record*, I, Doc. Pages 209-219.

[15] Bancroft to Dean Milman, August 15, 1861, published (in part) in Howe, *Life and Letters of George Bancroft*, II, 133-143. Bancroft had been active in politics as a Democrat since the time of Andrew Jackson. He had been unsympathetic to slavery, but had supported Douglas in the election of 1860. After Lincoln's inauguration, Bancroft, like Everett, shared the rather widespread distrust of Lincoln's abilities. With the attack on Sumter, however, he became an ardent and unequivocal backer of the administration and remained so throughout the war; see Russel B. Nye, *George Bancroft: Brahmin Rebel* (New York, 1944) *passim*.

placed in what was to him the worst possible light—it was not a movement of the "people," but merely the result of a conspiracy of proslavery politicians. By contrast, Bancroft pictured the Union cause as one sustained by "the uprising of the irresistible spirit of the people in behalf of law and order and liberty."

Francis Parkman, of Boston's Beacon Hill, had never, before 1861, devoted much attention to contemporary issues, but he was as deeply moved by the war as Motley and Bancroft. Near-blindness and shattered health made physical participation of any sort in the conflict impossible, but in public letters to the *Boston Daily Advertiser* beginning in August 1861, he gave vigorous expression to his views on the war.[16] In these letters extending over a period of three years, Parkman denounced "southern treason," praised the North's fight against "incarnate wrong," and described the war as a contest between Southern "oligarchy" and Northern "democracy" (terms with which George Bancroft could have agreed, though Parkman's brahmin-Federalist outlook was a far cry from Bancroft's concept of democracy). How completely Parkman shared the feelings of his contemporaries in the opening months of the war was revealed in a passage from his letter of September 4, 1861:

Our own blood has risen in arms against us, and we grapple for life or death with a fraternal foe, the most restless and warlike of mankind; ambitious, aggressive, and now maddened with an insane hate.[17]

Motley, Bancroft, and Parkman, just as Douglas and Everett, reflected attitudes which had appeared rapidly and spontaneously in their section. Although all of them, except Douglas, happened to be from Massachusetts, their personal backgrounds were diverse, they had represented widely different shades of Northern opinion before the outbreak of hostilities, and their views on the war were shared by individuals from Maine to Minnesota. These early sentiments received their classic expression when President Lincoln presented to the nation his administration's official statement of the origin of the struggle. In a carefully prepared address to the special war session of Congress which convened on July 4, 1861,

---

[16] Mason Wade, *Francis Parkman: Heroic Historian* (New York, 1942) 354ff. Parkman's brother served in the Union armed forces and was held prisoner by the Confederates for a time.

[17] *ibid.,* 355.

he assumed the role of official historian. As the head of one of the belligerent governments (like Woodrow Wilson in his message to Congress on April 2, 1917, or Franklin D. Roosevelt in his radio address to the nation on December 9, 1941), Lincoln set forth an interpretation of the events leading to war which embodied the views common among his Northern constituents at the time.

Lincoln insisted, as did Douglas, Motley, and others, that the blame for beginning the war rested upon the Confederates, for they were the aggressors: they had fired the first shot.[18] But he absolved the great mass of the people of the Confederate States from the guilt of initiating war, and questioned whether in any state, except possibly South Carolina, there was a majority of the legally qualified voters in favor of secession. Not the Southern people, but their leaders, the "seceder politicians," were responsible for the war; these leaders had deluded their followers and had enticed them into rebellion against the established government—and Lincoln emphasized that the Southern movement was a "rebellion" and should be called by that name rather than by the word "secession." The doctrine of secession, that a state possessed the constitutional right to withdraw peacefully from the Union, was, he asserted, simply an "ingenious sophism" invented by the Southern leaders to disguise their schemes of treason and rebellion.

Lincoln took pains to combat this "ingenious sophism," which seemed to him to rest upon the premise that there was some "sacred supremacy" belonging to each state of the Federal Union. The American "Union," he sought to demonstrate, was formed by the thirteen colonies even before they had secured their independence from Britain, and was thus "older than any of the States, and, in fact, . . . [had] created them as States." While agreeing that the states possessed the rights and powers reserved to them in the Constitution, he insisted that secession was not one of these reserved rights. It was, instead, a principle of destruction upon which no government could possibly endure, including, he predicted, the one which the seceders themselves had claimed to set up.

Throughout the message, Lincoln stressed his belief that the

[18] The message is printed in John G. Nicolay and John M. Hay, eds., *Complete Works of Abraham Lincoln* (new and enlarged edition, 12v., New York, 1905) VI, 297-325.

issue involved in the war transcended the events of 1861, transcended even the fate of the United States, and involved the "whole family of man." This issue, he maintained in language similar to that he was later to use at Gettysburg, was whether a constitutional democracy, a "government of the people by the same people," could maintain itself against its own domestic foes. Why, he asked, had the adversaries of the Union in their declaration of independence omitted the phrase, "all men are created equal," which had appeared in Jefferson's declaration? Why had they in the preamble to their constitution omitted the phrase, "We, the People," which had appeared in the constitution signed by Washington? This war, Lincoln told the Congress, was essentially a people's contest; it was, on the Union side, a struggle to preserve in the world the government of Washington and of Jefferson, the government whose primary object was to "elevate the condition of men." The people must now teach men that what "they cannot take by an election, neither can they take . . . by a war"; they must now demonstrate that "when ballots have fairly and constitutionally decided, there can be no successful appeal back to bullets."[19]

Lincoln thus summed up the early attitudes which had emerged in his section in the first reaction to the Fort Sumter episode, and these attitudes were of great significance. The initial atmosphere of patriotic enthusiasm in which they had been formulated evaporated to a considerable extent as the fighting continued. Bitter opposition to Lincoln's conduct of the war arose.[20] In particular, the Emancipation Proclamation, extending the war aims to include

[19] *ibid.*, VI, 304, 320-322. Lincoln did not mention the institution of slavery in this message, but in both earlier and later speeches and writings he specifically stated that slavery was the root of the differences between North and South and the basic cause of the war. "You think slavery is right, and ought to be extended," he wrote in December 1860 to his friend Alexander H. Stephens, soon to be Vice-president of the Confederacy, "while we think it is wrong and ought to be restricted. That I suppose is the rub. It certainly is the only substantial difference between us" (*ibid.*, VI, 86). Later, in his second inaugural address, Lincoln said that everyone had known in 1861 that slavery was "somehow, the cause of the war" (*ibid.*, XI, 45; see also *ibid.*, VIII, 3, and VIII, 32). Yet Lincoln's words seldom carried self-righteous overtones. In his annual message to Congress on December 1, 1862, for example, he declared that the people of the South were no more responsible than the people of the North for the original introduction of slavery, and he added that it might not be "quite safe to say that the South has been more responsible than the North for the continuance of slavery" (*ibid.*, VIII, 120).

[20] See below, chapter three.

the overthrow of slavery in the South as well as the preservation of the Union, furnished an important issue upon which the administration was criticized. Lincoln himself in the summer of 1864 expressed grave doubt that his administration would be returned to office at the coming November election. But, despite the defections and the discouragement, the supporters of the Union were eventually victorious; and, among the Union men of that generation, the ideas and attitudes which had crystallized in the first few months of hostilities remained dominant throughout the conflict and were not modified in a fundamental fashion for many years thereafter. It was these initial opinions which were reflected in the first great wave of histories of the war—those composed by Unionist sympathizers while the fighting was in progress—and it was largely through these wartime histories that the early sentiments were systematically elaborated.

Hardly had the ladies and gentlemen of Washington completed their hasty retreat from the battlefield of Bull Run in midsummer 1861, when the opening volumes of a veritable torrent of histories of the war began to appear in the Union states. The Bancrofts, Motleys, and Parkmans of the North did not write these histories; nor were there in that section (fortunately or unfortunately) any "trained" historians in the modern sense of the word. Instead, the writers of the pro-Unionist histories published during the war made up a miscellaneous assortment. The largest group was composed of experienced authors who had already in the decade or so before 1860 won large audiences with their popular historical writings. Men such as Joel Tyler Headley, John S. Cabot Abbott, Robert Tomes, Charles E. Lester, and others were well known for their dramatic simplifications of history, usually in the form of biographies of such colorful personalities as Napoleon, Cromwell, or Richard "the Lion Hearted." Their works had often been mere compilations characterized by a sentimental moralizing tone, and they were scorned by the intellectuals of the day.[21] But they were

---

[21] Poe, for example, called Headley "The Autocrat of All the Quacks" (Frank Monaghan, "Joel Tyler Headley," *The Dictionary of American Biography*, VIII, 479-480) while Emerson, in describing Abbott's *Life of Napoleon*, remarked that it seemed "to teach that the great object of Napoleon in all his wars was to establish in benighted Europe our New England system of Sunday-schools" (Edwin P. Whipple, *Recollections of Eminent Men* [*With other Papers*] [Boston, 1886] 150).

men who could write two-volume "best sellers," and their hold on the popular taste was secure. Joseph Tyler Headley, for example, had published in 1846 a two-volume biography of Napoleon which by 1861 had gone into its fiftieth edition; in all, he wrote more than thirty works, and as early as 1853 his books had reached a total sale of two hundred thousand copies. Although there were few writers as prolific or as popular as Headley, there were others of the same general type; for such writers, the Civil War afforded a dramatic theme of unsurpassed public interest, and they did not neglect their opportunity.[22]

In addition to these established popular authors, however, a host of other Union sympathizers wrote histories during the war.[23] All in all, there were volumes by former clergymen, members of Congress, literary critics, a newspaper editor, the provost of a university, a doctor, and even by the man who had helped publisher Erastus F. Beadle "invent" the American dime novel, Orville J. Victor. (Victor, displaying ingenuity worthy of a Beadle editor, issued his history of the "Rebellion" in monthly installments, each of which sold for twenty-five cents; these were periodically collected and published in volume form.) Their political views were as varied as their occupations: included in their number were pre-war abolitionists, Republicans, "War Democrats" (i.e., Democrats who, like Douglas and Bancroft, upheld the war), and even supporters of the Union from the Confederate States, some of whom had owned slaves before the war. Their places of birth and residence ranged from Maine to the Mississippi. One could say without much exaggeration that in the Union states from 1861 to 1865, almost every man was his own historian.

All these Unionist writers of histories were, like Douglas and Lincoln, partisan advocates of a cause. They visualized history in

[22] Accurate figures of the sale of the wartime histories are not available, but apparently the two-volume histories by Headley (*The Great Rebellion*, 2v., Hartford, 1863-1866) and by John S. Cabot Abbott (*The History of the Civil War in America*, 2v., Springfield, Mass., 1862-1865) had particularly large sales; see Frank Luther Mott, *Golden Multitudes: the Story of Best Sellers in the United States* (New York, 1947) 321.

[23] The reasons advanced in 1863 by a young Boston lawyer, John C. Ropes, for writing and publishing a history while the war was in progress, and the opposing arguments of his friend in the Union Army can be read in *War Letters 1862-1865 of John Chipman Gray, Major, Judge Advocate, and John Codman Ropes Historian of the War* (Boston, 1927) 207-211, 217-220, 236-238.

terms which justified their own stand while discrediting that of their enemies. Furthermore, they wrote at a time when men were dying on battlefields from Pennsylvania to Texas. When they discussed the causes of the war, they were writing of matters of life and death, and it was not surprising that they exhibited the passions of wartime and that they wrote histories which were primarily tracts for the times. They had no elaborate theories of causation in history nor of the nature of truth. Living in an age which expressed itself freely in moralistic terms, they described the war from the standpoint of the unconditional rightness of their own side and the unconditional evil of their opponents. Theirs was a story, as J.S. Cabot Abbott, the writer of popular histories, observed, of "infamous crimes, and of noble virtues." Candor in writing history, Abbott added, did not "demand that one should so ingeniously construct his narrative, as to make no distinction between virtue and vice."[24] This spirit was characteristic of most of the wartime historians; therefore, despite their numbers and despite their varied backgrounds, their attitudes were similar, and their explanations of the coming of war usually varied only in detail.

The theme which dominated all the wartime histories was the conviction that the Confederates were responsible for the conflict. This idea was fundamental and all pervasive; it was the point of departure from which the Unionist accounts began, and it was the unshakable conclusion to which they all ultimately led. Just as it has been for the participants in many another struggle, the war guilt of the enemy was the key concept in Unionist thinking. Certain that Southerners had brought about the trouble, the wartime historians inevitably located the causes of the war in forces which had impelled the Southerners to act as they did. Southern ambitions, Southern institutions, Southern civilization—whatever the particular explanation, it was something Southern which had produced war.

The specific evidence of Confederate aggressiveness and guilt which seemed most conclusive to Union sympathizers was the assault upon Fort Sumter, which had so aroused the North in April 1861. Here, it seemed to Unionists, was indisputable and unan-

[24] Abbott, *History of the Civil War in America*, I, iv.

swerable proof that the Southerners had fired the first shot and had brought on the conflict. Just as the attack upon Pearl Harbor of December 7, 1941, served a later generation of Americans as a symbol of aggressive warfare, so did the Sumter episode serve the Unionists as a symbol of the belligerent Confederacy in the very act of inaugurating unprovoked war. The assault upon Sumter and the capture of the fort were reenacted in detail in most of the histories, and it was a scene which readily lent itself to exploitation by experienced writers of purple prose. No one expressed this Sumter symbolism of war guilt in more dramatic and moralistic language than the prolific and verbose Joel T. Headley. It was fitting, wrote Headley, "that a deed so monstrous as the commencement of Civil war should have been committed in darkness [i.e., before daybreak]. Treason shuns the light of day and even the Confederate conspirators, though steeped in crime, were in haste to begin their accursed work before the bright sun should rise to throw his light upon it."[25]

But in the wartime histories, as in the actuality of 1861, what gave meaning to Fort Sumter as symbol was the fact that the attack upon the fort was viewed as an assault upon the nation. The cannon fired upon Sumter, as one writer expressed it, was "that hostile voice speaking in thunder tones the declaration of the South to war against the life of the nation."[26] This, to the Unionists, was the fundamental aggression of the South, and this the essence of its war guilt. By the 1860's, the Northern states had experienced the growth of a nationalistic feeling of the type which became such a powerful force in Western civilization in the nineteenth century. This sentiment was not based upon legal arguments over sovereignty but upon the feeling of ordinary people for their "country" —a feeling whose strength was apparently not realized even in the North until the attack upon Fort Sumter.

[25] Headley, *Great Rebellion*, I, 55. For other typical descriptions of the bombardment of Fort Sumter, see: Abbott, *History*, I, 88; Thomas S. Goodwin, *The Natural History of Secession* (New York, 1864) 195; James W. Hunnicutt, *The Conspiracy Unveiled* (Philadelphia, 1863) 290. A Civil War equivalent of Franklin Roosevelt's designation of December 7, 1941, as a "date which will live in infamy" was Edward Everett's description of the day on which news of the attack on Sumter reached the North as a "day forever to be held in inauspicious remembrance."

[26] E.A. Duyckinck, *National History of the War For the Union, Civil, Military, and Naval* (3v., New York, 1861-1865) I, 121.

Such an emotion recognized only one country with its one flag and its government at Washington; allegiance to a rival sovereign within the territorial limits of the United States, such as a state of the Federal Union, was practically inconceivable and could only be interpreted as treason. One of the most emotional and powerful expressions of this nationalism was made by Edward Everett Hale in his story of the mental anguish of an individual who as a result of his own hasty action had become in truth a "Man Without A Country." Hale wrote this widely read story in specific support of the Union cause and first published it in 1863; although directed primarily against men like Clement L. Vallandigham, the Ohio Democrat, whom Hale considered sympathetic to the South, its condemnation of Confederates was explicitly set forth in terms of the North's nationalism. Speaking of Generals Braxton Bragg, P.G.T. Beauregard, and other Southerners who had left the armed forces of the United States to serve the Confederacy, Hale declared that they had

done all that in them lay that they might have no country,—that all the honors, associations, memories, and hopes which belong to "country" might be broken up into little shreds and distributed to the winds.[27]

A vital component of the North's nationalism, one which brought it added emotional and intellectual force, was the vigorous republicanism or "democratic faith" which was characteristic of the mid-nineteenth-century United States. The Unionist historians had reached maturity in an era when orators in the non-slaveholding states had extolled "Liberty *and* Union, now and forever, one and inseparable," an era in which periodic rebukes had been administered to the "emperors and priests" of Europe in the name of American ideals and institutions. In their ardent republicanism, they pictured the United States as an experiment, surrounded by a hostile world, in constitutional government by majority rule, the inspiration and hope of forward looking men all over the earth. Thus, in assaulting the nation, the Confederates seemed to most of the Unionist historians to be attacking the principles of representative government upon which the United States was founded, seemed to be traitors attempting to overthrow from

[27] *The Atlantic Monthly*, XII, 676 (December 1863).

within the world's one constitutional republic.[28] Some of the more extreme of the wartime historians described the conflict between North and South as the latest phase of the age-old struggle between "aristocratic usurpation" and popular rights. It was small wonder, they declared, that the traditional foes of liberty, the Tories and the reactionaries of the old world, hoped for the success of the Confederacy; smaller wonder yet that the Papacy, "the seven-headed beast, the decrepit giant," long leagued with civil despotism, should seek to aid the South.[29]

In the light of these nationalist sentiments of the Unionist historians, the justifications advanced by Southerners for their attack upon the constitutional republic could only seem incredible misinterpretations or deliberate attempts to confuse the issue. The Confederate contention, that the secession of states was perfectly constitutional and was clearly called for because of the oppression of the Southern states in the old Union, was met in the wartime histories in the same spirit of energetic unionism which had characterized the uprising of the North in April 1861. The common attitude in the North on the constitutional aspects of secession was most clearly stated by a professor at the Harvard Law School who was formerly Chief Justice of the New Hampshire Superior Court, Joel Parker. His conclusion, shared by all the Unionist historians, was that state secession was unconstitutional and was, in reality, simply the insurrection and rebellion of individuals against lawful authority.[30] Lincoln had described the argument for secession as an "ingenious sophism," and most of the Unionist historians shared the belief that this argument was advanced by the Confederates merely to give a show of legality to their obviously unconstitutional actions.

[28] These ideas are set forth in greatest detail in Thomas S. Goodwin, *The Natural History of Secession: or, Despotism and Democracy at Necessary, Eternal, Exterminating War* (New York, 1864), and Loring Moody, compiler, *The Destruction of Democratic Republicanism the Object of the Rebellion* (pamphlet, 3rd ed., Boston, 1863). The wording of the two titles is significant. See also Abbott, *History*, I, *viii*, 15; Horace Greeley, *The American Conflict* (2v., Hartford, 1864-1866) I, 558; Joel Parker, *The Character of the Rebellion and the Conduct of the War* (pamphlet, Cambridge, Mass., 1862) 40.

[29] Goodwin, *Natural History*, 228-229; Greeley, *American Conflict*, I, 503. The popular author J.S. Cabot Abbott asserted that the "leading rebels" wished to establish a monarchy in the South (*History*, I, 53).

[30] Joel Parker, *Constitutional Law: With Reference to the Present Condition of the United States* (pamphlet, Cambridge, Mass., 1862).

This interpretation of secession as rebellion was an important feature of Unionist thinking because it concisely defined the nature of the Southern war guilt and gave it a name: the Confederates caused the war by attacking the Union and their actions constituted treason and rebellion. So fundamental to Union sympathizers was this point of view that it was embodied both in the common and the official designation for the war in the North, and also in the name usually given it in the Unionist histories: "The Rebellion." The titles of the wartime histories, centering around the word "Rebellion," recorded the essence of the Unionist interpretation of the causes of the war.

It was a rebellion, moreover, which in the eyes of the Unionists was completely unjustified, for the federal government had not been tyrannical and Southerners had controlled it during most of its existence. Even if Southerners had legitimate grievances, the remedy lay in constitutional measures rather than in secession and war.[31] The Confederates were rebels, their rebellion had no justification—therefore *the rebels, and they alone,* as the provost of the University of Pennsylvania wrote, were "guilty of all the bloodshed and manifold woes entailed upon both South and North by this unnatural and deplorable war."[32]

Yet even when wartime passions are at their strongest, it can seem unjust to indict an entire people, and most of the Unionist historians (following in the footsteps of Lincoln, Douglas, and Bancroft) blamed the war not upon the total population of the seceded states but upon a small group of Southern "conspirators." They pictured the majority of the Southerners in 1860-1861 as ordinary law-abiding citizens, loyal to the national (Washington) government; the secession of the Southern states and the formation of the Confederacy were the work of a cabal of Southern politicians.

It was a common charge that these conspirators had deliberately

[31] "Never," wrote Orville J. Victor, the dime novel editor, "since the revolt of Lucifer has there been a more causeless rebellion against a justly-constituted and beneficent Government" (*The History, Civil, Political, and Military, of the Southern Rebellion* [4v., New York, 1861-1868] 1, 1). For expressions of similar sentiments, see: Moody, *Destruction of Democratic Republicanism,* 20; Moore, *Rebellion Record,* 1, *iv*; Parker, *Character of the Rebellion,* 14.

[32] Daniel R. Goodwin, *Southern Slavery in its Present Aspects* (Philadelphia, 1864) 312.

split the Democratic Party in 1860 to insure the election of Lincoln and thus to make secession more certain.[33] Centering their criticism upon Buchanan, the Unionists asserted that his ineptness as President was responsible for the ease with which the conspirators, working in Washington, had been able to consummate their plans. Almost without exception, Buchanan was described in hostile terms. To the caustic abolitionist John Smith Dye, he seemed a "worse traitor than Benedict Arnold," or simply "an imbecile traitor"; in the more moderate view of most of the historians, Buchanan was an ineffectual man whose lack of resolution and firmness had encouraged the seceders while discouraging loyal men. The comparison between Andrew Jackson, the strong President who had stamped out nullification in 1833, and Buchanan, the weakling who had allowed treason to flourish in 1860-1861, was frequently drawn. Such a vacillating President had offered no bar to the determination of the conspirators to break up the old Union before Lincoln took office.[34]

Conspicuous among those censuring the conspirators were not only Northerners but also Southerners who remained loyal to the Washington government. Many of these "Southern Unionists," like Senator Andrew Johnson of eastern Tennessee, came from a geographical and social background which set them apart from other Southerners, and they were particularly numerous in the mountainous areas of the South; frequently, but not always, they were former Whigs (John W. Burgess, the distinguished Columbia University professor, came from a Whig, slaveholding, Unionist family in Tennessee, and at the age of eighteen, in 1862, he left his home and joined the Union Army). Two of the most outspoken Southern Unionists were W.G. Brownlow of eastern Tennessee and James W. Hunnicutt of Fredericksburg, Virginia; both were na-

[33] William G. Brownlow, *Sketches of the Rise, Progress, and Decline of Secession* (Philadelphia, 1862) 158; Headley, *Great Rebellion*, I, 37-39; Parker, *Character of the Rebellion*, 19-20. Stephen A. Douglas and others had made this charge during the campaign of 1860, and both Edward Everett and George Bancroft had repeated it early in the war.

[34] For discussions of the activities of the conspirators during Buchanan's administration, see: Duyckinck, *History*, I, 37; T.S. Goodwin, *Natural History*, 194ff.; Headley, *Great Rebellion*, I, 37ff.; Robert Tomes and Benjamin G. Smith, *The War with the South* (3v., New York, 1862-1867) I, 37, 92. Various personal estimates of Buchanan can be found in: Abbott, *History*, I, 69; John Smith Dye, *The Adder's Den* (New York, 1864) 85, 111; Greeley, *American Conflict*, I, 95; Victor, *History*, I, 78.

tive Southerners and, before the war, both had been slaveholders, clergymen, and newspaper editors. After the outbreak of war, they both fled to the Union states and there found ample opportunity to publicize their opinions of the war. Southern Unionists were in demand as public speakers in the North, especially in the early years of the war. Brownlow proved to be so popular with Northern audiences that a Beadle dime novel was published about him, and a Philadelphia firm published a sheet music song entitled the "Parson Brownlow Quick Step."[35] Once they reached the Union states, both Hunnicutt and Brownlow quickly published accounts of the coming of the war.[36] Brownlow's volume sold a hundred thousand copies in three months after it was published in the summer of 1862; eventually, at least three hundred thousand copies of the book were sold, and it probably had the largest sale of any of the wartime histories.[37]

Brownlow and Hunnicutt, like the Northern Unionists, blamed Southern politicians for the war, asserting that the strife had been forced upon the unwilling Southern people by the fraud and violence of the rebel leaders.[38] Their denunciations of fellow Southerners were particularly violent. Both men were highly emotional and were wont to indulge in vituperation; in addition, they wrote with all the venom engendered by a "brothers' war" which, in their sections of the South, had set neighbors, and even members of the same family, in opposition to one another. They castigated the Southern conspirators as "bold, bad men," "perjured scoundrels," "aspiring demagogues and ambitious tyrants" who had successfully carried out their "deep, dark, and damnable conspiracy against the United States Government." According to them, the Confederacy which these conspirators had established was founded upon cruelty and upon the suppression of all civil liberties; their histories were filled with accounts of the persecution of Unionists by Confederates.

Only a few writers matched the Southern Unionists in acrimony,

[35] E. Merton Coulter, *William G. Brownlow: Fighting Parson of the Southern Highlands* (Chapel Hill, N.C., 1937) 208-246.

[36] James W. Hunnicutt, *The Conspiracy Unveiled* (Philadelphia, 1863); William G. Brownlow, *Sketches of the Rise, Progress, and Decline of Secession* (Philadelphia, 1862).

[37] Mott, *Golden Multitudes*, 309, 765-766.

[38] Brownlow, *Sketches, passim*; Hunnicutt, *Conspiracy Unveiled, passim*.

but the "conspiracy thesis" in some form or other was a well-nigh universal theme in the Unionist histories. In this fashion, the secession of the Southern states, the formation of the Confederacy, and the ensuing war were depicted as representing not the will of the Southern people expressed in free and fair elections but the diabolical schemes of a few clever politicians. This interpretation furnished the comforting assurance that the Union cause was in accord with the republican principle of majority rule. What has seemed to later generations a complex historical situation was thus explained by contemporaries (as is frequently the case in history) in the simple and easily understood terms of an intrigue of evil men.

In view of the general agreement among Unionist historians that the Confederates, particularly a few conspirator-politicians, were responsible for the conflict, the ultimate causes of the war were to be found in those factors which had motivated the secessionists to act as they did. In the early days after the firing on Fort Sumter, Stephen A. Douglas had explained the deeds of the conspirators primarily in terms of their personal ambitions; his viewpoint was shared by several, but not most, of the historians. A typical expression of this personal-ambition interpretation was made by Joel Parker, the Harvard Law School professor. The real cause of the war, he wrote in 1862, was the "inordinate political ambition of the Southern politicians." Seeing that they were about to lose power in the old Union, these men had determined to destroy it and to set up a new government which they could control; they had used the slavery issue simply as an excuse to fire the heart of the South. Historians who agreed with Douglas and Parker held that state sovereignty, the tariff, slavery, and like questions were only masks adopted by the secession leaders to hide their selfish desires for personal power.[39]

That the Southern conspirators were evil men with excessive ambitions was a common enough opinion among Unionist historians; yet the great majority of them, unlike Douglas and Parker, did not explain the coming of war solely in those terms. Beneath the personal desires of individuals, and underlying the secession

[39] Parker, *Character of the Rebellion*, 19-20, 32-33; Tomes and Smith, *War with the South*, I, 5-6; Brownlow, *Sketches, passim*.

conspiracy, most of the historians found that the one factor ultimately responsible for the war was the institution of slavery. In their view, it was slavery which fed the "lust of power" of the Southern conspirators; slavery was the "parent" of secession and of treason, and loyalty to slavery was the foundation of the loyalty of a Southerner to his state.[40] This assertion that slavery was in some way the ultimate cause of the war was not confined to the prewar abolitionists, who would naturally have been expected to hold such a theory, nor did it appear only after Lincoln's proclamation had made emancipation one of the war aims. (Everett and Bancroft, for example, had both been decidedly moderate on the slavery question before 1861; yet they had stated in the first few months of fighting that slavery had caused the war.) Rather, it was to be found in most of the Unionist histories, and its prevalence can be judged from the fact that it was made not only by Northerners who were highly critical of the abolitionists of their section but also by the Virginia Unionist J.W. Hunnicutt, who had owned slaves until he fled the South.[41]

To these wartime historians, the institution of slavery was the cause of the war in the sense that it was the primary source of the differences between the South and the rest of the nation—irreconcilable differences which had existed long before 1861 and which were due ultimately to the South's "peculiar institution." Their views were similar to those expressed both by Lincoln in his famous "house divided" speech of 1858 and by Secretary of State William H. Seward in his equally well-known "irrepressible conflict" speech of the same year. Both Lincoln and Seward had stated that there were irreconcilable antagonisms between the Northern and Southern civilizations, and both had found the key to those antagonisms in the institution of slavery. Neither Lincoln nor Seward, it should be stressed, had said that armed hostilities were inevitable; both had declared that two ways of life so hostile could not be reconciled and that one must in some way finally prevail,

[40] John H. Aughey, *The Iron Furnace* (Philadelphia, 1863) 265-266; Greeley, *American Conflict*, I, 509.

[41] T.S. Goodwin, *Natural History*, 193ff., 210-211, 272; Hunnicutt, *Conspiracy Unveiled*, 276. For typical statements that slavery was the cause of the war, see: Abbott, *History*, I, iii-viii; Duyckinck, *History*, I, 6, 34-36; Joshua R. Giddings, *History of the Rebellion; Its Authors and Causes* (New York, 1864) viii; D.R. Goodwin, *Southern Slavery*, 311-312, 332.

but they did not say that it had to prevail by force of arms—"irrepressible conflict" did not necessarily mean "inevitable war."[42]

Whether the Unionist historians considered armed hostilities between North and South inevitable (a question which was to interest some twentieth-century historians) is not clear from their writings. It would seem that, in their opinion, the struggle had been precipitated in 1861 because Southern political leaders had refused to submit to the decision of a constitutional election and had led a rebellion against the federal government. Hence, war could presumably have been averted had Southern political leaders followed a different course. But most of the Unionist historians also viewed the war as the culmination of a long conflict growing out of fundamental dissimilarities between North and South due to the institution of slavery. Irreconcilable differences led to a "conflict"; that this conflict turned into armed hostilities was due primarily to the Southern conspirators.

Unionist historians made occasional mention of the tariff or other divergent economic interests of North and South, but the dissimilarities most of them emphasized were those arising from the moral or ideological conflict between a free and a slave society. Like Edward Everett, they held that the alleged grievances of the Southern states which had led to secession centered almost entirely around the slavery question; it seemed to them that the origin of all these grievances lay in the fact that (as Lincoln had stated in his letter of December 1860 to Alexander H. Stephens of Georgia) Southerners defended human slavery and sought to protect and extend it, while Northerners were opposed to the institution and sought to restrict it. While not claiming that the North's original aim in the war had been to destroy the institution of slavery, the Unionist historians definitely linked the Confederate cause inextricably with the institution. Human slavery, they maintained, was a Southern institution, the basis of Southern life, and in the last analysis it was to protect a society founded on slavery and to secure rights pertaining to slavery that the South had fought.

As proof that slavery was the foundation of the Confederacy,

---

[42] The text of the addresses by Lincoln and Seward can be found in: Nicolay and Hay, *Complete Works of Abraham Lincoln*, III, 1-15; George E. Baker, ed., *The Works of William H. Seward* (new edition, 5 v., Boston, 1884) IV, 289-302.

some writers, like the literary critic E.A. Duyckinck, cited the South Carolina Convention's justification of secession, which was devoted primarily to slavery. Many more, however, exploited to the full a portion of an address by the Confederate Vice-president, Alexander H. Stephens, which was ideally suited to their purposes. At Savannah, Georgia, in March 1861, Stephens, in explaining and defending the new Confederate Constitution, had stated that Thomas Jefferson and the leading men of the Revolutionary era had been mistaken in thinking that slavery was a violation of the laws of nature and, hence, immoral. Jefferson's ideas, said Stephens,

were fundamentally wrong. They rested upon the assumption of equality of races. This was an error. . . . Our new government is founded upon exactly the opposite idea; its foundations are laid, its cornerstone rests upon the great truth, that the negro is not equal to the white man; that slavery—subordination to the superior race—is his natural and normal condition.[43]

This famous "corner-stone" speech seemed to the Unionist historians conclusive proof, from the mouth of the Confederate Vice-president, that slavery was the basis of his government and that the moral and ideological conflict over human slavery was the root of the differences between North and South which had led to war.[44]

Believing that slavery was the ultimate cause of the war, some of the Unionist historians added slavery to the conspiracy thesis and ascribed the war to the machinations of a "slavepower conspiracy." George Bancroft had set forth this explanation in the first few months of the war, but it was primarily to be found in the histories written by men who (unlike Bancroft) had taken an advanced stand against slavery in the years preceding 1861.

The organized antislavery forces had long maintained, especially after the annexation of Texas in 1845, that a powerful conspiracy was at work to further the cause of slavery.[45] It was thus

[43] Stephens' speech is printed in Henry Cleveland, *Alexander H. Stephens, in Public and Private. With Letters and Speeches, before, during, and since the War* (Philadelphia, 1866) 717-729.

[44] For typical comments on Stephens' speech, see: Duyckinck, *History*, 1, 69-70; T.S. Goodwin, *Natural History*, 272; Victor, *History*, 1, 30-31.

[45] See Russel B. Nye, "The Slave Power Conspiracy: 1830-1860," *Science and Society*, x, 262-274 (Summer 1946).

an easy matter, after the attack on Fort Sumter, to blame the war itself on this slavepower conspiracy. The extremes to which this approach could be carried are evident in the history of the war by the abolitionist John Smith Dye. Dye's history (appropriately entitled *The Adder's Den: or Secrets of the Great Conspiracy to Overthrow Liberty in America*) was a vitriolic diatribe against the slavepower conspirators, and especially against the individual who, in Dye's opinion, had been their prime leader, John C. Calhoun. Calhoun, wrote Dye, "had a soul ever ready to betray human nature, with a heart as black as night"; he was the "deadly foe of the National government and peace of the country—the sworn enemy of Freedom, and champion of Slavery." The controlling influence of Calhoun and other proslavery leaders Dye found in practically every important action of the federal government in the forty years before the war. The annexation of Texas was a plot to get more slave territory; the passage of the Fugitive Slave Law of 1850 was a move to "appease the slavepower"; the administrations of Presidents Pierce and Buchanan were entirely dominated by the slavery forces (Dye called Pierce "President Jefferson Davis Pierce," or the "man of Sin"). The most sensational accusation made by Dye was that the conspirators (led by Calhoun until his death in 1850) had fatally poisoned Presidents William Henry Harrison and Zachary Taylor and had attempted, unsuccessfully, to assassinate President Andrew Jackson in 1835, President-elect James Buchanan in 1857, and President-elect Abraham Lincoln in 1861.[46] This war, Dye concluded, was begun and was being continued by "*those wicked traffickers in human flesh, the slaveholders,*" and, writing in 1864, he asserted that not until after the Emancipation Proclamation had been issued and Lincoln had removed the proslavery General McClellan did God bless the Union troops with victory in battle.[47]

Decidedly less extreme and less sensational accounts of the activities and influence of the slavery conspirators were given by Joshua Giddings, militant abolitionist Congressman from Ohio, and Horace Greeley, the widely known and influential editor of

[46] Dye, *Adder's Den*, 27-114. Similar charges were made by T.S. Goodwin in his *Natural History*, 255-257.
[47] Dye, *Adder's Den*, 117, 122.

the New York *Tribune.* Yet, in their volumes the entire history of the United States was still in essence the story of a long struggle between the forces of freedom and those of slavery. Like Dye, they ascribed the annexation of Texas and the Mexican War to the desires of the slavepower for more land, and they insisted that it had dominated the administrations of Presidents Pierce and Buchanan. The secession movement of 1860-1861 and the resulting war thus simply climaxed this long standing conspiracy of the slave interest which for seven decades, as Joshua Giddings wrote, had endeavored to make the government a "slaveholding oligarchy."[48]

While only a few of the Unionist historians traced out the operations of the "slavepower" in as great detail as Dye, Giddings, and Greeley, most of them were satisfied that the Confederate cause was linked to that of slavery and that slavery was the fundamental cause of the war. The war was thus more than a rebellion; it was a slaveholders' rebellion against the free institutions established by the South's own Jefferson and other Revolutionary leaders.

It was the defense, against this rebellion, of the free American nation, that, in the eyes of the Unionist historians, gave to the war its broad meaning and universal significance. Running throughout their volumes was the insistence that their cause involved principles which overshadowed the specific issues of the day and were of eternal importance. More was at stake than simply the tariff or other material interest of rival sections—free institutions were under attack from aggressive foes of liberty and their fate hung in the balance with that of the Union armies. Here were summed up all the basic features of Unionist thought about the war—the war guilt of the South for its rebellion, led by conspirators, against the free constitutional republic. Once again, it was Lincoln who, in the midst of war, gave unique and enduring expression to these widely held sentiments:

Four score and seven years ago our fathers brought forth on this continent a new nation, conceived in liberty, and dedicated to the proposition that all men are created equal. Now we are engaged in a great civil war, testing whether that nation, or any nation so conceived and so dedicated, can long endure.

[48] Giddings, *History of the Rebellion*, 459, and *passim*; Greeley, *American Conflict*, I, 142-150, and *passim*.

Generated in the first reaction to war, widely disseminated in the wartime histories during the years of fighting, the Unionist interpretations of the conflict were to be confirmed and strengthened in the minds of loyal supporters of the Washington government by victory in battle.

On Behalf of the Union
1865 to the 1880's

In the spring of 1865, victory finally came to the supporters of the Union. But their victory began amid sorrow, for within less than a week after the surrender of Lee's army, Abraham Lincoln was assassinated, and Northern rejoicing over the capitulation of the major Confederate fighting force turned into grief stricken mourning. Both the assassination of Lincoln and the fact of victory were important influences shaping the opinions of Union sympathizers concerning the war in the opening days of peace.

In a special train, Lincoln's body was carried seventeen hundred miles from Washington to New York to Albany to Chicago to Springfield. Walt Whitman described the tragic scene:

> *Over the breast of the spring, the land, amid cities, . . .*
> *Carrying a corpse to where it shall rest in the grave,*
> *Night and day journeys a coffin.*
>
> *Coffin that passes through lanes and streets,*
> *Through day and night with the great cloud darkening*
> *   the land,*
> *With the pomp of the inloop'd flags with the cities*
> *   draped in black,*
> *With the show of the States themselves as of crape-*
> *   veil'd women standing,*
> *With processions long and winding and the flambeaus*
> *   of the night,*
> *With the countless torches lit, with the silent sea of*
> *   faces and the unbared heads,*
> *With the waiting depot, the arriving coffin, and*
> *   the sombre faces,*
> *With dirges through the night, with the thousand*
> *   voices rising strong and solemn,*
> *With all the mournful voices of the dirges pour'd*
> *   around the coffin.*[49]

[49] Walt Whitman, "When Lilacs Last in the Dooryard Bloomed" (1865). For an account of the reaction to Lincoln's assassination, see Carl Sandburg, *Abraham Lincoln: the War Years* (4v., New York, 1939) IV, 298ff.

The assassination of Lincoln produced a deep emotional upheaval in the Union states, and thoughts of Lincoln's death occupied the minds of men to a remarkable degree.

It was soon known that the murder of Lincoln by Booth was part of a general plot which embraced an attempt upon the life of Secretary of State Seward and which was supposed to have included assaults upon other high government officials. At first, it was widely believed in the North that the leaders of the Confederacy were implicated in this plot. Orders for the capture of Jefferson Davis were dispatched, and President Andrew Johnson issued on May 2, 1865, a proclamation stating that

it appears from evidence in the Bureau of Military Justice that the atrocious murder of the late president, Abraham Lincoln, and the attempted assassination of the Hon. William H. Seward, Secretary of State, were incited, concerted, and procured by and between Jefferson Davis, late of Richmond, Va., . . . and other rebels and traitors against the Government of the United States.

Northern indignation focused on the President of the Confederacy, and its intensity can be estimated from the contemporary reactions of two Northerners who were to gain high distinction in intellectual circles, Lewis Henry Morgan, pioneer anthropologist, and Charles W. Eliot, soon to be named President of Harvard. When Davis was finally captured by Northern troops in 1865, Morgan urged that he be disfranchised and perpetually banished from the United States; Davis should be sent forth, said Morgan,

a sentenced and condemned criminal with the brand of Cain upon his forehead and representative at once of the conscious power, the mercy and the contempt of the American people. Shunned and despised by all honorable men, execrated by the many people whom he misled and betrayed . . . his punishment and disgrace and miserable future life will be a warning to future generations.[50]

Morgan's anger was more than matched in the outburst of Eliot when he learned of the assassination of Lincoln: "I hope Davis and as many of his *civil* advisers as can be caught will be hanged after trial."[51]

The evidence upon which Davis was accused in President John-

[50] Bernhard J. Stern, *Lewis Henry Morgan, Social Evolutionist* (Chicago, 1931) 38.
[51] Henry James, *Charles W. Eliot, President of Harvard University 1869-1909* (2v., London, 1930) I, 142.

son's proclamation was before long discredited, and the belief that important Confederates were linked to Booth's schemes soon died out. Yet, it was literally true, as Horace Greeley wrote in 1866, that "President Lincoln was the victim of a conspiracy of partisans of the Rebellion."[52] Who, asked a clergyman in Illinois on the Sunday following Lincoln's burial, "will be able to separate in thought the murder of the President" from Southern efforts to "murder the Union?"[53] Clergymen denounced before their congregations all Southerners for the tragedy in Ford's theater, and saw in it the Divine hand providentially removing Lincoln (whose own noble character failed to appreciate how evil the Confederates really were) in order that sterner hands might mete out justice to the South.[54] In the state of mind prevailing in the North at the end of the war, the assassination seemed to many Unionists final proof of the wickedness of the enemies they had fought for four years.

Now, it seemed, any story about Confederate iniquity was believable; now, some individuals in localities as separated as Detroit and North Colebrook, Connecticut, went so far as to agree with John Smith Dye's charges which, brought up to date, named Lincoln as the third President to fall a fatal victim to the slavepower conspiracy.[55] Disregarding such extreme sentiments, however, the murder of Lincoln seemed confirmation of the evil of rebellion and treason to Northerners of many shades of opinion, ranging all the way from Charles W. Eliot to the chaplain of the United States Senate (the Reverend Dr. E.H. Gray) to writers of popular history such as J.S. Cabot Abbott, E.A. Duyckinck, and Benson J. Lossing. Lincoln's assassination, in the words of these individuals, was "the crowning act of infamy in this wicked rebellion," the "embodiment of the dark spirit of the Conspirators against the Republic," the culmination of the treason which for so long had

[52] Greeley, *American Conflict*, II, 748.

[53] Jay Monaghan, "An Analysis of Lincoln's Funeral Sermons," *Indiana Magazine of History*, XLI, 38-39, 43 (March 1945).

[54] *ibid.*, 41-42; Paul H. Buck, *The Road To Reunion* (Boston, 1937) 10ff.

[55] Dye wrote that before the election of 1864 he had personally warned Lincoln of the assassinations of Harrison and Taylor at the behest of the slave interest by placing in his hands a copy of Dye's wartime volume, *The Adder's Den* (John Smith Dye, *History of the Plots and Crimes of the Great Conspiracy to Overthrow Liberty in America* [New York, 1865] 304-307). Monaghan reports that one clergyman in Detroit and another in North Colebrook, Connecticut, made charges similar to those of Dye in funeral sermons on Lincoln (Monaghan, "An Analysis," 39).

"deluged our land with blood." Here, wrote Eliot, balancing Confederate wickedness against its inevitable counterpart, Union righteousness, was the final proof that the Northern cause was a struggle of "humanity against barbarism."[56]

Intermingled with the grief of the Unionists, however, even while they were paying final homage to Lincoln, was exultation over victory in battle; even the loss of Lincoln could not obscure in the spring of 1865 the tremendous reality of a triumph gained after months and years of fighting. Just as indignation over the slaying of Lincoln burned the conviction of Southern wickedness into Northern opinion, so the contemplation of victory implanted deep in the Northern mind the assurance of Northern righteousness.

The manner in which the fact of victory was reflected in Northern opinion could be seen in the typical sentiments expressed by George Bancroft. Bancroft played a prominent role in the memorial services for Lincoln. Ten days after Lincoln's death, he delivered the oration of the day in New York City's Union Square to part of the multitude which, within the previous thirty hours, had paid their last respects to the President's remains. Less than ten months later, the historian delivered the official eulogy on Lincoln (as he had done twenty-one years before at the death of Andrew Jackson) before a joint session of both Houses of Congress attended by the President with his Cabinet, the Justices of the Supreme Court, and other dignitaries. Bancroft, it should be noted, was no more an extremist in the postwar North than he had been in the 1850's; he did not hold severe views toward the defeated South, and he favored the comparatively mild reconstruction policies of Andrew Johnson over those advocated by the "Radical" Republicans; in fact, his eulogy of Lincoln contained such praise for a lenient policy toward the South that it aroused the ire of Charles Sumner.[57]

[56] James, *Eliot*, I, 140. See also: Abbott, *History*, II, 596-597; Duyckinck, *History*, III, 625; Benson J. Lossing, *Pictorial History of the Civil War in the United States of America* (3v., Philadelphia, 1866-1868) III, 565; Sandburg, *Abraham Lincoln: the War Years*, IV, 391.

[57] Nye, *Bancroft*, 225ff., 234. The text of Bancroft's speech in New York is given in the *New York Herald*, April 26, 1865, and the address before Congress was published in pamphlet form: *Memorial Address on the Life and Character of Abraham Lincoln* (Washington, 1866).

Yet, however lenient were his views toward the South, Bancroft was a part of the victorious North, and he voiced the confident opinions of his section. In his message, both at New York and at Washington, there was a note of sorrow, and he acknowledged that the "wailings of the millions" accompanied Lincoln's body. Yet, overshadowing the note of sadness in his words was his powerful feeling of triumph at the outcome of the war. He described the victory of the North as the climax of a great moral drama. A confederacy with slavery as its cornerstone and supported by all the "worn out aristocracies of Europe" and even by the "Pope of Rome" had challenged the republic of the new world in a life or death struggle. But working in harmony with the moral laws of God, Abraham Lincoln and the people of the Union states had overcome the forces of evil and had won their battle for "freedom itself." All the questions in doubt during the war had been resolved in a satisfactory manner: slavery was destroyed, the republic was preserved, and the principles of constitutional government were vindicated. The contemplation of this victory gave unshakable assurance of the righteousness of the Northern cause. "Heaven," Bancroft declared triumphantly, "has willed it that the United States shall live."[58]

This was the dominant mood among the supporters of the Union in the opening months of peace: confident assurance of the evil of their late foes and of their own virtual faultlessness. The victorious Unionists of 1865 would have been less than human if their triumph of arms had not strengthened their belief in the rightness of their opinions; yet this feeling imparted to their discussions of the war a tone of moralizing self-righteousness. The bitter passions and memories remaining from wartime now were transformed into righteous indignation. Now the causes of the war were to be studied for the moral lesson they taught, and to many Unionist historians that lesson was essentially a reminder to future generations concerning the wages of sin: for its own protection, posterity was to be left a record of the manner in which the forces of darkness had attempted, unsuccessfully, to destroy the best government in the world with the purpose of erecting a new nation founded upon slavery. After 1865, Unionists explained

[58] *New York Herald*, April 26, 1865.

the coming of the conflict in essentially the same manner as they had during the war years, but now their thinking was permeated with this added conviction of rectitude. Treason, Andrew Johnson had declared shortly after becoming President, must be made odious; in a similar spirit the Unionists interpreted the causes of the war for many years after Appomattox.

In comparison with the great number of histories published during the war by authors with a large popular following, few volumes by such authors appeared after the fighting ceased. Perhaps this was due to a revulsion from wartime themes on the part of the reading public and a consequent drying up of the sales market for war books.[59] Whatever the reason, most of the popular historians of wartime concluded their narratives in final volumes issued a year or so after 1865. A few of them made periodic revisions for several years to keep their works up to date with postwar events. Only a few established popular writers began the publication of a history in the decade after the war's end, and of these few the best known was Benson J. Lossing.

Lossing was similar in background to J.T. Headley and J.S. Cabot Abbott. He had won a wide reputation with his *Pictorial Field Book of the American Revolution*, published in the 1850's; eventually he wrote more than forty volumes of popular histories. His opinions on the Civil War illustrated in particular the impact of victory upon Unionist attitudes. Lossing had traveled in the South after the war ended, visiting the memorable scenes and gathering material for his history both from the Federal occupying forces and from former Confederates. He could write in moderate terms, urging that there be forgiveness instead of strife now that the Union had been preserved.[60] But Lossing, spokesman of the victorious North, also wrote, as he confessed, with a "consciousness of fidelity to the laws of truth and righteousness," and in the light of these "laws" he could see clearly (as could so many in his section) that the late war had been a struggle between "wrong and

[59] The most recent and most thorough study of the sale of books in the United States lists six histories of the Civil War as "best sellers" or "better sellers" in the years from 1861 through 1866, and none in those categories after 1866 (Mott, *Golden Multitudes*, 309, 321).

[60] Benson J. Lossing, *Pictorial History of the Civil War in the United States* (3v., Philadelphia, 1866-1868) I, 4.

right in their broadest and most conspicuous aspects." At the very beginning of his history he explained to his readers why they would find so much space devoted to the Southern conspirators: not in an unworthy spirit of partisanship to keep alive animosities, but so that "posterity may know, and profit by the knowledge" of the evil of the rebellion which the conspirators had led to extend slavery and to destroy republican government.[61]

Perhaps the clearest indication of the spirit dominant throughout Lossing's three volumes is to be seen in the evaluation of the actions of Robert E. Lee. The Confederate general was singled out for particular condemnation, presumably on the grounds that censure of the South's hero was in effect censure of all Confederates. After remarking on the ease with which Lee had been "seduced" from allegiance to his flag in 1861, Lossing stated that Lee's farewell address to his troops was one which no "right-minded and right-hearted man would care to imitate," for it told Southern soldiers that they had done a patriotic act in trying to destroy the republic. Lee was consistently pictured as the man who for four years had sought to destroy his government and "to build on its ruins a hideous empire founded upon human slavery."[62] Along such paths did the "laws of truth and righteousness" lead the thoughts of the victorious Unionists in the late 1860's.

At approximately the same time that Lossing's volumes reached the public, there appeared another three-volume history, by John W. Draper, which was one of the most significant and revealing expressions of Northern sentiment in the decade after the fighting ceased. Draper was known to his generation as a college professor, an author on scientific topics, and a trained scientist who had made important investigations in the fields of chemistry, photography, and telegraphy.[63] Born in England, he had lived for a few years in the South before settling in New York City in the late 1830's; although he had been a firm supporter of the Union cause (and two of his sons served as surgeons in the Union Army), he never

[61] *ibid.*, III, 4, 613; I, 4.

[62] *ibid.*, I, 420-423; III, 558-559, 601-604.

[63] Donald Fleming, *John William Draper and the Religion of Science* (Philadelphia, 1950) *passim*; Donald E. Emerson, "Hildreth, Draper, and 'Scientific History,'" in Eric F. Goldman, ed., *Historiography and Urbanization: Essays in American History in Honor of W. Stull Holt* (Baltimore, 1941) 153ff.

played a prominent part in political affairs or sectional disputes. Draper's *History of the American Civil War* was the first such account by a scholar, and it was written with the avowed purpose of discussing the causes of the struggle in a fashion which would soften the bitter feelings between North and South and hasten the return of more cordial relations. If individuals of North and South understood that the war was a product of such natural forces as climate at work over many years, they would, on both sides, Draper hoped, lose their harsh opinions of their former foes.[64] If moderate opinions on the war were to be found at all among Unionists in the 1860's, surely they would be expressed by this scientist who believed that his interpretations would promote the reconciliation of the sections.

In some respects, Draper's views were notably moderate. His *History* explained the war ultimately in terms of climate, a natural force which was responsible for all the differences between Northerners and Southerners, and it was characterized by the absence of personal bitterness against individual Southerners. Similarly, it contained statements to the effect that both North and South were "guilty" for their participation in the war, and that in such controversies each party might conscientiously feel that it was right.[65] But such sentiments as these only served all the more to accentuate the degree to which wartime attitudes had persisted and had been strengthened in the mind of this Unionist scholar.

To Draper, as to many of his fellow Unionists, the study of the coming of war was an occasion for moralizing upon the evil which the Southerners had brought upon the land; the causes of the war were to be recounted to posterity in order that such evil might henceforth be guarded against and prevented:

If in the future there should be any one who undertakes to fire the heart of his people, and to set in mortal battle a community against the nation, let us leave him without the excuse which the war-secessionist of our own time may not unjustly plead, that he knew not what he did.[66]

Underneath the sentiment of leniency for the "war-secessionist,"

[64] John W. Draper, *History of the American Civil War* (3v., New York, 1867-1870) I, *iii-iv*.
[65] *ibid.*, I, 21-24, 100-101, 339-341, 438ff., 566-567.
[66] *ibid.*, I, 567.

lay Draper's unquestioned and apparently unconscious conviction that the Southern "war-secessionist" was solely and completely to blame for the struggle and, hence, alone needed to be "excused." Starting from such premises, Draper's explanation of the war's causes contained most of the familiar elements which characterized the views of ardent Northern partisans. Although "climate" was the factor ultimately responsible for the conflict, Draper clearly placed the guilt in an immediate sense upon a conspiracy of Southern leaders ("a conspiracy against the nation more audacious than that of Cataline") who wished to continue their power and profits. He linked the Southern position to slavery and described the activities of a "Slave Power." Finally, he summed up his explanation of the coming of war in 1861 with a discussion of "the Southern oligarchy—a most atrocious tyranny":

For more than thirty years that oligarchy had been training itself to hate the beneficent Republic, and in a frenzy had resolved to establish in its stead a slave empire—a vast and fantastic conception, a dark nocturnal dream.[67]

The significance of Draper's opinions is that they apparently represented not the views of an extremist minority but attitudes on the war which were widely held throughout the North in the 1860's and the 1870's. Draper's volumes were not a profitable publishing venture, but even individuals who considered the scientist naïve in his attempt to explain human actions in terms of such natural "laws" as climate could still commend his ideas on the war. An anonymous reviewer of Draper's *History* in *The Nation* in 1867, for example, was critical of what he called the volume's "puerile generalizations" concerning the effect of climate upon men's actions; but he had nothing but praise for the author's interpretation of the causes of the war. Draper's "sketch of the events which led to the war," wrote this reviewer, "and his summing up of the Northern and Southern sides of the controversy, are models of calm, perspicuous, and judicial statements. He is evidently exceedingly fair-minded."[68]

There is no reason to doubt the sincerity of either Draper or Lossing when they urged reconciliation and mutual "forgiveness"

[67] *ibid.*, III, 432. See also: I, 28ff., 339, 493, 523, 560; III, 600-601, 635ff.
[68] *The Nation*, V, 208 (September 12, 1867).

for North and South. But both men demonstrated in their writings attitudes toward the war among the victorious Unionists of the 1860's which (matched by similar partisan attitudes among the defeated Confederates) served as a barrier to genuine reconciliation or forgiveness.

Draper was the only scholar to publish a history of the Civil War in the decade after Appomattox, and Lossing was one of the few popular authors to do so. In the absence of accounts by scholars and popular authors, the principal writings on the causes of the war were to be found in the memoir-histories of men who had taken a leading role in the events of the war era. Prominent among these memoir-histories were volumes written by leaders of the extremist antislavery movements.

If a popular historian like Lossing, and if Northern moderates like Eliot, Bancroft, and Draper, received corroboration for their opinions as a result of the North's victory, so to an even more marked degree did those individuals who had taken a vigorous stand against slavery in the years before the war—the abolitionists and the original "free-soilers" of the 1840's. Before the war, they were frequently in the position of an unpopular minority in their section, and some of the abolitionists had suffered persecution to the point of serious physical violence. But, during the war, emancipation ("warranted," as the Emancipation Proclamation declared, "by the Constitution upon military necessity") had been adopted by the Lincoln administration as one of the war aims, thereby linking slavery with the rebellion; in 1865, the institution of slavery was abolished by constitutional amendment. There was opposition in the North, but these measures apparently had the support of majority opinion. Moreover, the course of events in wartime, as frequently happens, tended constantly to push men into a more extreme position than they had occupied at the outbreak of hostilities. In the great upheaval of Reconstruction, Northerners supported measures toward the South and toward the Negro which had received little or no popular backing in 1861. These developments had their effect upon interpretations of the war's causes, and already by 1865 Northern opinion, as its reaction to the assassination of Lincoln demonstrated, was much more receptive to tales of the "slavepower" and of its evil activities than formerly.

In all these ways the position of the abolitionists was enhanced after the war and their viewpoints given greater prestige. It was understandable that such abolitionists as the poet John Greenleaf Whittier, the newspaper editor Sydney Gay, and the oldtime free-soiler Henry Wilson should feel that the war had vindicated their position. Their writings after the war reflected the belief that events had demonstrated that the slavepower conspiracy had been as real, as evil, and as responsible for the country's troubles as they had long insisted before 1861.

Even Whittier's idyllic poem of rural New England in winter, "Snow-Bound" (published shortly after the close of the conflict in 1865), contained reminders of the time

> When all the land
> Was clay in Slavery's shaping hand.

It was as if the poet did not wish his readers to become so engrossed in his story that they would forget what he called

> The darkness and the ignorance,
> The pride, the lust, the squalid sloth,
> Which nurtured Treason's monstrous growth,
> Made murder pastime, and the hell
> Of prison-torture possible.

Slavery and treason must be made infamous even in poems about the snows of New England.

In histories published in the 1870's, Sydney Gay and Henry Wilson revealed a spirit akin to that expressed in Whittier's lines.[69] Of particular importance as a detailed statement of the postwar views of Northern antislavery extremists was the history of the causes of the war by Henry Wilson. The proverbial poor boy who had risen from farm laborer to Vice-president, Wilson had been active in politics since the 1840's, winning a reputation as a champion of New England workingmen and an opponent of slavery. During the war, he was chairman of the Senate committee on military affairs and repeatedly urged emancipation to Lincoln as a war measure. Opposed to Johnson's reconstruction plan, he be-

---

[69] William Cullen Bryant and Sydney Gay, *A Popular History of the United States* (4v., New York, 1876-1880) (although bearing Bryant's name as co-author, this history was written by Gay, except for the preface to Volume 1, and Bryant read only the first two volumes before his death in 1878); Henry Wilson, *History of the Rise and Fall of the Slave Power in America* (3v., Boston, 1872-1877),

came one of the leaders in congressional or "Radical" Reconstruction, and was elected Vice-president on the Grant ticket in 1872. In that same year, the first volume of his massive *History of the Rise and Fall of the Slave Power* appeared.

As the title of his work indicates, Wilson's views on the causes of the war were similar to those expressed during the struggle by Joshua Giddings, the Ohio abolitionist, and by Horace Greeley. Wilson wrote what was essentially a biography of what he called the "Slave Power" ("a commanding power, ever sensitive, jealous, proscriptive, dominating, and aggressive"), and throughout his volumes, the slavepower was the villain. All the familiar features of the Unionist interpretation of the causes of the war were present in Wilson's thought. Picturing a war which had grown out of the irrepressible conflict between slavery and freedom, he blamed it solely upon a conspiracy of Southern leaders; these men had succeeded in "dragooning" the Southern states into secession (against the will of the majority of the Southern people), and had finally forced the firing upon the flag at Fort Sumter. The cause of the war was thus the selfish ambition of evil men who were working always to advance the cause of slavery. The slavepower, as Wilson himself summed up his views,

after aggressive warfare of more than two generations upon the vital and animating spirit of republican institutions, upon the cherished and hallowed sentiments of a Christian people, upon the enduring interests and lasting renown of the Republic, organized treasonable conspiracies, raised the standard of revolution, and plunged the nation into a bloody contest for the preservation of its threatened life.[70]

Yet, unlike Giddings or other wartime authors, Wilson wrote with the perspective of victory which imparted to his volumes distinctive postwar overtones. Looking back from the vantage point of triumph, he could see the plan of "a higher than any human agency" in all that had occurred. Even the many successes of the slavepower in the years before 1860 were now seen by Wilson to have been part and parcel of this suprahuman scheme. For those successes served to stimulate the "grasping purposes" of the slavepower until it finally "o'erleaped itself and rushed to its own overthrow." In an age in which Horatio Alger stories told of the

70 Wilson, *History*, I, *vi-vii*.

triumph of virtue and right, a triumph always made the more impressive because of the seeming defeat of virtue in the midst of hardships, Wilson told a similar tale of the ultimate triumph, after many vicissitudes, of freedom over slavery. All the deeds of the slavepower were simply a preliminary step in "that march of events which has so rapidly and wonderfully opened the continent to the forces of a fresher energy and a higher civilization."[71] The crowning point in that "march of events," the climax of the schemes of that higher than human agency, Wilson naturally found in the Emancipation Proclamation; through it, the war, which had started out as one solely to preserve the Union, ultimately became a struggle for the truths of the Declaration of Independence and resulted in the destruction of slavery everywhere in the land. "Man," wrote Wilson, "proposes, but God disposes."[72]

However much Wilson, Gay, and Whittier believed that the war had vindicated their personal courses of action, none of them could write of the overthrow of slavery and of their own role in that overthrow with as great a sense of personal drama as Frederick Douglass, the escaped slave who became a leader among Northern abolitionists. Born a slave in Maryland, Douglass had escaped in 1838 (by traveling on the train from Baltimore to New York, using the identification papers of a free Negro friend). He began as a laborer in Massachusetts, later became an antislavery lecturer, founded and edited a newspaper in Rochester, New York, and published in the 1840's his widely-read autobiography. By the time of the Civil War, he was probably the best-known Negro in the United States, and during the war he talked with Lincoln on several different occasions. Lincoln was quoted as saying of Douglass

that considering the condition from which he had arisen and the obstacles that he had overcome, and the position to which he had attained that he regarded him one of the most meritorious men, if not the most meritorious man in the United States.[73]

[71] *ibid.*, I, 650-651.
[72] *ibid.*, III, 232ff., 380, 391.
[73] *In Memoriam Frederick Douglass* (Philadelphia, 1897) 70-71. For accounts of Douglass's life, see: *Life and Times of Frederick Douglass Written by Himself* (Hartford, 1881); Benjamin Quarles, *Frederick Douglass* (Washington, 1948); Philip S. Foner, ed., *The Life and Writings of Frederick Douglass* (3v., New York, 1950-1952).

After the war, Douglass became something of an elder statesman and was appointed to various federal offices by Presidents Grant, Hayes, and Garfield. In 1881, he published a new edition of his autobiography, *Life and Times of Frederick Douglass Written by Himself*, bringing it up to date and discussing the Civil War and its causes.

The *Life and Times of Frederick Douglass* was a more human, more moving, and more interesting document than Henry Wilson's *History*, but it expressed essentially the same view of the causes and character of the Civil War. The cause of the war, in Douglass's pages, was the institution of slavery, and the struggle was instigated by the "slavepower"; he wrote of a "slaveholding rebellion," a "war undertaken and brazenly carried on for the perpetual enslavement of colored men," and he described the events of the two or three decades preceding the outbreak of hostilities as part of a titanic conflict between freedom and slavery.[74] Douglass, like Wilson, told the gloomy story of the increasingly successful aggressiveness of the slavepower in Texas, Kansas, and elsewhere in the two decades before 1860 (he wrote of the "annexation of Texas for the avowed purpose of increasing the power of slavery in the Union"[75]). But looking back from the vantage point of the 1880's, he too could see the ray of light penetrating the gloom: "The more open, flagrant, and impudent the slavepower, the more firmly it was confronted by the rising antislavery spirit of the North."[76]

This very "madness" of the slave South, it turned out in Douglass's volume, was a blessing, for it forced the issue of freedom *versus* slavery, it prevented compromise, and it led to the ultimate destruction of slavery:

Happily for the cause of human freedom, and for the final unity of the American nation, the South was mad, and would listen to no concessions. . . . They had made up their minds that under a given contingency they would secede from the Union, and thus dismember the Republic. . . . They had come to hate everything which had the prefix "Free"—free soil, free States, free territories, free schools, free speech, and freedom generally, and they would have no more such prefixes.

[74] The quotations (in order) are from *Life and Times of Frederick Douglass*, 363, 426, 414.
[75] *ibid.*, 361.　　　　　　　　　　[76] *ibid.*, 363.

This haughty and unreasonable and unreasoning attitude of the imperious South saved the slave and saved the nation. Had the South accepted our concessions and remained in the Union, the slavepower would in all probability have continued to rule; the North would have become utterly demoralized; the hands on the dial-plate of American civilization would have been reversed, and the slave would have been dragging his hateful chains to-day wherever the American flag floats to the breeze.[77]

Among the individuals who were influenced by the example and the words of Douglass was a young Negro named George Washington Williams. Born in Pennsylvania, Williams had moved at the age of five or six to Massachusetts, and had enlisted in the Union Army when only fourteen; he was wounded in combat during the Civil War and rose from private to sergeant-major of his regiment.[78] After the war his career was varied indeed: he became a Baptist minister (graduated from Newton Theological Institution, Massachusetts, in 1874), a journalist, a lawyer (admitted to the Ohio bar in the 1870's), a legislator (elected in 1879 to the Ohio Legislature as a Republican for a two-year term), and a government official (United States Minister to Haiti in 1885-1886). In the 1870's, Williams became interested in the history of Negroes, and in the next decade published the results of his researches in two works: *History of the Negro Race in America from 1619 to 1880* (2v., 1883) and *History of Negro Troops in the War of the Rebellion* (1888).

Williams' *History of the Negro Race* contained a discussion of the causes of the Civil War, and from this discussion it was clear that his viewpoint was similar to that of Frederick Douglass. The cause of the war, in the opinion of Williams, was the institution of slavery:

Like some loathsome disease it [slavery] spread itself over the body politic until our nation became the eyesore of the age, and a byword among the nations of the world. The time came when our beloved country had to submit to heroic treatment, and the cancer of slavery was removed by the sword.[79]

[77] *ibid.*, 406-407.
[78] William E. Smith, "George Washington Williams," *The Dictionary of American Biography*, xx, 263; John Hope Franklin, "George Washington Williams, Historian," *The Journal of Negro History*, xxxi, 60-90 (January 1946).
[79] George W. Williams, *History of the Negro Race in America from 1619 to 1880* (2v., New York, 1883) I, *viii.*

And the guilt for beginning the war rested squarely upon the South, for the South had risen in rebellion in order to further the spread of slavery:

The South aggressively, offensively sought the extension and perpetuation of slavery. The North passively, defensively stood ready to protect her free territory, but not to interfere with slavery.[80]

Thus, this pioneer Negro historian reflected some of the same attitudes and ideas on the war which were expressed in the 1870's and 1880's by some former abolitionists.

Frederick Douglass, Henry Wilson, and the other prewar abolitionists mentioned above were representative of the humanitarian idealistic extremists in the North, a group which had given important support to the Reconstruction policies of the Republican Party. Another type of extremism in the North and in the Republican Party in the 1870's and 1880's was displayed by the politicians who "waved the bloody shirt." Some of these politicians, too, wrote memoir-histories in which they explained the coming of the Civil War.

The Republican Party after the war, like most successful political parties, contained groups which had quite different interests. The one uniting bond among all the diverse elements within the party was the desire to remain in power, and it soon became clear that one of the most effective ways for the Republicans to stay in power after the war was to keep alive the issues of the war period. The Republican Party was incontestably linked with the preservation of the Union; in addition, it was undeniable that the opposition to the war in the Union states had come in large part from Democrats and that the Democratic Party had been controlled before the war to a considerable extent by Southerners. Hence, there was an opportunity for Republican politicians to group the Democratic Party with the South and to equate both with treason and rebellion by constant references to the issues and emotions of the war. "Waving the bloody shirt" before Northern voters, as this practice was named, became a standard campaign technique for some Republican Party politicians, and former Union soldiers were periodically urged to "vote as you shot." "Every man," declared Robert G. In-

---

[80] *ibid.*, II, 240; for other examples of Williams' interpretation of the causes of the war, see *ibid.*, II, *iii-iv*, 228-240.

gersoll, the famous lecturer and a former colonel in the Union Army,

that [*sic.*] endeavored to tear the old flag from the heaven that it enriches was a Democrat. . . . Every enemy this great Republic has had for twenty years has been a Democrat. . . . The man that assassinated Abraham Lincoln was a Democrat. . . . Soldiers, every scar you have on your heroic bodies was given you by a Democrat.[81]

Two leaders in the effort by Republican politicians to keep alive a "bloody shirt" interpretation of the causes of the war were James G. Blaine and John A. ("Blackjack") Logan. Blaine had been a Congressman during the war, while Logan (despite his alleged sympathy for the South in the early days of the struggle) had an impressive combat record in the Union Army; after Appomattox, both men had risen quickly to prominence in their party, ultimately becoming the Republican candidates for President and Vice-president, respectively, in the election of 1884.

The picture of the war which both men sought to preserve in the volumes they published in the 1880's was fundamentally similar to that drawn by Henry Wilson. They described a rebellion of Southerners led by a conspiracy of politicians, and they affirmed that the Southern cause was that of slavery; in their pages, the South was exclusively responsible for the war and right was exclusively upon the side of the North. "From beginning to end," Blaine wrote in 1886, "the Rebellion was based upon the suppression of that which was true and the suggestion of that which was untrue."[82] Neither Blaine nor Logan went as far as Wilson in emphasizing the activities of the slavepower, and both men, as befitted leaders of the party of protection, stressed the role of the tariff in causing sectional discord and war. The Confederates were triply damned in Logan's eyes since they fought not only for slavery and for the dissolution of the Union but also for the "obnoxious and un-American doctrine of Free Trade."[83] Logan even extended the "Southern conspiracy" charge to the 1880's, suggesting that the victory of Grover Cleveland (the first Democrat to

[81] *The Works of Robert G. Ingersoll* (Dresden edition, 12v., New York, 1907) IX, 157-160.

[82] James G. Blaine, *Twenty Years of Congress* (2v., Norwich, Connecticut, 1884-1886) II, 26. For Logan's opinions, see his volume, *The Great Conspiracy: Its Origin and History* (New York, 1886).

[83] *ibid.*, 340-341, 663; Blaine, *Twenty Years*, I, 178ff.

be elected President since 1856) signified that the Southern conspirators, as in 1861, had once more been successful and could now practically govern the entire Union. In view of the Democratic victory, Logan raised the question, "Does the Free *Republic* of the United States exist, in fact, today?"[84]

The significance of the views of such "bloody shirt" extremists as Ingersoll, Blaine, and Logan lies in the fact that evidence indicates that these opinions on the war were simply exaggerated versions of attitudes common among many Northerners in the 1870's and (to a lesser extent) in the 1880's. The Republican Party and its leaders of that period have fallen into disrepute among present-day historians, and it has become the fashion to vilify the Republican leaders for cynically waving the bloody shirt in order to turn the minds of the voters away from the economic grievances of farmers and laborers. In measuring attitudes toward the Civil War, however, the important fact would seem to be not that some politicians, as always, attempted to exploit popular sentiment but rather that one current in the popular sentiment which was strong enough to be effectively exploited in the 1870's and 1880's reflected the survival of the viewpoints of the 1860's toward the war. However unbelievable the Republican bloody shirt orations may sound in the twentieth century, there is testimony to their appeal in the 1870's. When twenty-one-year-old Robert M. La Follette, for example, read in 1876 a Memorial Day address of Robert G. Ingersoll's which had been posted on the wall of the Madison, Wisconsin, post office, the effect was pronounced:

I can scarcely convey now [La Follette wrote later], or even understand, the emotional effect the reading of it produced upon me. Oblivious of my surroundings, I read it with tears streaming down my face.[85]

That same year, Albert J. Beveridge, a fourteen-year-old farm boy at the time, heard John A. Logan deliver a typical bloody shirt speech and was deeply impressed:

Next day, following the plow, with my bare feet in the mellow, fragrant furrow, I went over that speech. I wondered if ever I could say such wonderful things.[86]

[84] Logan, *Great Conspiracy*, 665.
[85] Robert M. La Follette, *La Follette's Autobiography* (Madison, Wisc., 1911) 34.
[86] Claude G. Bowers, *Beveridge and the Progressive Era* (New York, 1932) 10 (quoting Beveridge's manuscript autobiography).

Within less than ten years, Beveridge himself was saying "such wonderful things" and became a Republican orator who almost equaled Logan in his vigorous waving of the bloody shirt.

Young Northerners did not have to go to Republican politicians in the 1870's and 1880's to find evidence of the survival of partisan sectional viewpoints toward the Civil War. For such viewpoints were expressed in those decades by individuals with backgrounds quite different from that of James G. Blaine or John A. Logan. Certainly no Northerner, for example, was much freer of the "taint" of Republicanism than the former Union General George B. McClellan. A Douglas Democrat before the war, McClellan had run as the Democratic opponent of Lincoln in the presidential election of 1864 and had consistently supported the Democratic candidates for President in elections after the war; he had actively campaigned for Tilden in 1876 and for Cleveland in 1884, and was Democratic Governor of the State of New Jersey from 1878 to 1881.[87] Yet, the views on the war expressed by this staunch Democrat in his autobiography published in the 1880's, while not precisely the same as those of James G. Blaine or of Henry Wilson, seem to fall within the same general pattern.

McClellan, although criticizing the activities of Northern abolitionists, held "the South directly accountable for the war"; while he did not express agreement with the common Northern conspiracy thesis, he did place upon Southern extremists primary blame for the struggle. And the institution of slavery was, in his opinion, the cause of the war: "I suppose none now doubt that slavery was the real knot of the question and the underlying cause of the war." Whether or not McClellan thought that the war grew out of an irrepressible conflict, he seems to have been convinced that armed hostilities were inevitable; "with men as they are," he declared, "it would be difficult indeed to indicate how a permanent pacific solution [to the North-South conflict] could have been reached."[88] The attitudes toward the war expressed by this Northern Democrat would seem to have differed only in degree from those expressed by Northern Republicans.

[87] William Starr Myers, *A Study in Personality: General George Brinton McClellan* (New York, 1934) *passim*.

[88] George B. McClellan, *McClellan's Own Story* (New York, 1886) chap. 1; the quotations in this paragraph are (in order) from pages 37, 29, and 30.

And, during the 1870's and 1880's, when some Northern Republicans and some Northern Democrats were demonstrating the persistence of wartime emotions in their section, seven volumes of a massive eight-volume history of the United States were published. The author was the German historian Hermann Eduard Von Holst, and his volumes constituted the first major synthesis by a trained historian covering the period from the founding of the nation through the outbreak of the Civil War. Beginning with Von Holst's study, the principal published discussions of the causes of the war were, more and more as the years passed, written by trained historians. It is worthy of note that among some of the members of this new profession of historians in the United States, the wartime Unionist attitudes and ideas survived in the 1870's and 1880's, just as they survived among the Northerners who responded to the bloody shirt speeches of Republican politicians. One of the clearest indications of this fact is the reaction of some of the trained historians to the volumes of Von Holst.

H.E. Von Holst was to many Americans in the 1870's and 1880's the outstanding representative of the emerging school of trained historians. He enjoyed great prestige in an age which was beginning to have a tremendous respect for German scholarship; not only had he studied in a German seminar but he had also conducted one. Von Holst came to the United States shortly after the close of the war in the 1860's and remained for a few years. He took part in American politics in New York City as a Republican campaign orator in the election of 1868.[89] Opinions on the Civil War current in the North at that time had fitted in precisely with his predilections in favor of a strong national government and in opposition to the institution of slavery. Although he based his history on more research in the sources than most other Northern writers, his views on the causes and nature of the war did not differ essentially from the interpretation which Henry Wilson had expressed.

Von Holst viewed the entire course of United States history from the end of the Revolution to the outbreak of the Civil War as essentially a great moral struggle between absolute good and

[89] Eric F. Goldman, "Hermann Eduard Von Holst: Plumed Knight of American Historiography," *The Mississippi Valley Historical Review*, XXIII, 511-532 (March 1937).

absolute evil. Good was represented by the principles of nationality and freedom, whereas evil was linked with state sovereignty and slavery. The history of the United States was the conflict between these opposing sets of principles, intensified by an economic conflict between agriculture and manufacturing (for there was some mention of economic factors in Von Holst); virtue and right had ultimately triumphed. Just as there were irreconcilable differences between good and evil, so, in Von Holst's *History*, there was an irrepressible conflict between North and South; and he seems to have gone a step beyond Lincoln and Seward in the belief that war was the only solution to this conflict.[90] The only important way in which Von Holst differed from the traditional Unionist interpretation of the war's causes was that he made little mention of a "conspiracy" of Southerners in bringing on secession and war. He did, however, write of "slavocrats," "slave barons," and of the "unholy hand" of slavery; he also made it clear that the evil principles of slavery and state sovereignty were responsible for the war.

In the 1870's and 1880's, Von Holst enjoyed a tremendous popularity among scholars in the United States; praise was lavished upon him and he was sought by such American universities as Johns Hopkins and the University of Chicago.[91] Undoubtedly, some of his popularity was due to his prestige as a German scholar and to the fact that his history was the first large-scale effort published by a trained historian in the postwar period. But it also seems clear that a number of American historians in the 1870's and 1880's agreed with the views of the Civil War which Von Holst expressed—and this number included young men who had not been old enough to participate in the war itself.

Henry Adams (born 1838) and Henry Cabot Lodge (born 1850), both Massachusetts men, described in 1876 the first volume of Von Holst's *History* as "the best book which any foreigner has yet written on the United States, if indeed it be not the best book which has ever been written on that subject, whether by foreigner

[90] For discussions of the "irrepressible conflict" in Von Holst's volumes, see: *The Constitutional and Political History of the United States*, John J. Lalor and Alfred B. Mason, trs. (8v., Chicago, 1876-1892) I, 340ff.; IV, 213ff.; VI, 265ff., 285.

[91] Eric F. Goldman, ed., "Importing a Historian: Von Holst and the American Universities," *The Mississippi Valley Historical Review*, XXVII, 267-274 (September 1940).

or native."[92] In the course of their review, Adams and Lodge made it clear that they specifically agreed with Von Holst's indictment of "all the successive concessions to the slavepower," and with the spirit in which he told of "all the steps by which that power slowly converted the national government into an instrument of its own will." The story of the political influence of the slavepower was a chapter of American history, they wrote, "which admits of no defense or palliation." Similar high praise of Von Holst came from Herbert B. Adams (born 1850 in Massachusetts), who had studied in a German seminar and who was one of the outstanding leaders of the new group of trained historians in the United States. Writing a sketch for Baltimore newspapers in 1878, Adams stated that Von Holst's work "is now very generally recognized among American scholars as the most critical and, at the same time, as the most impartial and thoroughly scientific treatment to which the constitutional and political history of the U.S. has hitherto been subjected."[93]

That Herbert B. Adams was not writing mere publicity for newspapers was demonstrated when Charles Kendall Adams, of Vermont and Iowa, published in 1888 the third edition of one of the first bibliographical guides produced by the new group of professional historians. Charles Kendall Adams, president of Cornell University and later president of the University of Wisconsin and of the new American Historical Association, was a man of standing in historical and academic circles. He completed his college course in 1861, was a graduate student and teacher at the University of Michigan during the war, and apparently did not serve in the armed forces; he studied in German and French universities in the late 1860's and became a pioneer in introducing the seminar method of graduate instruction in American universities. In Adams' *Manual of Historical Literature*, Von Holst's *History* was praised as "unquestionably the ablest work that has yet been written on our constitutional and political history"; the topical headings of the *Manual* contained references to "The Slave Power"

[92] Henry Adams and Henry Cabot Lodge, "Von Holst's History of the United States," *The North American Review*, CXXIII, 328 (October 1876).

[93] Herbert B. Adams to Von Holst, December 6, 1878, printed in W. Stull Holt, ed., *Historical Scholarship in the United States 1876-1901: As Revealed in the Correspondence of Herbert B. Adams* (Baltimore, 1938) 36.

and Von Holst's treatment of the subject was especially praised.[94] The *Manual* criticized Wilson's *Rise and Fall of the Slave Power* because of its antislavery bias; yet, the first volume of Horace Greeley's *American Conflict* was cited as perhaps "the best existing portrayal of the causes that led gradually up to the conflict," and Greeley's treatment of the slavery question was particularly commended.[95] In this, the standard bibliographical guide of the decade, as in the views of Henry Adams and Henry Cabot Lodge, could be seen the persistence of the views of the 1860's.

The same was true of the articles on American history in one of the leading scholarly compilations in the United States during this period, the three-volume *Cyclopaedia of Political Science, Political Economy, and of the Political History of The United States*, edited by J.J. Lalor and published from 1881 to 1884. The articles on American history in this *Cyclopaedia* were written by Alexander Johnston, professor at Princeton (then the College of New Jersey) and author of what has been called the "first reliable textbook on American history from the pen of an American author."[96] Born in 1849 in Brooklyn, Johnston was of the same generation as Herbert B. Adams and Lodge; his father had served in the Union Army and his own views on the war and its causes were similar to those of Northerners of the war generation. The struggle was to him a "rebellion," and, writing in the 1880's, he explicitly rejected the newer designation, "civil war," which, as he acknowledged, was beginning to win favor. At the heart of this rebellion had been the institution of slavery, and Johnston described the conflict over that institution in terms of a Southern "slavepower," "aggressive," with an "inherent grasping nature," constantly demanding more slaves and more land.

Thus, among many individuals in the North, the viewpoints

[94] Charles Kendall Adams, *A Manual of Historical Literature* (3rd. ed., New York, 1888) 607, 661, 663. The *History* was not criticized because of its anti-Southern spirit but because it seemed hostile to republican institutions.

[95] *ibid.*, 575-576, 613-614.

[96] Fulmer Mood, "The Development of Frederick Jackson Turner as a Historical Thinker," *Publications of the Colonial Society of Massachusetts*, XXXIV, 295 (Boston, 1943). Articles by Johnston in the *Cyclopaedia* which show his opinions on the war include: "Nation, The (In U.S. History)," II, 930-936; "Rebellion, The (In U.S. History)," III, 532-537; "Reconstruction, The (In U.S. History)," III, 540-556; "Slavery (In U.S. History)," III, 725-738; "State Sovereignty (In U.S. History)," III, 788-800.

formulated in the early days of the war and confirmed by victory could still be found in the 1880's. These viewpoints were expressed by partisan politicians of the type represented by Blaine and Logan; they were also written into the volumes of trained historians. A diverse group of Northerners still pictured the Civil War as a rebellion for which Southerners were completely responsible, a rebellion which had grown out of irreconcilable differences between North and South rooted in the institution of slavery.

CHAPTER TWO

"THE WAR BETWEEN THE STATES"

Confederate Viewpoints
1861 to 1865

IN THE Confederate states, as in the Union states, the opening of the Civil War was marked by enthusiasm and unity of sentiment of a high degree. The capture of Fort Sumter and Lincoln's subsequent call for troops had the effect of solidifying public opinion in the seven seceded states of the lower South. In addition, these events touched off a second secession movement in the border slaveholding states of Virginia, North Carolina, Tennessee, and Arkansas. The governors of these states indignantly rejected Lincoln's appeal for soldiers, and, within a few weeks, the four states seceded and joined the Confederacy. Thus was effected a political union of upper and lower South, and in this enlarged Confederacy (outside of a few pro-Union areas, primarily in the hill country) there was firm popular approval of the war policy in the early months of the conflict. Charleston, Montgomery, and New Orleans witnessed similar scenes of excited crowds ardently voicing their support of the government. "The South is now united to a man," wrote the sister-in-law of Salmon P. Chase (Lincoln's Secretary of the Treasury) from New Orleans; her phrases were strikingly like those used by George Ticknor to describe the prevailing mood in the Union states:

There is no division among the people here. There is but one mind, one heart, one action. . . . Every night the men are drilling. Young and old, professional men and laborers, lawyers, doctors, and even the ministers are all drilling. . . . The ladies hold fairs, make clothes, lint, etc., for the army, and animate the men by appeals to their chivalry and their patriotism to resist the enemy to the death. What is seen in New Orleans pervades the whole South. Never were a people more united and more determined.[1]

---

[1] Mrs. R.L. Hunt to Salmon P. Chase, May 30, 1861, in *The American Historical Review*, IV, 336-339 (January 1899). Mrs. Hunt, a native of Ohio, lived in New Orleans with her Southern husband. For typical accounts by contemporaries of the reaction in the South to the outbreak of war, see: Mary Boykin Chestnut, *A Diary From Dixie*, Ben Ames Williams, ed. (Boston, 1949) 38-40; Raphael Semmes, *Memoirs of Service Afloat During the War Between the States* (Baltimore, 1868) 89.

Southerners, just as Northerners, were now faced with the limited choice of supporting either the government of Lincoln or that of Jefferson Davis, and individuals as different in background, temperament, and political opinions as Robert Barnwell Rhett of South Carolina and Robert E. Lee of Virginia joined in upholding the Confederacy. In stating their position, Confederate sympathizers formulated and gave voice to their opinions on the nature and causes of the war.

To the more ardent Southern secessionists—Rhett, and Edmund Ruffin and Roger A. Pryor of Virginia—the outbreak of war was welcome, for it put an end to talk of reconstruction of the old Union. During the winter of 1860-1861, both Ruffin and Pryor in Charleston had urged an attack on Fort Sumter in order to precipitate war and thereby force their own State of Virginia to secede.[2] Pryor even claimed many years later that the specific decision to open fire on Fort Sumter (a decision made by himself and three other members of the staff of Confederate General P.G.T. Beauregard) was based upon the fear that the Union would be restored by negotiation, and thus that the situation at Sumter offered the last opportunity for war.[3]

To such Southern "fire-eaters," state secession had been simply the preliminary step toward the founding of an independent Southern nation which would differ in important respects from the old Union. Rhett, for example, believed and hoped that a Southern nation based upon cotton, free trade, and slavery would be formed. He was an ardent defender of slavery as a positive good, and he desired both the permanent exclusion of nonslaveholding states from this new country, and the legal reopening of the slave trade with Africa. Rabid secessionists of the Rhett type spoke of their movement as a "revolution," and called themselves "revolutionists" and "rebels."[4] Their explanation of the conflict between

[2] Ruffin, disgusted at the refusal of Virginia to leave the Union after the election of Lincoln, went into voluntary exile from that state and became a citizen of the Confederacy. Avery Craven, *Edmund Ruffin, Southerner* (New York, 1932) 204; Mrs. Roger A. Pryor, *Reminiscences of Peace and War* (rev. and enl. edition, New York, 1905) 120; Laura A. White, *Robert Barnwell Rhett, Father of Secession* (New York, 1931) 205; Henry T. Shanks, *The Secession Movement in Virginia, 1847-1861* (Richmond, 1934) 191, 198, 266n.5, 268n.75.

[3] Conversations between Roger A. Pryor and William E. Dodd, December 30, 1909, described in William E. Dodd, *Statesmen of the Old South* (New York, 1911) 220-221.

[4] White, *Rhett*, 188ff.; Pryor, *Reminiscences*, 124.

North and South was clearly set forth in the widely circulated "Address to the Slaveholding States" written by Rhett in December 1860.[5]

The "Address" was a justification of the secession of South Carolina and was officially adopted by the convention which took that state out of the Union. Its basic theme was to be found in Rhett's assertion that secession was made necessary by the actions of the commercial and nonslaveholding Northern states. For more than thirty years, he declared, those states, totally different in ideas, interests, and institutions from the agricultural and slaveholding Southern states, had attempted to change the federal government into a "despotism" and to subjugate the Southern states—as was demonstrated by Northern actions on the questions of tariff, taxation, and slavery. Thus, Carolinians in 1860 were resisting a tyrannical regime, just as had their ancestors in 1776, and their action rested primarily upon the right of self-government. "We but imitate the policy of our fathers," he wrote, "in dissolving a union with nonslaveholding confederates, and seeking confederation with slaveholding states."[6] Rhett further defended secession as a reserved right of sovereign states, but his main emphasis was upon an inherent right of self-government.

In sharp contrast to the extremists of the Rhett type were men from the border slaveholding states whose views were predominantly moderate. Large numbers of them, too, became supporters of the Confederacy after Lincoln's call for troops. Of particular significance was the position of John Bell of Tennessee, a Southern counterpart of Edward Everett in almost every respect. A conservative Whig who owned many slaves, Bell had nevertheless

[5] "Address to the Slaveholding States," Moore, *Rebellion Record*, I, Doc. Pages 396-401. Fifteen thousand copies of the "Address" were published and distributed at the time.

[6] *ibid.*, I, 399. Rhett's impatience with the border states led him, after the attack upon Fort Sumter, to assert that their delay in joining the Confederacy had forestalled the opportunity to convince the North of Southern unity and thus had caused the war (White, *Rhett*, 205). Opinions similar to those of Rhett were held by the South's well-known novelist William Gilmore Simms. Simms had favored secession as far back as 1850; he defended the institution of slavery as a positive good and hoped that through secession a Southern nation founded upon slavery and agriculture would be established. See: William P. Trent, *William Gilmore Simms* (Boston, 1892) *passim*; John W. Higham, "The Changing Loyalties of William Gilmore Simms," *The Journal of Southern History*, IX, 210-223 (May 1943).

been condemned by many Southerners before 1860 because of his lukewarm attitude in defense of slavery and of "Southern rights."[7] Unlike many Southerners of his day, he acknowledged the authority of Congress to prohibit slavery in the territories (although he was opposed to the exercise of that authority); again unlike many Southerners, he did not believe that a state possessed the constitutional right of secession. In 1860, as the presidential candidate of the Constitutional Union Party (with Everett as vice-presidential candidate) he won votes in both North and South and carried the three border slaveholding states of Kentucky, Tennessee, and Virginia.

But Bell was just as critical of what he regarded as the "coercion" of states by the federal government as he was of state secession. Lincoln's call for troops after the fall of Sumter seemed to Bell to portend such coercion, and he was disturbed by it. At first he advocated "armed neutrality" for his state, but within a few days he placed himself squarely on the side of the Confederacy.[8] To a gathering in Nashville, Tennessee, on April 23, 1861, Bell advocated a policy of defending the South, all the South, against the "unnecessary, aggressive, cruel, unjust, and wanton war which is being forced upon us"; common cause, he declared, should be made with the slaveholding states against the "invading foe," and to every Tennessean his exhortation was "to arms, to arms."[9]

Another moderate from a border state was Robert E. Lee, who in his long career as an Army officer, had taken little part in political affairs. As with many men of the border states, it is difficult to characterize Lee's position accurately. He was a slaveholder, but he had never owned more than a half-dozen slaves; he was opposed to Northern abolitionists, but he hoped and believed

[7] For example, he had defied the instructions of the Tennessee Legislature and had spoken and voted in Congress in the late 1850's against the Lecompton Constitution, which would have allowed slavery in Kansas. See: Philip M. Hamer, "John Bell," *The Dictionary of American Biography*, II, 157-159; Joshua W. Caldwell, "John Bell of Tennessee," *The American Historical Review*, IV, 652-664 (July 1899); Joseph H. Parks, "John Bell and the Compromise of 1850," *The Journal of Southern History*, IX, 328-356 (August 1943), and Joseph H. Parks, *John Bell of Tennessee* (Baton Rouge, La., 1950) *passim*.

[8] "Address to the People of Tennessee," by Bell and others, April 18, 1861, in Moore, *Rebellion Record*, I, Doc. Pages 71-72; "Jno. Bell and Edwin H. Ewing, at Nashville, Tenn., April 23 [1861]," *ibid.*, I, Doc. Pages 137-138.

[9] *ibid.*, I, Doc. Pages 137.

that emancipation would gradually come about through the influence of Christianity, and he had sent to Liberia those of his slaves who desired to go; he was acquainted with the institution of slavery only at its best (i.e., in the border states), but he still held it to be evil rather than good. "In this enlightened age," Lee wrote to his wife in 1856, "there are few, I believe, but will acknowledge, that slavery is a moral and political evil in any country."[10] But slavery was a greater evil to the white race, in his opinion, than to the black. While maintaining that citizens of all states should have equal rights in the territories, he nevertheless expressed, in December 1860, his opposition to the renewal of the foreign slave trade "on every ground." Finally, three days after Lincoln issued the call for troops, he made the statement that if he owned all the slaves in the country, he would gladly give them up without compensation in order to preserve the Union.[11]

Lee was opposed to the Southern extremists in the secession crisis, criticizing the "selfish, dictatorial bearing" of the cotton states. When he learned in January 1861 of the secession of four states, he explicitly stated his belief that the Constitution was not a "compact" between the states, that it was intended to be perpetual, and that secession, as he phrased it, was "nothing but revolution." But unlike the "fire-eaters," who also considered secession to be revolution, Lee did not feel that there was sufficient cause to justify such a step. "I must confess," he was quoted as saying even after the Virginia Convention had voted to withdraw from the Union, "that I am one of those dull creatures that cannot see the good of secession."[12] Yet, he had frequently declared that his primary loyalty was to Virginia, and that he would defend any state if "her rights were invaded"; when Virginia seceded, he resigned without hesitation from the United States Army. He recognized two governments only—the Union and the State of Virginia (he was not a Southern nationalist)—and he took pride in them both. Faced with the cruel dilemma of choosing between the two, he chose Virginia.

On the same day on which he resigned from the Union Army,

[10] Douglas S. Freeman, *R.E. Lee: A Biography* (4v., New York, 1934) I, 372.
[11] *ibid.*, I, 434, 634-635.
[12] *ibid.*, I, 439. See also *ibid.*, I, 416-417, 421, 428-429, 439-444.

Lee explained his action in a letter to a sister who was Unionist in her sympathies and whose son remained in the army from which Lee had withdrawn:

The whole south is in a state of revolution, in which Virginia, after a long struggle, has been drawn; and, though I recognize no necessity for this state of things, and would have forborne and pleaded to the end for a redress of grievances, real or supposed, yet in my own person I had to meet the question whether I should take part against my native state.

With all my devotion to the Union and the feeling of loyalty and duty of an American citizen, I have not been able to make up my mind to raise my hand against my relatives, my children, my home. I have therefore resigned my commission in the Army, and save in defense of my native state, with the sincere hope that my poor services may never be needed, I hope I may never be called on to draw my sword. I know you will blame me; but you must think as kindly of me as you can, and believe that I have endeavored to do what I thought right.[13]

Here, free from legal or philosophical subtleties, was the initial explanation of the coming of war by one of the leading Confederates. Lee, like Bell, did not argue the constitutional right of secession, nor defend a compact theory of the Union, nor mention slavery, nor trace the cause of the war further back than the secession of Virginia. Secession was revolution, but he could not fight against his home, and would fight in her defense if necessary.[14]

Most of the people of the Confederate States, however, were neither "fire-eaters" nor moderates of the border slaveholding states. More representative of the entire body of Confederate supporters than Rhett, Bell, or Lee was Jefferson Davis of Mississippi. Davis was the proponent of Southern nationalism and had been one of the leading advocates of Southern interests in Washington in the 1850's.[15] He was a slaveholder who defended the institution

---

[13] *ibid.*, I, 443.

[14] The members of the secession convention of the border slaveholding State of Tennessee, like Bell and Lee, did not defend secession as a constitutional right, and they called their secession ordinance a "Declaration of Independence." "We, the people of the State of Tennessee," the ordinance began, "waiving an expression of opinion as to the abstract doctrine of secession, but asserting the right as a free and independent people to alter, reform, or abolish our form of Government in such a manner as we think proper, do ordain and declare" (Moore, *Rebellion Record*, I, Doc. Pages 203-204).

[15] See: William E. Dodd, *Jefferson Davis* (Philadelphia, 1907); Robert McElroy, *Jefferson Davis: The Unreal and the Real* (2v., New York, 1937); Dunbar Rowland, ed., *Jefferson Davis, Constitutionalist* (10v., Jackson, Miss., 1923).

of slavery as a positive good, and had consistently maintained that Congress could not prohibit slavery in the territories. As far back as 1850, he had upheld the constitutional right of a state to secede. Yet, he was definitely not a "fire-eater," and he was viewed with suspicion by the Southern radicals in the secession crisis of 1860-1861; that his views were not considered extreme was one of the factors which had led to his election as President of the Confederacy.

On April 29, 1861, two weeks after Lincoln's call for troops, Davis presented before a special session of the Confederate Congress his government's official account of the causes of the war. In some respects this account represented a synthesis of the views of both radicals like Rhett and moderates like Bell. Displaying opinions similar to those of Rhett, for example, Davis portrayed the background of the war as a long-standing conflict produced solely by the Northern states. Almost from the beginning of the old Union, he said, those states had sought control of the common government in order to further their own interests at the expense of the Southern states.[16] By means of tariffs and bounties, the Northern states had endeavoured to enrich the manufacturing and shipping classes of their section at the expense of the agricultural South; in addition, for many years they had attempted to make the Southern slave system insecure. Property in slaves, declared Davis, was recognized and protected in the Constitution, and he defended the institution of slavery as one under which "brutal savages" had been elevated, under the supervision of a "superior race," into "docile, intelligent, and civilized agricultural laborers."[17]

In defending slavery, Davis maintained that the long-standing conflict between North and South did not hinge on the morality of the institution. The Northern states, he said, had prohibited slavery and had sold their slaves to the South not because of humanitarian considerations but because this was in their own self-interest when their climate and soil proved unsuitable to slavery. Similarly, it was the desire to control the Union rather than humane motives which had prompted the Northern agitation against slavery, and it was because the election of Lincoln in 1860 meant the culmination of

16 For the text of this message, see Rowland, *Davis*, v, 67-84.
17 *ibid.*, v, 82.

this agitation that the Southern states withdrew from the Union. The Confederate President described and justified secession as a conservative movement and a legal one based upon the clear historical right of sovereign states. The Constitution of 1787, he insisted, was a compact between independent states which had never relinquished their sovereignty; the Southern states, in seceding, were thus simply resuming their place as sovereigns by the exercise of an ancient, well-established right. Unlike Rhett and the radicals, Davis emphasized that the Southern movement was *not* a revolution; it sought not to change but to preserve the laws and the Constitution of the old Union, from which the Yankees had departed. Davis compared the Confederates to the colonists of 1776, but it was in the sense of men seeking to achieve their national independence, not of men attempting to overturn or even to modify established institutions.[18] Despite the fact that history and the Constitution justified secession, however, self-interest had led the people of the North (where the population was increasing at a greater rate than in the South) to assent to the "lamentable and fundamental error" that the national government was sovereign over state governments, and that the Constitution required the rule of the majority. Upon these erroneous theories was based the Northern policy which, extending over many years, finally culminated in aggression.

Holding the North solely responsible for its long conflict with the South, Davis placed the guilt for initiating war in 1861 directly upon the Lincoln administration. He recalled that the Confederate government, shortly after its organization, had sent commissioners to Washington to settle peacefully any differences with the government of the United States. Lincoln, Davis charged, had refused to receive the commissioners officially, and the Washington government had not acted in good faith in its unofficial dealings

[18] For other characterizations of secession as a conservative movement in the early addresses of Davis as President of the Confederacy, see Rowland, *Davis*, v, 50, 52-53, 68-69, 72-74, 199-200. Lincoln's secretary, John Hay, noted in his diary that Davis, in the April 29 address, claimed nationality for the Confederacy not upon the basis of a successful revolution but upon an interpretation of the Constitution of the United States government—the government against which the Southern states were revolting. This, Hay thought, made the war a domestic matter and thereby weakened the Confederate demand for recognition by the nations of the world (Tyler Dennett, ed., *Lincoln and the Civil War in the Diaries and Letters of John Hay* [New York, 1939] 21).

with the Confederate representatives. While Secretary of State Seward gave unofficial assurance that Fort Sumter would be evacuated, Lincoln secretly prepared for hostile operations against the fort. "The crooked paths of diplomacy," said Davis, "can scarcely furnish an example so wanting in courtesy, in candor, and directness as was the course of the United States Government toward our commissioners in Washington."[19]

Davis praised the restraint of the people of South Carolina in tolerating for so long a period the federal garrison at Fort Sumter, "a standing menace against their peace and independence." When Lincoln's intention to reinforce the fort became known and the federal commander refused to surrender, no alternative remained for the Confederates but to capture the fort. Lincoln's purpose, Davis explained, was "to invade our soil, capture our forts, blockade our ports, and wage war against us"; his proclamation for troops following the fall of Sumter was a "plain declaration of war" which the Confederate government could not ignore.[20] Seeking no conquest, the Confederates asked only to be let alone; they were fighting, Davis declared, to prevent "subjugation by arms" and to secure their inherent right to "freedom, independence, and self-government."

Rhett, Bell, Lee, and Davis reflected the various attitudes that were common in the seceded states in the early months of the war. Their aims and their motives were not the same, and there were differences in their explanations of the causes of the war. Rhett and Davis pictured the war as the outgrowth of a long series of wrongful Northern actions and held that secession was justified after the election of 1860. By contrast, Bell and Lee traced the struggle only to actions of the Lincoln administration in April 1861; Bell defended secession and war solely because of those actions, whereas Lee, it appears, did not approve of secession and was willing to fight only in what seemed to him the defense of his state. Despite their differences, however, all four men joined, after the events of April 1861, in supporting the Confederate government and the war policy, demonstrating graphically how the outbreak of hostilities fused individuals of diverse viewpoints in the seceded states (as

[19] Rowland, *Davis*, v, 75.
[20] *ibid.*, v, 78, 81.

in the Union states) into a unified group. Moreover, dissimilarities in their opinions of the causes of the war were overbalanced by the basic agreement among Rhett, Bell, and Davis that the blame for the conflict rested solely upon the North and that the coming of war could be explained only in terms of the actions of Northerners. (Lee's position on this point is not explicit, but since he fought in "defense" of his state, the federal armed forces were presumably from his point of view the aggressors responsible for the war.) This fundamental harmony of outlook provided the foundation for a distinctive interpretation of the causes of the war by Confederates.

In the seceded states, as in the Union states, the initial widespread popular enthusiasm and support of the war effort was short-lived. Conflicts arose between important state and Confederate officials, on the one hand, and the Davis government on the other; as the military outlook grew progressively worse after the summer of 1863, desertions from the Confederate cause steadily increased.[21] But, despite defections and differences, there remained a loyal core of supporters of the Confederacy, and they retained the initial attitudes toward the causes of the conflict. It was these attitudes (particularly as expressed by Jefferson Davis) which were embodied in the first histories of the war by Confederate sympathizers.

The most popular and prolific writer of histories in the Confederates states was Edward A. Pollard, the Richmond journalist. An advocate of secession for several years before Lincoln's election, Pollard supported the war wholeheartedly. Throughout the conflict, however, from his post as editor of the *Daily Richmond Examiner*, he was a caustic critic of Jefferson Davis and of his administration, and this animosity was clearly demonstrated in his writings. Pollard's numerous histories were comparable to the popular histories published during the war in the Union states. They were clearly the work of a partisan, reflecting the intense emotions of wartime, and were colorful, dramatic, and infused with the author's own vigorously stated opinions; they had a wide popularity and a large sale.[22]

[21] See Georgia L. Tatum, *Disloyalty in the Confederacy* (Chapel Hill, 1934) *passim*, and below, chapter three.

[22] J.G. de Roulhac Hamilton, "Edward Alfred Pollard," *The Dictionary of American Biography*, xv, 47-48. Pollard's histories published during the war were: *Southern His-*

However much Pollard may have criticized the official actions of Jefferson Davis, his interpretation of the causes of the war differed little from that of the Confederate President. Pollard traced the roots of the struggle to the development over several decades of hostile Northern and Southern "nations." While the North became radical and materialistic, the South remained conservative and kept its system of "African servitude," for which Pollard had nothing but praise. The Northern theory of government, majority rule, was "coarse," "materialistic," and "erroneous"; under it, the North for forty years "reaped the fruits of partial legislation [tariffs, taxes, subsidies] while the South tasted the bitterness of oppression." Because of this profit, the North worshiped the Union in a "base spirit of commercial idolatry," while the South venerated it for its "sublime moral principle," state rights. By 1860, the Union no longer afforded security and protection to Southerners; instead, their institutions, their property, and even their lives were threatened by Northern fanaticism.[23]

To escape this Northern oppression, the Southern states seceded, and Pollard justified their action on the basis of state rights and on the "still higher principle" of self-government. Although he spoke of the secession movement as a "revolution," he emphasized, as had Davis, its conservative character and purpose. The South, he insisted, sought not to destroy but to preserve existing institutions; it waged a war for independence, not a crusade for new social experiments.[24]

Pollard attributed the immediate outbreak of hostilities to Lincoln, "this Yankee monster of inhumanity and falsehood," and he charged in 1862 that Lincoln had "procured" the assault upon Fort Sumter in order to make it appear that the South had started the war. He characterized Lincoln's plea of sending bread to a starving garrison as "an ingenious artifice to commence the war that the Federal Government had fully resolved upon."[25]

The influence of Pollard's wartime volumes was enhanced by

tory of the War: The First Year of the War (Richmond, 1862); Southern History of the War: The Second Year of the War (Richmond, 1863); Southern History of the War: The Third Year of the War (New York, 1864).

[23] Pollard, First Year, 107-108; Second Year, 309, 313; Third Year, 196n, 294ff.
[24] First Year, 108; Second Year, 296n.
[25] First Year, 67; Third Year, 188.

the fact that they were the first popular histories of the war from a Confederate point of view. In the absence of competing accounts, his opinions were taken as the standard Southern interpretation of the causes of the war. In fact, aside from Pollard's works, there were no other widely read pro-Confederate histories published while the fighting was in progress. Several related factors were responsible for this situation: there were in the Confederacy few of the established popular historians of the type who wrote so many of the wartime Unionist histories, nor was there the large reading public to support such authors; in addition, the South had fewer physical facilities for publishing than the North. However, the Confederate cause was upheld vigorously during the war in the writings of two separate groups: publicists in the service (and pay) of the Confederacy abroad, and Northerners whose sympathies lay with the seceded states.

Late in 1861, the Davis administration, losing its original confidence that the demand for cotton would force European intervention on the side of the Confederacy, began a vigorous attempt to "educate" public opinion in England and France on the causes and character of the war; it hoped in this fashion to bring popular pressure for intervention to bear upon those two governments.[26] The primary mouthpiece of Confederate propaganda abroad was a weekly journal, *The Index*, established in London in 1862 by Henry Hotze and edited by him throughout the rest of the war. Hotze was the director of the Confederate propaganda effort, and under him *The Index* was influential in disseminating information favorable to the Confederacy; in its columns there were frequent editorial discussions of the causes of the war. Hotze was assisted by another Confederate propagandist, James Williams, of Tennessee, who had been United States Minister to Turkey during the Buchanan administration. In addition to supplying articles to London newspapers and to *The Index*, Williams wrote two histories of the war which were published both in London and in the Confederacy.[27]

[26] For an account of Confederate propaganda efforts abroad, see Frank L. Owsley, *King Cotton Diplomacy* (Chicago, 1931), especially chap. vi.

[27] Frank L. Owsley, "James Williams," *The Dictionary of American Biography*, xx, 267. One of the histories by Williams, *The South Vindicated*, published originally at Nashville, Tennessee, was translated into German under Hotze's direction and circulated in Germany.

As was to be expected, the views expressed by Hotze and Williams were similar to those of their chief, Jefferson Davis. They wrote, as had John Lothrop Motley in the London *Times,* to convince foreign readers of the justice of their cause, and they sought in particular to refute the common Unionist explanations of the coming of the war. Repeatedly, Hotze and Williams placed the responsibility for sectional conflict and war upon the North and stressed the conservative and constitutional nature of the Southern movement.[28] To Europeans they explained that the United States Constitution had been a compact among sovereign states and that Americans owed their loyalty to these sovereign states. Thus the Confederates, far from being insurgents in rebellion against legal authority, were patriotic and loyal citizens defending their homes. State secession was clearly constitutional, and it was Northern aggression rather than Southern secession which had violated the Constitution.

The Confederate agents emphasized that secession had not resulted from a mere conspiracy or intrigue of Southern politicians; not the "unworthy promptings of personal ambition" but "a spontaneous outburst of human feelings, which . . . caused every heart to thrill with the same emotions" had motivated Southern actions. Secession, indeed, was simply the political separation of societies which, from the very establishment of the Constitution, had been distinctly different in their nature and interests. Williams contrasted the radical North and the conservative South in terms similar to those used by Pollard; it was little wonder, he concluded, that "the debased, and the dissolute, and the radicals" of all nations had been drawn to the Union side.[29]

Recognizing foreign sensitivity on the subject of slavery, Hotze and Williams declared that Northerners and Southerners (however different the societies in which they lived) thought alike about the institution and about the Negro. Until the Emancipation

[28] James Williams, *The South Vindicated* (from the 2nd American edition, London, 1862); *The Rise and Fall of "The Model Republic"* (London, 1863). See the following representative editorials in *The Index*: "Who Commenced the War?" I, 88-89 (June 5, 1862); "Are the Confederates Rebels?" I, 136-137 (June 26, 1862); "Cause of the Disruption of the Union," I, 314 (September 11, 1862); "Northern Duplicity before the War," I, 409-410 (October 23, 1862).

[29] Williams, *South Vindicated,* 436.

Proclamation was issued, both men pointed out that the North proposed no change in the status of the Negro as a result of the war.[30] Williams, in particular, maintained that slavery was not the cause of the war, but was simply the pretext for a Northern attempt to subjugate the South. Slavery, he wrote, was no more the cause of the war than was the purse of an unfortunate traveler the "cause" of his being robbed on the highway; through its generally conservative influence slavery had retarded rather than produced the breach between North and South.[31]

Both Hotze and Williams found the causes of the war in the attempts of the North to dominate the South, attempts which had led to the secession of the Southern states. That this constitutional, orderly, and popularly approved separation had resulted in war was due to the personal ambition of Abraham Lincoln and his advisers, and to the general Northern desire to maintain control over the South and to garner the profits accompanying control. War had come in April 1861 not because of the Confederate attack upon Fort Sumter but because the "duplicity" of the federal government toward the Confederate peace commissioners rendered inevitable the Sumter attack.[32]

Much more extreme in their opinions than the Confederate agents abroad were those Northerners who sympathized with the seceded states. These "Northern Confederates" were counterparts of the Southern Unionists in many respects; their views on the causes of the war were certainly as radical and stemmed from emotions as bitter as those of a "Parson" Brownlow. Support for the Confederacy in the Union states was centered politically in the antiwar faction within the Democratic Party, and geographically in the Midwest and in New York City, areas which had ties of commerce and of blood with the South (even in far-off San Fran-

[30] *ibid.*, 399-400; "Cause of the Disruption of the Union," *The Index*, I, 314 (September 11, 1862).

[31] Williams, *Rise and Fall*, 9-10, 144ff., 176ff.

[32] At one point, Williams maintained that the ultimate cause of the war was the presidential election system which allowed the "radical element of mere numbers" to control the United States government. He implied that war might not have come if the Constitution had provided for a presidential term of ten years, with the continuous succession to the presidency of the Senator who had been longest in office (*Rise and Fall*, II, 400-403, 410, 419). In a somewhat similar vein, a twentieth century "revisionist" historian was to state that "frequent elections" were a factor in stirring up emotions and thereby bringing on war; see below chapter seven.

cisco a Presbyterian clergyman offered prayers for Jefferson Davis during the war).[33]

From New York City (whose mayor had proposed secession for that community in 1861) came two articulate Confederate partisans, T.W. MacMahon and J.H. Van Evrie. As many Southern Unionists fled to Union territory at the outbreak of hostilities, so MacMahon left New York in 1861 and made his home thereafter in the Confederacy. Van Evrie, a newspaper publisher, remained in New York and was in conflict with federal authorities throughout the war. He had been an extreme pro-Southern Democrat in the 1850's, as had most of the Northern Confederates, and had supported Breckinridge in the election of 1860; by 1864, he advocated that the Democrats run Jefferson Davis for President and that the Union adopt the Confederate Constitution.[34]

The views of MacMahon and Van Evrie rested on a zealous defense of the institution of slavery, a defense predicated on their unshakable conviction of the inferiority of the Negro race. Only among the most extreme defenders of slavery in the South were there more sweeping assertions of racial inequality than those made by the two New Yorkers. The Negro, MacMahon wrote in 1861, was "physiologically and psychologically degraded" and was of an inferior species of the human race, "wholly dependent upon the Caucasian for progress, enlightenment, and well being." The slavery of "inferior" races such as the Negro seemed to Van Evrie the cornerstone of American civilization and of human progress; toward the end of the war, he proposed that the African slave trade be immediately reopened, that the Northern states adopt slavery in their constitutions, and that all the Negroes in the North be immediately reenslaved.[35]

Holding that slavery was a positive good, the very foundation

[33] Gray, *Hidden Civil War*, 13-30, 211ff., 218.

[34] J.H. Van Evrie, *Subgenation: the Theory of the Normal Relation of the Races* (pamphlet, New York, 1864) 59, 61. There is an account of Van Evrie's life in Howard C. Perkins, "The Defense of Slavery in the Northern Press on the Eve of the Civil War," *The Journal of Southern History*, IX, 503ff. (November 1943). Meager biographical information about MacMahon can be found in his history of the war, *Cause and Contrast: an Essay on the American Crisis* (Richmond, 1862) 81.

[35] MacMahon, *Cause and Contrast*, ix; Van Evrie, *Subgenation*, 30-31, 68-69. Mac-Mahon employed the phrase, "Negro subordination," while Van Evrie referred to the "subgenation" of the Negro; neither used the word "slavery."

of the old Union, both men blamed the war upon the antislavery fanatics and the "miscegenationists" (i.e., abolitionists) of the North who opposed that institution. Among those extremists, Mac-Mahon charged, there had been a persistent conspiracy, culminating in the election of Lincoln, to overthrow the Constitution and bring on war. Van Evrie declared that the Northern miscegenationists (despite the steady degeneration of Northerners after slavery was abolished in that section) had attempted to impose their system upon the South. Against this attempt the Confederates had simply defended themselves; "God grant," he wrote in 1864, "they may be successful in this pious work."[36]

MacMahon and Van Evrie exhibited in radical form the general tendency among supporters of the Confederacy to blame the war upon the actions of a small group of Northern zealots, generally abolitionists. Although there did not develop among Confederates quite the same sort of "conspiracy thesis" that was so prevalent in the Unionist histories, Jefferson Davis and Edward A. Pollard expressed a common sentiment when they held Lincoln and a comparatively few "evil" Yankees primarily responsible for the actual outbreak of hostilities. Going a step further in this direction, Joseph E. Brown, wartime Governor of the State of Georgia, specifically absolved the Democratic Party of the North, and even the rank and file of the Republican Party, from the moral guilt of causing war. A large part of the Northern populace, Brown declared, led by such men as Clement L. Vallandigham of Ohio, had tried to halt the Northern fanatics. But the "wicked leaders of the Republican Party," the "abolition leaders in power," proved too strong and finally precipitated armed conflict.[37]

One of the most significant and important statements of this Southern version of the conspiracy thesis was made by the members of the Confederate Congress in 1864 in an *Address* to the people of the seceded states. Northern extremists, stated the Congressmen, had decided that the Union and its Constitution must be destroyed in battle in order to carry out the purposes of the Republican Party (i.e., the destruction both of slavery and of the

---

[36] Van Evrie, *Subgenation*, 34ff., 54ff.; MacMahon, *Cause and Contrast*, 120-139.

[37] Message of Brown to the Georgia Legislature, March 10, 1864, quoted in Herbert Fielder, *A Sketch of the Life and Times and Speeches of Joseph E. Brown* (Springfield, Mass., 1883) 286-289.

equality of States).[38] The mass of the Northern people, however, loved the Union and did not wish to destroy it; so, in order to rally the population to support the war, its object was proclaimed to be the restoration of the Union. Even in 1864, said the *Address*, all the Northern people did not desire to conquer the South, and it cited the opposition of the Democratic Party in the North to the Lincoln administration—an opposition which was unfortunately rendered ineffectual because of the "arbitrary despotism" set up in the Union states by Lincoln.

In addition to placing the blame for the war upon Northern radicals, the Congressmen reiterated what were becoming the standard arguments in the Confederate interpretation of the war's causes. They insisted that the Southern movement was a popular uprising of all the people to protect their rights, a movement whose "unanimity and zeal" was unparalleled in history. They compared the Southerners of 1860-1861 to the colonists of 1776, but they emphasized that the Confederacy was a product not of sedition, insurrection, or violence but of law and of right. Yet, while agreeing with Davis and Pollard that secession was conservative in nature and purpose, the Congressmen took a stand on the question of slavery which was similar to that of Rhett and other proslavery "fire-eaters." Declaring that God had stamped indelibly upon Negro slaves the marks of "physical and intellectual inferiority," they made the forthright assertion that their government was unlike the Union in that it was based upon "the proper relation of labor and capital."[39]

In view of the statements made by Confederates after the war, this stand of the Congressmen on the slavery question is worthy of special attention. The majority view among Confederates during the war was expressed by Davis and Pollard when they emphasized that secession was simply an attempt to restore and to

[38] "Address of Congress to the People of the Confederate States," published in *Southern Historical Society Papers* (hereafter cited as *SHS Papers*), I, 23-38 (January 1876), and in Moore, *Rebellion Record*, VIII, Doc. Pages 385-391. In the *Rebellion Record*, the date of this address is given as February 26, 1864; it was signed by all the members of both houses of the Congress. J.L.M. Curry, the distinguished educator in the South after the war, was a member of the Confederate Congress, and was the actual author of this address (Edwin A. Alderman and Armisted C. Gordon, *J.L.M. Curry: A Biography* [New York, 1911] 173-174).

[39] *SHS Papers*, I, 24.

preserve intact the principles of the old Union, and that the morality of the institution of slavery was not in dispute between North and South. But, before 1865, there were a number of Southerners who declared, as did Rhett and the Congressmen, that the Confederate government was unlike the old Union in that it was specifically founded upon the institution of slavery. Such declarations were made not only by some radical "fire-eaters" but also by men whose views were considerably more moderate. Such a moderate as the Speaker of the Confederate House of Representatives, Thomas S. Bocock of Virginia, declared in 1862 that his government was sustained by a "peculiar and more conservative state of society" than the old Union.[40] The most striking expression of this sentiment was made by the Vice-president of the Confederacy, Alexander H. Stephens, in the previously mentioned address of March 1861 in which he praised the Confederacy as a new type of government, the first in the world's history with slavery as its "cornerstone."[41] After the war, when the attempt to set up a "new type of government" had failed and when slavery had been abolished by law, the opinions expressed by Bocock, Stephens, and the Congressional *Address* found few, if any, champions among former Confederates and were not generally alluded to.

The common conviction that the war was caused by Northerners provided a basic similarily of viewpoint among all Confederate sympathizers throughout the struggle. But within the limits of this fundamental agreement, Southerners exhibited during the conflict differences of opinion similar to those which Rhett, Bell, Lee, and Davis had shown in the early days after the firing on Fort Sumter. Not until after Appomattox did Confederates, unified by defeat and faced by the manifold hardships which accompanied defeat, arrive at a common interpretation of the causes and character of the secession movement and the war.

[40] Thomas S. Bocock, speech in the Confederate House of Representatives, February 18, 1862, printed in Moore, *Rebellion Record*, iv, Doc. Pages 189-190.
[41] See above, p. 24.

Confederate Viewpoints
1865 to the 1880's

WITH the surrender of its armies, the South's bid for independence was transformed into a cause that was lost. Confederates were now confronted with the harsh reality which had played little part in their thoughts in the winter of 1860-1861: they were a people vanquished in battle and subject to the will of the victors. Their voice, for at least a decade after the end of the war, was to count for little in national politics, and their society was to undergo reconstruction by the hand of their former foe. Defeated, exhausted, much of their land devastated, they faced what seemed to them a dismal present and a future auguring only ill. They felt oppressed, in the words of Robert L. Dabney, the former Confederate chaplain to General "Stonewall" Jackson, with "present sufferings and a prospective destiny more cruel and disastrous than has been visited on any civilized people of modern ages."[42]

To cap their despair was the galling fear that Northern victory in arms would be accompanied by the general adoption of Yankee opinions on the issues in dispute between North and South. Everywhere, it seemed, "Northern" viewpoints were gaining acceptance as unquestioned truth, and Confederates were being branded as "rebels" and "traitors." The full measure of bitterness was set down by a young woman of Georgia in her diary:

I hate the Yankees more and more, every time I look at one of their horrid newspapers and read the lies they tell about us, while we have our mouths closed and padlocked. The world will not hear our story, and we must figure just as our enemies choose to paint us. The pictures in "Harper's Weekly" and "Frank Leslie's" tell more lies than Satan himself was ever the father of. I get in such a rage when I look at them that I sometimes take off my slipper and beat the senseless paper with it.[43]

[42] Robert L. Dabney, *A Defence of Virginia* (New York, 1867) 356.
[43] Eliza Frances Andrews, *The War-Time Journal of A Georgia Girl, 1864-1865* (New York, 1908) 371 (diary entry for August 18, 1865).

Amid such gloomy circumstances, one of the few remaining sources of consolation to Confederate sympathizers was their hope and belief that "impartial history" would ultimately vindicate the justice and truth of their cause. However much in happier days they had cited victory in battle as evidence of Divine favor, Southerners, like most humans in similar circumstances, were unwilling after the war to believe that physical defeat signified any lack of merit in themselves or in the principles for which they had fought. Were the Huns superior to Caesar's race, a Virginian asked, just because they overran the Roman Empire?[44] Like vanquished men in all ages who feel that might has unjustly triumphed over right, Confederates looked to the future for justification. They turned, as their former President observed, "to the judgment of posterity for the reversal of the decree of their contemporaries, appealing with the self-sustaining hope of conscious rectitude from 'Philip drunk to Philip sober.' "[45] With the subsiding of passion, with the reassertion of the voice of truth and reason, then would the justice of Southern viewpoints be recognized, then would Yankee falsehoods be discredited. As ancient Hebrew prophets comforted their followers in time of trouble, so Dabney, the staunch Calvinist, gave assurance to Southerners:

Let the arrogant and successful wrongdoers flout our defense with disdain; we will meet them with it again, when it will be heard, in the day of their calamity, in the pages of impartial history and in the Day of Judgment.[46]

Stemming from the common experience of defeat, this desire to vindicate the South through history was shared after Appomattox by Confederates of all shades of opinion. It was founded upon some of the strongest of human sentiments. Defense of the South necessarily included a defense of one's own individual actions, and such personal justification held the same widespread appeal after 1865 which it customarily holds after any war, among any people. Southerners derived additional satisfaction from their conviction that by presenting to the world the "truth of Southern his-

[44] H.R. Pleasants, "Character of the Southern People," *The Land We Love*, IV, 243-248 (January 1868).

[45] Varina Howell Davis, *Jefferson Davis Ex-President of the Confederate States of America: A Memoir by His Wife* (2v., New York, 1890) II, 747.

[46] Dabney, *Defence*, 356.

tory," they were paying respect to the memory of their comrades and loved ones who had given their lives for the Confederacy. At the same time, they believed that they were thereby insuring that the youth of the South would grow up with a proper understanding and appreciation of the ideals and the valor of their parents. Historical defense of the South became an act of the highest patriotism.[47]

No one conveyed the intensity of the various emotions supporting this desire to vindicate the South with greater skill and force than Wade Hampton, prominent South Carolinian and former Confederate general. In a typical speech before a Richmond audience in 1873, Hampton appealed to Confederate sympathizers in words which reveal clearly the attitudes prevalent in the postwar South. Emphasizing the duty of parents, he told his listeners that if Southern children were

made to comprehend the origin, progress and culmination of that great controversy between the antagonistic sections of this continent . . . they cannot fail to see that truth, right, justice were on the side of their fathers.

He invoked sectional patriotism and respect for the dead:

Can any higher incentive to exertion be held out than those which call upon us to rescue our country [i.e., the South] from the unjust obloquy that has been heaped upon her; to justify our actions in the eyes of our contemporaries; to secure a verdict of acquittal from posterity, and to do honor to the memory of our dead? . . . Do you wish to see your kindred, who sacrificed not only all that makes life worth having, but life itself, for our common cause, and who are now sleeping peacefully in these sacred cemeteries . . . or on the fields their valor won, denounced as traitors? You know that they were not traitors.

Then, in a stirring peroration, he called upon all Southerners to fulfill their solemn obligation:

As it was the duty of every man to devote himself to the service of his country in that great struggle which has just ended so disastrously . . . so, now, when that country is prostrate in the dust, weeping for her dead who died in vain to save her liberties, every patriotic impulse

[47] Conversely, lack of criticism for the Union position in the war could be interpreted as disloyalty to the South, as the poet Paul Y. Hayne discovered when, shortly after Appomattox, he received an anonymous note directing him never to visit Richmond again because he had spoken too mildly against the Union cause in a poem. William P. Trent, *William Gilmore Simms* (Boston, 1892) 305.

should urge her surviving children to vindicate the great principles for which she fought, to justify the motives that activated her, to explain to the world the everliving truths she sought to maintain, to show the unexampled triumphs of her heroic armies, and to place on the eternal record an appeal from the distorted and vindictive judgment of her enemies, to the impartial tribunal of history, and to that dread Judge on high who alone can condemn or acquit.[48]

That former supporters of the Confederacy were decidedly responsive to pleas of the type made by Hampton was shown most clearly by the pronounced interest in various forms of historical endeavor in the South after the war ended. Books, articles, and speeches dealing with the history of the war and its causes were produced by a host of Confederates, led by their former President and Vice-president. With great frequency, the biographies of Confederates tell of the collection of materials for a history of the war; many of these were never completed, yet, completed or not, the spirit which sustained this labor was the hope that history would "some day bring present events before her impartial bar; and then her ministers will recall my obscure little book, and will recognize in it the words of truth and righteousness."[49] Supplementing the "obscure little books" were magazines founded and edited with the primary purpose "to vindicate the truth of history in regard to the events of the War." Such were *The Land We Love*, edited by D.H. Hill, distinguished Confederate general, and *The Southern Review*, established by A.T. Bledsoe, Assistant Secretary of War in the Confederacy.[50]

But the principal center of historical activity in the South after the war was the Southern Historical Society, organized in 1869 by a host of prominent Confederates including R.M.T. Hunter, Confederate Secretary of State, Generals Beauregard, Jubal A.

---

[48] Wade Hampton, "Address of Gen. Wade Hampton," *Trans. Southern Historical Society*, I, 11-14 (1874). For typical expressions of sentiments similar to those of Hampton's, see: J.A.P. Campbell, "The Lost Cause," *SHS Papers*, xvi, 235-236 (1888); Joseph Hodgson, *The Cradle of the Confederacy* (Mobile, Alabama, 1876) "Preface" (unpaged); "Editorial," *SHS Papers*, I, 41-42 (January 1876); Jefferson Davis, "Address" (delivered April 25, 1882), *SHS Papers*, x, 228-229 (May 1882).

[49] Dabney, *Defence*, 6.

[50] Both magazines began publication shortly after the fighting ceased, *The Land We Love* in 1866 at Charlotte, North Carolina, and *The Southern Review* in 1867 at Baltimore. It was Hill's boast that his magazine was endorsed by eighty generals and that it was recognized as the organ of the late Confederate Army.

Early, and Dabney H. Maury, Admiral Raphael Semmes, and many other leaders. Denied access to the federal archives, they feared that the official collection of war documents planned by the Washington government (which ultimately appeared under the title, *The War of The Rebellion . . . Official Records of the Union and Confederate Armies*) would not do justice to their cause; their express purpose in organizing the Southern Historical Society was to provide for the collection, preservation, and presentation to the world of materials which would vindicate Southern principles in the war.[51] With affiliated branches in the former Confederate states (balloting within the society was done, inevitably, by states), the society received the support of most of the well-known Confederate leaders. The monthly *Southern Historical Society Papers* (beginning in 1876) were, for at least ten years, one of the most important forums of authoritative Confederate opinion on the war.

The guiding purpose, be it repeated, behind the writing of histories and the founding of magazines and historical societies in the postwar South was the desire to show, in the words of the couplet (by the English poet, P.S. Worsley) which former Confederates so loved to quote, that

> *No nation rose so white and fair*
> *Or fell so pure of crimes.*

For some two decades after Appomattox, this attitude was widespread among Confederate sympathizers. They sought to demonstrate that their "nation" had been more humane in its treatment of war prisoners than the Union, that its soldiers had never used "poison bullets," or that their language had never been so vulgar as that of the Northern troops. (General Jubal A. Early even gave battle to Northern poets, insisting that, contrary to Whittier's famous lines, Barbara Frietchie had in reality never defied Southern soldiers with the immortal

---

[51] The society's founding, purposes, and early history are sketched in: *SHS Papers*, I, 39-45 (January 1876); VI, 191-192 (October 1878); VI, 239-240 (November 1878); VI, 244-245 (December 1878). In some respects it took the place of a veterans organization until the first South-wide society of Confederate veterans was established in 1889. There is a description of the society and of historical activities in the postwar South in E. Merton Coulter, "What the South has Done about Its History," *The Journal of Southern History*, II, 3-28 (February 1936).

"Shoot, if you must, this old gray head,
But spare your country's flag," she said.)[52]

The common experience of defeat and the omnipresent desire to vindicate the South through the agency of history were extremely important factors shaping the outlook of Confederate sympathizers after 1865. They provided the most important foundation for the emotional and intellectual unity characterizing the postwar South—a unity greater than that of either the South of the 1850's or the South during wartime. Now (as in other defeated "nations") there was a strong tendency for Southerners, whatever had been their differences in the crisis of 1860-1861 or during the years of war, to close ranks and to forget past differences in the face of what seemed to them their present perils.

The closing of ranks after 1865 was well illustrated in the activities of the Confederacy's two highest civil officials, Vice-president Stephens and President Davis. Alexander H. Stephens, after the first year of the war, had been one of the leaders in attempts to thwart and to embarrass the Confederate government.[53] Although he held the second highest office in that government, he seldom visited Richmond after 1862. Bitterly critical of the centralization of power in the Davis administration, he vehemently opposed the policy of conscription and the suspension of the writ of *habeas corpus*. He sympathized with Governor Joseph E. Brown of Georgia in the latter's open defiance of the Confederate authorities, and, desiring a negotiated peace in 1864, he apparently considered the advisability of ousting the Davis government or of leading Georgia in secession from the Confederacy.

But in defeat, Stephens underwent experiences similar to those of other Confederate leaders.[54] Imprisoned for some months by federal authorities, he was not allowed to take the seat in the United States Senate to which he was elected in January 1866, and from his Georgia home he observed the processes of Reconstruction. Under the pressure of these events, Stephens' ideas and

---

[52] A.M. Keiley, *In Vinculis* (New York, 1866) *passim*; *The Land We Love*, v, 544-545 (October 1868); *SHS Papers*, I, 113-221, 225-327 (March, April, 1876), VII, 435-439 (September 1879).

[53] Rudolph Von Abele, *Alexander H. Stephens: A Biography* (New York, 1946) chap. four.

[54] *ibid.*, chaps. five and six.

actions after 1865 came to differ little from the general pattern of most Confederate sympathizers. By the early 1870's, he occupied a position in politics more irreconcilable and more anti-North than most prominent Southerners. And like so many other Confederates, he wrote a history of the war to vindicate the South. In this history, there was praise for the Confederate government, and emphasis was placed upon those matters upon which President Davis and Stephens had been in agreement. Although the disagreements between Stephens and Davis were mentioned, they were dismissed in Stephens' observation that the ablest and truest men often have honest differences of opinion; Stephens stated that he had no doubt that the Confederate President, the Cabinet, and the Congress did the "very best they could, from their own convictions of what was best to be done at the time."[55] Even the most loyal Confederate supporter could have found no fault with Stephens' summation of the purpose of his history: "vindication of the Rightfulness of the great Cause of those with whom my fortunes in the terrible and most lamentable contest were cast."[56] Like Stephens, there were other Southerners who became more ardent Confederates after Appomattox than they had ever been before.

While Stephens was learning at first hand the vicissitudes attendant upon defeat, so too was the Confederate President, and Jefferson Davis became one of the principal symbols around which Southern emotions and ideas solidified in the first few years of defeat. Before the fighting had completely ended, Abraham Lincoln had apparently decided against the imprisonment or trial of prominent Confederates.[57] But in the Northern reaction to the

[55] Alexander H. Stephens, *A Constitutional View of the Late War Between the States* (2v., Philadelphia, 1868-1870) II, 625. For other typical discussions by Stephens of the ideas and actions of Davis, see *ibid.*, II, 423-424, 500ff., 526-527.

[56] *ibid.*, II, 667.

[57] At Lincoln's last Cabinet meeting (held on the day he was shot by Booth) the question of what should be done with the Confederate leaders came up, and Lincoln expressed his opposition to their imprisonment and trial in forceful and vivid language. "I am a good deal like the Irishman who had joined a temperance society, but thought he might take a drink now and then if he drank unbeknown to himself," Secretary of the Treasury McCulloch quoted Lincoln as saying. "A good many people think that all the big Confederates ought to be arrested and tried as traitors. Perhaps they ought to be, but I should be right glad if they would get out of the country unbeknown to me" (Hugh McCulloch, *Men and Measures of Half A Century* [New York, 1889] 408). According to Secretary of the Navy Welles, Lincoln declared that he would take no part in hanging any of the Confederate leaders: "Frighten them out of the country, open the

assassination of Lincoln, as we have seen, there arose a strong sentiment in favor of punishing the principal "rebels," particularly Jefferson Davis, who was thought to be implicated in the assassination plot. Orders for the capture of Davis were issued, and within less than a month after the assassination, he was seized in Georgia by federal troops. No action was ever taken upon the charge that he was connected with the death of Lincoln, but in June 1865, Davis, with Lee and a number of other prominent Confederates, was indicted by a federal grand jury for treason against the United States.[58]

The efforts of the federal government to convict Southerners of treason naturally centered upon the President of the defeated Confederacy (and no attempts were ever made to bring any Confederates other than Davis to trial on this charge). For two years, Davis remained in prison, and then spent another period of almost two years on bail awaiting trial. During this long interval, he became in effect the personal representative of the defeated South, the "martyr of the lost cause"—and his "martyrdom" was aided by the fact that he spent five days in chains when first imprisoned. In this role, Davis probably won more support in the South than he had ever enjoyed as President of the Confederacy; the South itself probably became more unified on this issue than it had been on any subject since 1861. Southerners signed petitions for his release and Southern legislatures passed resolutions of sympathy. To former Confederates, Davis seemed, in the phrase of General D.H. Hill, the "vicarious sufferer" for the actions of all of them; if Davis is guilty, declared a memorial of the Georgia State Convention in October 1865, "so are we."[59]

---

gates, let down the bars, scare them off, said he [Lincoln] throwing up his hands as if scaring sheep." Gideon Welles, "Lincoln and Johnson," *The Galaxy* (New York) XIII, 526 (April 1872).

[58] Roy Franklin Nichols, "United States vs. Jefferson Davis, 1865-1869," *The American Historical Review*, XXXI, 266-284 (January 1926); Freeman, *Lee*, IV, 202ff., 334, 381.

[59] For contemporary Southern sentiment toward Davis, see: D.H. Hill, *The Land We Love*, I, 278 (August 1866); James Ford Rhodes, *History of the United States from the Compromise of 1850* (7v., New York, 1893-1906) v, 538; Edward A. Pollard, *Life of Jefferson Davis* (Philadelphia, 1869) 526ff.; J. William Jones, *Life and Letters of Robert Edward Lee* (New York, 1906) 388; Sidney Lanier, *Tiger Lilies* (New York, 1867) in Charles R. Anderson, ed., *The Centennial Edition of the Works of Sidney Lanier* (10v., Baltimore, 1945) v, 97; James Wilford Garner, *Reconstruction in Mississippi* (New York, 1901) 92-93.

Davis was the symbol around which were rallied the emotions of the defeated South, and became in addition the center of the earliest important efforts to vindicate the Confederate cause through history—for the questions involved in his trial were momentous for his section. If he were convicted of treason, the way was prepared for similar convictions of any and all Confederates whom the federal government might choose to bring to trial. In addition, the question of whether Davis was a "traitor" necessarily involved the more fundamental issue of the causes and nature of the war; if he were found guilty, Confederate actions would thereby be stigmatized legally as treason, and the "Northern" interpretation of the conflict would have the sanction of the courts. The defense of Davis would inevitably require a full-scale justification of the South's role in secession and war—and this justification was the crucial point in any vindication of the South. The "war guilt" was the crux of the matter for Confederates (just as for Unionists); if the South were to be vindicated, she must be adjudged innocent of causing the war—and this was precisely the central issue in the trial of the Confederate President. The defense of Davis enlisted widespread support among former Confederates, and the arguments advanced in his behalf were a significant indication of the manner in which Confederates interpreted the causes of the war after Appomattox.

When the war ended, few Southerners were better prepared for the vindication of Davis on historical grounds than Albert Taylor Bledsoe and Bernard J. Sage.[60] Bledsoe, a professor of mathematics at the University of Virginia before he became Assistant Secretary of War in the Confederate government, had been sent to London during the war by Davis, apparently for the primary purpose of preparing an historical and constitutional justification of secession. (He never tired, as his biographer has pointed out, of quoting what he said were Lee's words to him: "We all look to you for our vindication.") Returning from England, he published in 1866 the material he had collected, giving his volume the title, *Is Davis a Trai-*

[60] Edwin Mims, "Albert Taylor Bledsoe," *The Dictionary of American Biography*, II, 364-365; Sophia Bledsoe Herrick, "Explanatory Preface" in Albert T. Bledsoe, *The War Between the States* (Lynchburg, Va., 1915); Herman C. Nixon, "Bernard Janin Sage," *The Dictionary of American Biography*, XVI, 289-290.

tor: or Was Secession a Constitutional Right Previous to the War of 1861? Like Bledsoe, Sage (a Louisiana sugar planter born in Connecticut) had been sent abroad during the war on special missions by the Confederate President, and he was prepared to publish a defense in 1865, shortly after the fighting had ceased. The title of his volume, just as that of Bledsoe's, indicated its spirit and purpose: *Davis and Lee: a Vindication of the Southern States, Citizens, and Rights, by the Federal Constitution and Its Makers, and an Exposure of the Perversions of the Said Constitution, and the Falsifications of Historical Records, by the Massachusetts Expounders.*

To defend Davis, Lee, and all Confederates from charges of treason, Bledsoe and Sage advanced two major arguments: first, state secession had been in accord with the Constitution and thus involved no punishable "crime"; second, whatever the nature of secession, it was an action of sovereign states for which no personal blame could justly be placed upon individual Confederates. In support of their claim that secession was constitutional, Bledsoe and Sage employed the familiar arguments which had been common in the Southern states long before 1861. Citing the language of the Constitution and the opinions of men of the revolutionary generation, they described the Constitution of 1787 as a "compact" between independent, sovereign states which were justified, legally and morally, in resuming their sovereignty by secession whenever (as in the winter of 1860-1861) circumstances warranted. The disruption of the Union was blamed in particular upon such Northern constitutional theorists as Justice Joseph Story and Daniel Webster. Their nationalizing doctrines, it was asserted, had provided the justification for the attempts of the aggressive, ambitious North to rule the South, and it was these attempts which had made secession necessary.

The concept of state sovereignty also underlay the contention of Bledsoe and Sage that Confederates could not with justice be held personally responsible for secession. Developing the line of reasoning employed during the war by the Confederate agents abroad, they explained that Davis, Lee, and their followers had been taught from childhood to give primary allegiance to their states; even at West Point, the military academy of the federal government, declared Sage, the future Confederate leaders had been instructed from a textbook which specifically recognized that the right of secession belonged to sovereign states.[61] In the crisis of 1860-1861, these men naturally remained loyal to their states in accordance with their lifelong beliefs. How then, it was argued, could they be convicted of treason, solely because they maintained allegiance to the only sovereign they knew, their state?

The histories of Bledsoe and Sage were of direct assistance to the lawyers preparing the defense of Jefferson Davis. But their arguments were never actually tested in court, because the United States government ultimately dismissed its suit against the Confederate President without a trial, and no Confederate was ever tried on the charge of treason. Although Davis was not affirmatively cleared, however, the continued reluctance of the government to try his case, and the final dismissal without trial, seemed to Southerners a clear indication that their foes recognized the weakness of their own arguments. Here was cause for rejoicing, here was one of the first rays of encouragement, however faint, to those who sought to vindicate the South.[62]

The defense of Jefferson Davis against the charge of treason has a triple significance in the history of attitudes toward the war. Since it enlisted the support of many Southerners, it demonstrated the emotional unity of the postwar South and served as a focus for that unity. In the second place, the propositions set forth by such defenders as Bledsoe and Sage indicated the basic attitudes toward the war which colored the thinking of Confederate sympathizers after Appomattox. Bledsoe and Sage were partisans who (both figuratively and literally) presented lawyerlike briefs for the de-

[61] This textbook was William Rawle's *A View of the Constitution of the United States of America* (Philadelphia, 1825), and it was apparently used as a text at West Point at irregular intervals before the Civil War. The lawyers who prepared Davis's defense declared that they had intended to cite Rawle's volume if the treason trial had been held. Actually, Davis, by his own statement, later made it clear that he was not instructed from this book, and it seems probable that Lee was not (Robert McElroy, *Jefferson Davis: The Unreal and the Real* [2v., New York, 1937] I, 15-16, II, 610-611; Freeman, *Lee*, I, 78-79). After the war, Southerners frequently defended the Confederate leaders on the ground that they had been taught secession at West Point from Rawle's *View*. See, for example: Dabney H. Maury, "West Point and Secession," *SHS Papers*, VI, 249 (December 1878); Robert Bingham, "Sectional Misunderstandings," *The North American Review*, CLXXIX, 361-362 (September 1904).
[62] Rowland, *Davis*, VII, 104-110; Pollard, *Davis*, 534-536.

fense in the form of histories. Their ultimate goal was to prove that the South's actions in secession and war were legal and proper, while the blame or guilt for causing the war rested entirely upon the North.

This brief-for-the-defense approach to an interpretation of the war's causes was to be dominant among Confederate sympathizers for many years. It was extolled with disarming candor by Jefferson Davis long after the soldiers of Lee and Grant had laid down their arms. Speaking to a gathering in New Orleans in the 1880's, the Confederate President held up no ideal of a broad and balanced understanding of history for his fellow Southerners—that task he reserved for historians of a future generation. The powerful and victorious North, he declared, had amply presented its views on the war, and the duty of Southerners was to set forth in opposition their own opinions. "I will frankly acknowledge," said Davis, "that I would distrust the man who served the Confederate cause and was capable of giving a disinterested account of it. . . . I would not give twopence for a man whose heart was so cold that he could be quite impartial."[63] Jefferson Davis was more outspoken after the war than most of his supporters, and he was not a man to relinquish old hatreds easily and speedily. But, in this case, he accurately reflected the spirit of partisan advocacy characterizing the interpretations of the causes of the war by most Confederate sympathizers in the two decades after the fighting ceased.

Finally, in the third place, the arguments presented in defense of Davis revealed not only the general spirit in which Southerners viewed the war after 1865 but also the specific explanation for the coming of war which most won their favor. This explanation centered around the justification of secession as a constitutional, conservative, peaceful, and orderly movement which was prevented from taking its normal course due to the unconstitutional use of force by the Washington government. Defeat led to a larger measure of agreement among Confederate supporters in interpreting the causes of the war than had existed before 1865. Whatever differences there were in 1861 between the opinions of a Rhett, on the one hand, and those of a Lee, on the other, tended to disappear

---

[63] "Address of President Davis" [among loyal Confederate sympathizers, the end of the war did not affect Davis's title], *SHS Papers*, x, 228 (May 1882).

after 1865 in the common attempt to vindicate a lost cause by picturing it as a constitutional and conservative cause. Confederates carried on long and acrimonious disputes among themselves after the fighting ceased over the relative merits of their commanders, the comparative fighting ability of troops from various units and from various states, and over a variety of other topics. But in explaining the causes of the war, they presented a practically unbroken front. In historical interpretation, as in politics, the South was more solid after Appomattox than before.

The interpretation of the war's causes in terms of the constitutionality of secession was not new—Jefferson Davis had made such an interpretation in April 1861, and other Confederates had followed his lead. What was new after 1865, however, was the unanimity with which Confederate supporters employed this defense. Now, unlike the war years, practically no voice was lifted in praise of revolution or rebellion or the setting up of a new government founded upon principles different from those of the old Union. Instead, the emphasis now was just the reverse, was placed upon demonstrating that the secessionists had been more loyal to the principles of the Union of 1789 than had been their foes.

One of the clearest indications of the unity of sentiment in the postwar South is to be found in the notable evolution in the opinions of Robert E. Lee from the days of 1861—a change both in his attitude toward the question of assessing blame for the war and in his interpretation of the secession movement.

When Lee went to war, his dominant mood had been one of sadness rather than of recrimination, and he seems to have been uninterested in efforts to pin responsibility for the state of affairs upon any one group or section. His conduct after surrendering to Grant has understandably won the unstinted admiration of later generations; rejecting proposals to migrate from the South, removing bitterness from his mind, he advocated and personally practiced a policy of hard work, patience, and conciliation. In nearly every respect, he was the complete opposite of the "unreconstructed rebel." Yet, after 1865, on occasion (and it should be emphasized that it was only on occasion), the desire to defend the South and to place the blame for war upon the former enemy burst through even the careful self-control of Lee and showed itself in what was for him unusually sharp language on this subject. "The epithets that have been heaped upon us of 'rebels' and 'traitors' have no just meaning," he wrote to a friend after the war, "nor are they believed in by those who understand the subject, even at the North."[64] More explicitly, he expressed his feelings in 1866 to the distinguished British historian Lord Acton, who had requested his views on the war. After stating that Virginia had worked to save the Union, Lee cited the remark of Senator Douglas that it was the Republican Party which had prevented the adoption of the proposals of Senator Crittenden for compromise of the differences between North and South in 1861. "Who then," he demanded, "is responsible for the War?"[65]

Lee revealed a profound shift of opinion not only in regard to the assessment of blame for causing the war but also in regard to the secession movement. In 1861, he had been one of that group of Confederates (primarily men from the border states) who held that the Constitution did not allow secession and who did not justify their actions on that ground. Few Confederates had stated more emphatically their disagreement with the compact theory and their belief that secession was unconstitutional.

The framers of our Constitution [Lee had written in January 1861] never exhausted so much labor, wisdom and forbearance in its formation and surrounded it with so many guards and securities, if it was intended to be broken by every member of the Confederacy at will. It was intended for "perpetual union" . . . and for the establishment of a government, not a compact, which can only be dissolved by revolution, or the consent of all the people in convention assembled. It is idle to talk of secession.[66]

But in the course of the next few years, Lee's views underwent considerable change; he "absorbed," states his biographer, "the Southern constitutional argument and was convinced by it." After the war, Lee conceded that the result of the struggle had decided that the Union was indissoluble, and he made no effort to conceal the fact that he had opposed the *exercise* of the right of secession in 1861. But now he defended the traditional Southern interpreta-

[64] McElroy, *Davis*, II, 615.

[65] John N. Figgis and Reginald V. Laurence, eds., *Selections from the Correspondence of the First Lord Acton* (London, 1917) I, 304-305; Freeman, *Lee*, IV, 302-306.

[66] Freeman, *Lee*, I, 421.

tion of the Constitution. In the letter of 1866 noted above, which contained his fullest discussion of the subject, he cited in support of the state sovereignty viewpoint (just as many other Confederates were doing) the opinions of Washington, Jefferson, and Chief Justice Chase, and he took particular pains to point out that New Englanders had asserted the right of secession when it suited their interests. For the last seventy years, Lee concluded, state sovereignty had been advocated by "the leading men of the country."[67] In 1861, Lee had been a symbol of the diversity of opinion among Confederates in interpreting the causes of the war; by 1866, he was a symbol of the unity of Confederate opinion on that subject.

Lee wrote letters in support of state sovereignty; his fellow Southerners wrote volumes, or at least long articles. The justification of secession as a conservative, constitutional movement rested in the last analysis upon the doctrine that the Constitution of 1787 had been a compact among sovereign states—and upon this ground former Confederates entrenched themselves after 1865. Again and again the familiar arguments were repeated and the time-honored evidence was marshaled in order to demonstrate that the compact theory of the Union had been sanctioned both by the men who wrote the Constitution and, afterwards, by leading statesmen in all sections of the country. Alexander H. Stephens presented one of the most detailed and forceful arguments for the theory in his two-volume history of the war; essentially similar arguments were advanced by many other Confederates, including Jefferson Davis, Robert L. Dabney, former General Jubal A. Early, and Peter Turney, a colonel in the Confederate Army who later became Governor of Tennessee and Chief Justice of the State Supreme Court.[68] A discussion of the war's causes by a Confederate was incomplete if it did not include some of the standard proofs of the compact theory. Through repetition, the arguments became so familiar that, by the late 1880's, even when a Confederate veteran sketched them

[67] Figgis and Laurence, *Correspondence of the First Lord Acton*, I, 302-305; Freeman, *Lee*, IV, 302-306, 402n.17.

[68] Stephens, *Constitutional View*; Jefferson Davis, *The Rise and Fall of the Confederate Government* (2v., New York, 1881); Robert L. Dabney, *Life and Campaigns of Lieut.- General Thomas J. Jackson (Stonewall Jackson)* (New York, 1866) 125ff.; Jubal A. Early, *The Heritage of the South* (Lynchburg, 1915) (written in the 1860's) 61ff.; Peter Turney, "They Wore the Gray—The Southern Cause Vindicated," *SHS Papers*, XVI, 319-339 (1888).

before an audience of Confederate veterans, he felt called upon to apologize for carrying his hearers over such well-known ground.[69]

Confederates generally derived from the compact theory of state sovereignty the same conclusions as had Bledsoe and Sage: that state secession was constitutional and that individual Confederates were personally justified in the course they pursued.[70] From this standpoint, the war was most accurately described as a conflict between independent states; and so prevalent was this view among Confederate sympathizers, so essential was it to their concept of the fundamental nature of the war, that it became a matter of principle to refer to the struggle only as "The War Between the States." (Many years after the cannons had ceased their fire, the former President of the Confederacy expressed regret for having once, in the hurry of writing, used another name for the war.)[71]

Confederate supporters continued to insist after 1865, as before, that their conduct in this War Between the States possessed the sanction not only of the Constitution but also of public opinion in the South. They asserted that they had been neither rebels nor conspirators and that Unionist charges of a Southern "conspiracy" were without foundation. Secession had resulted not from the mere intrigue of a few disgruntled men but from a widely popular movement supported by the mass of the Southern people. Among the many who expressed these sentiments were Jefferson Davis, R.M.T. Hunter, Judge Campbell of Mississippi, and Confederate General D.H. Maury. Typical were the words of Hunter, picturing a brave people who, abhorring war, were nonetheless brought together by their determination to maintain their liberty:

Men too old to be driven blindly by passion; women whose gentle and kindly instincts were deeply impressed by the horrors of war, and young men, with fortune and position yet to be won . . . if peace could be maintained . . . united in the common cause.[72]

Almost as fundamental in the thinking of former Confederates

[69] Turney, *SHS Papers*, XVI, 338.

[70] Freeman, *Lee*, IV, 253; Hampton, *Trans. Southern Historical Society*, I, 14; Stephens, *Constitutional View*, I, 20.

[71] J. William Jones, *SHS Papers*, XIV, 451 (1886).

[72] R.M.T. Hunter, "Origin of the Late War," *SHS Papers*, I, 1 (January 1876). See also: Campbell, "Lost Cause," *SHS Papers*, XVI, 241 (1888); Davis, *Rise and Fall*, I, 199; D.H. Maury, *SHS Papers*, I, 426-427 (June 1876).

as the contention that secession was constitutional and was approved by most Southerners, was the insistence that the war was not caused by a conflict between North and South over the morality of the institution of slavery. This, again, was a point of view which had been urged by Davis, Lee, and others as early as 1861; the new development after 1865 was the practical unanimity of opinion on this point. No longer did Southerners claim, as some of them had done in 1861, that slavery had been the "cornerstone" of the Confederacy or that the Confederate government had been founded specifically upon this unique basis for the proper relations between the races. Now, they were agreed that slavery simply happened to be the specific issue over which the South had finally been pushed into opposition to Northern aggression.

This did not mean that Confederate sympathizers ceased to defend the institution of slavery. Although they accepted the fact that slavery was legally abolished once and for all, they vigorously justified the institution as it had existed in the *ante-bellum* South. They were scornful of what General D.H. Hill called the "hypocritical cant" of protestations by Southerners that they had "always believed slavery to be a sin" and that they were happy because it had been abolished.[73] They praised slavery as a beneficent institution for both the "superior" and the "inferior" races in the South; through its mild discipline, it was stated, kind masters had introduced a savage people to the rudiments of civilization. To emphasize their contention that their institution had not been the harsh and cruel system commonly pictured, some Southerners refused to employ the word "slavery" and wrote instead of "African servitude" (Jefferson Davis), "negro servitude" (E.A. Pollard), or the "legal subordination of the African to the Caucasian race" (Alexander H. Stephens). "Never," declared Jefferson Davis, "was there a happier dependence of labor and capital on each other."[74]

But despite their defense of the institution of slavery, Southern-

[73] "Editorial," *The Land We Love*, III, 85 (May 1867).
[74] Davis, *Rise and Fall*, II, 193. For other typical defenses of slavery, see: Stephens, *Constitutional View*, I, 539-541, and II, 80-83; Pollard, *The Lost Cause* (New York, 1866) 43-49; Early, *Heritage of the South*, 107-113. One of the most elaborate justifications of slavery published after Appomattox was R.L. Dabney's *A Defence of Virginia* (New York, 1867) which repeated the standard proslavery arguments employed before the war, including the Biblical defense.

ers insisted that slavery was not a cause of the war in the sense of being a source of an irrepressible moral conflict between North and South. They admitted that Northerners had attacked slavery in *ante-bellum* days; in fact, one of their primary justifications of secession was that it had been the only recourse of the Southern states in view of the North's concerted attack upon their domestic institution.[75] They ascribed those attacks, however, not to any humanitarian or ideological considerations which indicated divergent opinions on the morality of slavery, but to the desires of ambitious politicians and selfish manufacturers for political power and economic gain. They charged that Northern majorities in Congress had passed legislation for the economic benefit of their section's commercial and manufacturing interests and at the expense of the Southern states.[76] The Yankees had become grasping and aggressive, and Jefferson Davis, drawing a parallel to the contemporary Franco-Prussian War, compared the Yankees of the 1850's to the Prussians of the 1870's (he described the Prussians as the "arrogant, robbing Yankees of Europe" who appropriated their small sister states).[77]

Only by chance, Confederate sympathizers maintained, had the South's resistance to the North's unconstitutional and aggressive acts come to a head over questions connected with the institution of slavery. The split might have come about, as one Confederate put it, over mules; eventually it did come over slavery. To Edward McCrady, Jr., a South Carolina historian who had served in the Confederate Army, it was now a cause for regret that his state's convention had justified secession in 1860 so exclusively in terms of the North's actions toward slavery. McCrady summed up the prevalent opinion among former Confederates when he stated that the institution of slavery, although it might have been the occasion of the war, was assuredly not its cause.[78]

---

[75] Hunter, "Origin of the Late War," *SHS Papers*, I, 3ff. (January 1876); Matthew Fontaine Maury, "A Vindication of Virginia and the South," *SHS Papers*, I, 57-58 (February 1876); Early, *Heritage of the South*, 73-74; Stephens, *Constitutional View*, I, 495ff.

[76] Hodgson, *Cradle of the Confederacy*, 155-156, 206, 214-215, 219-221; M.F. Maury, *SHS Papers*, I, 54-56 (February 1876); R.L. Dabney, "Memoir . . . ," *SHS Papers*, I, 455 (June 1876).

[77] McElroy, *Davis*, II, 621.

[78] Edward McCrady, Jr., "Address," *SHS Papers*, XVI, 248, 255 (1888). Practically identical words were used by many other former Confederates. See: Dabney, *Defence*, 354-355; Davis, *Rise and Fall*, I, 78; Stephens, *Constitutional View*, I, 10.

Not slavery but the North's unjustifiable assaults upon the Southern states had caused secession and war, in the view of Confederates. And yet it is worthy of note that Confederates, although they denied the Unionist interpretation of an irrepressible conflict stemming from the institution of slavery, found the ultimate factors which led to war in fundamental differences between North and South. For in their view, the primary reasons for the North's hostility to the Southern states lay in the fact that the Northern and Southern states had differing, antagonistic, and competing ways of life.

The Southern way of life was generally defined by former Confederates in terms of an agricultural economy, locally controlled, and conservative in its social and political customs. At the beginning of the Confederacy's existence in 1861, Jefferson Davis had described the divergent economies of the agricultural South and the commercial and industrial North, and this difference was frequently mentioned by Southerners after 1865. In addition, they emphasized in particular that the *ante-bellum* South had differed from the North in that its civilization had been essentially conservative. It was conservative, they asserted, in its concept of constitutional liberty, centering around the sovereignty of states and opposed both to national centralization and to extreme doctrines of the "natural rights" of individuals. It was conservative also, they stated, in its aristocratic principles, opposing mere majority rule, opposing what the former Confederate Secretary of State R.M.T. Hunter called the "despotic majority of numbers" in the North.[79]

D.H. Hill, A.T. Bledsoe, and R.L. Dabney took the lead in describing the antagonism between Southern "conservatism" and Northern "radicalism." The North, they declared, had abandoned the system of government prescribed in the Constitution and had adopted radical, democratic, European "isms," based upon principles of equal rights for all individuals and rule by the majority. These doctrines had stemmed from the French Revolution; they were held, implied General Jubal Early, by the men who had crucified Jesus Christ. Against Northern Jacobinism the Confederacy had fought the whole world's battle; the South, asserted Hill, was the *Vendée* of the United States and had waged a similar fight

[79] Hunter, "Origin," *SHS Papers*, I, 9.

for "conservatism against lawlessness, infidelity, irreverence towards God and man, *radicalism*."[80]

Confederates did not identify the underlying differences between North and South in the same terms as Unionists—the Unionists placed stress upon ideological differences between a free and a slave society, which Confederates denied, while Confederates more frequently mentioned material and economic differences between the sections. But Confederates no less than Unionists tended to describe an "irrepressible conflict" (without using that phrase) between the differing interests of the agricultural and conservative South, on the one hand, and the mercantile and "radical" North, on the other.

This conflict, arising from basic differences between North and South, could, in the view of Southerners, easily have been solved without war by the peaceful secession of the Southern states. The North, however, had provoked armed hostilities by its indefensible actions in the winter of 1860-1861, and these actions clearly placed the guilt of initiating war upon the North. Northerners, particularly the leaders of the Republican Party, had made secession inevitable, Confederate sympathizers asserted, by their refusal to compromise on any of the issues in dispute in 1860-1861.[81] Even after the secession of the Southern states, they declared, war need not have come had not the Lincoln administration determined to force those states back into the Union. Employing the familiar reasoning which Jefferson Davis had expressed in his April 1861 message to the Confederate Congress, Southerners now insisted that the Fort Sumter episode was conclusive proof both of Northern war guilt and of Northern duplicity. They stated that the initial aggression in 1861 lay in the attempts of the federal government to reinforce the fort. Only by a shallow and dishonest "trick," wrote E.A. Pollard expressing a common sentiment, had Lincoln provoked the firing of the first shot by the South. Rather than an act of aggres-

[80] "Editorial," *The Land We Love*, v, 447 (September 1868). For similar ideas, see: Anon., "The Crimes of Philanthropy," *The Land We Love*, ii, 81-93 (December 1866); Early, *Heritage of the South*, 119.

[81] For typical Southern accounts of the events of 1860-1861, see: John A. Campbell, "Reply of Judge Campbell," *Transactions of the Southern Historical Society*, i, 26 (1874); Dabney, *Jackson*, 173ff.; Davis, *Rise and Fall*, i, 268ff., 289ff.; Pollard, *Lost Cause*, 111; Stephens, *Constitutional View*, ii, 34-53; Turney, "They Wore the Gray," *SHS Papers*, xvi, 337.

sion, the Confederate reduction of Fort Sumter was in reality a defensive measure, "*as purely an act of self-defense and self-preservation,*" it was stated, "as is to be found in all history."[82]

These charges that Lincoln and the Republican leaders had provoked war in 1861 were, after Appomattox as before, the nearest Southern counterpart to the Northern "conspiracy" versions of the war's origin. And, just as during the war, the most bitter criticisms of Northern "conspirators," came not from Southerners but from a Northerner who had sympathized with the Confederacy, George Lunt of Massachusetts. Lunt's history, *The Origin of the Late War* (published in 1866), was the most important statement after the war of the views of Northerners who had favored the South.

Lunt was a graduate of Harvard and a journalist whose political sympathies had shifted from the Whig to the Democratic Party in the 1850's. During the first two years of the war, he was editor of his city's leading Democratic newspaper, the Boston *Daily Courier,* a journal which seemed to one ardent supporter of the Union an "infamous reservoir of treason, mendacity and scurrility."[83] The opinions expressed by Lunt in his history were similar to those of Southerners in many respects. Firmly convinced that Negroes were an inferior race, he defended slavery in the *antebellum* South as a positive good, sanctioned by the Bible and by the "moral law." Like Confederates, however, he held that slavery was not a cause of the war but was simply the issue over which North-South disputes had come to a head. His explanation of the origins of the war reflected (just as had that of MacMahon and Van Evrie during the war) his intense antagonism toward the extremists of his own section. Upon them he placed the sole blame for the struggle, charging that they had conspired against the

---

[82] "Editorial," *SHS Papers*, VII, 98 (February 1879).

[83] George Livermore, January 12, 1864, as quoted in Edith Ellen Ware, *Political Opinion in Massachusetts During Civil War and Reconstruction* (New York, 1916) 207. "People have croaked at every advance of the human race," said Boston's well-known clergyman James Freeman Clarke in a sermon in 1863, ". . . I look upon the Boston *Courier* as a kind of marsh which has been providentially provided for these people, where they can sit and croak to each other in a sort of frog concert of mutual condolence" (*ibid.*, 207n2). Ware, whose volume is the most thorough study of Massachusetts politics in this period, describes the *Courier's* general position as "anti-Republican, antiadministration, anti-war and sometimes anti-Union." (*ibid.*, 206). For biographical information about Lunt, see Laurence S. Mayo, "George Lunt," *The Dictionary of American Biography*, XI, 507-508.

Union for many years before 1860. The abolitionists and their political allies, the "self-seeking and ambitious demagogues," he wrote, had long been hostile to the Constitution and the Union; gradually over a period of many years they had forced the Southern states into opposition to the federal government. Finally in 1861, the same "radical Republican oligarchy" had precipitated war by inducing Lincoln to attempt the provisioning of Fort Sumter.[84] Lunt's history was long popular among Confederates; even at the turn of the century, Confederate veterans' "history" committees (set up to examine school textbooks) were still recommending it in terms of highest praise.[85]

Even more than Lunt, Southern Confederate supporters placed emphasis upon their contention that in fighting they had acted in self-defense. They insisted that the Southern type of society, and Southern ideas, had been sanctioned in the Constitution of 1787, and that it was the North, not the South, which had departed from that Constitution. They appealed much more to the Constitution than to the Declaration of Independence, and they invoked the sanction of a revolutionary tradition even less after 1865 than they had during the conflict. Their aim in secession and in war, they maintained, had been the protection of the traditional American way of life from Northern attacks; they sought merely to be let alone, to be independent and free in order to preserve their civilization and their principles.

As proof of the soundness and lasting significance of the "Southern" principles which they had fought to preserve, as proof that their worst fears of radical, centralizing tendencies in the North had been well founded, Confederate sympathizers frequently pointed to the policies followed by the victorious section after the war. The Washington government, they declared, had abolished the Constitution in its dealings with the South. The states had been replaced by despotic military regimes under the control of the

---

[84] George Lunt, *The Origin of the Late War* (New York, 1866) 3-10, 104, 332, 390-393, 451-453. The only important respect in which Lunt's views differed from those generally held by Confederates was that, while justifying the action of the Southern states in leaving the Union, he denied that secession was a constitutional right (*ibid.*, 392*n*).

[85] See, for example, the report of the chairman of the history committee, Grand Camp of Virginia of Confederate Veterans, October 12, 1899, in Hunter McGuire and George L. Christian, *The Confederate Cause and Conduct in the War Between the States* (Richmond, 1907) 25, 30.

national government; former slaves had been enfranchised and placed in positions of power, accompanied by those white Southerners whom D.H. Hill called "worming, squirming, wiggling, writhing, twisting, crawling, fawning renegades." Corruption and fraud had made government a mockery, and the very conditions of civilized life were endangered. Their experiences in Reconstruction, Confederates concluded, had amply justified the fears which had led to secession in 1860-1861; the sequel to battle had demonstrated convincingly to them the validity of the tenets they supported in war.[86]

Thus, in the two decades after 1865, the attitudes formulated in time of war were hardened under the impact of defeat. The "official" pattern of interpretation of the causes and nature of the Civil War, which the Confederate President had set forth a fortnight after the beginning of hostilities in 1861, persisted for a quarter-century and had an even greater appeal for Confederates after 1865 than during the war. The major features of this pattern —the attempt to fasten the war guilt exclusively upon the North, the justification of secession by the compact theory of state sovereignty, and the insistence that the institution of slavery had not been a cause of war—were still held resolutely by many Confederate sympathizers in the 1880's. Southerners whose views diverged markedly from this pattern were regarded as sycophants of the North and were criticized, as in the 1860's, for their "cringing, crawling, dirt-eating spirit."[87] Typical testimony of the survival of the older views came from a young Southerner, Walter Hines Page, who traveled throughout the South in the early 1880's as a newspaper correspondent. Although his own opinions were considerably different from those of Jefferson Davis, Page reported that Davis's views of the causes of the war were generally approved by most Southerners at that time.[88] Among Confederate supporters, as among Unionists, the viewpoints generated in the heat of conflict were not speedily set aside.

[86] J.A.P. Campbell, "The Lost Cause," *SHS Papers*, XVI, 236 (1888); Jefferson Davis, "Address," *SHS Papers*, VI, 163-171 (October 1878); R.M.T. Hunter, "Origin of the Late War," *SHS Papers*, I, 11-12 (January 1876). The quotation by Hill is from "Editorial," *The Land We Love*, V, 91 (May 1868).

[87] R.L. Dabney, "George W. Cable in the Century Magazine," *SHS Papers*, XIII, 148-153 (1885).

[88] Burton J. Hendrick, *The Training of an American: the Earlier Life and Letters of Walter H. Page 1855-1913* (Boston, 1928) 143-144.

CHAPTER THREE

"THE NEEDLESS WAR"

The "Peace Interpretation"
1861 to 1865

By THE TIME the initial enthusiasm attending the outbreak of hostilities in 1861 had waned, it became evident that there were some individuals who, in reality, could not accurately be called supporters of either the Union or the Confederacy. They, too, developed a distinctive interpretation of the causes and character of the war.

These persons were not the "disloyal" in each section—they were not the Southerners, like "Parson" Brownlow, who sympathized with the Union, nor the Northerners, like J.H. Van Evrie, who hoped for the success of the Confederacy. They might be called, instead, the "discontented"; unlike the truly disloyal in both North and South, they insisted that they did not desire the victory of the enemy forces, and they did not desert to the foe nor give him direct aid. Yet, throughout the conflict, they devoted most of their energies to criticism and obstruction of the war effort of their respective governments and to the support of various peace movements looking to the immediate cessation of fighting. They were apparently a decided minority during most of the struggle, although in each section their number increased whenever the military outlook became particularly unfavorable.

The loyalist majority in each section did not usually make distinctions between discontented peace advocates and outright disloyal individuals, designating both groups indiscriminately by such terms as "copperhead" and "butternut" in the North, and "croaker" in the South. This is understandable, for in some cases the distinction is a fine one, difficult to determine, and discontent frequently stemmed from the same general background as disloyalty—a background of economic, political, social, and cultural factors which led to varying degrees of sympathy for the opposing section. Yet, many of the discontented peace men held opinions on the causes and nature of the war unmistakably different from those which characterized either the supporters of the Union or those of the Confederacy; moreover, similar opinions, it turned out, were shared by discontented men in both North and South. Here was an interpretation of the war's causes which cut across sectional boundaries.

In the Union states, the discontented peace advocates included such men as Clement L. Vallandigham and Samuel S. Cox, Democratic Congressmen from Ohio, Stephen D. Carpenter, a newspaper publisher in Wisconsin, and William C. Fowler of Connecticut, a member of the State Senate in 1864. Their backgrounds were significant. The Midwest, home of Vallandigham, Cox, and Carpenter, had strong ties with the South—ties of commerce, for example, and ties of long political association in the Democratic Party. More important still, forty per cent of the Midwesterners of 1860 were of "Southern blood," according to the estimate of one historian.[1] Of this group was Vallandigham, whose family was originally from Virginia and Maryland, and who prided himself on this ancestry; both Vallandigham and Cox lived in a section of Ohio noted for its strong Southern sympathies. Fowler, a Yale graduate and son-in-law of Noah Webster, typified the peace men of the Middle Atlantic and New England states, who generally held less extreme opinions than those of the Midwest. All four men belonged to the "peace" faction of the Democratic Party, the political center of discontent in the Union states, composed of Party members who, unlike Douglas and Bancroft, did not give wholehearted support to the war effort of the Lincoln administration.

Underlying much of the thinking of the three Midwesterners was the conviction that Negroes were an inferior race, and Cox candidly voiced their opinions on the rights of black men. "I have been taught," he declared in the House of Representatives in June 1862, "that these Commonwealths and this Union were made for white men; and this Government is a Government of white men; that the men who made it never intended by anything they did, to

---

[1] Gray, *Hidden Civil War*, 21. Chapter 1 of this work describes in admirable fashion the various forces which linked the Midwest to the South. I am indebted to Miss Margaret Gleason, reference librarian, Wisconsin State Historical Society, for furnishing information about Stephen D. Carpenter.

place the black race on an equality with the white."[2] Going a step further, Vallandigham openly defended slavery as a positive good; on the floor of Congress in January 1863, he praised the institution and predicted that it would come out of the war fifty-fold stronger than when it entered. In this speech, he identified himself with the people of the "west," who, he said, believed in the "subordination of the negro race to the white, where they both exist together."[3]

Expressing opposition to secession, Vallandigham, Cox, Carpenter, and Fowler maintained that they desired not an independent Confederacy but simply the restoration of the "Constitution as it is" and the "Union as it was." They declared that they were in favor of a constitutional war to crush secession, but they charged that Lincoln was waging a battle for the conquest and subjugation of the South and that he was conducting it in a despotic fashion, subverting the constitutional liberties of individuals and the rights of states. Opposing military conscription, they also criticized the suspension of the writ of *habeas corpus* and declared that freedom of speech had been abolished in the Union. In particular, they attacked Lincoln's policy of emancipation. Spurning the argument that emancipation was a legitimate measure adopted to aid the prosecution of the war, they pictured it as an unconstitutional act by which the President had changed the war aims of the North from preservation of the Union to abolition of slavery. If, said Fowler in the Connecticut State Senate in 1864,

the President should avow the fact that he has violated the Constitution, in order to save the Union, as the President did in a letter to Mr. Hodge, let us say to him "out of thine own mouth will I judge thee, thou wicked servant."[4]

[2] Samuel S. Cox, *Eight Years in Congress, from 1857-1865* (New York, 1865) 156.

[3] *Speeches, Arguments, Addresses, and Letters of Clement L. Vallandigham* (New York, 1864) 438-439, 452. Carpenter, in 1864, wrote that he considered the institution of slavery an evil, but he declared that Negroes would not work when they could avoid it; tracing slavery back to Biblical times, he asserted that the world had not yet been able to overthrow it. Similarly, Cox, in a speech in Congress in January 1865, criticized slavery, but he voted at that time against what became the Thirteenth Amendment to the Constitution, abolishing slavery, on the grounds that its adoption would hinder negotiations then impending with representatives of the Confederacy (Stephen D. Carpenter, *Logic of History* [2nd ed., Madison, Wis., 1864] 20, 22-23; Cox, *Eight Years*, 396ff.).

[4] William C. Fowler, *Local Law in Massachusetts and Connecticut, Historically Considered . . . . [and Other Essays]* (n.p., n.d.) 162-163. The emancipation issue emphasized the opposition to the war on the part of some Roman Catholic groups in the

The opinions of these men about the nature and causes of the war followed directly from this background of criticism of the Lincoln administration and of opposition to any attempts to interfere with the institution of slavery. Like their contemporaries who supported the Union and the Confederacy, they sought to assess personal blame for the war, and they spoke at times of conspiracies of evil men. But, in contrast to the dominant opinion in either section, the views of the discontented peace men were based on a denial that the war had resulted from any differences between North and South over fundamental moral, social, economic, or other issues. Instead, they maintained that the struggle had stemmed from artificial disputes created by the agitations of extremists on each side; it was even charged that the radicals of North and South had conspired together to bring on the conflict.[5]

The peace advocates placed special blame for war upon the abolitionists of the North, stating repeatedly that it was not the institution of slavery but the agitation of the slavery question by the abolitionists that had caused hostilities. (Tracing throughout history the evil effects of excitement over slavery, Carpenter declared that it was the primary cause of the fall of the Roman Empire.) The notion that there was an "irrepressible conflict" between freedom and slavery, or between free labor and slave labor, was ridiculed by Vallandigham; he declared that the real, though secret, purpose of the war from its beginning had been the abolition of slavery in the Southern states.[6] For the immediate outbreak of fighting, the three Midwesterners placed responsibility upon Lin-

Union states. In the several decades preceding the war, Catholic leaders had taken the position that the institution of slavery was not intrinsically evil *per se*, and American Catholic opinion in the slavery controversy had been characterized chiefly by its intense opposition to abolitionism. After the outbreak of hostilities, Catholics in the Union states differed in their opinions and actions, as did individuals in other denominations; but some vocal and important Catholics were consistently opposed to the Union war effort or noticeably lukewarm in their support, and when the Emancipation Proclamation was issued, this hostility of Catholics to the war increased (Madeline H. Rice, *American Catholic Opinion in the Slavery Controversy* [New York, 1944] *passim*; Arthur M. Schlesinger, Jr., *Orestes A. Brownson: A Pilgrim's Progress* [Boston, 1939] 245ff.).

[5] Carpenter, *Logic of History*, 23, 25-26, 54-55, 290; Cox, *Eight Years*, 10, 238, 287-288, 296-297; Vallandigham, *Speeches*, 308-309, 436-437, 439-440; Fowler, *The Sectional Controversy* (New York, 1862) *v-vi*.

[6] Vallandigham, *Speeches*, 425, 436-437.

coln and the Republicans because of their refusal to compromise with Southerners in the crisis of 1860-1861.[7]

Opinions on the nature and causes of the war similar to these were shared by other peace Democrats in the North. One of the most important indications of this was a party manifesto signed by fourteen Democratic members of the House of Representatives in May 1862 (ten of the fourteen signers were from the Midwest). Drafted by Vallandigham, this "Address . . . to the Democracy of the United States" embodied his views of the coming of the war. Primary blame was placed upon the abolitionists of the North: "The bitter waters of secession flowed first and are fed still from the unclean fountain of abolition." In like manner, the "Address" declared that the Union could have been saved by compromises in the crisis of 1860-1861 had it not been for the stand taken by the Republican Party.[8]

Vallandigham, Cox, Carpenter, and Fowler maintained that no basic conflict between the sections had produced the war, and they expressed disapproval of the war aims of each of the rival governments. Thus, throughout most of the war, they backed movements to halt the fighting. But they were not specific in defining the terms of peace, nor did they explain how the cessation of hostilities would achieve the restoration of the "Union as it was" and the "Constitution as it is." Cox, Carpenter, and Fowler seemed to think that both sides would agree to stop fighting and that this would restore the Union. More detailed suggestions for peace were made in Congress by Vallandigham early in 1863; let the fighting cease, he urged before a packed House of Representatives, let the armies be withdrawn from the South, leave slavery alone, let trade and social relations be restored between the sections, choose a new President in 1864, and all would be well. But he did not explain how his proposals could be carried out, and when they were ridiculed by Confederate Congressmen and by Confederate administration newspapers in Richmond, he replied simply that once the

[7] *ibid.*, 310-314; Carpenter, *Logic of History*, 95, 133-134, 145; Cox, *Eight Years*, 27-30.

[8] This "Address" can be found in Vallandigham, *Speeches*, 362-369; the quotation is from p. 365. See also Gray, *Hidden Civil War*, 93, and Edward C. Kirkland, *The Peacemakers of 1864* (New York, 1927) 34.

fighting was stopped, the people of both North and South would elect officials who could agree on peace terms.[9]

At one point, Vallandigham seems to have advanced beyond mere peace proposals. In the summer of 1864, he talked in Canada with Confederate agents, and apparently gave tacit sanction to their scheme to create by revolution a Northwestern Confederacy which would withdraw from the Union and ally itself with the South. All the while, however, he consistently maintained that he sought only the restoration of the old Union.[10] It was in that same summer that the peace movement reached its pinnacle. Meeting at the end of August, the Democratic National Convention nominated as its candidate for Vice-president an avowed peace man, and adopted as part of its platform the famous plank which affirmed

That this convention does explicitly declare, as the sense of the American people, that after four years of failure to restore the Union by the experiment of war, . . . justice, humanity, liberty and the public welfare demand that immediate efforts be made for a cessation of hostilities, with a view to an ultimate convention of the States, or other peaceable means, to the end that at the earliest practicable moment peace may be restored on the basis of the Federal Union of the States.

The opinions of the discontented peace advocates, particularly those of the Midwest, were satirized during the war by the Ohio antislavery editor and humorist David Ross Locke. Locke created in 1861 the well-known fictitious character Petroleum V. Nasby, and through this cowardly and illiterate figure he heaped ridicule upon Copperhead sentiments. Readers of Nasby's wartime letters to the newspapers (and one of the most enthusiastic readers was Lincoln) were told of his adventures in resisting the draft and of his undying hatred for "niggers" and "Abolishnists." Nasby's views on the "war queshun" were clearly modeled on those of the peace Democrats. He constantly professed that he was in favor of "puttin down the rebelyun" in all "constitooshnal ways"; yet he was violently opposed to a "war uv subgagashen," and was thus hostile to all this "military bisnis." He held Oberlin College responsible for the war:

9 Vallandigham, *Speeches*, 449, 495-496.
10 Gray, *Hidden Civil War*, 167-169; Kirkland, *Peacemakers*, 124-127.

Oberlin commenst this war [he wrote in 1862].
Oberlin wuz the prime cause uv all the trubble.
What wuz the beginnin uv it? Our Suthrin brethrin wantid the territories—Oberlin objectid. . . . They wantid Breckenridge fer President. Oberlin refused, and elektid Linkin. Then they seceded; and why is it that they still hold out? . . . Becoz . . . Oberlin won't submit. We might to-day hev peese if Oberlin wood say to Linkin, "Resine!" and to Geff Davis, "come up higher!" When I say Oberlin, understand it ez figgerative for the entire Ablishn party, wich Oberlin is the fountinhead. There's wher the trouble is. Our Suthern brethren wuz reasonable. So long as the Dimokrasy controlled things, and they got all they wanted, they wuz peeceable. Oberlin ariz—the Dimokrasy wuz beet down, and they riz up agin it.[11]

In the Confederacy were to be found counterparts to Vallandigham and the peace Democrats, and there, just as in the Union, the discontented men based their opposition to the government's war policy upon constitutional grounds. Military conscription and the suspension of the writ of *habeas corpus* by the Confederate government aroused the same bitter opposition as in the North, and it was charged that Jefferson Davis was destroying the constitutional rights of states and the constitutional liberties of individuals. The Governors of Georgia and North Carolina demonstrated that state sovereignty arguments could be turned against the administration at Richmond just as easily as against the administration at Washington. To some Confederates, the conflict seemed, just as it did to some Unionists, a "rich man's war and a poor man's fight"; and there were some Confederates who charged that their government was showing favoritism to men of certain political affiliations and was thus waging a "party war." In the South, as in the North, was heard the cry for "the Constitution as it is and the Union as it was."[12]

One of the leaders of the discontented Confederates was H.S. Foote of Tennessee. A strong Unionist in the 1850's, Foote had opposed secession; nevertheless, he accepted the action of his state

[11] David R. Locke (Petroleum V. Nasby), *The Moral History of America's Life-Struggle* (Boston, 1874) 45-46.

[12] Internal opposition to the Confederate government is described in: Frank Lawrence Owsley, *State Rights in the Confederacy* (Chicago, 1925), and "Defeatism in the Confederacy," *The North Carolina Historical Review*, III, 446-456 (July 1926); Albert B. Moore, *Conscription and Conflict in the Confederacy* (New York, 1929); Georgia Lee Tatum, *Disloyalty in the Confederacy* (Chapel Hill, 1934).

and represented it in the Confederate Congress during most of the war. As the Northern peace Democrats were critical of the manner in which Lincoln conducted the war, so Foote charged that Jefferson Davis sought to establish a despotism and that he trampled the Constitution underfoot. Foote ultimately declared that a victory of either side was undesirable, and became a strong supporter of various peace movements. Late in 1864, he resigned from the Confederate Congress and proceeded within the federal lines in an attempt to communicate with Lincoln and Seward to make peace (and one of his proposed peace terms was the restoration of slavery). Professor Sydnor has aptly described Foote as the "Vallandigham of the South."[13]

Foote's interpretation of the causes of the war was based, as was that of the Midwestern peace Democrats, upon the belief that no fundamental social, political, or economic forces had caused a struggle between the sections. The war, he wrote in 1866, did not result from an "irrepressible conflict of antagonisms imbedded in the very nature of our heterogeneous institutions," as Horace Greeley had asserted. Instead, the combined action of fanatics on both sides was responsible. The "incessant agitation of sectional factionists," North and South, the "unskillful and blundering management of men in power" had led ultimately to war.[14]

Foote, like Vallandigham, Cox, Carpenter, and Fowler, placed the major share of blame for the war's coming upon the radicals of his own section. In 1865, while the fighting was still in progress, he declared that the responsibility for initiating the war rested upon Jefferson Davis and upon the "ultra pro-slavery men" of the South. Secession, he continued, had resulted from a long-standing conspiracy of Southern "political zealots"; knowing that their disunion schemes would fail without war, they had taken all the necessary steps to bring it about.[15]

Opinions about the war generally similar to Foote's were expressed by C.C.S. Farrar of Mississippi. A planter of considerable means, Farrar at the beginning of the war owned land valued at

[13] Charles S. Sydnor, "Henry Stuart Foote," *The Dictionary of American Biography*, VI, 500-501; Henry S. Foote, *War of the Rebellion* (New York, 1866), 374-376, 381-383, 388ff.; Kirkland, *Peacemakers*, 218-220, 236n-237n.
[14] Foote, *War of the Rebellion*, 418-422.
[15] *ibid.*, 401-402.

$30,000 and eighty-five slaves under sixty years of age.[16] He lived in the Mississippi Delta, where wealthy planters had long been Whig and Unionist in politics, and the county in which he lived cast its vote for the moderate Bell-Everett Constitutional Union Party in the election of 1860. Whether Farrar, like Foote, opposed secession in 1860-1861 or what his actions were during the war are not known. He shared with both Vallandigham and Foote a strong desire for peace, and like them he presented no practical plan for stopping the war. (He went a step further toward outright pacifism than any of the other discontented men under discussion here, stating that war was always absurd, was always caused by error, and that nothing but evil could ever come from it.)[17]

Writing in 1864, Farrar traced the cause of the war, as had Foote, to the actions of extremists in both North and South. He pictured the conflict as a struggle between the two "evil principles" of abolitionism and secessionism, and he was decidedly critical of both principles. He placed the specific blame for the war upon abolitionist and secessionist "demagogues." In the South, he charged, demagogues did all in their power to instigate the secession movement by their refusal to compromise on the slavery question and by picturing Lincoln as an abolitionist pledged to immediate emancipation. The secession of the Southern states seemed completely unjustified to him; secession was an "orgy of liberty," and the state rights doctrine on which it was based was the "worst derivative of democracy." For abolitionism he had similar harsh words, comparing its attack upon established institutions to that of free love or communism. Despite the fact, he wrote, that the Negro was an inferior race whose normal condition was obviously slavery, Northern Protestant ministers had taken up the abolition doctrine and had done more than all other groups combined to precipitate the present crisis.[18]

Here, then, was a distinctive contemporary explanation of the

---

[16] I am indebted to Mr. William D. McCain, director of the Department of Archives and History, State of Mississippi, for supplying information about Farrar from the federal Census of 1860 and from the personal tax roll of Bolivar County, Mississippi, for 1861.

[17] C.C.S. Farrar, *The War: Its Causes and Consequences* (Cairo, Ill., 1864) 232.

[18] *ibid.*, 126, 132-133, 190-191, 203-250.

nature and causes of the war (it might be called the "peace" interpretation) expressed by men of a recognizable type in both Union and Confederate states. Vallandigham, Cox, Carpenter, Fowler, Foote, and Farrar were in general agreement that no underlying irreconcilable differences between North and South had caused sectional conflict. They insisted, on the contrary, that sectional strife and war had arisen from artificial issues generated and emotionalized by zealots of both North and South. It was charged that the extremists on each side had been in the wrong, that the men in power had blundered; had it not been for them, the internal harmony of the country could have been preserved, and compromises could have been devised which would have prevented a needless war.

The "Peace Interpretation"
1865 to the 1880's

HELD APPARENTLY by only a comparatively small number of men in each section during the war, the peace interpretation of the conflict did not increase in popularity in the two decades after the fighting ceased. In that period, characterized, as we have seen, by a general solidifying of opinion among both the supporters of the Union and those of the Confederacy, few voices championing the views of the peace men were heard. S.S. Cox and H.S. Foote issued volumes in which they restated essentially the same opinions they had expressed in wartime.[19] But it was from an unexpected quarter—from the pens of former President James Buchanan and of the Yankee intellectual Orestes A. Brownson—that this peace interpretation drew what little support it received in the few years after the war ended. Buchanan and Brownson had held vastly different opinions during the war, and neither of them had shared the views of men like Vallandigham. Yet, different as were Buchanan and Brownson, each of them had a certain affinity to the discontented men of wartime. When, after the conflict, they followed the common practice and set about to defend their actions, each of them emerged with an explanation of the causes and nature of the war which had many points in common with the peace interpretation.

Of the two, Buchanan's viewpoint was nearer that of the discontented men of the Union states than Brownson's. After leaving Washington in March 1861, Buchanan retired to his home, "Wheatland," in Pennsylvania and played little part in public life thereafter. First and foremost he remained a Democrat, but his opinions during the war place him somewhere between the

[19] Samuel S. Cox, *Eight Years in Congress, from 1857-1865* (New York, 1865), and *Union—Disunion—Reunion. Three Decades of Federal Legislation 1855-1885* (Providence, 1885); Henry S. Foote, *War of the Rebellion* (New York, 1866), and *Casket of Reminiscences* (Washington, 1874).

rival "war" and "peace" factions of that party in the North.[20] When Sumter was attacked, he came to the support of the Lincoln administration, and throughout the struggle he insisted that the Union be preserved and opposed clearly and consistently any recognition of the independence of the Confederacy. Upholding the constitutionality of military conscription, he urged Democrats not to make a political issue of it.

But Buchanan, like many of the peace Democrats, disapproved of abolitionists and of the policy of emancipation. (He later stated that he delayed becoming a member of the Presbyterian Church until after the war because of the antislavery stand of the Northern wing of that church.) The Emancipation Proclamation, he asserted in 1864, demonstrated that "the administration, departing from the principle of conducting the war for the restoration of the Union as it was, and the Constitution as it is, had resolved to conduct it for the subjugation of the Southern States and the destruction of Slavery."[21] Early in the war, Buchanan had taken a firm stand against the discussion of peace proposals with the Confederacy; as the years passed, however, without modifying his demand that the Union must be preserved, he expressed approval of negotiations with the South. After the reelection of Lincoln in 1864 (Buchanan had supported McClellan), he urged conciliation based upon ignoring the slavery issue. Now, he wrote in November 1864,

would be the time for conciliation on the part of Mr. Lincoln. A frank and manly offer to the Confederates that they might return to the Union just as they were before they left it, leaving the slavery question to settle itself, might possibly be accepted.[22]

Buchanan spent much of his time during the war in preparing a defense of his actions as President; when this was published shortly after the fighting ended, it contained his most complete statement on the causes of the war.[23] Like the discontented men of both sections, he placed the blame for war upon extremists.

[20] See John Bassett Moore, ed., *The Works of James Buchanan* (12v., Philadelphia, 1908-1911) XI (1860-1868) *passim*.

[21] *ibid.*, XI, 356.

[22] *ibid.*, XI, 377. See also *ibid.*, XI, 370.

[23] James Buchanan, *The Administration on the Eve of the Rebellion: A History of Four Years before the War* (London, 1865).

He was unfailingly critical of secessionism, and he held the Confederate government responsible for the actual beginning of hostilities because of the firing upon Fort Sumter. At the same time, he declared that the North could and should have prevented secession in the crisis of 1860-1861 by guaranteeing to Southerners the right to take slavery into the territories of the federal government (and here Buchanan, unlike Cox or Foote, was as critical of the Douglas Democrats with their doctrine of popular sovereignty as he was of the Republicans). But the basic cause of the sectional struggle and war was in operation long before 1860, and Buchanan insisted that this basic cause was not the institution of slavery or any other difference between North and South but the agitation over slavery. For this agitation he blamed the radicals of both sections, but he always placed primary blame upon the Northern abolitionists. The original cause of all the country's troubles, he wrote, was to be found in

the long, active, and persistent hostility of the Northern Abolitionists, both in and out of Congress, against Southern slavery, until the final triumph of their cause in the election of President Lincoln [consistently, Buchanan made little or no distinction between abolitionists and opponents of slavery of the Lincoln type]; and on the other hand, the corresponding antagonism and violence with which the advocates of slavery resisted these efforts, and vindicated its preservation and extension up till the period of secession.[24]

If there had been no opposition to slavery, was the theme of Buchanan's reasoning, there would have been no sectional conflict or war.

There were no similarities between the wartime actions of Orestes Brownson and those of the discontented peace men.[25] Brownson was a strong supporter of war, with no thought of making peace; his criticism of the Lincoln administration was that the struggle was not being prosecuted with enough vigor. As early as January 1862, he publicly urged the emancipation of slaves as a war measure to preserve the Union. But his position during the war was in sharp conflict with many of his earlier opinions, for

[24] *ibid., iv.*
[25] For accounts of Brownson's life, see: Arthur M. Schlesinger, Jr., *Orestes A. Brownson: A Pilgrim's Progress* (Boston, 1939); Theodore Maynard, *Orestes Brownson: Yankee, Radical, Catholic* (New York, 1943).

in the 1840's he had been a personal friend of John C. Calhoun, had ardently advocated state sovereignty, and had criticized the equalitarian tendencies of majority rule. In that same decade, he became a convert to Catholicism; he also became tolerant of slavery and bitterly opposed to abolitionists.

Brownson's wartime actions not only conflicted with his past, they also placed him in opposition to some of his coreligionists. Deploring the lukewarm support given the government by some members of his faith, he stated that Catholics did not understand the war. It was undeniable, he wrote,

that no religious body in the country stands so generally committed to slavery and the rebellion, or as a body have shown so little sympathy with the effort of the government to save the unity and life of the nation, as the Catholics.[26]

His stand led him into controversy with several members of the Catholic hierarchy; and, undaunted, he even challenged the views of the Pope. In an article published in 1863, he implied that the Pope expressed opinions on the war which were contrary to Catholic doctrine, and suggested that "the Holy Father . . . has been induced to lend the [Southern] conspiracy his powerful aid."[27]

Brownson's life had been marked by drastic changes of position, however, and toward the close of the war his opinions began once more to shift. His biographer has suggested that his changing opinions represented an attempt to reconcile his earlier views with those of the war period; whatever the explanation, Brownson now sought to make amends for his strictures against Catholics and to defend their role in the war.[28] The completeness of this alteration in his viewpoint can be seen in his volume, *The American Republic*, published in 1866. In sharp contrast to his earlier statements, Brownson now asserted that Catholics could interpret the war better than non-Catholics:

The best things written on the controversy [i.e., the war] have been written by Catholics, and Catholics are better fitted by their religion

[26] Henry F. Brownson, *Orestes A. Brownson's Later Life: from 1855 to 1876* (Detroit, 1900) 378.

[27] Henry F. Brownson, ed., *The Works of Orestes A. Brownson* (20v., Detroit, 1882-1887) xvii, 438, 444.

[28] Schlesinger, Jr., *Brownson*, 256ff.

to comprehend the real character of the American constitution than any other class of Americans, the moment they study it in the light of their own theology.[29]

(This was part of a declaration of general Catholic superiority by Brownson; in a few years, he stated, Catholics, because of their religion, would be the "most learned, enlightened, and intelligent portion of the American population.") The war had now taken on a new significance for him. While still denying the validity of the state sovereignty doctrine and criticizing the secessionists who had fought in its defense, he now looked at the same time with disfavor upon a centralized national government founded upon majority rule. Having long feared the rule of the mob, he now declared that the real cause of the war was the growth in this country of the majority rule theory (a principle borrowed from European "Liberals and Revolutionists," and one which did not apply in the United States). It was this theory, he asserted, which provoked secession and rebellion in the South and which aided the abolitionists in the North. Brownson, like the discontented men of the North, reserved his sharpest criticism for the abolitionists, and he praised the Confederate cause in so far as it was directed against the abolitionists and their plans for a "socialistic democracy."

The great danger now that the war was over, Brownson stated, was that the North and the world at large would interpret the outcome as a victory for centralization, majority rule, and social democracy; Mazzini and Garibaldi humiliated the North, he declared, with their congratulations, and those Americans who were pleased with such praise from "revolutionary leaders of European liberals" were "worse enemies to the American democracy than ever were Jefferson Davis and his fellow conspirators, and more contemptible."[30]

Viewing the war in such a manner, Brownson could now explain why some bishops and clergy of the Catholic Church had sympathized so little with the Northern government in its prosecution of the war. It was not because they were disloyal, not because

[29] Orestes A. Brownson, *The American Republic: Its Constitution, Tendencies, and Destiny* (new edtition, New York, 1866) 378.

[30] *ibid.,* 366.

they wanted the dissolution of the Union, not because they wanted to see slavery prolonged, but because Catholics feared (and rightly so, Brownson implied) that the war might result in encouraging *"La République démocratique et sociale."*[31] After a "liberal" period in his career, Brownson had at last made peace with his former views and with his church. Now his position on the war constituted a defense, if not for all the wartime peace advocates of the North, at least for those of the Catholic faith.

Buchanan and Brownson thus eventually arrived at opinions similar in many respects to those of Vallandigham, Fowler, and the other discontented men of their section. But neither during the conflict nor afterward did the "peace" interpretation of the causes and nature of the war find favor with many individuals of the war generation. Both the supporters of the Union and those of the Confederacy were inclined to suspect that the views of the Vallandighams and the Footes were based fundamentally upon sympathy for the opposing side, and to most of their contemporaries the opinions of the peace men on the war seemed as unrealistic as their conduct during the struggle. Eventually, interpretations of the war's causes similar to those of the discontented peace men were championed by some "revisionist" historians of a later generation in the twentieth century, but not until another war had helped to produce an intellectual atmosphere favorable for such an interpretation.

[31] *ibid.*, 365.

A Summary of Attitudes
1861 to the 1880's

THE different interpretations of the causes and character of the Civil War which won most favor in the period from 1861 to the 1880's (the "war of the rebellion," the "war between the states," and the "needless war") reflected the divergent sympathies and attitudes of the individuals who formulated and who accepted them, and were in this sense "relative" to the respective sympathies and attitudes of those individuals.

And yet, paradoxical as it may at first seem in the light of the above paragraph, one can distinguish certain broad similarities in the patterns of thought of most interpreters of the causes of the Civil War in the years from 1861 to the 1880's, whatever their viewpoint. These interpreters were, to use the descriptive word applied by Alfred Cobban to some historians of the French Revolution, the "primitives" of Civil War historiography. Most of them had experienced the coming of war and the passions of wartime at first hand; despite their differences in allegiance and point of view, they set about explaining the causes of the war in a similar manner. A primary concern, for example, of Unionist Horace Greeley in discussing the coming of the war was the same as that of Confederate E.A. Pollard, or even of peace advocate Clement L. Vallandigham: each sought to place personal guilt for the conflict upon his foes, while at the same time defending his own role, or that of his section or political or social group. Many of these "primitives" tended to explain the coming of war in terms of the actions of evil individuals motivated by personal ambition and greed, and frequently they pictured a small group of men banded in a conspiracy. They often emphasized a single cause for the war—personal ambition, the institution of slavery, sectional aggression, or some other *one* factor. They generally pictured the struggle in black and white lines, with little or no intermediate shading: their side was absolutely right, their opponents absolutely wrong.

These general similarities in the method of interpreting the causes of the Civil War employed by Unionists, Confederates, and peace advocates in the period from 1861 to the 1880's tend to distinguish their explanations, as a group, from most of the explanations advanced after the 1880's. Interpretations have thus been relative not only to the differing backgrounds of individuals living at the same time but also to the ideas, interests, and thought patterns which are characteristic of many individuals in a particular chronological era, whatever their differences in point of view.

And yet, if relativism in interpreting the war's causes is evident here, so too are limitations upon this relativism and continuity in outlook. For it would seem that individuals suggested in the 1860's and 1870's most of the major factors which were later to be singled out as causes of the Civil War—climate and geography, the institution of slavery, economic forces, emotions, and "weaknesses" in the political machinery, among others. Later generations have developed these suggestions in a more sophisticated fashion, have shifted and reshifted the emphasis placed upon certain factors, but at least the seeds of most of the later explanations, and sometimes the full-blown explanations themselves, are to be found in the 1860's and 1870's (the later Beardian economic interpretation, for example, is similar in some fundamental respects to the insistence of Confederates that differing economic interests of North and South were a cause of conflict and war; even the Marxian interpretation of the Civil War, as will be indicated later, had its origin in the 1860's). A realization of the fact that most of the later interpretations of the Civil War were suggested in the 1860's and 1870's should perhaps serve as an antidote to the common tendency of later generations, with the advantage of wisdom after the event, to scorn the historical views of earlier ages.

So long as the emotions of wartime retained their hold, so long as Civil War issues were burning questions bitterly contested in the arena of day-to-day politics, interpretations of the war's causes were dominated by the effort to locate the blame for the struggle upon the enemy. By and large, the individuals of the period from 1861 to the 1880's seem to have explained the causes and nature

of the Civil War in much the same manner as other war generations in history have looked upon their momentous conflicts. One
war generation in history produced Thucydides, and this deposed
general (comparable in that respect to, say, George B. McClellan
or Joseph E. Johnston), in the midst of a civil strife in which he
was a participant, wrote of the struggle with a calm detachment
and a keen understanding which has won the applause of later
ages. No such figure emerged in the period from the 1860's to
the 1880's, but, after all, there has been only one Thucydides.

CHAPTER FOUR

"THE CIVIL WAR—IRREPRESSIBLE CONFLICT"

New Viewpoints within the War Generation

It HAS generally happened in history that the opinions on the causes of a war which are formulated in the heat of the conflict seem inadequate and unsatisfactory after the passage of time. So it was in the case of the Civil War; within a quarter century after the outbreak of hostilities at Fort Sumter, there were signs in North and South alike that the older viewpoints were beginning to lose their appeal both to many members of the war generation and also to a new generation which was now coming to maturity.

Walter Hines Page noted when he traveled in the South in the 1880's that, albeit Southerners agreed with the traditional Confederate opinions, yet they talked of the causes of the war with a detached air, precisely, he wrote, "as they might discuss an historical situation detailed by Thucydides or by Macaulay—a thing that is interesting only as a matter of history."[1] Page's observation was significant, and it was true of many individuals in both North and South in the decade in which he wrote. For, despite the persistence of the older attitudes on the war, there appeared during the late 1870's and the 1880's the first important signs of change in these traditional patterns of thought.

By the 1880's, there was an ever expanding basis in political, social, and economic developments for the formulation of new points of view toward the Civil War. The passage of time, in itself, softened to a considerable extent the bitter emotions generated in the era of sectional strife; in addition, the advancing years had brought specific developments which worked toward this same end.

One of the most important of these developments was the removal of the last federal troops from the Southern states in 1877 by the Hayes administration; signifying as it did the formal abandonment of a policy which had aroused violent antagonism in the South (and which had seemed to Southerners proof of the

[1] Hendrick, *The Training of an American,* 143-144.

soundness of their suspicions and fears in 1861), the removal of troops prepared the way for the development of more cordial intersectional relations. The removal of Northern military control was interpreted by many Southerners as a partial vindication of the state sovereignty principles for which they had long contended, and as an indication that the Union was now established upon its prewar principles. Each judicial decision that the federal government was one of limited powers, declared A.M. Keiley of Virginia in 1879, was a "wreath laid on the graves of Confederate soldiers"; a common reaction among Southerners to the ending of Reconstruction was expressed by Senator John T. Morgan of Alabama (a former officer in the Confederate Army) when he declared in 1877 that the South, with "home rule" restored to her, was now content and the American people were again one people.[2]

Moreover, the restoration to Southerners of control over their local governments meant that the "Negro question" was to be left in the hands of Southern whites. This fact reflected the increasing measure of agreement between Southern and Northern whites on the role of the Negro, agreement made possible primarily by a reversal of the Northern attitudes toward the Negro which had prevailed in the Reconstruction period.[3] Disillusioned after a decade of attempts to impose a solution to this question upon the South from the outside, the majority of Northerners apparently were willing, by the end of Reconstruction, to permit Southern whites to handle the problem by themselves. This new Northern approach received legal sanction in a series of decisions by the Supreme Court which, in effect, left the question of Negro segregation in the hands of white Southerners. By 1889, a former officer in the Union Army, T.B. Edington, speaking before a reunion of veterans of that army, stated that although he favored the giving of suffrage to a "responsible class of colored voters," the enactment of unrestricted Negro suffrage was "the great crime of the age."

[2] A.M. Keiley, "Our Fallen Heroes," *SHS Papers*, VII, 380 (August 1879); John T. Morgan, "Address" (delivered October 31, 1877), *SHS Papers*, V, 1-33 (January-February 1878). For expressions of sentiments similar to those of Keiley and Morgan, see: Jefferson Davis, "Address" (delivered July 1878), *SHS Papers*, VI, 163-171 (October 1878); Bernard J. Sage, *The Republic of Republics: Or, American Federal Liberty* (4th ed., Boston, 1881) x.

[3] This reversal is described in detail in Buck, *Road to Reunion*, Chapter XII. I am indebted to this book for many of the ideas expressed in this chapter.

"Listen attentively," he urged his audience in a Memorial Day service at a national cemetery, "for the faintest whispering that comes from these graves, and you will hear no syllable of approbation of this overthrow of the white race and the destruction of all its dearest aspirations and hopes."[4]

In view of such attitudes, it was not strange that former Confederates now began to find common bonds of sentiment with their foes of the 1860's. In an era which was increasingly hearing references to "Anglo-Saxonism," Senator John W. Daniel of Virginia (a former Confederate officer) declared that both North and South were Anglo-Saxon and thus had common traits. "The instinct of race integrity," he stated in 1890, "is the most glorious, as it is the predominant characteristic of the Anglo-Saxon race, and the sections have it in common."[5] As early as 1868, Edward A. Pollard had proclaimed that the Southern cause in the war had been that of white supremacy, and that the "lost cause" would be regained if control by whites could be secured; the Northern acquiescence, after the 1870's, in the restoration of local rule and of the supremacy of Southern whites gave a certain justification to the feeling of some Southerners that they had not lost everything in the conflict.[6]

Thus, by the 1880's something of a compromise had been reached between the sections on some important issues of 1861: the Union was preserved, secession and the institution of slavery were forever destroyed, but, within the Union, home rule for the South and the maintenance of white supremacy were to be permitted. Under such conditions, it was much easier for Southerners to reconcile themselves to the Union than it had been in the 1860's.

While this *modus vivendi* on the questions of state sovereignty and the Negro was evolving, important social and economic changes were underway in both North and South. The war had stimulated the growth of a new, rapidly expanding, industrial and urban America, and by the 1880's, it was becoming apparent that the forces of industrialization and urbanization would pro-

[4] T.B. Edington, "The Race Problem in the South—Was the Fifteenth Amendment a Mistake?" *SHS Papers*, XVII, 26, 28 (1889).

[5] John W. Daniel, "Life, Services and Character of Jefferson Davis," *SHS Papers*, XVII, 140 (1889). See also H.E.M. Law, "Address," *SHS Papers*, XVII, 86-110 (1889).

[6] Edward A. Pollard, *The Lost Cause Regained* (New York, 1868), especially 13-14.

duce changes in the South as well as in the rest of the nation; in the new United States which was emerging, the economic and social structure of the South would not be as different from that of the other geographical sections as had been true before the war. At the same time, commercial relations between the former Confederate States and the rest of the nation were being restored and extended. The increasing similarity in the organization of society in the South and in other sections, the growth of economic ties between some groups in the South and some groups in other sections—such factors as these helped to provide yet another series of steppingstones upon which Southerners could discover common ideas with non-Southerners.

Accompanying these developments, there was a gradual change in political issues and alignments. In the bustling and busy America of Carnegie and Rockefeller, of Gompers and Powderly, the issues of 1860-1861 came to seem remote. More and more, the issue of North *versus* South, on the lines of division of 1861, was being replaced in national politics, despite the efforts of wavers of the "bloody shirt," by other questions on which there were different sectional groupings—questions such as the tariff, currency inflation, the regulation of corporations, and the difficulties of the farmers. Perhaps the most significant indication in the 1880's of the gradual passage of Civil War issues from politics was the election to the presidency of Grover Cleveland in 1884, the first Democrat elected since James Buchanan in 1856—and elected over the warnings of traditionalists that this might mean the resurgence of Southern treason through the Democratic Party. Whether or not this election signified that "rum" and "Romanism" were now more potent questions in politics than "rebellion," one result at least of the election of Cleveland was the appointment of two ex-Confederates to cabinet positions.

Indicative of the new currents in both economic and political life, some Northern business groups now took the lead in working for friendly relations between North and South. Perhaps a passage from William Dean Howells' widely read novel, *The Rise of Silas Lapham* (published in 1884), is significant in this connection— significant because of Howells' reputation as an accurate and faithful portrayer of the life and ideas of middle class New England of

the 1880's. In one scene from this novel, Howells' leading character, the self-made businessman Silas Lapham (depicted as a
former officer in the Union Army) opposed further waving of
the bloody shirt by politicians:

"I hate to see them stirring up those Southern fellows agin," said the
Colonel [Silas Lapham], speaking into the paper on his lap. "Seems
to me it's time to let those old issues go."
"Yes," said [Lapham's companion]. . . . "What are they doing now?"
"Oh, stirring up the Confederate brigadiers in Congress. I don't like
it. Seems to me, if our party hain't got any other stock-in-trade, we
better shut up shop altogether."[7]

All of these various developments paved the way, by the 1880's,
for the growth of an ever increasing measure of reconciliation
between North and South, reflected in part by the tremendous
popularity of themes of sectional reunion emphasized by novelists,
dramatists, and poets.[8] Veterans of the Union and Confederate
armies now began to hold joint "Blue and Gray reunions." Reconciliation became popular enough to become a theme for politicians, so arousing the ire of humorist "Bill" Nye that he declared
in the early 1890's that the "chronic reconciler" who paraded a
tired olive branch and constantly made a "tableau" of himself was
worse than the man who could not forgive or forget.[9] Intertwined
with this growing sectional reconciliation were the beginnings of
a new spirit of nationalism broad enough to include all sections
of the country.

With these fundamental political, economic, and intellectual developments as a basis, new conceptions of the nature and causes

---

[7] William Dean Howells, *The Rise of Silas Lapham* (centenary ed., New York, 1937)
80. Historians disagree in their interpretations of the role of economic factors and of
businessmen in the reconciliation of North and South. Since the question comes up
several times in the course of the present study, I should state here that I am in general
agreement with the account presented in Buck, *Road to Reunion*, chap. VI; viewpoints
differing from this account can be found in: Howard K. Beale, "Tariff and Reconstruction," *The American Historical Review*, XXXV, 276-294 (January 1930); Charles A.
and Mary R. Beard, *The Rise of American Civilization* (2v., New York, 1927) II, 113;
C. Vann Woodward, *Reunion and Reaction* (Boston, 1951), and *Origins of the New
South* (Baton Rouge, La., 1951), especially chaps. I-II.

[8] Buck, *Road to Reunion, passim*. One example of the reconciliation motif in American
literature, the appearance of a romantic and sympathetic picture of the *ante-bellum*
Southern plantation, is traced in Frances P. Gaines, *The Southern Plantation: A Study
in the Development and the Accuracy of a Tradition* (New York, 1924).

[9] Edgar Wilson Nye, *Bill Nye's History of the United States* (New York, 1894) 302-
303.

of the war began to appear here and there. The heart of the wartime attitudes among Unionists, Confederates, and peace men alike had been the conviction that one's own section, party, or group had been absolutely and solely right in its stand on the war and that one's opponents had been completely and exclusively at fault. By the 1880's, however, there was evidence that some men of the war generation, North and South, were beginning to discard this viewpoint, and by their actions and words were beginning to admit implicitly or explicitly that there were at least two sides to the questions involved in the Civil War.

The first signs of this newer attitude were naturally unspectacular and limited in nature; one of the most important of them was the action of representatives of the federal government in a matter relating directly to the writing of the war's history. After 1865, Southerners had repeatedly sought permission to examine materials on the war in the federal archives and had consistently been refused. But when Hayes became President, this policy was reversed, and the Secretary of War even appointed a former Confederate general, Marcus J. Wright, to an office in the federal service with the duty of collecting Confederate records for the federal archives.[10]

A few years later, when publication of the official government collection of war documents began, long-standing Southern suspicions were quieted. The fear among ex-Confederates that this official collection would be unfair in its presentation of their records had been one of the principal reasons for the founding of the Southern Historical Society. When the volumes of *The War of the Rebellion* began to appear, however, the former Confederate officer who was secretary of the society, although objecting decidedly to the use of the word "Rebellion," expressed the general satisfaction of Southerners that the work was fair in its presentation of Confederate as well as Union reports and documents.[11]

[10] See: *SHS Papers*, VI, 191-192 (October 1878); VI, 239-240 (November 1878); and XI, 530 (December 1883).

[11] *SHS Papers*, XI, 575-576 (December 1883). *The War of the Rebellion . . . Official Records of the Union and Confederate Armies* was published in 128 volumes from 1880 to 1901; the series pertaining to the navies was published in 30 volumes from 1894 to 1922.

Here for the use of future generations was a collection of basic records of the war on whose fairness both sides were agreed. This was not a dramatic incident, but it represented a considerable achievement over the spirit which had prevailed in the decade after Appomattox. In this action of the federal government was an implicit recognition that there were two sides to the Civil War story, and that both of them deserved to be heard.

A similar sentiment was evidenced in the publication, beginning in the late 1870's, of symposiums on various aspects of the war written by prominent individuals, both Unionists and Confederates. By this date, there was a revival of interest in the battles of the war, and such symposiums had great popularity. Two of the most successful were composed of articles published originally in the *Philadelphia Weekly Times* and the *Century* magazine which were later issued as volumes bearing the titles, respectively, *The Annals of the War Written by Leading Participants North and South* (1879) and *Battles and Leaders of the Civil War* (4v., 1887-1889) (it was significant that the word "Rebellion" was avoided in both titles). In these symposiums, such war leaders as Grant, Beauregard, and Longstreet presented the rival Union and Confederate accounts of Shiloh, Gettysburg, and other battles; additional contributors gave the competing versions of such hotly disputed issues as the exchange of prisoners during the war. At a time when the "Blue and Gray reunions" of veterans of both the former armies were becoming increasingly more popular, these symposiums represented something of a literary reunion of Blue and Gray for the discussion of historical topics. The contributors were not in agreement, and the question of the causes of the war was avoided in these symposiums, but here again in a limited sphere was the recognition, virtually unthinkable among the ardent partisans of the 1860's, that the events of the war could be viewed with honesty from more than one standpoint.

One of the firmest foundations upon which was based a new outlook on the war was the recognition by ex-soldiers, now growing old, that the former enemy had demonstrated personal bravery in battle. Many persons had noted, beginning in wartime, that combat soldiers of each side frequently evidenced less bitter personal hostility toward their foes and more respect for their courage than did others who had taken a less active part in the strug-gle. As the years passed, testimonials of soldiers to the bravery of the onetime enemy were heard with increasing frequency (the new spirit which was emerging was illustrated by the title of a volume by D.M. Kelsey published in 1886: *Deeds of Daring by Both Blue and Gray . . . during the Great Civil War*). From such testimonials, it was not a far step to the position that the opponent of the 1860's had been honest in his beliefs. Without losing, on either side, the conviction that the cause which they had sup-ported in arms had been "right," there were now a growing num-ber of men of the war generation who no longer found it necessary to cast doubt upon the motives of their foe of other days.

Typical was the statement made in 1883 by Theodore A. Dodge, a former officer in the Union Army who two decades before had been wounded and captured by the Confederates at Gettysburg. "Each side in our great Civil War," Dodge now declared simply, "believed itself in the right, and fought with the courage so en-gendered."[12] An answering echo came in the next year from Charles Fenner, a former Confederate officer who was now a Justice of the Supreme Court of the State of Louisiana. In an address in New Orleans, Fenner disavowed any desire to proclaim dogmatically that "we were right and that the supporters of the Union were wrong. . . . Far be it from me," he added, "to impugn the motives of those who advocated and enforced the indissolubil-ity of the Union."[13] As the veterans grew older, as death began to make inroads on their numbers and to occupy a larger place in their thoughts on successive Memorial Days, milder sentiments toward their old rivals came easily and naturally. The theme which later became so popular was clearly set forth by A.M. Keiley in a Memorial Day address in 1879:

Before the awful revelation of death, how petty and contemptible are the antagonisms of life. . . . Side by side on a hundred battlefields these children of a common mother still are lying. The grass which covers the blue grave and the gray grave mingles its leaves above and inter-laces its roots below.[14]

Dodge, Fenner, and Keiley expressed sentiments, still compara-

[12] Theodore A. Dodge, *A Bird's-Eye View of Our Civil War* (Boston, 1883) *ix*.
[13] Charles E. Fenner, "Oration," *SHS Papers*, XIV, 77 (1886).
[14] A.M. Keiley, *SHS Papers*, VII, 374, 383.

tively new in the 1870's and the 1880's, which were before long to become commonplace. They did not concern themselves primarily with efforts to demonstrate the war guilt of evil opponents or to justify their own cause by ingenious arguments. Instead, following the practice of the *Official Records* and the joint war symposiums, they tended to push into the background the causes of the war, on which there was still dispute, and to emphasize their conviction that individuals on each side had been valiant and honorable, a conviction on which there was growing agreement. It was in accord with this same widespread feeling that Walt Whitman, lecturing on Lincoln in 1879 and later years, passed rapidly over the "well-known events" which had led to war with the parenthetical comment that they were "too well known—I believe, these days, we almost hate to hear them mention'd."[15]

A beginning had been made, but even when men who had fought in the war admitted the bravery and sincerity of their former enemies, it was still difficult for them to alter their conceptions of the *causes* of the war, for these conceptions were the heart of the older attitudes in each section. How difficult it was to make this change, and yet how surely the change was being made, was revealed in this period in the writings of two veterans of the Union Army who became prominent historians, James Schouler and John W. Burgess. In the thinking of both Burgess and Schouler could be seen a mixture of the old and the new attitudes—a mixture common among men of the war generation at a time when opinions were gradually shifting.

James Schouler was a New Englander who had voted for Lincoln in both 1860 and 1864; after completing his army service, he practiced law in Massachusetts and later began the writing of history as a hobby. In the volumes of his *History of the United States of America under the Constitution* (published beginning in 1880), Schouler described the causes of the Civil War primarily in terms of traditional Unionist opinions and time-honored, stereotyped judgments. He pictured a war, concerned almost exclusively with an irrepressible moral conflict over slavery, in which the Northerners were righteous and the Southerners were wicked. His discussion of the expansion of the United States to the southwest

[15] William E. Barton, *Abraham Lincoln and Walt Whitman* (Indianapolis, 1928), 220.

typified his viewpoint. Writing of "degenerate sons of slavery," and of the "slave power, the oligarchy of human capital," he ascribed the annexation of Texas and the "iniquitous war with Mexico" to Southern slaveholders, whom God punished by causing the North and the South to quarrel over the disposition of the lands acquired from Mexico.[16]

Yet, in some respects, Schouler revealed attitudes which were distinctly different from those traditional in the Union states. He expressed a sentiment of nationalism which could encompass both Northerners and Southerners, and which permitted him, like Dodge, Fenner, and Keiley, to maintain that men of both sections had been faithful to their ideas and convictions. It was this sentiment which enabled him to condemn slavery not only for the standard reason that it was immoral but also because it "obstructed the destiny and growth of the American people in homogeneous grandeur."[17] Slavery was bad because it hindered the growth of the American nation. Moreover, the general "tone" of Schouler's *History*, especially some of the descriptions of the *ante-bellum* South and of individual Southerners, was characterized at times by an absence of personal bitterness that contrasted with many of the Unionist histories of the 1860's and the 1870's. He admitted, for example, that there were humane slaveholders, and he discussed Lee with admiration; Lee, Schouler insisted, made a mistake in going with his state, but "terrible though his mistake, one cannot doubt Lee's sincerity in his choice, for he was the soul of honor."[18]

But the clearest indication of new viewpoints in Schouler's writing was his account of the secession movement. Specifically disavowing the theory that secession had resulted from a conspiracy of Southern leaders, he urged that instead of "conspiracy," "treason," or "rebellion," the term "civil war" be used to designate the struggle of 1861-1865. He expressed agreement with the long-

[16] For examples of conventional Unionist viewpoints in Schouler's writings, see his *History of the United States of America Under the Constitution* (7v., New York, 1880-1913), I, 142-143, 239ff.; III, 172; V, 96-130, 371. The *History* was primarily a work of the 1880's; volumes I-V (covering the period 1783-1861) were published in 1880-1891, while volume VI was published in 1899 and volume VII in 1913.

[17] *ibid.*, V, 511. For an example of Schouler's nationalism, see his description of the United States in 1818 in *ibid.*, III, 106.

[18] *ibid.*, VI, 67. See also: II, 231-242; III, 484ff.

standing contention of Confederate sympathizers that the Southern people had been united to a considerable degree behind their leaders, and he declared that it was not the crime of a few men which had produced secession and war.[19]

Here was a former Union soldier, a New Englander, who held distinctly "Northern" views of the war in most respects, abandoning the "conspiracy theory" which had been such a consistent feature of the Unionist interpretation, abandoning even the designation "rebellion" and explaining the secession movement in terms which were at least partially similar to those long used by defenders of the Confederacy. What a contrast to the views of a man like Von Holst, who had formed his opinions of the war in large part in the atmosphere of the Northern states of the 1860's and the early 1870's and had never revised them! That Schouler's interpretation of the war was primarily the traditional pro-Union one is clear; so much more impressive, therefore, is the evidence of newer attitudes in his work.

Viewpoints formed in the 1860's were still held in the 1890's by John W. Burgess, but in his case, just as in that of Schouler, older and newer viewpoints were commingled. Burgess, the Tennessee Unionist who had left the South at the age of eighteen, pointed out that he had learned before his majority to regard "secession as an abomination, and its chief cause, slavery, as a great evil," and he frankly stated in the 1890's that he had found no reason to modify these early sentiments. With equal candor, he declared his belief that the history of the Civil War period should be written by a Northerner, for the Northern view was, in the main, "the correct view"; readers of one of his volumes were warned that not "one scintilla of justification for secession and rebellion" was to be found in its pages.[20] He used the word "rebellion" deliberately, for although the title of one of his volumes carried the phrase "Civil War," he still insisted, unlike Schouler, that the struggle of 1861-1865 had been a rebellion, pure and simple. Nationalism was the keynote of Burgess's views. Expressing

---

[19] *ibid.*, v, 509-511.

[20] John W. Burgess, *The Middle Period 1817-1858* (New York, 1897) *viii-xi*. In addition to this volume, Burgess's views on the war and related issues were set forth in *The Civil War and the Constitution* (2v., New York, 1901), and *Reconstruction and the Constitution* (New York, 1902).

the conviction that slavery and state sovereignty were fetters which had retarded the United States in the march of modern civilization, he condemned secession and the Southern justification for it in a manner similar to Von Holst. The secessionists, he declared, were in the wrong legally and ethically; they were the aggressors, and the South should acknowledge its error in regard to secession and rebellion.[21]

Yet, critical as Burgess was of the doctrines of the South, his judgments of individuals, North and South, reflected attitudes different from those of the Unionists writing in the early years after the war. He did not express bitter feelings toward individual Southerners (nor toward Northerners who had favored compromise with the South, such as Stephen A. Douglas); he granted that the Southern leaders and people were sincere in their interpretation of the Constitution. Even Jefferson Davis, the personification of the constitutional theories which Burgess detested, did not receive harsh censure; Davis, Burgess explained, simply held to an older point of view toward the Constitution, with no conception that changing conditions might require changes in constitutional interpretation. Indeed, the individuals toward whom Burgess was most severe in his remarks were not Southern secessionists but Northern abolitionists, particularly John Brown.[22]

The greatest departure from older Unionist viewpoints made by Burgess was his discussion of Reconstruction. Just as he was convinced that slavery and secession were wrong, so Burgess (whose family had owned slaves before the war) was certain that there were "vast differences in political capacity between the races." It was, he declared, "the white man's mission, his duty and his right, to hold the reins of political power in his own hands for the civilization of the world and the welfare of mankind."[23] From this basis, Burgess was bitterly critical of the policies followed by the Washington government in the Reconstruction period, and he asserted that the North should acknowledge that Reconstruction was an error as well as a failure.

Thus, the opinions of Burgess, like those of Schouler, repre-

[21] Burgess, *The Civil War*, I, 74ff., 120, 134-135, 168-171.

[22] Burgess, *The Middle Period*, xi, 384ff., 440ff., 473-474, and *The Civil War*, I, 16-17, 148-149.

[23] Burgess, *Reconstruction*, viii-ix.

sented a mixture of old and new attitudes; in his views as a whole, he struck something of a balance—the North was right in the war while the South was right in Reconstruction. Southerners noted and approved his tolerant attitude toward Jefferson Davis, his criticism of Reconstruction, and other evidences of the newer viewpoints in his writing.[24] That the views of a partisan as ardent as Burgess showed at least some signs of softening was an indication that changes were under way.

No Confederate veterans attained the prominence of Schouler or Burgess as writers of history, but there was evidence that some of the men who had worn the Gray were also looking at the war in a different fashion from the 1860's. By the 1890's, there were frequent statements from former Confederates expressing satisfaction at the outcome of the war. R.E. Colston, writing in 1893, particularly rejoiced that because of the war Southerners had gotten rid of the "incubus of slavery, which we would not otherwise have shaken off in more than a century." Glorying in the prosperous and powerful nation which had emerged since 1865, envisioning the "magnificent destiny" stretching before the youth of this reunited country with its one flag, Colston ascribed the war and its outcome to "Fate," and declared, "It is well."[25] A few years later, Confederate General James Longstreet, evidencing a similar satisfaction at the result of the war, stated his belief that "there is to-day, *because of the war*, a broader and deeper patriotism in all Americans," South Carolinians as well as citizens of Massachusetts.[26] Colston and Longstreet did not discuss the causes of the war, but they reflected a feeling of nationalism which was ultimately to serve as the basis for a changed interpretation of the war's causes. For this "new nationalism" of the 1880's and 1890's, as another former Confederate, William R. Garrett, accurately observed in 1899, disposed "the hearts of the American people to recall the Civil War with emotions of national pride, rather than sectional malice."[27]

[24] *Publications of the Southern History Association*, VI, 167 (March 1902), and 343-346 (July 1902).

[25] *SHS Papers*, XXI, 38 (1893).

[26] James Longstreet, *From Manassas to Appomattox* (Philadelphia, 1895) *vi.*

[27] William R. Garrett, "The South As a Factor in the Territorial Expansion of the United States," Clement A. Evans, ed., *Confederate Military History* (12v., Atlanta, 1899) I, 68.

These men of the generation which had fought reflected the new opinions on the war which were beginning to appear after the late 1870's. In this period of small beginnings, it was still seemingly impossible for them to explain the causes of the war in accord with the new sentiments and in a manner which would appeal to both Northerners and Southerners. But it was evident that some members of the war generation in both North and South were now beginning to find Civil War themes and attitudes upon which they could reach agreement. With these attitudes the future lay, and they were soon to dictate new interpretations of the coming of war.

James Ford Rhodes
and the New Generation

IF NEW ATTITUDES toward the war were beginning to be adopted here and there by men of the generation which had actively fought in it, the same was true, as we would expect, of some of the "young men growing up" in both North and South. The writings, beginning in the 1890's, of such individuals of the new generation as James Ford Rhodes, Frederick Jackson Turner, Woodrow Wilson, and Edward Channing mark a new era in the interpretation of the causes of the Civil War. These men differed in their points of view, but each of them explained the coming of war in a manner and in a spirit which were distinctly different from those formerly prevailing in either North or South. They were each influential in shaping their generation's concept of the causes and nature of the war, but it was clear from the reception accorded their ideas that they were reflecting attitudes which were already becoming widespread and which needed only to be crystallized. These writers of histories told their age what it was already prepared to accept about the Civil War.

To the historians of this second generation, the Civil War was primarily "history" rather than remembered personal experience. It is instructive to look at the birthdates of some of the men who became prominent as writers of history in the quarter-century after 1890. James Ford Rhodes (1848), John Bach McMaster (1852), Albert Bushnell Hart (1854), Woodrow Wilson (1856), Edward Channing (1856), and William A. Dunning (1857) were all born before the war, but of the six only Rhodes had reached the age of fifteen when the fighting ceased. Frederick Jackson Turner (1861) and William P. Trent (1862) were born during the struggle, and in the 1860's, after the war, William Garrot Brown (1868) and William E. Dodd (1869) were born. Not until a decade or more after the election of Lincoln, were T.C. Smith (1870), Emerson D. Fite (1874), Charles E. Merriam (1874), and Frederic L. Paxson

(1877) born. The memories held by these historians of the events and emotions of wartime were those of childhood—memories of asking grownups in 1860 what the election of Lincoln meant (Woodrow Wilson), of hearing war news read aloud in school (James Ford Rhodes), or of being allowed to go into the street alone for the first time to buy a paper telling of Lincoln's assassination (Edward Channing).

Whether or not these men of the new generation had inherited the attitudes toward the war traditional in their sections, they had reached maturity amid circumstances different from those which their parents had known, and in a period in which the wartime emotions and viewpoints were beginning to change. Only a few of the historians mentioned above reached maturity and began writing before the 1890's, and that decade was marked by any number of incidents which demonstrated that the primary issues and alignments in American life were no longer those of 1861 save for infrequent, sporadic outbursts.

The 1890's witnessed eruptions of the domestic unrest which had been on the increase for several years. Some of the prominent issues in national politics in that decade were spotlighted by the emergence of the Populist Party. How different from the 1860's were the forces here represented was symbolized in that party's candidates for national office in 1892: a former Union general from Iowa was the candidate for President, while a former Confederate general from Virginia was the candidate for Vice-president. General Coxey's "army" of unemployed marching on Washington had a more immediate and compelling significance for the decade than did the armies of Grant or Lee; the decision of the Supreme Court in 1895 declaring the income tax unconstitutional was now of greater practical import than the famous Dred Scott decision almost four decades earlier; William Jennings Bryan and the cross of gold were much nearer to the main stream of day-to-day politics than were Jefferson Davis and the sour apple tree. And whether the electoral campaign of 1896 be interpreted as a contest of East *versus* West, or of farm *versus* city, or farmer *versus* industrialist, it demonstrated in a striking fashion that the primary alignment of American politics was no longer a union of Northeast and Northwest in opposition to the South, as it had been in 1861.

At the close of the 1890's, the war against Spain revealed the extent to which the Civil War was becoming "history," the extent to which the animosities of the 1860's were now being submerged in the emotional "new nationalism" of a reunited North and South. The Spanish war produced tangible and dramatic symbols of the reunion of Blue and Gray. Of the four major-generals appointed from civil life to lead the armies against Spain, two were former officers in the Confederate Army, Fitzhugh Lee and Joseph ("Fightin' Joe") Wheeler. Former Confederates and the sons of former Confederates now demonstrated that they would wear the blue uniform and "fight for their country" just as if there had been no division in 1861. Illustrating the extent to which the Civil War had receded into the past was the fact that the onetime hostility between Confederate and Yankee was now a subject about which jokes could be made. Typical of many such humorous anecdotes, based on fact or imagination or both, were two which grew out of the war against Spain. One concerned an old Confederate veteran who reputedly stated that what he looked forward to with greatest eagerness in the next world was hearing "what Jubal Early would say when he met Fitz Lee wearing a Yankee uniform."[28] In a similar vein was the story over which the country laughed in 1898, the story of "Fightin' Joe" Wheeler, who, in the heat of battle in Cuba, momentarily fancied that he was once again faced by his foes of the 1860's and exulted to his followers that the Yankees were on the run (one account of this incident had Wheeler saying "Charge the Yankees—no, dammit, I mean the Spaniards").[29]

Thus, a combination of influences—the passage of time bringing with it the removal of old issues, the rise of a new generation which had not known the war at first hand and which reached maturity in an era of nationalism and of reconciliation between North and South—paved the way for a new outlook on the Civil War in the 1890's. Already at the beginning of the decade, a young

[28] Basil W. Duke, *Reminiscences of General Basil W. Duke* (Garden City, New York, 1911) 477.

[29] John P. Dyer, *"Fightin' Joe" Wheeler* (University, La., 1941) 352-353.

writer, Finley Peter Dunne (born 1867), demonstrated the lack of appeal of "bloody shirt" issues to at least some members of this second generation. In the 1890 congressional campaign, Dunne, a newspaper reporter at the time, recounted in a sober column a "bloody shirt" speech by former Governor Joseph B. Foraker of Ohio, but concluded the account with this sentence: "Then the audience went out to get the latest news of the battle of Gettysburg."[30] Whether or not Dunne in this case reflected the views of his contemporaries as accurately as he was to do a decade later in the guise of "Mr. Dooley," it was demonstrated in the 1890's that individuals of this second generation could now interpret the causes of the Civil War in a manner and spirit quite unlike that of the 1860's. The transition from the older to the newer points of view can be seen most clearly in the writings of James Ford Rhodes.

In Rhodes' personal background were elements well suited to make him a figure of transition in interpreting the causes of the Civil War. He was not of the generation which had fought in the war, yet he had memories of wartime from his school days. Living in Cleveland, the center of an area in Ohio which was strongly Republican, Rhodes came from a family which, although of New England origin, was Democratic in politics and remained so throughout the war. His father, Daniel P. Rhodes, close friend and strong admirer of Stephen A. Douglas, possessed such strong Democratic Party sentiments that they caused, during the war, a temporary delay in the marriage of his daughter to a young man by the name of Marcus Alonzo Hanna, whose Cleveland family was outspokenly Republican.[31] Apparently the elder Rhodes supported the war, and James Ford Rhodes' brother served for a time in the Union Army, but legends survive which testify to Daniel Rhodes' lack of love for the "niggers"; "I like you very well, Mark," he is quoted as saying to Mark Hanna, "but you are a damned screecher for freedom." James Ford Rhodes, writing in

[30] Brand Whitlock, *Forty Years of It* (New York, 1914) 47.

[31] Herbert Croly, *Marcus Alonzo Hanna: His Life and Work* (New York, 1912) 47ff.; Thomas Beer, *Hanna, Crane, and the Mauve Decade* (New York, 1941) 415-418. The most complete account of James Ford Rhodes' life is M.A. DeWolfe Howe, *James Ford Rhodes American Historian* (New York, 1929); see, in particular, the autobiographical sketch, written by Rhodes in 1892, printed on pp. 17-29.

1893, described his father as a "Copperhead" during the war.[32] As a youth, Rhodes later recalled, he "drank in eagerly" the political opinions of his father, and during the war opposed the Emancipation Proclamation in a school essay and defended Vallandigham in a school debate (on the grounds that he had been outrageously treated and was not a traitor). He was one of a handful of Democratic boys in a public high school where the master and most of the pupils were strong Republicans, although the Democratic boys were generally allowed opportunity to express their opinions. It has been suggested that the necessity as a boy to reconcile the Democratic opinions upheld so strongly in his home and the predominantly Republican viewpoints of his school served to promote fairness of mind in Rhodes; whether or not this is so, whatever lasting attitudes Rhodes absorbed from his father presumably offered less of a barrier to the new currents of thought about the Civil War in the 1880's and the 1890's than orthodox Republican or abolitionist sentiments would have presented.[33]

Rhodes' background (like that of his contemporary, the historian Henry Charles Lea) also included success in business. Daniel P. Rhodes had been a pioneer in the coal mining industry of Ohio, and by the time of the Civil War was a wealthy man, "one of the most substantial and influential citizens of Cleveland." Although James Ford Rhodes desired to be a writer, he entered business in response to his father's wishes; only after a successful career in the coal and iron industry had rendered him financially independent did he, in 1885, quit business to devote his entire time to the study and writing of history. (This was in striking contrast to his brother-in-law Hanna, a member of the same firm as Rhodes, who successfully pursued his own avocation, politics, while remaining in business.) Rhodes lived in the upper middle class, late nineteenth century Victorian world of confidence in

---

[32] Letter, Rhodes to J.W. Burgess, June 5, 1893, published in Joseph Borome, "James Ford Rhodes and Historical Scholarship," *The New England Quarterly*, xxi, 379 (September 1948). See also: Beer, *Hanna, Crane, and the Mauve Decade*, 416; Howe, *Rhodes*, 33-34. The quotation concerning Hanna in the preceding sentence is from Croly, *Hanna*, 47.

[33] Howe, *Rhodes*, 34; Dumas Malone, "James Ford Rhodes," *The Dictionary of American Biography*, xv, 531-533. Rhodes' account of his schooldays is given in Howe, *Rhodes*, 18-20.

business, of security, of optimism, and of faith in progress. The significance of this business background lies in the fact, as has been suggested, that some business groups, North and South, were markedly receptive to the sentiments of sectional reconciliation after the war.[34]

Rhodes was not a consistent supporter of either the Republican or Democratic Party. In the Reconstruction period, he apparently supported the Republican policies in general, but he was opposed to the granting of suffrage to Negroes. Later he became a Grover Cleveland Democrat, favoring a lower tariff despite his connection with the iron industry. In 1896, and during the Theodore Roosevelt administrations, he sided with the Republicans, but in 1912 supported Woodrow Wilson. Because he thought Wilson had surrendered to organized labor in signing the Adamson Act, Rhodes voted for Hughes in 1916, but he upheld Wilson's policies during the First World War and hoped for the entrance of the United States into the League of Nations. "I started life," he told his grandson in 1919, "as a strong Democrat, then I became a strong Republican, then a lukewarm Democrat, and now I suppose I am a lukewarm Republican."[35]

This personal background of Rhodes as a businessman of Democratic heritage in Civil War times contained influences which would logically produce sympathy with the new attitudes toward the war; although there were elements of both the old and the new in his conception of the war, it was his expression of the new attitudes which accounted, in the main, for the impact he made upon his generation as a historian.

The first volumes of Rhodes' *History of the United States from the Compromise of 1850* appeared in 1893 (and before they were published, Rhodes, the Midwesterner with literary ambition, had moved to Cambridge and soon thereafter established himself in Boston in a home on Beacon Street). Viewed in the perspective of the 1890's, the most striking feature of the *History* was the dominant spirit which pervaded it: throughout, the opinions of Rhodes on the causes and nature of the Civil War were grounded on the conviction that in history, as he phrased it, "all the right is never

[34] See note 7 above.
[35] Howe, *Rhodes*, 306; see also 77, 94, 154, 173-174, 232-233, 270-271.

on one side and all the wrong on the other."[36] This spirit led to an obviously sincere attempt to be fair to each side in the war, and it led also in the case of Rhodes (who, good Victorian that he was, believed that the historian should openly and explicitly pass moral judgments upon men) to an attempt to balance the "right" and "wrong" of each of the contestants. The war was not a burning contemporary issue to Rhodes as it had been to the men of the 1860's; instead, it was for him an event in history (comparable, as he said, to the Peloponnesian War in ancient Greece). Thus, questions which had aroused the most bitter emotions North and South in the years after 1865 (such as the responsibility for the burning of Columbia, South Carolina, during the war) were now to Rhodes primarily historical problems—a matter of sifting documents and of weighing evidence—a true "delight," as he confessed, to the historian.[37]

The primary, and indeed practically the sole cause of the Civil War, in the view of Rhodes, was the institution of slavery; on this subject, Rhodes' opinions were, in some respects, not markedly different from those traditional in his section. He scorned the attempts of Southerners to justify their "rebellion" as an exercise of the right to revolution (declaring that there had been no "oppression" which would justify revolution), or as the defense of their constitutional rights under the Calhoun theory of state sovereignty (had there been no slavery, he asserted, there would have been no effective Calhoun theory of the Constitution); the South, he insisted, fought to extend slavery—an institution condemned by ethics, Christianity, and science—and slavery was the cause of the Civil War.[38] Similarly, Rhodes, a New Englander by choice, paid little attention to the West in discussing the causes of the war (William A. Dunning once speculated whether Rhodes' view-

[36] James Ford Rhodes, *History of the United States from the Compromise of 1850* (7v., New York, 1893-1906) v, 485. These seven volumes cover the years from 1850 to 1877; two volumes were published later, in 1919 and in 1922, which carried the narrative down to 1909. In addition, Rhodes published two one-volume histories of the war: *Lectures on the American Civil War* (London, 1913), and *History of the Civil War 1861-1865* (New York, 1917).

[37] James Ford Rhodes, "Who Burned Columbia?" *Proceedings of the Massachusetts Historical Society*, Second Series, xv, 264-274 (1901-1902).

[38] Rhodes, *History*, I, 52-53; III, 265, 280.

point would have been different if he had moved west from Cleveland in the 1890's rather than east).[39]

The heart of the sectional dispute lay, as he saw it, in differences over the morality of human slavery; this issue had involved an irrepressible conflict which had divided the nation into a hostile "North" and "South," and in this struggle the South had clearly been in the wrong:

The judgment of posterity is made up: it was an unrighteous cause which the South defended by arms; and at the tribunal of modern civilization, Calhoun and Davis must be held accountable for the misery which resulted from this appeal to the sword.[40]

Rhodes seems to have employed the phrase "irrepressible conflict" with two different meanings, and it is difficult to determine whether he considered the Civil War itself "inevitable." At some points in his writings, he apparently equated "irrepressible conflict" and "inevitable war" (at least by December 1860), as when he wrote that "those of us who hold to the idea of irrepressible conflict" could see that the adoption of compromise proposals in December 1860 would have meant "no more than the delay of a war that was inevitable"; in a similar vein, he declared that "destiny pointed [presumably by 1860-1861] to certain war," and that it was "practically impossible" for the Union and Confederate governments to have remained long at peace even had the Union government agreed to a separation in the crisis of 1860-1861.[41] Yet, in other passages, Rhodes implied that war was not inevitable, as when he stated that the alternatives in 1861 were war or peaceable separation; similarly, he at times seemed, like William H. Seward in 1858, to mean by "irrepressible conflict" the existence of irreconcilable differences between North and South which might or

---

[39] *Educational Review*, xxxiv, 114-115 (September 1907).

[40] Rhodes, *History*, i, 380. Other examples of opinions expressed by Rhodes which were similar to those common in his section during and after the war can be found in: *History*, i, chaps. i, iv; iii, 135-136. In his judgment on Stephen A. Douglas (before Douglas's break with the Buchanan administration), Rhodes was on the whole more harsh than had been the traditional Unionist viewpoint: he pictured Douglas as an ambitious politician who, prompted by the desire to get the vote of the South for the presidency, reopened, in the Kansas-Nebraska Act, the question of slavery in the territories and thus hastened the coming of the war. Douglas, wrote Rhodes, "sinned as a statesman." See: *History*, i, 429-430, 494; ii, 261; iii, 414-415.

[41] The quotations are taken from *History*, iii, 135-136, 343.

might not have led to war: he wrote, for example, that gradual and compensated emancipation offered even in 1861 "a real solution of the irrepressible conflict."[42]

Rhodes' views on slavery as a cause of the war, similar as they were in some respects to the traditional opinions of Unionists, also reveal how far he had departed from the attitudes formerly common in his section. He did not seek to place personal and sectional guilt for the war exclusively upon Southerners because of slavery. Proceeding beyond the simple assertion that slavery caused the war to the more complex question of the responsibility for slavery, he found the influence of inanimate forces. Cotton had fostered slavery, and the invention of the cotton gin had made slavery profitable in the nineteenth century, thus bringing to nought moral and humane expectations of its destruction. "It is more than probable," he declared, "that the invention of the cotton gin prevented the peaceful abolition of slavery."[43] Thus, the ultimate "blame" for the continuance of slavery, for the irrepressible conflict, and for the war growing out of this conflict, was placed not upon evil Southerners but upon the cotton plant and the cotton gin.

Moreover, if any personal or sectional blame were to be assessed for slavery, Rhodes insisted that England and the Northern states should not cast stones at the South, since both of them had been involved in establishing the institution in the South. Critical as he was of the institution of slavery, Rhodes made a distinction between slavery and individual slaveholders, and the slaveholders were absolved, for the most part, of the blame for slavery which they customarily received. The verdict of history, Rhodes was convinced, would be that slavery was the calamity of Southern men, not their crime; they deserved sympathy rather than censure.[44] That Southerners were associated with slavery was not ascribed in Rhodes' volumes to innate personal depravity, and he insisted that Southerners were not inherently different in personal character even from New Englanders. If the Puritans had settled Virginia, he wrote, and the Cavaliers had settled Massachusetts, then it was not inconceivable that the slavery conflict would have arisen

---

[42] The quotation is taken from *ibid.*, III, 270; for additional expressions of the point of view described in this sentence, see: *ibid.*, I, 2; III, 262-264, 269-271, 291.
[43] *ibid.*, I, 26.   [44] *ibid.*, I, 370, 379.

just as it did, with the Puritan fighting for slavery and the Cavalier for liberty![45]

With personal blame for slavery largely removed, *ante-bellum* Southern society was now praised on the grounds that it had been more "hospitable" than that of the North, and individual Southerners were acclaimed even for their conduct in the war! Like Schouler, Rhodes extolled Lee for although Lee chose the "wrong" side, he was one of the finest products of American life, a man who in "all essential characteristics" resembled George Washington.[46] Similarly, a revised judgment was now made of Northerners like Daniel Webster. To many individuals of the war generation of his section, Webster had seemed a fallen giant because of his support of the compromise of 1850, but Webster's nationalism and love of the Union were praised by Rhodes: it was Webster's principle of "Liberty and Union" which won in the Civil War, not Garrison's principle of "no union with slaveholders."[47] The battles of the war were now depicted as the struggles of courageous men with glory enough to spare for each side. For the harsh features of the conflict (the prison camp cruelties, the destruction, and plundering), the blame was placed primarily upon the nature of war itself rather than upon individuals of either side.[48]

From the basic approach of Rhodes to the war, a revised estimate of the secession movement naturally followed. Like Schouler, Rhodes specifically rejected the older view that secession had resulted from the conspiracy of a few treasonable men. Instead, just as did Southerners of the 1860's, he described a true popular movement in which the Southern people were overwhelmingly united behind their leaders; he hesitated even to justify Lincoln and the Republican Party for their rejection of the Crittenden compromise proposals in the winter of 1860-1861.[49] Symbolizing his changed concept of the causes and character of the war was the fact that Rhodes did not refer to it as "the Rebellion." This name, as we have seen, had been traditional among supporters of the Union, and Rhodes noted the importance that Lincoln and other loyal Unionists had placed upon that designation for the struggle;

[45] *ibid.*, I, 380-381. [46] *ibid.*, III, 411-413. [47] *ibid.*, I, 137-161.
[48] *ibid.*, v, chap. XXIX. [49] *ibid.*, III, 169-171, 262ff., 272-279.

but he himself consistently and matter-of-factly employed the newer term now beginning to win favor in the North, "the Civil War"—and this fact speaks volumes concerning the revised attitudes toward the war which he expressed.[50]

Rhodes had opposed suffrage for Negroes during Reconstruction, and he shared the feeling dominant in his section by the end of the nineteenth century that the Southern whites should be in control of race relations in their states.[51] Just as he had made a distinction between slavery and individual slaveholders, so he differentiated slavery and what he called the "Negro question" or the "race question"—and in each case the distinction made possible a revision of traditional points of view. Human slavery involved a question of morals, and he was unyielding in his opposition to this institution; but the "Negro question" was one involving race, and here his sympathy was with the Southern whites. The North, he wrote in 1893, had been wrong at the close of the war in thinking that the Negro question was settled, and it now appreciated the wisdom of Madison's remark that if he could make all Negroes white, he could abolish slavery in one day.[52]

This point of view led to a reinterpretation of the actions of the national government in the Reconstruction period similar to that made by Burgess. Rhodes felt that these actions had been decidedly mistaken. "No large policy in our country," he wrote, "has ever been so conspicuous a failure as that of forcing universal negro suffrage upon the South," and he criticized Charles Sumner, leader of congressional Reconstruction, on the ground that he showed no appreciation of "the great fact of race."[53] Re-

[50] See, for example: *ibid.*, I, 1; III, 408-409; *Lectures on the American Civil War* (note the title), 136.

[51] Rhodes stated that among his Ohio friends who acquired mansions in the South, even those who were formerly critical of the South for its treatment of Negroes soon adopted Southern attitudes or became even less sympathetic toward Negroes than Southern whites ("Remarks," *Proceedings of the Massachusetts Historical Society*, Second Series, XVIII, 232-237 [1903-1904]).

[52] *History*, I, 383.

[53] *ibid.*, VI, 39; VII, 168. See also: "Negro Suffrage and Reconstruction," *Proceedings of the Massachusetts Historical Society*, Second Series, XVIII, 465-467 (1903-1904); XIX, 34-37 (1905). Rhodes wrote during the same period in which the studies of Reconstruction by Burgess and by William A. Dunning and his students were being published; he attributed his views on the subject, in part at least, to the influence of *The Nation* magazine under the editorship of E.L. Godkin (Rhodes, *Historical Essays* [New

construction as a whole represented to Rhodes "the oppression of the South by the North," and he hailed the abandonment of that policy as a "triumph of Southern intelligence and character."[54] It was not strange that David Y. Thomas of Kentucky, who had previously declared that only a Southerner could write the history of Reconstruction, retracted his statement upon the appearance of Rhodes' volumes on the period, implying that no Southerner could present the Southern point of view with greater sympathy than Rhodes.[55]

Such in broad outline were the opinions of Rhodes. Slavery had caused a "Civil War," yet there had been praiseworthy slaveholders, and the final responsibility for the institution was not to be placed solely upon Southerners. Throughout, Rhodes attempted to balance the right and wrong of each side, and he emerged with an over-all judgment similar to that of Burgess: the North had been right in the war, while the South had been right in Reconstruction. Rhodes went a step further than Burgess, and in his volumes most of the blame for what happened was ultimately placed upon inanimate forces. Here was an interpretation of the war's causes which went far toward solving the long standing question of war guilt in accord with the new attitudes and points of view developing since the late 1870's. How different it was from either the Confederate or the Unionist interpretations which had been so common in the 1860's and the 1870's!

Written at a time when sentiments were changing, Rhodes' *History* was both one of the last major statements of some of the older Northern viewpoints toward the war and, at the same time, one of the first major statements of the newer interpretations. To a later era, Rhodes has come to represent the older Unionist ideas to such an extent that his significance to his contemporaries has been overlooked. To the men of the 1890's and of the first decade of the twentieth century, the prime importance of Rhodes was not that he presented some of the older opinions but that he

York, 1909] 282). For Dunning's tribute to the volumes of Rhodes' covering the Reconstruction period, see below, note 59.

[54] *History*, VII, 290.

[55] *The Dial* (Chicago), XLII, 182 (March 16, 1907); *Review of Reviews* (United States), XXVI, 464 (October 1902).

presented so many of the new.[56] For in the fifteen years or so after the publication of the first two volumes of the *History* in 1893, it was the new features of Rhodes' interpretation which were noted and commented upon; it was the attempt to be impartial, to be fair to both sides, and the comparative success of this attempt, that immediately appealed to the men of his era and won their widespread praise. The reaction of the contemporaries of Rhodes to his interpretation of the causes of the war provides in itself an important indication of the widespread appeal of the new ideas.

The volumes of Rhodes' *History* received what no other history of the war up to that time had received—commendation from men of widely different sectional backgrounds and points of view. To Charles Francis Adams of Massachusetts, who had fought in the Union forces at Gettysburg, just as to John C. Reed of Georgia, who had fought in the Confederate forces in the same battle; to a former radical abolitionist from Indiana (George W. Julian), just as to a young scholar from Alabama whose father had fought in the Confederate cavalry (Walter L. Fleming); to trained historians of "Northern" or "Western" background (such as A.C. McLaughlin, Frederick Jackson Turner, or William A. Dunning), just as to those of "Southern" backgrounds (such as John S. Bassett, J.G. de R. Hamilton, William G. Brown, or David Y. Thomas)—to all these men it seemed that Rhodes had tried to hold the scales of judgment even, and they applauded the effort. There was not agreement that Rhodes had been entirely successful in his attempt to be fair, but there was almost universal recognition that he had made an honest effort and that he had written the fairest account of the war and its causes which had yet appeared.

The dominant reaction to the views of Rhodes can be seen in the remarks of a young Southern scholar, William E. Dodd, and in those of the former abolitionist George W. Julian: Dodd wrote Rhodes that he believed that his *History* had done more than any other agency of any sort to bring about a time when the issues of 1861-1865 no longer served as red rags; in a similar vein, Julian expressed the prevailing sentiment when he wrote in 1895 that one of Rhodes' volumes, by its "fairness in dealing with sectional

[56] Appendix A contains a listing of some comments upon Rhodes and his writings by his contemporaries before the First World War.

and party issues, happily voices the general feeling of reconcilia-tion and peace."[57]

It would be difficult to overestimate the importance of Rhodes and his *History* to his generation of historians in the United States. Rhodes was unknown as a historian, for the good reason that he had written very little history, until the first two volumes of his *History* were published in 1893 (Justin Winsor, librarian of the Harvard Library, upon first seeing the name "Rhodes" on the title page is supposed to have expressed surprise that a Cambridge printer of that name should have produced such a work). Within a remarkably short time, however, Rhodes was recognized as one of the country's leading scholars; soon he was elected president of the American Historical Association, was asked to write the volume on the United States in the *Cambridge Modern History*, lectured at Oxford on the Civil War, and received numerous per-sonal honors from scholarly organizations.[58] To Rhodes and his volumes Albert Bushnell Hart, Edward Channing, William A. Dunning, F.L. Paxson, Edward G. Bourne, and other leading historians of the day paid tribute and acknowledged their in-debtedness.[59]

Rhodes became something of a symbol of balanced judgment and fairness in the writing of history, a standard by which to com-pare writers on controversial topics; by 1904, it seemed entirely fitting for the historian William Roscoe Thayer to praise a volume with the remark that it deserved to rank with the work of Rhodes.[60] A typical contemporary estimate, made in 1902 by H.

[57] Letter, William E. Dodd to Rhodes (date not given), quoted in Howe, *Rhodes,* 114; George W. Julian in *The Dial* (Chicago), xix, 70 (August 1, 1895).

[58] Howe, *Rhodes,* 93, 125. For the Justin Winsor anecdote, see *ibid.,* 66.

[59] William A. Dunning was not a man given to superlatives, but in the preface to his volume in *The American Nation* series on Reconstruction—a field in which Dunning was supposedly the master—he stated: "The appearance of Dr. James Ford Rhodes's last two volumes, covering the years 1866-1877, in time to be used in the final revision of my manuscript, is a mercy the greatness of which cannot . . . be adequately expressed"; the best general guide to the sources of the Reconstruction period, Dunning declared, was the footnote references in Rhodes' *History*, volumes v-vii (William A. Dunning, *Reconstruction Political and Economic 1865-1877* [New York, 1907] *xvi,* 342). Hart dedicated his volume in *The American Nation* series to Rhodes. See also: Edward Chan-ning, *The United States of America 1765-1865* (New York, 1896) *vii-viii;* Edward G. Bourne, in J.N. Larned, ed., *The Literature of American History* (Boston, 1902) 289; F.L. Paxson, *The Civil War* (New York, 1911) *x,* 251-252.

[60] *The American Historical Review,* x, 199 (October 1904).

Morse Stephens, professor of history at Cornell University, was that, among the living and working writers of American history, "the palm undoubtedly belongs to Mr. James Ford Rhodes"; a few years later, a Southern historian, William Garrott Brown, born three years after Appomattox, declared that Rhodes was the best historian writing in the English tongue.[61]

The basis for this esteem, it is worth stressing, lay in the fact that Rhodes, by explaining the causes of the war with greater fairness than had previously been done, struck a decidedly responsive chord in his generation. He faced the problem of the war's causes squarely and handled it, unlike Schouler and Burgess, in a way that seemed remarkably fair to many of his contemporaries. The ovation Rhodes received is testimony both to his own skill as a historian and to the strong attraction newer opinions on the war held for his contemporaries.

[61] H. Morse Stephens, *The World's Work* (New York), IV, 2324 (July 1902) (illustrating the comparative judgments of Stephens was his description of Frederick Jackson Turner as a professor to whom "the highest hopes and expectations" of students of American history were turned); William G. Brown, *The American Historical Review*, XI, 181 (October 1905).

The Rise of the Trained Historian

JAMES FORD RHODES was a figure of transition in the writing of history in the United States, just as he was in respect to attitudes toward the Civil War. He was one of the last of the great self-trained "amateurs" who wrote history in the nineteenth century as an avocation, and by the time that his volumes were published, the writing of history in the United States was becoming more and more the province of trained historians. Beginning in the 1880's and 1890's, students emerged from the history seminars at Johns Hopkins, Harvard, Columbia, Chicago, Cornell, and other universities in ever increasing numbers, and gradually a new profession, devoted to the study, teaching, and writing of history, was created. The teaching of history in American colleges and universities rapidly expanded (it was estimated by J. Franklin Jameson that there were only eleven professors of history in the United States in 1880), and this era has been described accurately as the "Great Awakening" in the American historical world.[62] Henceforth, more and more (although not all) of the individuals who had a serious interest in the Civil War and who wrote histories of the war were trained historians.

It was noteworthy that the new university graduate schools and

[62] For a contemporary summary of some of these new developments, see Charles K. Adams, "Recent Historical Work in the Colleges and Universities of Europe and America," *Papers of the American Historical Association*, IV (New York, 1890) 39-65. For various later accounts, see: Charles M. Andrews, "These Forty Years," *The American Historical Review*, XXX, 225-250 (January 1925); H. Hale Bellot, "Some Aspects of the Recent History of American Historiography," *Transactions of the Royal Historical Society*, 4th Series, XXVIII, 121-148 (London, 1946); William A. Dunning, "A Generation of American Historiography," *Annual Report of the American Historical Association for the Year 1917* (Washington, 1920) 345-354; W. Stull Holt, "The Idea of Scientific History in America," *Journal of the History of Ideas*, I, 352-362 (June 1940); J.H. Randall, Jr., and George Haines, IV, "Controlling Assumptions in the Practice of American Historians," Social Science Research Council, Bulletin 54, *Theory and Practice in Historical Study: A Report of the Committee on Historiography* (New York, 1946) 15-52; Theodore C. Smith, "The Writing of American History, 1884-1934," *The American Historical Review*, XL, 439-449 (April 1935); James A. Woodburn, "Promotion of Historical Study in America Following the Civil War," *Transactions of the Illinois State Historical Society for the Year 1922* (Springfield, 1923) 37-50.

the new historical profession reflected and probably stimulated among historians the contemporary spirit of nationalism and of sectional reconciliation (although we have seen that some of the early trained historians in the Union states uncritically accepted sectional opinions on the war), for both the graduate schools and the historical profession quickly became national in scope and sentiment, and apparently militated against intellectual sectionalism. The graduate schools, one of the powerful intellectual influences in the latter part of the nineteenth century in the United States, were great "imperialistic" institutions drawing their faculties and their students from all sections of the country and sending out graduates to all corners of the land. (To illustrate what he called the "colonial system of the Johns Hopkins University," Herbert B. Adams kept a map of the United States on which he marked the location of institutions on whose faculties were former graduate students from Johns Hopkins.)[63]

One specific example of the intersectional commingling promoted by the new graduate schools was to be seen at Johns Hopkins in the 1880's. There, in the same Baltimore boarding house, lived Woodrow Wilson the Southerner, Frederick Jackson Turner from Wisconsin, and Charles H. Haskins from Pennsylvania. Both Wilson and Turner later testified to the influence of their Baltimore conversations in shaping and stimulating their historical thinking.[64] In Cambridge, New York, Madison, Chicago, and other graduate centers, the scene at the Baltimore boarding house was duplicated with lesser Wilsons, Turners, and Haskinses.

Similarly, the new historical profession was organized on national lines from its very beginning. In the age when John D. Rockefeller and other titans were organizing their businesses on a national scale, the historians formed in 1884 the first truly national historical society in this country, the American Historical Association. This association, through its conventions and its pub-

[63] United States Bureau of Education, Circulars of Information, No. 1 (1887), *The College of William and Mary*, 73-74.

[64] Ray Stannard Baker, *Woodrow Wilson: Life and Letters* (8v., New York, 1927-1939) II, 124-125; William E. Dodd, *Woodrow Wilson and His Work* (New York, 1920) 27-28; Wendell H. Stephenson, "The Influence of Woodrow Wilson on Frederick Jackson Turner," *Agricultural History*, XIX, 249-253 (October 1945); Frederick Jackson Turner, "Turner's Autobiographic Letter," *The Wisconsin Magazine of History*, XIX, 90-103 (September 1935).

lications, provided yet another intersectional meetingplace and intersectional forum for historians.

If the graduate schools and the historical profession, by stimulating nationalizing tendencies, weakened the influence of intellectual sectionalism, they apparently worked also to that same end by their promotion of professional standards. The primary goal held up before students in the seminars (in the United States as in the nations of Western Europe) by the leaders in the profession was the teaching and writing of "impartial," "objective," and "scientific" history. And the tremendously significant fact is that by the turn of the century the trained historians considered sectional bias "unscientific" and a threat to their professional aims and standards—particularly when the subject under discussion was the Civil War.

In the seminars, students were taught to recognize the issues and alignments of 1861 as history and to treat these subjects as historical questions. The new trained historians were, on the whole, acutely aware that sectional backgrounds could influence one's opinions on the Civil War, and they adopted numerous expedients to dilute the bias which such backgrounds might induce. Frequently, they carefully acknowledged in the prefaces to their volumes their own sectional background as if to put their readers on guard. Thus, in the opening pages of his biography of Stephen A. Douglas, Allen Johnson pointed out that his heritage was a New England home and an antislavery atmosphere hostile to Douglas's creed; similarly, Albert Bushnell Hart, in his volume on the antislavery movement, frankly stated that he was the son and grandson of abolitionists.[65]

Diligent efforts were made to counterbalance sectional influences wherever possible in order to approach the history of the United States in a national spirit fair to all sections. When a scholar of "Northern" birth, J.N. Larned, compiled a bibliography of American history, he secured advice and assistance from scholars of "Southern" birth—and this was noted and approved.[66] At

[65] Albert B. Hart, *Slavery and Abolition 1831-1841* (New York, 1906) *xv*; Allen Johnson, *Stephen A. Douglas* (New York, 1908) *vii*. See also John Fiske, *The Mississippi Valley in the Civil War* (Boston, 1900) *ix*.

[66] *Publications of the Southern History Association*, VI, 519 (November 1902).

the University of Wisconsin, Frederick Jackson Turner emphasized the role of geographical sections in the history of the United
States and gave courses in the history of the West; at the same
time it was arranged that a New Englander, Carl R. Fish, should
give a course in the history of his section, and that a Southerner,
Ulrich B. Phillips, should teach Southern history.[67]
Shortly after the turn of the century, when a group of historians
of this generation undertook a large scale cooperative synthesis of
American history, authors were selected from all sections of the
country, and the entire work was visualized as a history of *The
American Nation*. It was typical of the prevailing spirit that the
editor of this history, Albert Bushnell Hart, descendant of abolitionists, picked Southerners to write several volumes of the series,
and even attempted to persuade an Alabamian, William Garrott
Brown, to write the volume on the Civil War.[68] Hart, in this instance, was only following his previous practice, for a decade
earlier, as editor of another cooperative history, he had selected
Woodrow Wilson, primarily because he was a Southerner, to write
the volume on United States history in the Civil War period entitled *Division and Reunion*.[69]
Editors of histories were apparently willing to go to any lengths
to avoid the appearance of sectional bias toward North or South.
In the twenty-volume *History of North America*, a contemporary
rival of *The American Nation*, two volumes were devoted to the
Civil War—*The Civil War from a Southern Standpoint*, written
by Southerners, and *The Civil War: The National View*, written
by a Northerner. Similarly, the editor of *The American Crisis
Biographies*, E.P. Oberholtzer, assigned biographies of Southerners in that series to Southern authors, and biographies of Northerners to Northern authors (presumably it was comparable logic
which dictated the selection of Booker T. Washington to write

[67] Fulmer Mood, "The Development of Frederick Jackson Turner as a Historical Thinker," *Publications of the Colonial Society of Massachusetts*, xxxiv (Boston, 1943) 343.

[68] Brown was under contract to write a volume in *The American Nation* entitled *Elements of the Civil War*, but for some unknown reason asked to be relieved of the assignment. Hart also sought, unsuccessfully, to have Woodrow Wilson write a volume in *The American Nation*. See: Wendell H. Stephenson, "William Garrott Brown: Literary Historian and Essayist," *The Journal of Southern History*, xii, 328 (August 1946); Arthur S. Link, *Wilson: The Road to the White House* (Princeton, 1947) 98.

[69] Baker, *Woodrow Wilson, Life and Letters*, i, 307; Link, *Wilson*, 29.

the life of Frederick Douglass, the Negro leader of Civil War days). It was apparently a similar effort to avoid sectionalism which prompted the council of the American Historical Association in 1903 to hold its first meeting in the South.[70] Whether or not the historians of this generation were able to overcome their sectional backgrounds, they were, by and large, quite conscious of them; unlike the men of the 1860's, they (or many of them) considered the possible effects of such backgrounds undesirable, and sought to counteract and to overcome sectionalism in numerous ways.

Thus, the emergence of a national historical profession whose members recognized sectional bias as a threat to their standards was one more factor paving the way for a new outlook on the Civil War among the historians of this second generation. Rhodes, although not trained in a seminar, helped, as we have seen, to set the standards for this new historical profession, and by his attempt to be fair to both combatants in the Civil War, made a strong appeal to many of the new historians. Like Rhodes, many of them based their opinions on the recognition that there had been at least two sides to the story of the war, and thus, were no longer satisfied with the explanations of the war's causes which had once been prevalent in their sections.

Dissatisfaction with traditional Confederate explanations of the coming of war was widespread by the 1890's among trained Southern historians of this second generation. The Southern historians who made the most far reaching revision of attitudes common in their section were a group sometimes designated as the "liberals," including, among others, such individuals as Woodrow Wilson, William P. Trent, John Spencer Bassett, Edwin Mims, William Garrott Brown, and William E. Dodd.[71]

[70] James Ford Rhodes, "Remarks," *Proceedings of the Massachusetts Historical Society*, Second Series, XVIII (1903-1904) 232.

[71] For interesting accounts of Southern historians who attended graduate schools in the North in this period, see the following articles by Wendell H. Stephenson: "A Half Century of Southern Historical Scholarship," *The Journal of Southern History*, XI, 3-32 (February 1945); "Herbert B. Adams and Southern Historical Scholarship at the Johns Hopkins University," *Maryland Historical Magazine*, XLII, 1-20 (March 1947); "William Garrott Brown: Literary Historian and Essayist," *The Journal of Southern History*, XII, 313-344 (August 1946); "William P. Trent as a Historian of the South," *The Journal of Southern History*, XV, 151-177 (May 1949).

The outlook of these "liberal" Southerners was similar in many respects to the "New South" philosophy which had crystallized among many of the young men growing up after Appomattox in the former Confederate States. As expressed by its best-known exponent, Henry W. Grady the Atlanta newspaper editor (born 1850), the "New South" spirit emphasized nationalism, sectional reconciliation, and the integration of the South into the national pattern of life.[72] It was a spirit sympathetic to business and to the development of industry within the South. Optimistic in tone, it rested on the belief that the South had progressed since 1865 in many fields, and that it could continue to do so.

For those imbued with this new spirit, as Grady demonstrated, the Civil War took on a new aspect and became in many respects a different war from the one pictured by Alexander Stephens or Jefferson Davis. It became a war whose results were more important than its causes, a war whose prime significance lay in the fact that it had prepared the way for a new and better South by removing slavery and the type of sectionalism represented by secession. While maintaining respect and admiration for the men of the Old South, the new Southerners showed unconcealed satisfaction over the outcome of the war.

This "New South" view of the Civil War received one of its earliest major expressions at the hands of Grady in his famous speech before the New England Society of New York in 1886. The South, Grady declared in that address, believed that its convictions in the war were as honest as those of the North, and it had nothing for which to apologize; he paid honor to the memory of his father, who died during the war in the service of the Confederacy. But he also paid tribute to Lincoln, the "first typical American," and expressed his satisfaction that "the omniscient God held the balance of battle in His Almighty hand, and that human slavery was swept forever from American soil—the American Union saved from the wreck of war."[73] And throughout this

---

[72] Raymond B. Nixon, *Henry W. Grady Spokesman of the New South* (New York, 1943) *passim*; Buck, *Road to Reunion*, chap. VII. An evaluation of the "New South" different from the one given here may be found in the writings of C. Vann Woodward; see, in particular, *Tom Watson: Agrarian Rebel* (New York, 1938), and *Origins of the New South 1877-1913* (Baton Rouge, La., 1951).

[73] Nixon, *Grady*, 348-349. The entire speech is printed on pp. 340-350.

speech, Grady combined a defense of the men of the Old South with rejoicing that slavery and secession were gone forever. The sensationally favorable reaction to his speech—he was boomed for Vice-president and even for President as a result of it—would seem to indicate that the time was ripe for the sentiments he expressed.[74]

Like Grady, the "liberal" Southern historians were nationalistic, and were optimistic concerning the future of the "New South," seemingly free of its old shackles and part of a reunited nation; they were confident, as one of their number, William P. Trent, wrote, that "out of the ashes of the old South, a new and better South has arisen."[75] Their optimism rested not upon satisfaction with conditions in the South of their own day but upon the conviction that the South was advancing and that further reforms could be made; they advocated reforms in Southern life as diverse in nature as the extension of the public school system, the liberalization of religious dogmas, the diversification of crops, and the transcending of a provincial spirit in cultural matters. According to them, an essential preliminary for reform was the development among Southerners of a more critical spirit both toward the contemporary South and toward Southern history, and this critical spirit was one of their distinguishing characteristics.[76]

In their views of history, the sympathies of the Southern "liberals" were with the South of Thomas Jefferson and of the revolutionary generation; there they found the spirit of nationalism and of humanitarianism which they so much admired. By contrast, they were hostile toward certain phases of the later South

[74] For an account of the response to Grady's address, see *ibid.*, 250ff.

[75] William P. Trent, *William Gilmore Simms* (Boston, 1892) 289. Typical statements of the nationalism and of the reform spirit of the "liberal" Southerners can be found in Edwin Mims, *Sidney Lanier* (New York, 1905), especially 272-279, 283-284, 298-299.

[76] To further such a spirit, two journals were established in the South by former graduate students of H.B. Adams: William P. Trent founded *The Sewanee Review* in 1892, and John Spencer Bassett founded *The South Atlantic Quarterly* a decade later. For an example of one "liberal" Southerner's criticism of the South, see William E. Dodd, "Some Difficulties of the History Teacher in the South," *The South Atlantic Quarterly*, III, 117-122 (April 1904). Dodd particularly deplored the censorship of history textbooks by history committees of Confederate veterans' organizations. "The Confederate Veteran," he wrote, "works almost as great havoc in the field of history, though he unquestionably does some good, as does the union Veteran in the neighborhood of the United States Treasury" (*ibid.*, 121).

of Calhoun and of Jefferson Davis. Like Grady, they respected and venerated individual Confederates, they found much to admire in the *ante-bellum* South, and they insisted that there was nothing in their section's past which required repentance; yet it seemed to them that in the South of Davis and Calhoun, Jefferson's reformist political party had been transformed into a proslavery organization, and a civilization had developed which was "dangerous to our American experiment."[77]

Their criticism of the Old South centered upon the institution of slavery and the movement for secession. None was more unsparing in his strictures than William P. Trent, a Virginian born in the capital of the Confederacy in 1862. That secession was "wrong in itself" seemed to Trent to be obvious to any beginner in political theory; and the evils he found flowing from the institution of slavery made up a formidable catalogue. Slavery had kept the South "feudal," "conservative," and in a "primitive condition"; it had prevented the growth of cities, it had kept out immigrants, and it had made the South intellectually stagnant; the attempt to create a Southern literature under the shadow of slavery was compared to the impossibility of creating "a soul under the ribs of death."[78]

Trent's views were extreme in comparison with those of his contemporaries, but criticisms of slavery and of secession were echoed by other Southerners of the postwar generation. D.Y. Thomas, the Alabamian, wrote, for example, of the "blunder crime of secession," while Edwin Mims of Arkansas and Tennessee shared Trent's belief that slavery had hindered literary efforts in the Old South. A native of Calhoun's own state, David F. Houston (who was later Secretary of Agriculture in Woodrow Wilson's Cabinet), asserted, after a scholarly study, that none of the arguments used by the South Carolinians of the 1830's in

[77] See: William Garrott Brown, *The Lower South in American History* (New York, 1902) 111-112; William E. Dodd, *Statesmen of the Old South* (New York, 1911) *passim*, *Expansion and Conflict* (Boston, 1915) 161, and *The Cotton Kingdom* (New Haven, 1918), 58-59, 62, 69; Samuel Chiles Mitchell, "Education in the South Since the War," in Julian A.C. Chandler and others, eds., *The South in the Building of the Nation* (13v., Richmond, 1909-1913) x, 211-212; Trent, *Simms, passim*, and *Southern Statesmen of the Old Regime* (New York, 1897) *passim*.

[78] Trent, *Simms*, 23, 31, 37, 50, 167, 169, and *Southern Statesmen of the Old Regime*, 177-181.

support of the doctrine of nullification possessed any validity; the institution of slavery, Houston declared in 1896, was an economic evil and was the real cause of South Carolina's "backwardness." One of the most moderate of the "liberal" Southerners was William Garrott Brown of Alabama, a man whose words were carefully qualified and balanced. Yet his sober conclusion was that slavery was a curse to the master and a wrong to the slave, and he described slavery's "economic, political, intellectual, and moral unfitness to survive."[79]

Critical as Rhodes had been of some features of the Southern past, here was similar censure from men of Virginia, Arkansas, Alabama, and South Carolina, some of whom were sons of Confederate veterans. In fact, one is impressed with the marked similarity between the pictures of the Old South by Rhodes and by the Southern "liberal" trained historians. And it is striking to note that the Rhodes and Southern "liberal" approach to the institution of slavery—condemnation of the institution without condemning slaveholders—was shared, too, by the best-known Southern, or American, Negro of the period around the turn of the century, Booker T. Washington. Like many of the "liberal" Southern historians, Washington was born in the 1850's—but as a slave on a Virginia plantation; also like these historians of the second generation, Washington's memories of the Civil War were those of a child—but a slave child:

So far as I can now recall, the first knowledge I got of the fact that we were slaves, and that freedom of the slaves was being discussed, was early one morning before day, when I was awakened by my mother kneeling over her children and fervently praying that Lincoln and his armies might be successful, and that one day she and her children might be free.[80]

But the notable fact (and a fact which constitutes one more testimony of the prevalence of the viewpoints expressed by Rhodes) was that Washington in his most widely read book, his autobiography *Up From Slavery* published in 1901, discussed slavery

[79] David Y. Thomas, *The Dial* (Chicago) XLII, 181 (March 1907); Edwin Mims, "Introduction," *The South in the Building of the Nation*, VIII, p. xlvii; David F. Houston, *A Critical Study of Nullification in South Carolina* (New York, 1896) 16-32, 47; Brown, *Lower South in American History*, 32, 252.

[80] Booker T. Washington, *Up From Slavery* (New York, 1901; "Pocketbooks" edition, 1940) 6.

in much the same vein as did Rhodes and the Southern "liberals." His condemnation of slavery was explicit: it was a "sin," an evil institution originally established for selfish reasons.[81] But at the same time, he looked on most of the individuals associated with the institution, white and black, with sympathy rather than criticism; he expressed no feeling of bitterness toward his former white owners, and he even found no especial fault with his unknown father, said to be a white man on a nearby plantation, who had made no provision for his children's care—the unknown father was "simply another unfortunate victim of the institution which the Nation unhappily had engrafted upon it at this time."[82] Washington's own words convey much better than any summary the spirit in which he looked back at the institution of slavery, and they reveal once again the similarity between his point of view and that of Rhodes and the Southern "liberals":

I pity from the bottom of my heart any nation or body of people that is so unfortunate as to get entangled in the net of slavery. I have long since ceased to cherish any spirit of bitterness against the Southern white people on account of the enslavement of my race. No one section of our country was wholly responsible for its introduction, and, besides, it was recognized and protected for years by the General Government. Having once got its tentacles fastened on to the economic and social life of the Republic, it was no easy matter for the country to relieve itself of the institution.[83]

As was to be expected, the trained Southern "liberal" historians who criticized slavery and secession no longer attempted to pin the blame for war exclusively upon the North; they did not seek to justify secession as a constitutional movement, nor did they describe a "war between the states."

Not all the trained Southern historians of the new generation, as will be emphasized in a later chapter of this book, shared the attitudes of the "liberals"; in particular, the writings of Ulrich B. Phillips gave influential expression to an interpretation of the Old South quite unlike that of Wilson, Trent, or Dodd. But these differences among this generation of trained Southern historians

---

[81] *ibid.*, 11-13, 62. Washington did not discuss at length the causes of the war in *Up From Slavery*, but it seems certain that he, like Rhodes, considered the institution of slavery to be the principal cause; see *ibid.*, chap. 1.
[82] *ibid.*, 2.   [83] *ibid.*, 11.

should not obscure the fact that most of them, whether they sympathized more with the viewpoints of the "liberals" or with those of Phillips, discarded the older Confederate view of a war caused primarily by a disagreement over the interpretation of the Constitution of 1787. A few traditionalists still held to the older views —men such as Lyon G. Tyler, the son of the former President of the United States, or Julian A.C. Chandler of Virginia, or Dunbar Rowland of Mississippi—but they seem clearly to have been in the minority.[84]

More typical was the conviction shared both by the "liberals" and by Ulrich B. Phillips that questions of constitutional interpretation were matters of secondary importance whose significance depended on more basic social forces. The opinions of Alexander H. Stephens on the causes of the war now seemed, in the words of William P. Trent, those of a lawyer rather than of a historian; the question of broad or strict interpretation of the Constitution, stated T.C. McCorvey of Alabama, was to some extent a question of "ins" and "outs." By 1914, Phillips was only expressing the prevailing sentiment when he wrote that, despite Stephens and the other official vindicators of the South, the state rights doctrine was advocated in the Old South primarily as a means to an end —to "give the insignia of legality to a stroke for national independence."[85]

As a counterpart to the trained Southern historians who were dissatisfied with traditional Confederate attitudes toward the war, trained Northern historians of this second generation were also, by the 1890's, unsympathetic to many of the traditional Unionist views once common in their section. Frederick Jackson Turner, Edward Channing, John Bach McMaster, and many other his-

[84] Tyler, Chandler, and Rowland all contributed articles expressing the older views to *The South in the Building of the Nation*. See: I, pp. *xxi-liv*, and IV, 442-472 (Chandler); IV, 499-524 (Tyler); II, 370-406 (Rowland).

[85] Ulrich B. Phillips, "The Literary Movement for Secession," *Studies in Southern History and Politics Inscribed to William Archibald Dunning* (New York, 1914), 33-34, 59-60. For the views of Trent and McCorvey cited in this paragraph, see: Trent, *Simms*, 251-252, and *Southern Statesmen*, 250-251; T.C. McCorvey, *The South in the Building of the Nation*, IV, 344. Other examples of the rejection by Southern historians of the traditional constitutional interpretation can be found in: Dodd, *Expansion and Conflict*, *vi*; Walter L. Fleming, *The Dial* (Chicago), XLII, 332 (June 1, 1907); James W. Garner, *Reconstruction in Mississippi* (New York, 1901) I; John H. Latané, "The Economic Causes of the Civil War," *The South in the Building of the Nation*, v, 656-668.

torians of this generation explained the coming of war in quite a different fashion from Unionists of the 1860's. Few indeed were the Northern historians of this generation who still described Southern secession in terms of "rebellion" or "treason," and few were those who now wrote of a Southern "conspiracy" to disrupt the Union; moreover, the few historians who still employed the old terminology and the old concepts were liable to be sharply criticized by their colleagues.[86] Dissatisfaction with the older points of view led, in the North as in the South, to a reevaluation of the reputations of the authors of histories which expressed those points of view. Just as Alexander H. Stephens' *Constitutional View* now seemed inadequate to Southern historians, so the volumes of Horace Greeley, Henry Wilson, and H.E. Von Holst now seemed partisan and biased to trained historians of Northern birth. One of the earliest and most impressive indications that such a reevaluation was taking place became apparent with the publication in 1896 of the first edition of what became one of the best known bibliographical manuals for historians, *Guide to the Study of American History* by Edward Channing and Albert Bushnell Hart. Channing (born in Massachusetts) and Hart (born in Pennsylvania) carefully classified (and dismissed) most histories of the war so far published as "Northern accounts" or "Southern accounts"; of extended studies covering the Civil War, only Rhodes' *History* and one other work won from Channing and Hart what was probably the highest accolade this generation of trained historians could confer —"written in a scientific spirit."[87] Out of this dissatisfaction among trained historians of the second generation with viewpoints traditional in both North and South there emerged new interpretations of the causes and character of the Civil War. Each major new current of historical interpretation in this era—emphasis upon the importance of the frontier and the West, emphasis upon "economic" history or upon "social"

[86] See, for example, Carl R. Fish's remarks on E.P. Oberholtzer in *The American Historical Review*, x, 902 (July 1905).

[87] Edward Channing and Albert Bushnell Hart, *Guide to the Study of American History* (Boston, 1896) 46; see also pp. 402ff. and *passim*. For another criticism of older Unionist points of view, see Theodore C. Smith's review of Alexander Johnston, *American Political History, 1763-1876*, in *The American Historical Review*, xi, 688-690 (April 1906).

history—led to explanations of the causes of the Civil War quite different from the explanations of the 1860's and 1870's. And the significant fact was that now many of the trained historians could not be described accurately as "Northerners" or "Southerners" in their interpretations of the coming of the Civil War; instead, they were "social" or "economic" or "frontier" historians, for many of the streams of ideas in the new profession now cut across sectional lines. One of the clearest illustrations of this fact was to be seen in the interpretations of the causes of the Civil War by four historians of this generation whose geographical backgrounds were diverse: Frederick Jackson Turner of Wisconsin, Woodrow Wilson of Virginia, Edward Channing of Massachusetts, and John Bach McMaster of Pennsylvania.

4

Turner, Wilson, Channing, and Mcmaster

AMONG THE REVIEWERS of James Ford Rhodes' *History* in the 1890's were Frederick Jackson Turner and Woodrow Wilson.[88] Like nearly all other individuals who commented on Rhodes in that decade, Turner and Wilson noted and praised Rhodes' "sense of fairness," his "calm and dispassionate judgment," and they agreed that these qualities distinguished Rhodes from previous writers on the Civil War era. Interspersed with this commendation, however, were some criticisms of certain aspects of Rhodes' historical thought. Rhodes paid attention too exclusively, it was said, to the struggle over slavery and did not understand that the real significance of the slavery question lay in the conflict over the extension of slavery, lay in the relationship of slavery to the forces making for "national uniformity"; furthermore, it was suggested that Rhodes did not properly relate political ideas and institutions to underlying social and economic conditions, the implication being that Rhodes still pictured history in too narrow a fashion as "past politics." Turner and Wilson, in short, had high praise for the spirit in which Rhodes studied the era of the Civil War and for his achievement within his own framework of thought, but the framework itself seemed somewhat narrow and the point of view somewhat limited.

These comments on Rhodes illustrated the fact that the thinking of Turner and Wilson was attuned to some of the newer currents of ideas among historians in the late nineteenth century which were not reflected, or at least not emphasized, in Rhodes' volumes; and, like Turner and Wilson, Edward Channing and John Bach McMaster also expressed newer and less conventional approaches to history than did Rhodes. Turner, Wilson, Channing, and Mc-

[88] Woodrow Wilson in *The Atlantic Monthly*, LXXII, 272-274 (August 1893); Frederick Jackson Turner in *Political Science Quarterly*, XI, 167-170 (March 1896), and in "Recent Studies in American History," *The Atlantic Monthly*, LXXVII, 837-844 (June 1896).

Master all made important statements of the newer attitudes toward the causes and character of the Civil War which were beginning to win favor in the 1890's. These newer attitudes, as we have seen, were reflected in the volumes of Rhodes, but whereas Rhodes' *History* was a mixture of some of the older viewpoints once common in his section with many of the newer viewpoints, the writings of Turner, Wilson, Channing, and McMaster reflected the newer points of view toward the war almost exclusively. If Rhodes was a figure of transition in the interpretation of the causes of the Civil War, Turner, Wilson, Channing, and McMaster were figures of the new era who demonstrated in their writings how far explanations of the causes of the war had changed since the 1860's and 1870's.

The ideas of Turner and Wilson were similar in many respects, but their personal backgrounds were quite different. Turner, the son of Andrew Jackson Turner, came of what he described as a pioneering family which "moved at least every generation."[89] Born in Portage, Wisconsin, a town near the frontier in his childhood, Turner's youthful memories, as he set them down in later life, had little relation to the Civil War, to Reconstruction, or to any other North-South disagreements. He looked back instead to Indian tepees and to fishing along "rivers and lakes in the virgin pine woods, where French names made real the earlier frontier."

Turner began the study and writing of history at a time (the 1880's and the 1890's) of increasing self-consciousness and articulateness on the part of Westerners in the United States. In the century after the establishment of the new government in 1789, a vast area stretching roughly from the Appalachian mountains to the Pacific Ocean had been settled and a succession of new fron-

[89] Turner's own brief account of his life, written in 1922, is published as "Turner's Autobiographic Letter," *The Wisconsin Magazine of History*, xix, 91-103 (September 1935); the quotations in this paragraph are from this letter. In addition to this letter, I have found the following accounts of Turner particularly interesting and instructive: Carl L. Becker, "Frederick Jackson Turner," in Howard W. Odum, ed., *American Masters of Social Science* (New York, 1927) 273-318; Merle E. Curti, "The Section and the Frontier in American History: the Methodological Concepts of Frederick Jackson Turner," in Stuart A. Rice, ed., *Methods in Social Science* (Chicago, 1931) 353-367; Fulmer Mood, "The Development of Frederick Jackson Turner as a Historical Thinker," *Publications of the Colonial Society of Massachusetts*, xxxiv (Boston, 1943), 283-352; Lee Benson, "The Historical Background of Turner's Frontier Essay," *Agricultural History*, xxv, 59-82 (April 1951).

tiers and new "Wests" had been opened up. These new "Wests," like previous "Wests" in American history, differed in economic and social organization and in many other ways from the perennial "Easts" which began on the Atlantic seaboard. After the Civil War, some Western farmers (like earlier Westerners) came to feel that they were being economically exploited by Easterners and voiced their grievances in periodic "Granger," "Populist," and other such movements. A prominent theme, and at times the dominant theme, in the political and economic life of the United States from the 1870's to the 1890's was the conflict of East *versus* West, a theme which reached its dramatic climax in the election of 1896.

Out of this background there grew in the latter decades of the nineteenth century a sentiment of Western self-consciousness; this sentiment was reflected in the writings of Hamlin Garland, and it formed part of the background for the historical thought of Turner. The point, of course, is not that Turner or his family were Grangers or Populists but that the growth of Western discontent and of Western self-consciousness was part of the broad background in which Turner's ideas took shape. Just as Western farmers declared their grievances against the East, just as Hamlin Garland expressed in literature the sense of Western resentment at the East, so Turner's historical writings were, to use Professor Curti's phrase, something of a "historiographical declaration of independence" from the East. It should be emphasized that the sentiment of Western self-consciousness complemented rather than conflicted with the ardent nationalism of the period, since Westerners could and did identify their own section with the nation, urging that the West was the most "American" (i.e., most unlike Europe) part of the nation. Turner, for example, writing in 1919, explained the origin of his historical thought partly in terms of Western self-consciousness and partly in terms of national self-consciousness; his ideas, he wrote, "were part of the growing American consciousness of itself."[90]

By contrast, Woodrow Wilson was born in Virginia, the son of a loyal supporter of the Confederacy; his youth was spent

[90] Wendell H. Stephenson, "The Influence of Woodrow Wilson upon Frederick Jackson Turner," *Agricultural History*, XIX, 251-252 (October 1945).

largely in Georgia and South Carolina until he entered Princeton in 1875. But Wilson was a Southerner with uncles who fought in the Union Army, a Southerner whose mother was born in England and whose father was born in Ohio. Wilson's father, although vigorously defending the right of secession, did not take a strong stand in defense of the institution of slavery, and has been described as never as "violent a partisan as many men of the older Southern tradition."[91]

Growing up in the South after Appomattox, Wilson apparently absorbed the nationalism and sectional reconciliation which were part of the "New South" spirit represented by Henry Grady (although Wilson expressed dislike of the Atlanta of the 1880's because of its materialism and because the "studious man" was there considered "impractical" and "visionary").[92] It was the "New South" spirit certainly which infused an address made by Wilson when a graduate student at the University of Virginia in 1880:

I yield to no one precedence in love for the South. But *because* I love the South, I rejoice in the failure of the Confederacy. Suppose that secession had been accomplished? Conceive of this Union as divided into two separate and independent sovereignties! . . . We cannot conceal from ourselves the fact that slavery was enervating our Southern society and exhausting to Southern energies. . . . Even the damnable cruelty and folly of reconstruction was to be preferred to helpless independence. All this I can see at the same time that I recognize and pay loving tribute to the virtues of the leaders of secession, to the purity of their purposes, to the righteousness of the cause which they thought they were promoting—and to the immortal courage of the soldiers of the Confederacy.[93]

However different their personal backgrounds, Turner and Wilson discovered at Johns Hopkins in the late 1880's that their historical ideas were quite similar (Turner was a graduate student at Johns Hopkins in 1888 and 1889; Wilson was a graduate stu-

[91] Baker, *Woodrow Wilson: Life and Letters*, I, 52. In addition to Baker's volumes, see the following accounts of Wilson: William E. Dodd, *Woodrow Wilson and His Work* (New York, 1920); Arthur S. Link, *Wilson: the Road to the White House* (Princeton, 1947); Francis P. Weisenburger, "The Middle Western Antecedents of Woodrow Wilson," *The Mississippi Valley Historical Review*, XXIII, 375-390 (December 1936); Louis M. Sears, "Woodrow Wilson," in William T. Hutchinson, ed., *The Marcus W. Jernegan Essays in American Historiography* (Chicago, 1937) 102-121.

[92] Baker, *Wilson: Life and Letters*, I, 168-169.

[93] Ray Stannard Baker and William E. Dodd, eds., *The Public Papers of Woodrow Wilson: College and State . . . (1875-1913)* (2v., New York, 1925) I, 56-57.

dent there from 1883 to 1885, but he lectured at Hopkins during 1888 and 1889 and at that time came to know Turner).[94] The immediate point of agreement between Turner and Wilson lay in the fact that both of them were dissatisfied with the type of history which they were taught at Hopkins under the direction of Herbert B. Adams—a history which emphasized the beginnings of American institutions and ideas in Europe, notably in the Germanic forests, and which was focused, within the United States itself, upon the experiences of the seaboard East. In part, this dissatisfaction can be explained, as Turner himself has suggested, in terms of a young Westerner and a young Southerner reacting against neglect of the history of their sections by Easterners; for Herbert B. Adams was like the "older writers" on the history of the United States, described by Turner in 1892, who, "coming, like all wise men, from the East, have largely restricted their view to the Atlantic coast."[95] (Turner also suggested, and this is frequently overlooked, that his own point of view came in part from his attempt to apply to the history of America the methods and ideas he had been taught as an undergraduate in studying the history of medieval Europe.)[96]

But the writings of Turner and Wilson in the 1890's demonstrated that their common dissatisfaction with the views of Herbert B. Adams rested also upon a more fundamental similarity in their historical ideas. The historical thinking of both Turner and Wilson was impregnated with the currently popular Darwinian concept of evolutionary development and change in all spheres of life. They pictured human society as an organism: "Society," Turner wrote in 1891, "is an organism, ever growing. History is the self-consciousness of this organism."[97] From this stand-

---

[94] Baker, *Wilson: Life and Letters*, I, 171ff., and II, 124-125; Dodd, *Wilson*, 27-28; "Turner's Autobiographic Letter," *The Wisconsin Magazine of History*, XIX, 100 (September 1935); Stephenson, "The Influence of Woodrow Wilson on Frederick Jackson Turner," *passim*.

[95] Frederick Jackson Turner, "Problems in American History," in Everett E. Edwards, compiler, *The Early Writings of Frederick Jackson Turner* (Madison, 1938) 71.

[96] "Turner's Autobiographic Letter," 96; Stephenson, "The Influence of Woodrow Wilson on Frederick Jackson Turner," 252.

[97] Frederick Jackson Turner, "The Significance of History," in Edwards, *Early Writings*, 57. The similarity between the ideas expressed in the 1890's by Turner and Wilson is quite striking—so striking that the present author believes that a modern reader who read several of the essays and book reviews of the two historians without looking at

point, social ideas and institutions were visualized as the products of growth and development. This Darwinian concept implied as great an alteration in historical thinking as it did in other fields of thought, for it explained institutions and ideas not as static absolutes but as products of historical evolution and of historical environments. Constitutions, for example, were not, in Wilson's words, "mere legal documents" but were "the skeleton frames of a living organism."[98]

The Turner-Wilson concept of evolution and development, however, did not in itself necessarily conflict with the Herbert B. Adams emphasis upon European "origins." The conflict arose because in the minds of Turner and Wilson, unlike Adams, the concept of evolution was fused both with a strong sentiment of American nationalism and with the feeling that the seaboard East was not the proper focus for this nationalism. Whereas Adams emphasized beginnings in Europe, Turner and Wilson were interested primarily in the development on this continent of the American nation (one organism). The history of the United States, Wilson wrote in 1893, was not a history of "origins" but of development.[99] And both Turner and Wilson were agreed that to understand the American developments, attention must be focused on the American West: the "proper perspective" (Wilson's phrase) of American history was the West, and its most important theme was the expansion of the nation; it was in the advancing frontier and in the settlement of successive "Wests" that one could observe the true growth and development of the American nation.[100]

From this "proper perspective," it seemed to both Turner and Wilson that the history of the United States could not be understood accurately in terms solely of the traditional conflict of North

the titlepages would be able to distinguish which was Wilson's and which Turner's only on the basis of literary style and not on the basis of the thoughts set forth.

[98] Woodrow Wilson, *Division and Reunion, 1829-1889* (New York, 1893) 211.

[99] Woodrow Wilson, "Mr. Goldwin Smith's 'Views' on Our Political History," *The Forum*, XVI, 495 (December 1893).

[100] Woodrow Wilson, "The Proper Perspective of American History," *The Forum*, XIX, 544-559 (July 1895). These ideas run throughout Turner's writings. See, in addition to Turner's *Early Writings* compiled by Edwards, the two one-volume collections of Turner's essays: *The Frontier in American History* (New York, 1920); and *The Significance of Sections in American History* (New York, 1932).

versus South. "Eastern" historians, North and South, wrote Wilson, had distorted the focus of the nation's history: Northern historians had pictured primarily the "expansion of New England," while Southern historians had described the "suppression of the South"—and both groups of historians had been mistaken.[101] In a similar vein, Turner later recalled his realization of the fact that "there was a persistent pervasive influence in American life which did not get its full attention from those who thought in terms of North and South."[102] Here lay the significance of the Turner-Wilson approach to the American past for the interpretation of the causes and character of the Civil War—the long standing picture of a static North *versus* a static South was enlarged and refocused by the addition of a third dimension, the West, and by viewing the nation's history as a story of change and development. From this underlying intellectual position, Turner and Wilson explained the coming of the Civil War; there was a different emphasis in the explanations they each advanced, but both their explanations originated in the same general framework of ideas.

In describing the origins of the Civil War, Wilson placed stress upon the growth of the American nation comparable to that which Rhodes had assigned to the institution of slavery, for the development of the American national union was to Wilson the major thread of United States history. This development and growth was partly a matter of physical and material changes, but it also involved the rise of a sentiment of nationality; in each case it was a process which, as Wilson saw it, had occurred after the formation of the new government in 1789. It was because of its relation to this process of national growth that slavery was a significant factor.[103]

Rhodes had insisted that without the institution of slavery there would have been no Civil War. Wilson held that the existence of slavery in the Southern states would not in itself have disrupted the Union—the importance of slavery lay in the fact that it be-

[101] Wilson, "The Proper Perspective of American History," 544-545.

[102] "Turner's Autobiographic Letter," 101.

[103] See the following writings by Wilson in the 1890's: *Division and Reunion, passim*; review of Rhodes' *History*, Vols. I-II, in *The Atlantic Monthly*, LXXII, 272-274 (August 1893); "Mr. Goldwin Smith's 'Views' on Our Political History"; "The Proper Perspective of American History"; "The Making of The Nation," *The Atlantic Monthly*, LXXX, 1-14 (July 1897).

came inextricably intertwined with the national acquisition of new lands, and thus, rather than showing signs of disappearing, became a problem ever more acute. The real slavery question was that of slavery in the territories (i.e., in the West) and this was a question primarily between the South and the West, not between the South and New England. Thus, it was not the antislavery societies of New England but the men whom Lincoln represented who pushed the question to a settlement. "Kansas," as Wilson summed up his analysis of the slavery question, "showed us what the problem was, not South Carolina."[104]

Although Wilson ascribed a role to the institution of slavery different from that set forth in the pages of Rhodes, he, like Rhodes, pictured it as a prime cause of the Civil War. To Wilson, slavery was a cause of the war in the sense that it had insulated the South from the many developments which changed the rest of the United States in the nineteenth century. As the United States acquired new territory and underwent various material changes in the nineteenth century, the sovereign states of 1789 were gradually fused, Wilson declared, into a united nation. While the nation, the living organism, thus developed, so too the Constitution of 1787 (the "skeleton frame" of the organism) underwent subtle changes. What had originally been a compact between sovereign states was thus changed into the charter of a national union. The course of events, wrote Wilson, "nationalized the government once deemed confederate."[105] But the *ante-bellum* South, primarily because of the institution of slavery, did not experience the varied developments which affected the North and the West, and thus the South came to be quite different from the North and the West.

From this standpoint, Wilson explained the constitutional aspects of the sectional disputes over slavery in the territories and over secession—and the remarkable feature of his explanation was that both sides were pictured as "right" in these disputes. Southerners correctly interpreted the Constitution as it was understood in 1789 (as a compact between sovereign states) while Northerners and Westerners correctly interpreted the Constitution as it had

[104] Wilson, "The Proper Perspective of American History," 555.
[105] Wilson, *Division and Reunion*, 211.

developed after 1789 (as the charter of an integral nation). Neither side, Wilson declared, could have fought the battles of 1861-1865 unless they had satisfied themselves that "they had a legal right to do so."[106]

There was in Wilson's interpretation no personal or sectional guilt to be assessed for war; it was not the result of a "conspiracy" on either side. Rather, the war had been, on the part of the North, "a splendid revelation of national strength and coherency," while history showed no nonreligious devotion equal to that exhibited by the South.[107] The war was to be explained, rather than blamed upon any persons; not corrupt individuals but natural forces of national expansion and development had caused a struggle which Wilson, at least on one occasion, pictured as inevitable: "There was war between the South and the rest of the nation because their differences were removable in no other way."[108]

Wilson's nationalism and lack of sectional bitterness were particularly evident in his judgments of personalities. He praised John Marshall and Daniel Webster as great constitutional statesmen, men who viewed the Constitution as a "great organic product, a vehicle of life."[109] This was in contrast to his appraisal of Calhoun, whose reasoning seemed "a negation which embarrassed the whole movement of national affairs"; even so, there were no harsh words for Calhoun—he was simply a "great provincial" rather than a great American. There was a kind word for Grant (he was "national in spirit") as well as for Lee (he believed not in secession but in the local rootage of all government—a principle no less American, wrote Wilson, than the principle of Union). Like his fellow Southerner Henry Grady, however, Wilson reserved his greatest praise for Lincoln; the whole country, he asserted, was summed up in Lincoln, whose role was providential and who was, indeed, "the supreme American of our history."[110]

The interpretation of the causes of the war expressed by Wilson

106 Wilson, "Mr. Goldwin Smith's 'Views' on Our Political History," 499; *Division and Reunion*, 211; "The Making of the Nation," *passim; A History of the American People* (5v., New York, 1902) IV, 201-202.

107 Wilson, *Division and Reunion*, 239-241.

108 Wilson, "The Making of the Nation," 3.

109 Wilson, "A Calendar of Great Americans," *The Forum*, XVI, 715-727 (February 1894).

110 *ibid.*, 724-725.

explained the much debated constitutional issue involved in secession in a fashion which was neither "Northern" nor "Southern," and this explanation had appeal for individuals in this second generation of both Northern and Southern birth. It was accepted by such Southern "liberals" as William P. Trent and Peter J. Hamilton (an Alabamian educated at Princeton); present in their writings were the major elements which had characterized Wilson's explanation of the coming of war: the singling out of slavery as the cause of the war in the sense that it had isolated the South from national developments, and the assertion that North and South had both been "right" in their view of the Constitution with no group of individuals solely responsible for the sectional conflict.[111] Among scholars of "Northern" birth in this generation, two of the most distinguished, Edward Channing of Massachusetts and Charles E. Merriam of Iowa, explained the sectional differences in constitutional interpretation as did Wilson, Trent, and Hamilton; Channing and Merriam, too, reached the customary conclusion—that both sides had been "right" in their point of view.[112] Thus was laid to rest for many historians of this second generation the constitutional question which had proved to be so troublesome for the war generation.

Wilson is known to a later generation primarily as a political leader and international statesman rather than a historian; even as historian, he is remembered principally for his five-volume *History of the American People*, a hastily composed work decidedly inferior to his historical writings of the 1890's. For these reasons, the importance of Wilson as an historian in the 1890's has not always been sufficiently appreciated. It was Wilson whom Turner recommended in 1890 to the president of the University of Wisconsin as a man of established reputation around whom the history department there could be reorganized (Wilson, Turner wrote in 1903, was "the first Southern scholar of adequate training and power who has dealt with American history as a whole

---

[111] Trent, *Simms*, 167, 251-252, and *Southern Statesmen of the Old Regime, passim*; Peter J. Hamilton, "Lee and the Confederacy," *Publications of the Southern History Association*, IV, 316-334 (September 1900).

[112] Edward Channing, *The United States of America, 1765-1865* (New York, 1896) 258-262, 300; Charles E. Merriam, *A History of American Political Theories* (New York, 1903) 257-289.

in a continental spirit"); it was to Wilson that President Gilman of Johns Hopkins offered the chairmanship of his university's history department upon the death of Herbert B. Adams in 1901; and a present-day historian, from his study of the correspondence of Herbert B. Adams, has added further testimony of Wilson's prestige in the 1890's:

When reading his [Adams'] correspondence [Professor W. Stull Holt has written] I was immediately struck by the remarkable impression Wilson made on the people with whom he associated. In the case of no other graduate of the Department [at Johns Hopkins] were there so many letters containing praise and a recognition of power.[113]

Wilson's standing among historians in the 1890's makes all the more significant his expression of new points of view concerning the causes of the Civil War.

However important Wilson was as historian in the 1890's, he pales (as do most historians of that generation) in comparison with Frederick Jackson Turner, for Turner exerted a much more lasting influence upon historical thought than did Wilson. And Turner's influence, it should be emphasized, extended to the interpretation of the causes of the Civil War. Turner did not write a volume (nor, so far as the present author knows, even an article) devoted solely to explaining the causes of the Civil War. But Turner's whole approach to American history and his underlying philosophy of causation in history carried with them certain attitudes toward the coming of the Civil War, and throughout Turner's writings are sentences and paragraphs suggesting or spelling out his interpretation of its causes. Whether Turner merely reflected ideas which were "in the air," or whether he introduced new opinions, or both, the attitudes toward the war which he expressed came to be held by many historians. Thus, Turner and his ideas occupy an important place in the story of changing interpretations of the causes of the Civil War.

Wilson's explanation of the coming of war had stressed the growth of a national union, but Turner's thought (although it was strongly tinged with nationalism) was focused more upon

---

[113] Holt, ed., *Historical Scholarship in the United States, 1876-1901*, 91*n*, 123; the quotation from Turner concerning Wilson is taken from Turner's review of Wilson's *A History of the American People* in *The American Historical Review*, VIII, 764 (July 1903).

the importance of physiographic and economic factors. In Turner's opinion, "past politics" and history were far from being identical, and political ideas, institutions, and policies were always related to underlying social and economic forces. Because of these underlying forces, particularly those of climate, geography, and economics, there had developed in America sections with different interests and different institutions comparable to European nations (that Turner attributed at least a part of Southern sectionalism to other than physiographic and economic forces is suggested by a remark he made in 1907: "The Negro is still the problem of the South and while he remains there will be a Southern sectionalism").[114]

Turner explained much of the history of the United States before 1861 in terms of the conflicts between these rival sections, and this led to a reinterpretation of the traditional picture of a North-South dispute over slavery or over state sovereignty. Turner's interpretation broadened the traditional picture, for in his pages the endless play of sectional forces involved many more issues than just slavery and state sovereignty. He noted older and more enduring examples of sectionalism in American history than the struggles over slavery or constitutional interpretation, citing other sectional conflicts involving such questions as land, tariff, and political power. Thus, the dispute over slavery, while it was an important aspect of American history before 1861, was, in Turner's opinion, only one aspect—of "primary, but far from exclusive, importance."[115]

Turner's interpretation also served to refocus the traditional picture, for he, like Wilson, found the prime significance of most of the sectional conflicts in the West—here was the "proper per-

[114] The sentence is quoted from Turner's address, "Is Sectionalism in America Dying Away?" (delivered December 1907), *The Significance of Sections in American History*, 307.
[115] The quotation is from Turner's famous paper read in 1893, "The Significance of the Frontier in American History," *The Frontier in American History*, 24. The ideas described in this paragraph and the next are expressed frequently in Turner's writings; they can be seen particularly in the 1893 paper just cited and in the following essays from Turner's volume, *The Frontier in American History*: "The Middle West" (first published in December 1901), "The Ohio Valley in American History" (an address delivered in October 1909), and "The Significance of the Mississippi Valley in American History" (an address delivered in May 1910).

spective" for understanding those conflicts. This was especially true of his explanation of the slavery question; Turner found the crucial aspect of the struggle over slavery in the West where expanding, competing societies were in contact:

Such a struggle as the slavery contest can only be understood by bearing in mind that it was not merely a contest of North against South, but that its form and its causes were fundamentally shaped by the dynamic factor of expanding sections, of West to be won.[116]

Had there been no area of expansion in the West, slavery might gradually have died away; similarly, it was the alignment of the Midwest with the Northeast, rather than with the Southeast, which determined the final outcome of the slavery struggle. And in explaining that eventual alignment, Turner pointed to a variety of factors in addition to the slavery question alone: the Midwest had been predominantly (but not completely) free-soil in its sympathies, but it had also been nationalistic in outlook and its economic life had been tied by railroads to the North Atlantic states —hence its material interests and its sentiment of nationalism, as well as its stand on the slavery question, had bound it to the Northeast by the 1860's.

Turner described in a dispassionate spirit those sectional disputes in which "North" was aligned against "South." This was not because he was a man who possessed no strong emotions, or one who succeeded in hiding them. Far from it, for it was clear throughout his writings that his sympathies lay with the various "Wests" in American history and with the characteristics which he associated primarily with those Wests—"idealism," "democracy," "nationalism." This was the significant fact—that Turner's sympathies, more so even than Wilson's, cut across the North-South division and did not fit into the traditional patterns of thought. His thinking was pointed in a direction so different from that of most of his predecessors that the older ways of looking at the North-South conflict were for him no longer satisfactory. After Turner's viewpoints had won wide acceptance, it became difficult to speak of a simple "North" *versus* "South" struggle before 1860 without taking into account the "West" and its influence.

[116] Turner, "The Significance of the Section in American History" (an address delivered in January 1925), *The Significance of Sections in American History*, 33-34.

In broadening the time-honored concepts of a North-South struggle over slavery and state sovereignty, Turner broadened long established explanations of the coming of war. Sectional conflict had led to the Civil War, and, as the reasons for sectional disputes were diverse, so the question of what caused the war was, for Turner, a complex one. Turner represented a more sophisticated and more comprehensive type of historical thinking than did either Rhodes or Wilson; in view of the complexity of human life, he held that the causes of historical events could not accurately be reduced to a single explanation—economic, psychological, political, or otherwise. Instead, he urged the historian to follow the example of the geologist, who "creates a whole family of possible explanations of a given problem and thus avoids the warping influence of partiality for a simple theory."[117] Under this "multiple hypothesis" approach employed by Turner, the explanation of the coming of the Civil War thus involved a consideration of the many and varied reasons for sectional discord. The war grew out of sectional disputes and its causes were the numerous forces which produced those disputes.

Judging from what scattered evidence is available, it would seem that Turner did not consider the Civil War inevitable, but that he did think that fundamental and even irreconcilable differences had developed between the slaveholding and nonslaveholding sections by 1861. And it is interesting to note that Turner, however different was his thinking from that of Rhodes, apparently found the heart of these fundamental sectional differences in the institution of slavery. It was not certain, he wrote in 1922, that the Civil War was inevitable, and it was probable that the majority of Americans preferred and expected a different solution than war in 1861; but at the same time he pointed out that

---

[117] The quotation is from Turner's presidential address before the American Historical Association in December 1910, "Social Forces in American History," *The Frontier in American History*, 331. The flexibility of thought to which this "multiple hypothesis" approach could lead was illustrated in a statement by Turner in 1922: "Men are not absolutely dictated to by climate, geography, soils, or economic interests. The influence of the stock from which they sprang, the inherited ideals, the spiritual factors, often triumph over the material interests. There is also the influence of personality. Men do follow leaders, and sometimes into paths inconsistent with the section's material interests. But in the long run the statesman must speak the language of his people on fundamentals, both of interests and ideals" ("Sections and Nations," *The Significance of Sections in American History*, 337).

"perhaps no more difficult test of peaceful methods of adjustment could arise than that between a slave society and a free society."[118]

The latter opinion was similar in tone to another discussion of this question by Turner a quarter of a century earlier. There were some issues, he had written in 1897, which "cannot be settled by compromise, tendencies one of which must conquer the other. Such an issue the slave power raised."[119] Turner published this statement at a time (1897) when the conflict of East *versus* West had raised issues which also seemed difficult to compromise; Turner noted the similarity, in this sense, between the era preceding the Civil War and his own day, but he stated explicitly that the issues of the 1890's did not present "the same imperious 'Which?'" as had "the issue of freedom or slavery."[120] So far as the present author knows, Turner did not use the phrase "irrepressible conflict" to describe the dissimilarities between "North" and "South" by 1861, but that phrase (in the sense of "irreconcilable differences") seems to fit the implications of the passages cited above.

There was no attempt in Turner's writings to assess personal or sectional blame for the war. Turner was the scientist-historian, thinking in terms of the influence of geography, climate, economics, and a variety of other forces; his writings pointed to the conclusion that war causation was a complicated historical problem involving many diverse factors. In his framework of ideas there was no place for a "war guilt" controversy of the type which had absorbed so much of the attention of the writers of the 1860's.

Of late, Turner has received so much criticism on the score that his ideas were "narrow" and "provincial" that the great breadth and depth of his thinking seem in danger of being forgotten. The current criticisms seem much more applicable to some of Turner's students and disciples than to Turner himself, for whatever the validity or lack of validity of Turner's theories of the influence of the frontier, of sections, and of the West, he was a giant (and a pioneer giant in the United States) in his description and analysis

[118] Turner, "Sections and Nation" (originally published in October 1922), *The Significance of Sections in American History*, 318.
[119] Turner, "Dominant Forces in Western Life" (originally published in April 1897), *The Frontier in American History*, 230.
[120] *ibid.*, 241.

of some of the fundamental problems faced by the historian—the nature and scope of history, the problem of causation in human history, and the question of bias and limited point of view on the part of the historian.[121] His presidential address before the American Historical Association in 1910 remains, in the opinion of this author, one of the most mature and balanced statements of the problem of historical causation yet made by a United States historian, and it serves as evidence of the difference between the attitudes of some of Turner's generation of trained historians and the attitudes common in the 1860's.

Turner, unlike Rhodes, did not write a many-volumed history, and he did not win a reputation as rapidly as did Rhodes. Turner's ideas became known primarily through his essays and his teaching (and through the teaching and writings of his students). Beginning with the reading, in 1893, of his famous paper on the significance of the frontier, the concepts he expressed won favor gradually but steadily, and by 1910 recognition had come to him in the form of election to the presidency of the American Historical Association. A decade later, when the publication of a volume of Turner's collected essays presented the opportunity for some historians to evaluate his work, they were agreed that his ideas were widely held among historians and that he was one of the most influential historians of his generation.[122] Turner's interpretation of American history, wrote Allen Johnson in 1921, "has come to be almost a commonplace in American historiography, so completely have the younger historians made this point of view their own." The notable place in American historical writing won

[121] See, for example, the following essays of Turner's: "The Significance of History" (first published in 1891), in Edwards, *Early Writings*, 43-68; "Social Forces in American History," *The Frontier in American History*, 311-334; "Geographical Influences in American Political History," *The Significance of Sections in American History*, 192; "Problems in American History," *ibid.*, 25. An interesting discussion of this aspect of Turner's thought can be found in Randall and Haines, "Controlling Assumptions in the Practice of American Historians," Social Science Research Council *Bulletin 54*, 17-52.

[122] See the following reviews of Turner's *The Frontier in American History*: Allen Johnson in *The American Historical Review*, xxvi, 542-543 (April 1921); C.W. Alvord in *The Mississippi Valley Historical Review*, vii, 403-407 (March 1921); Carl L. Becker in *The Nation*, cxi, 536 (November 10, 1920). The quotations in the sentences which follow are from these reviews. Charles A. Beard also reviewed Turner's *Frontier* in *The New Republic*, xxv, 349-350 (February 16, 1921), and admitted the influence of Turner's ideas although he disagreed with them; Beard's criticisms of Turner are discussed in the following chapter.

by Turner was suggested by C.W. Alvord: "No one since Bancroft has so completely redirected the course of historical research as has this westerner." In a similar vein, Carl L. Becker (a former student of Turner's) voiced what was apparently the opinion of many historians in 1920:

I think it is safe to say . . . that in giving direction to the methods of investigating American history and in furnishing new light for its interpretation, the share of Mr. Turner has been the most profound and abiding of this generation.

Turner was neither the first nor the only historian of his generation to emphasize the importance of the West and of economic factors, and to stress a many-sided explanation of human actions. But he did play a prominent role both in shaping these concepts and in popularizing them for his own and later generations of historians. The effect of the concepts he expressed upon the interpretation of the causes of the Civil War was pronounced.

In contrast to Turner the Westerner and to Wilson the Southerner, Edward Channing was indelibly associated with the Northeast. This scion of an old New England family, as George P. Winship has pointed out, was born, educated, lived, and died in Massachusetts; moreover, Channing, as another biographer, Samuel Eliot Morison, has noted, was "friend, cousin, nephew, and brother-in-law to Thomas Wentworth Higginson, the [New England] abolitionist."[123] Yet, despite the marked differences between the personal background of Channing and that of Turner or Wilson, there were fundamental similarities in the ideas of the three historians. Channing placed very little emphasis upon the role of the frontier and of the West in American history, and this fact constituted the most important difference between his historical thought and that of Turner and Wilson. But with that exception, the major currents present in the ideas of Turner and Wilson were also present in the ideas of Channing—the Darwinian concept of evolution and development, the stress placed upon economic factors in history (in this respect comparable especially to Turner), and the strong sentiment of sectional reconciliation and

123 Samuel Eliot Morison, "Edward Channing: A Memoir," Massachusetts Historical Society, *Proceedings*, LXIV (October 1930 to June 1932) 279; George P. Winship, "Edward Channing," *The Dictionary of American Biography*, supplementary volume I, 166-168.

of nationalism. To Channing, just as to Turner and to Wilson, the major theme in the history of the United States was the "growth of the nation," the "victory of the forces of union over those of particularism"—and Channing explained that while the factors making for disunion in American history should be studied thoroughly and sympathetically, emphasis should be placed upon forces and institutions making for union.[124]

In view of these fundamental similarities in the thinking of the three historians, it is not surprising to find that Channing, writing from the 1890's onward on the causes and character of the Civil War, displayed attitudes and advanced interpretations similar in some respects to those of Turner and/or Wilson. The ultimate causes of the war, in Channing's pages just as in the pages of Turner and Wilson, were not the actions of evil men but the workings of inanimate forces—forces which in Channing's opinion had eventually localized the institution of slavery in the Southern states and had created a "South" fundamentally different from the national pattern.[125] The forces upon which Channing placed most stress were economic. The Southern states, he pointed out, were agricultural and this condition led to the early introduction of slavery there; once slavery was firmly established, it in turn prevented those states from changing their economy; by contrast, the Northern states developed a diversified economic life containing a mixture of agriculture, manufacturing, and commerce. Thus, by the middle of the nineteenth century, two distinct, disparate, and conflicting societies had developed in the United States: "The country was . . . divided into two sections whose social and business interests were irreconcilable."[126]

Channing in this fashion broadened the Rhodesian conflict into a struggle between two societies with different economic foundations (and yet it is worth noting that Channing, like Wilson and Turner, pictured the institution of slavery as one of the most

[124] Edward Channing, *A History of the United States* (6v., New York, 1905-1925) I, *v-vi*.

[125] Channing's interpretation of the causes of the war were set forth primarily in two of his volumes, *The United States of America, 1765-1865* (New York, 1896), and *A History of the United States, VI: The War for Southern Independence, 1849-1865* (New York, 1925).

[126] Channing, *United States of America*, 300; see also pp. 258-262.

fundamental of the differences between the rival societies: slavery, he wrote, "was at the bottom of the social and material distinctions which separated the country into two irreconcilable sections").[127] Out of this conflict between two nation-societies with "irreconcilable" interests there came war, and Channing apparently did not consider war inevitable:

Two such divergent forms of society could not continue indefinitely to live side by side within the walls of one government. . . . One or the other of these societies must perish, or both must secure complete equality, . . . or the two societies must separate absolutely and live each by itself under its own government.[128]

Channing (like other historians of this generation) insisted that the war should not be called a "rebellion," and he employed such designations as the "Civil War," the "War for the Union," or the "War for Southern Independence."

This last mentioned name for the struggle, the "War for Southern Independence," reflected both Channing's concept of a conflict between rival nationalisms and his attempt to be fair to the South. Channing, like the "liberal" Southerners and many other members of this generation, was sympathetic to the attempt to preserve the Union (the "nation") in the Civil War and he was critical of the institution of slavery—the attempt to enlarge the area of slave territory was, he wrote,

against the whole economic, social, and moral sentiment of the times, not merely in the Northern United States, but throughout the greater part of the civilized world.[129]

But at the same time, Channing reflected both the spirit of sectional reconciliation common in his day and the awareness of the trained historian of his generation that the sectional background of the historian could lead to biased historical writing; he at-

[127] *ibid.*, 261.

[128] Channing, *War for Southern Independence*, 3-4; for another passage which seems to indicate that Channing did not consider war inevitable, see pp. 252-254.

[129] *ibid.*, 3-4. The institution of slavery, Channing stated in another passage, was "utterly opposed to the moral sense of the civilized world in the year 1857," and he declared that in the Old South, for the first time in the world's history, it was proposed to found a state on the enslavement of human beings of one color by masters of another (the quotation is from *ibid.*, 194; see also *ibid.*, 13). Channing's opposition to slavery should not be confused with support for the abolitionist position—see, for example, his criticisms of abolitionists in *ibid.*, 85, 113-115.

tempted to be fair to the South and did not seek to blame the war solely upon Southerners. Channing was conscious, he stated, of the hazards of a "Northern student of history" in judging the motives of Southerners; he declared that the great mass of white Southerners in the cotton states had desired their independence from the Union (hence the "War for Southern Independence"), and his evaluation of the much-debated North-South differences in interpreting the Constitution was similar, as we have seen, to Wilson's judgment that both sides had been "right."[130] Channing, in short, pictured the Civil War as a contest between rival nations; he did not attempt to place exclusive blame for starting war upon either "nation," but he regarded with satisfaction the outcome of the combat.

Channing wrote one of the last of the multivolumed histories of the United States in the grand manner, eventually publishing six volumes covering the period 1000-1865. As volume after volume of his *History of the United States* appeared (beginning in 1905), Channing's fame as historian steadily increased. By 1925, when the sixth volume was published, Channing was generally recognized as one of the leading historians in the United States; he and his *History*, as one historian pointed out in that year,

were so widely known and respected that scholars everywhere are proud to contribute a suggestion or a table of facts, just as a hundred years ago the whole scientific world sent specimens to Cuvier.[131]

Here, then, was another of the most influential historians of this generation who reflected the new ideas and attitudes toward the Civil War which spread after 1890.

Just as Channing broadened the Rhodesian concept of an irrepressible conflict between freedom and slavery to include a struggle of different social orders and rival nationalisms, so John Bach McMaster led the way for "social" historians to enlarge the Rhodesian concept to include a struggle of diverse civilizations. In the 1880's and 1890's, when "economic history," the influence of the frontier and of the West, and other new currents of his-

[130] Examples of Channing's attempt to be fair to the South as described in this paragraph can be found in his volumes, *The United States of America*, 215-216, 258-262, and *The War for Southern Independence*, 11-21, 193-194, 264-265, 279.

[131] Dixon Ryan Fox, review of Channing, *History of the United States*, vi, in *The American Historical Review*, xxxi, 151 (October 1925).

torical thought were in the air, there was present also in the minds of some individuals the concept of "social history"—the history of all aspects of the day-to-day life of ordinary people, as opposed to accounts which emphasized battles, treaties, and the doings of governmental leaders. The historian who was to write the most important large-scale history of the United States from this "social" viewpoint was John Bach McMaster.

McMaster's geographical background, unlike that of Rhodes, Wilson, Turner, or Channing, was the Middle Atlantic states: born in Brooklyn (1852), he spent most of his life in New York, New Jersey, and Pennsylvania.[132] Like Rhodes, McMaster was a self-trained historian; he studied engineering and taught that subject as a member of the Princeton faculty in the 1870's and 1880's. But from the time of his graduation from college (City College of New York) in the early 1870's, he had wished to write history, and he formed the purpose of writing a history of the United States comparable to Macaulay's *History of England*. In 1883, the first volume of his *A History of the People of the United States from the Revolution to the Civil War* was published (and in that year McMaster left Princeton's department of engineering for the University of Pennsylvania's department of history, where he remained until his retirement in 1918). Seven more volumes of the *History* appeared in the three decades after 1883, and an additional volume was published in 1927, *A History of the People of the United States During Lincoln's Administration*.

In a work as all-embracing as was McMaster's, many subjects were discussed and many emphases were evident—emphasis upon the influence of the West in the history of the United States, for example, and upon the importance of economic factors and forces; but the primary emphasis of McMaster's *History*, and the one which was to have the most influence upon historical writing in the United States, was that upon the "life of the people." McMaster accurately described the theme of his study in its opening sentences:

In the course of this narrative much, indeed, must be written of wars,

---

[132] Eric F. Goldman, *John Bach McMaster, American Historian* (Philadelphia, 1943) *passim*; see pp. 21ff. of this volume for a description of the beginnings of "social" history in the United States after the Civil War.

conspiracies, rebellions; of presidents, of congresses, of embassies, of treaties, of the ambition of political leaders in the senate-house, and of the rise of great parties in the nation. Yet the history of the people shall be the chief theme. . . . It shall be my purpose to describe the dress, the occupations, the amusements, the literary canons of the times; to note the changes of manners and morals.[133]

(And to pioneer in writing this "new" type of history, the life of the people, McMaster pioneered in the extensive use of a "new" type of source material—periodicals, particularly newspapers.)

As was to be expected from McMaster's approach to history, the coming of the Civil War was not a primary focus of attention in his volumes—and this fact in itself would seem to be indicative (even if in a negative sense) of the new era in explaining the causes of the war. It served as one more example of the fact that to historians born in the 1850's or later, the traditional emphasis upon a struggle between freedom and slavery or between North and South no longer provided the exclusive, or even the primary, focus for interpreting the history of the United States. Turner, because his interest and sympathies were centered in the West, could describe the disputes between "North" and "South" in a more dispassionate manner than had previously been common; in a similar fashion, McMaster, because his primary interest was in "social" history, discussed the various sectional conflicts in political and economic life, including the conflict over slavery, without rancor and without the degree of sectional partisanship which had characterized Von Holst or even Schouler.[134]

But if McMaster's volumes illustrated something of the outlook of the new generation on the Civil War in the negative sense just described, they also revealed newer points of view in a positive sense. For, although there was no explicit and comprehensive discussion of the causes of the war in McMaster's *History*, this social historian did describe at length the development of fundamental differences in the economy and the society of the South, on the one hand, and that of the rest of the nation, on the other. McMaster, in a volume published in 1900, drew the now familiar contrast between the agricultural, static, and isolated South con-

[133] John Bach McMaster, *A History of the People of the United States from the Revolution to the Civil War* (8v., New York, 1883-1913) I, I.
[134] See, for example, *ibid.*, VIII, chaps. 86, 90, and 97.

servative in its folkways, and the agricultural, commercial, and manufacturing North and West in touch with and responsive to all the varied currents of mid-nineteenth-century life:

To the great forces which in the course of the nineteenth century were to radically change the conditions of civilized man she [the South] was indifferent. Not so the North. There every art and science which could add to the wealth, increase the prosperity and comfort of the people, and develop the material resources of the country was already [*circa* 1825] assiduously cultivated.[135]

Thus, McMaster, like Channing, described two different and conflicting societies (and perhaps it would not be a misrepresentation of McMaster's viewpoint to say even two different civilizations). His summary of the contrast between "South" and "North" accurately indicated his over-all point of view, and whether or not he employed the phrase "irrepressible conflict," this seemed, as in the case of Turner, to be the implication of his words: "Socially and industrially, the North and South were now [in 1850] two distinct peoples."[136] It was, presumably, in these fundamental differences between the sections that the origins of the Civil War were to be found.

As between these two different and conflicting societies, it seems clear that McMaster's sympathies were with the North and the West, which he pictured as attuned to the new material, social, and intellectual developments of the nineteenth century. Above all, McMaster's sympathies seem to have rested with the nation, the Union, for his thought, like that of Wilson, Turner, and Channing, was infused with a strong sentiment of nationalism (McMaster's biographer has pointed out that the Pennsylvania historian thought of the achievement of national unity as the main theme of American history and that this was illustrated in the various titles he proposed for his volumes, such as "The Rise and Growth of the Federal Union.")[137] Yet, despite his sympathies, McMaster did not attempt to lay the blame for the coming of war upon any one section or any one particular group of persons; like Turner, he was in many respects the scientist-historian describing

[135] *ibid.*, v, 228-229.
[136] *ibid.*, vii, 270; this statement summarizes a contrast of North and South found on pp. 267-270.
[137] Goldman, *McMaster*, 39-40.

the past without attempting to fix the "guilt" for the Civil War. And finally, he might be compared to Channing in the sense that, picturing a conflict between rival civilizations, he did not hold either side "guilty" for instigating or prolonging the conflict, but he seems to have looked with satisfaction upon the result of the struggle.

The writings of Turner, Wilson, Channing, and McMaster on the causes and character of the Civil War can be summarized in two related statements: in the first place, those writings illustrated the manner in which the new currents of historical interpretation in the latter part of the nineteenth century furnished new perspectives on the Civil War and new explanations of its coming; all of these new outlooks and explanations, in the second place, reflected attitudes toward the war quite different from those which had been common in any section in the 1860's and 1870's.

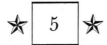

★ 5 ★

The "Nationalist Tradition"

RHODES, Turner, Channing, McMaster, and the "liberal" Southerners such as Wilson, all gave influential expression to some of the interpretations of the causes and character of the Civil War which were most widespread among their generation of historians (the generation born from the late 1840's through the 1870's). The differences in their perspectives and viewpoints are obvious and cannot be minimized with accuracy. But one is struck by the general and over-all similarities in their explanations of the coming of war if they are compared, on the one hand, with the explanations which prevailed in the 1860's and 1870's, and on the other hand, with some of the interpretations which won favor after the First World War. From this standpoint, the similarities in the outlook of these historians, most of whom began to write in the 1890's, are more impressive than their differences, and the manifest differences which do exist seem to exist within a common broad pattern of ideas and attitudes—a pattern which distinguishes their interpretations from those which preceded as well as from many of those which were to follow. This pattern might well be called the "nationalist tradition" of the Civil War.

The "nationalist tradition," as expressed in the writings of the historians discussed in this chapter, was characterized primarily by its spirit of nationalism and sectional reconciliation (as between the "North" and the "South" of 1861). This unusually powerful sentiment of nationalism and sectional reconciliation was in sharp contrast to the abnormally bitter sectional antagonism in which individuals, North and South, had interpreted the causes of the war in the 1860's and 1870's, and this new spirit led to a decidedly different approach to the causes of the Civil War.

Whereas the heart of the viewpoints of the 1860's, as we have seen, was the placing of guilt upon one's rivals for the coming of war, the historians in the "nationalist tradition" now interpreted the causes of the struggle in such a way that no individual or section was saddled with exclusive blame for what had happened. Rhodes sought to balance the right and wrong of each side; Wilson, Channing, and other historians insisted that both North and South had been right in the constitutional arguments they advanced; and Turner and McMaster explained the reasons for war in a fashion which tended to remove questions of personal or sectional guilt from consideration; each of these historians reflected attitudes unlike those which had prevailed in the 1860's and 1870's. Instead of condemning the actions of those who had been enemies of their own particular section in 1861, historians now sought to explain those actions in a fashion which was not discreditable to the supporters of either side.

The characteristic mood of the era was symbolized particularly in the widespread tributes to Lincoln, on the one hand, and to Robert E. Lee, on the other; this so-called "cult of Lincoln and Lee" reflected the widespread agreement among historians that supporters of the Union, typified in Lincoln, and supporters of the Confederacy, typified in Lee, had acted in the main from honorable and justifiable motives. Historians could now agree with Frederic L. Paxon of Pennsylvania (born 1877) that honesty and intelligence were about evenly divided on each side in the war, and that both sides were "thoroughly American" and were "devoted to the Union as they knew it."[138] This generation, as Emerson D. Fite of Ohio (born 1874) accurately remarked in 1911, was impressed primarily with the "infinite pathos" of the Civil War: "Both sides were right! Neither could have given in and have remained true to itself."[139]

Imbued with this spirit and possessing a more sophisticated concept of history than most of their predecessors, historians in the "nationalist tradition" now pictured inanimate forces as the primary cause of conflict between North and South rather than the actions of evil individuals. These historians advanced more complex explanations to replace the relatively simple hypotheses of the 1860's and 1870's; they singled out, as the forces which had ultimately produced sectional hostility, not ambitious and wicked politicians, but the spread of cotton cultivation, or the influence of

[138] Frederic L. Paxson, *The Civil War* (New York, 1911) 28.
[139] Emerson D. Fite, *The Presidential Campaign of 1860* (New York, 1911) 195-196.

physiographic and economic factors. They did not express agreement on whether the Civil War was inevitable, but now there were historians from all geographical sections who were agreed in explaining the causes of the war in terms of deep-seated, fundamental, irreconcilable differences between the sections—and many of them described the institution of slavery as one of the most important of these differences.

Finally, the "nationalist tradition" was marked by a feeling of satisfaction at the outcome of the Civil War. In their descriptions of the basic differences between the sections which had provided the background for war, it was clear, as we have seen, that the sympathies of the above-mentioned historians were with the nonslaveholding sections of the country; in addition, their strong feeling of nationalism led them to rejoice over the preservation of the Union. Even the dissatisfaction of Rhodes and most of the other historians in the "nationalist tradition" with the policies adopted by the national government in the Reconstruction era was subordinated to the feeling that the Civil War experience had resulted in much more good than evil. The Civil War had destroyed the institution of slavery and had preserved and strengthened the American nation, and these were results with which the historians in the "nationalist tradition" were in deep sympathy.[140] This feeling of satisfaction with the results of the Civil War was part and parcel of the general cast of thought of these historians; they were not complacent and completely uncritical in their outlook, but they studied the American experience by and large in a sympathetic spirit, and they found in this experience more cause for encouragement than for dismay. This distinctive outlook was to distinguish the "nationalist tradition" of the Civil War from several of the interpretations which were advanced later in the twentieth century.

By the time of the First World War, the "nationalist tradition," with its adherents in all sections, had replaced to a very consid-

[140] For examples of expressions of satisfaction with the ultimate results of the Civil War by "liberal" Southerners (in addition to those already mentioned in this chapter) see: Brown, *Lower South in American History*, 110-112; Peter J. Hamilton, "Lee and the Confederacy," 329-330; Edwin Mims, *The South Atlantic Quarterly*, v, 196 (April 1906); S.C. Mitchell, *The South in the Building of the Nation*, x, 211-212; Trent, *Simms*, 289-290; Wilson, *Division and Reunion*, 289-290.

erable extent the older views of the war which had once been common in each section. Both the replacement of older concepts of the war by newer ones and the large measure of agreement on the new concepts among many historians of all sections were reflected and symbolized in the fact that a single new name for the war, the "Civil War," came into wide use throughout the nation, supplanting by and large the various names once popular in the different sections.

The appeal of the ideas and attitudes comprising the "nationalist tradition" extended beyond the generation of Rhodes and Turner. By the time of the First World War, yet another generation of historians was reaching maturity and beginning to write—individuals born in the late 1870's and afterward (this was the second generation of trained historians, and the third generation of individuals measured from the participants in the Civil War). The writings of a number of historians of this second trained generation published in the two decades after the First World War can be described, in general, as restatements of the "nationalist tradition" bringing the tradition up to date in terms of some of the recent findings of historical scholarship. Probably the most widely noticed and the most influential such restatement of the "nationalist tradition" in the 1920's and 1930's by a member of this second generation of trained historians was Arthur C. Cole's volume, *The Irrepressible Conflict, 1850-1865*, published in 1934.

Cole, born in Michigan in 1886, received his undergraduate and graduate training at the universities of Michigan and Pennsylvania. His book was part of a large-scale cooperative history of the United States planned and written from the viewpoint of social history, and bearing the appropriate name, *A History of American Life*. Edited by Arthur M. Schlesinger and Dixon R. Fox, this history (thirteen volumes were published from 1927 to 1948) reflected the interest of many historians of the generation of Cole, Schlesinger, and Fox in the type of social history in which McMaster had pioneered in the United States.

The title of Cole's volume, *The Irrepressible Conflict*, accurately indicated its point of view, and in all essentials that point of view was in accord with the "nationalist tradition." Somewhat in the

manner of McMaster, Cole described the development of two unlike and conflicting civilizations in the United States of the 1850's,
the one centered in the Northeast and the Midwest, and the other
centered in the South. The general outline of the portrait he
painted was familiar, although this outline was filled in with a
multitude of facts uncovered in extensive new research in the
sources: the economy of the agricultural slave-plantation South
diverged from that of the agricultural, commercial, and industrial
Northeast and Midwest; at the same time, different and conflicting political, social, and cultural systems had taken root in the
various sections—the North and the West becoming a flexible,
changing society, a land of "isms" of all sorts, open to the manifold new currents of life of the midnineteenth century, while the
South remained relatively static and unchanging, isolated from
many of the movements of the day. As Cole summed up these developments:

The spirit of democracy and the cause of free land spread their influence over the industrial North. The railroad pushed its iron bands
across the country binding together the young commonwealths and
the old. The fruits of a new and glowing prosperity were tasted in the
great agricultural empire as well as in the Eastern marts of trade and
manufacture. The throbbing forces of enlightenment, culture, and
humanitarian reform spread over the North, while free labor, girding its
loins, began to feel its power. South of the Ohio's murky waters a
plantation oligarchy basked contentedly in the waning sun of prosperity. For the few, life was easy and pleasant; culture—measured in
terms of passive leisure-class enjoyment and not in science and the
creative arts—was within ready reach. An army of Negro vassals and a
dependent white class made obeisance to planter rule, though the white
yeomanry stirred restlessly as its opportunities of rising to a share in
the plantation regime steadily declined and slave labor threatened to
become a fatal incubus upon the back of Dixie.[141]

The sympathies of Cole, like those of McMaster and other historians of his generation in the "nationalist tradition," were with
the North and the West, and the South was pictured as being out
of step with the nineteenth century. But Cole did not attempt to
blame the coming of war upon individual Southerners or upon

[141] Arthur Charles Cole, *The Irrepressible Conflict, 1850-1865* (New York, 1934) 406-
407; for another concise statement of the "irrepressible conflict" point of view, see the
"Editors Foreword" in Cole's volume by Arthur M. Schlesinger and Dixon Ryan Fox.

the South as a whole, nor yet upon individual Northerners nor upon the North as a whole. Without implying that war itself was inevitable, he pictured it as stemming from the irreconcilable sectional differences described above:

The revolutionary victory in 1860 of the forces that challenged the social institutions of the South severed the last bonds that held the cotton kingdom within the Union. Since the North and the administration that represented it refused to "allow the erring sisters to depart in peace," the issue was staked upon the arbitrament of arms.[142]

The ultimate outcome of the war seemed, in Cole's pages, to give cause for satisfaction, however qualified; here again, Cole seemed to view the situation in much the same spirit as his predecessors in the "nationalist tradition":

In the fiery furnace of war and the crushing defeat of the South, the permanence of the Union was welded. Yet dislike, suspicion, fear, remained; the gaping wound lingered. Only when it could be bound up and healed could real peace and happiness come to the nation. Then emerged at length the glories of a modern America.[143]

Not all the historians of Cole's generation accepted the "nationalist tradition," as will be indicated in subsequent chapters, but apparently many of them did. The ideas and attitudes comprising the tradition were written into the textbooks and the lecture notes of the historians of this generation; these ideas supplanted previous interpretations to such an extent that they themselves constituted, by the 1930's, the conventional and traditional explanations of the causes of the war. By and large, the "nationalist tradition" of a Civil War growing out of an irrepressible conflict represented the thinking of a great many of the historians in the United States in the half-century after 1890—and even after fifty years and two generations of historians, the appeal and influence of the tradition were not negligible. Looking back from the vantage point of the early 1950's, one could say that, so far, this tradition had been one of the most widespread and most persistent of all patterns of attitudes toward the Civil War.

[142] *ibid.*, 407.
[143] *ibid.*

CHAPTER FIVE

"THE SECOND AMERICAN REVOLUTION"

Historians and Social Reform

EARLY in the twentieth century, when the "nationalist tradition" was most widely accepted among historians in the United States, forces were at work shaping quite different points of view concerning the causes and nature of the Civil War. Beginning in the 1920's, the twentieth century was to be characterized not by the uncontested dominance of the "nationalist tradition" but by the emergence of sharply conflicting interpretations of the war. These conflicting interpretations were formulated and accepted by individuals, with only a few exceptions, of the generation after Rhodes, Turner, and Channing—i.e., by historians who were born in the late 1870's or afterward.

Of all the rival explanations set forth in the twentieth century, one of the most important was the distinctive economic interpretation which was given its most influential expression by Charles A. Beard. The Beardian type of interpretation of history had its counterparts in other nations within Western European civilization (just as there were counterparts to the emergence in the United States of "scientific" history, "social" history, and other such historical perspectives and techniques). But the origins within the United States of the Beardian viewpoint, and the principal factors which explain its wide acceptance by historians in the United States, are to be found in the changed climate of opinion which stemmed from the important transformations of society in America after the Civil War.

In the half-century after Appomattox, the hitherto predominantly rural and agricultural United States was changing into a nation whose urban and industrial characteristics were ever more pronounced. These profound alterations in the national life, whatever their beneficial results, brought in their wake social problems and social ills, and a varied group of individuals gradually lifted their voices in protest and proposed "reforms." The heterogeneous reform efforts gained adherents slowly in the late nineteenth century, but in the decade and a half after 1900, the bipartisan progressive movement in political and economic life won impressive mass support from the voters. And at approximately the same time that this reform movement was winning electoral victories, there appeared new points of view in many fields of intellectual endeavor which contributed to the support of social reform. Pragmatism in philosophy, "realism" in literature, sociological jurisprudence, the "new economics," the "social gospel" movement in religion, "progressive education"—all of these new currents implicitly or explicitly questioned older standards, conditions, and ideals; in a sense, they were all counterparts, within their own spheres, of the progressive movement in political life.

At this time, when both the voters and the intellectuals were giving support to movements for social reform, an increasing number of historians, too, became sympathetic to those causes and to the "progressive" point of view on political and economic questions.[1] The beginnings, on a significant scale, of this alignment of the sympathies of historians was most concretely shown in the publication of two volumes in the years 1912 and 1913: James Harvey Robinson's *The New History: Essays Illustrating the Modern Historical Outlook* (1912), and Charles A. Beard's *An Economic Interpretation of the Constitution of the United States* (1913). These volumes embodied the new historical viewpoint which characterized the leaders of the reformer-historians.

The appearance of Robinson's book marked the coming-of-age of the "new history" movement. Gradually taking form over a number of years, this movement had a number of facets and represented several different aims of historians. But whatever else the movement indicated, it demonstrated that the interests and the sympathies of some historians in the United States were shifting toward the cause of social reform and "progressivism," for the attention of the most vocal historians in the new movement was frankly focused upon contemporary social problems, primarily those which centered ultimately in the distribution of wealth and

[1] The word "progressive" is used in this chapter to mean one broadly in sympathy with the progressive movement and/or the "New Deal" of the 1930's; a distinction has been made between "progressives" and "Marxists."

of economic and political power among the various economic groups or classes in society. And in their consideration of contemporary social problems, the new historians were generally ardent proponents of reform.

Robinson (born in 1863), the acknowledged leader of the movement, made quite explicit in his 1912 volume his contention that a primary reason for studying history (and at times it seemed that he meant the sole reason for studying history) was to aid in the reformation of society. One studied the past, according to him, in order to understand the present; but the prime reason for understanding the present was so that one could aid in its "improvement" in the sense in which progressives understood that word:

Society is to-day engaged in a tremendous and unprecedented effort to better itself in manifold ways. . . . The part that each of us can play in forwarding some phase of this reform will depend upon our understanding of existing conditions and opinion, and these can only be explained . . . by following more or less carefully the processes that produced them. We must develop historical-mindedness upon a far more generous scale than hitherto, for this will add a still deficient element in our intellectual equipment and will promote rational progress as nothing else can do.[2]

The individual who did not aid the cause of reform—the conservative—stood convicted of sin in a quite literal sense:

At last, perhaps, the long-disputed sin against the Holy Ghost has been found; it may be the refusal to cooperate with the vital principle of betterment. History would seem, in short, to condemn the principle of conservatism as a hopeless and wicked anachronism.[3]

The publication of Charles A. Beard's *An Economic Interpretation of the Constitution of the United States* provided additional evidence of the adoption of the reform cause by historians. It also furnished a further indication of the spread of the idea that the purpose of acquiring knowledge of the past was to reform the present. While the use of history to reform society was only one (although extremely important) among the several points of emphasis of the "new history" movement, it was far and away the principal emphasis of Beard's volume, for Beard the historian was

[2] James Harvey Robinson, *The New History* (New York, 1912) 23-24; a similar statement can be found on p. 252.
[3] *ibid.*, 265.

never far removed from Beard the progressive, and to understand the former one must understand the latter.

Beard became a reformer from a personal background so similar to that of many of the leaders of the progressive movement that he could serve as something of a case history in that respect.[4] His biography is essentially the story of a young man of a well-to-do middle-class family in a small town who went to college and, either there or later in his life, was "converted" to the cause of social reform (Henry George, Tom L. Johnson, and many leaders in the progressive movement described their entry into the reform ranks through experiences comparable to a religious conversion). Beard's ancestry was apparently in the conservative tradition in politics: Federalist and Whig. His father (born in 1840 and given the name of the Whig President elected in that year), William Henry Harrison Beard, was a prosperous man of many occupations ranging from farmer to president of the local bank in a small Indiana community; he has been described as a "copper-riveted, rock-ribbed, Mark Hanna, true-blue" Republican, although he seems to have retained some of the idealism of the early Republican Party in regard to Negroes. Charles A. Beard, born in 1874, is said to have been brought up in an atmosphere in which it was assumed that no self-respecting person could be a Democrat.

But in 1895, Beard entered De Pauw College, and at this small Methodist institution in Indiana came under the stimulus of new influences, in particular that of a remarkable teacher, Col. James Riley Weaver.[5] Weaver, a veteran of the Union Army and a Republican in politics, was at the same time a teacher who empha-

[4] The literature on Beard is rapidly becoming extensive. I have found the following articles particularly helpful in depicting various aspects of his life and ideas: Hubert Herring, "Charles A. Beard: Free Lance among the Historians," *Harper's Magazine*, v. 178, pp. 641-652 (May 1939); Samuel Eliot Morison, "Did Roosevelt Start the War?," *The Atlantic Monthly*, v. 182, pp. 91-97 (August 1948); Bernard C. Borning, "The Political Philosophy of Young Charles A. Beard," *The American Political Science Review*, XLIII, 1165-1178 (December 1949); Richard Hofstadter, "Beard and the Constitution: the History of an Idea," *American Quarterly*, II, 195-213 (Fall 1950); Max Lerner, "The Political Theory of Charles A. Beard," *American Quarterly*, II, 303-321 (Winter 1950); Eric F. Goldman, "The Origins of Beard's *Economic Interpretation of the Constitution*," *Journal of the History of Ideas*, XIII, 234-249 (April 1952).

[5] For a description of Weaver and his role as Beard's teacher, see Merle Curti, "A Great Teacher's Teacher," *Social Education*, XIII, 263-267 (October 1949).

sized reading the source works of history whatever their point of view; under his supervision, Beard's reading was apparently wide. It was also through Weaver's influence that Beard took a trip that was to be an important milestone in his pathway to reform: he visited Chicago in the summer of 1896—the Chicago of slums and factories, the Chicago of Jane Addams (Beard met her and lived near Hull House), the Chicago in which Bryan captured the Democratic convention. In that atmosphere, the son of the well-to-do small town farmer-banker learned, writes Hubert Herring, "to discount his traditions, to question current orthodoxies." Now, in college debates Beard upheld the right of labor to organize and argued for a federal income tax (in contrast to James Ford Rhodes, who, some thirty years before in school debates, had upheld Vallandigham and the opponents of the Emancipation Proclamation). Henceforth, whatever else Beard was, he was always a vigorous advocate of social reform.

Beard spent several years in England, beginning in 1898, studying history at Oxford, and also becoming acquainted with the leaders of British labor and lecturing before labor groups (he and a classmate at De Pauw had offered to raise a volunteer military company for service in Cuba in 1898, but their offer was not accepted). Back in the United States, he received the degree of Doctor of Philosophy from Columbia in 1904, and for the next thirteen years was a member of the Columbia faculty and at the same time an active supporter of various reform enterprises. He was at Columbia when his controversial volume on the Constitution was published.

In *An Economic Interpretation of the Constitution of the United States*, Beard the reformer set forth a view of history which could be, and was, used as a potent instrument for social change. Historical materialism had been a part of the intellectual scene in Europe for some time, and Marxists both in the United States and in Europe had, of course, employed an economic interpretation of history as a weapon to promote social change before Beard wrote (Marxian viewpoints are discussed in section 3 of this chapter). But Beard was one of the first non-Marxists in the United States to explain history from such a standpoint, and this was what differentiated his economic interpretation from previous non-Marxist studies which had placed stress upon the importance of economic forces. Before Beard's volume was published in 1913, McMaster, Channing, and a number of other historians had emphasized, as we have seen, the importance of economic factors in the history of the United States, and as early as 1902, E.R.A. Seligman had published his discussion of *The Economic Interpretation of History*. Turner and his associates and students had placed particular stress upon economic forces, and Beard acknowledged this in his *Economic Interpretation of the Constitution*.

But Beard's own economic interpretation, unlike that of the other historians named here, was distinctly "reformist" in tone: the compelling impression which many readers gained from Beard's writings was that social reform was urgently necessary and that history could be of service in promoting such reform. (One of the clearest indications of this distinguishing characteristic of Beard's economic interpretation was his criticism of Turner on the ground that Turner had placed too much emphasis upon American "individualism," thereby supporting conservative opponents of social reform:

Although Turner did not invent the phrase "rugged individualism," he did in effect . . . identify it with the frontier spirit. . . . Turner set many historians to thinking that individualism had been the driving force in American civilization. Wittingly or not he fortified the teachings of [William Graham] Sumner in economics and sociology and of [John W.] Burgess in political science.[6]

Beard's interpretation of the Constitution did, in fact, provide a weapon with which the opponents of social change could be discredited and their arguments undermined by the assertion or the implication that they were acting from motives of personal or class economic gain.

Robinson and Beard were in the foremost echelons of the reformer-historians; they more ardently advocated social reform, they favored more drastic social changes, and they held a more

---

[6] Charles A. Beard, *The American Spirit* (New York, 1942) 363. For other discussions of Turner and his ideas by Beard, see: "The Frontier in American History," *The New Republic*, xxv, 349-350 (February 16, 1921); "Culture and Agriculture," *The Saturday Review of Literature*, v, 272-273 (October 20, 1938); "Turner's 'The Frontier in American History,'" in Malcolm Cowley and Bernard A. Smith, eds., *Books That Changed Our Minds* (New York, 1938) 61-71.

extreme view of the function of history as an aid to reform than did most of their fellow historians in 1912 and 1913.[7] But it is clear that by the time of the First World War, historians, whether or not they agreed in all respects with Robinson and Beard, were turning in increasing numbers to the support of movements for social reform. (Even Frederick Jackson Turner, despite the fact that he was sharply criticized by Beard and other reformer-historians on the ground that his views gave support to those who opposed reform, spoke approvingly in 1910 of history holding the "lamp for conservative reform.")[8] It is clear also that this trend was a continuing long-range one, lasting for at least three decades after *The New History* and *An Economic Interpretation of the Constitution* were published.

The embracing of the reform movement by a sizeable number of historians was influential in altering attitudes toward the Civil War in at least two important respects. It gave impetus to a trend already under way among historians in the United States (whether they were reformers or not) toward placing greater emphasis upon economic factors in history. The reformer-historians, living in an age of great economic change, were concerned as reformers with the solution to problems which many of them traced back to the fundamental economic transformation in the United States produced by industrialization. Therefore, in studying history, including the history of the Civil War, many of them tended to focus their attention in particular upon economic causes and economic results.

In the second place, many of the reformer-historians naturally looked with sympathy upon the reform movements in history which seemed similar to those of their own day—their outlook on history became progressive or reformist as well as their view of current events. The eventual triumph of this progressive outlook among historians in the United States, and the revision in histori-

---

[7] The varied reactions of some of Beard's fellow historians to *An Economic Interpretation of the Constitution* are summarized in Maurice Blinkoff, "The Influence of Charles A. Beard Upon American Historiography," *The University of Buffalo Studies*, XII, 16ff. (May 1936).

[8] *The American Historical Review*, XVI, 226 (January 1911); this was Turner's presidential address before the American Historical Association.

cal writing it occasioned, were noted by Samuel Eliot Morison, speaking in December 1950:

Fifty years ago it was difficult to find any general history of the United States that did not present the Federalist-Whig-Republican point of view, or express a very dim view of all Democratic leaders except Cleveland. This fashion has completely changed; it would be equally difficult today to find a good general history of the United States that did not follow the Jefferson-Jackson-F.D. Roosevelt line.[9]

As the reformer-historians became progressive in their sympathies, many of them became sharply critical of certain aspects of the economic system which had emerged in the United States after the Civil War, for they considered that system the source of the unhealthy social conditions which they as reformers were seeking to change. This critical attitude toward business and industry was in marked contrast to the outlook of most of the historians who expressed the "nationalist tradition." The climate of opinion in which the "nationalist tradition" had crystallized was, as we have seen, generally sympathetic to business and to the post-Civil-War economic system. (Rhodes was himself an industrialist, the "liberal" Southerners viewed business as a force making for progress in the New South, and Channing and McMaster were sympathetic to business. Wilson, although he later became a leader in the progressive movement, was not a reformer in the 1890's when he was writing history—and he described himself in 1889 as a "Federalist." Even Turner was not critical of the economic system in the sense in which Beard was.) When the Civil War was restudied by the reformer-historians in the light of their hostility to post-Civil-War business and industry, a picture emerged which was profoundly different from that drawn by the historians of the "nationalist tradition."

Not all the historians, be it repeated, who came to sympathize with movements for social reform were Beardians, nor were they all devotees of the New History—there were progressive historians who were anti-Beardian and/or anti-Robinsonian; similarly, some of the followers of Robinson were not followers of Beard, and vice versa. Yet it is still true that the post-Civil-War movements for social reform to which historians were turning, particularly the

[9] *The American Historical Review*, LVI, 272 (January 1951).

progressive movement, provided an intellectual climate quite different from that in which the "nationalist tradition" of the Civil War had been nurtured. From this new intellectual climate came the Beardian interpretation of the Civil War which was to have great appeal for many of the progressive historians.

The Beardian Point of View

BEARD's interpretation of the nature and causes of the Civil War was set forth in 1927 in the well-known two-volume work written in collaboration with his wife, *The Rise of American Civilization.* This book provided an appealing setting for Beard's picture of the Civil War—broad in its conception and scope, it was written in a stimulating style with a tone of irony and light-heartedness which served to deflate pomposity. It had an exciting youthful quality, for throughout the work ran the implicit conviction that here was the truth which had so far eluded historians. Here, it seemed, in the Beardian liberal economic interpretation, was the key which gave access to the hitherto impenetrable roots of human history and to the inmost sources of human conduct and social change. The portrait of the Civil War which emerged from this framework possessed two aspects which were particularly noteworthy: the virtually exclusive emphasis throughout upon economic forces and factors, and the distinctive alignment of sympathies which permeated the whole.

Beard explained the Civil War in terms of his concept of "the Second American Revolution," or, "in a strict sense," as he wrote, the First American Revolution (this idea of "the Second American Revolution" which Beard expressed in 1927 was quite similar in some ways, as will be indicated presently, to the viewpoint previously expressed before the First World War by Algie M. Simons, the American Marxist). This revolution was a profound economic and social transformation of the United States, a

social cataclysm in which the capitalists, laborers, and farmers of the North and West drove from power in the national government the planting aristocracy of the South.[10]

The Civil War was one aspect or phase of this cataclysm; it was a "social war" which made great changes in "the arrangement of

[10] Charles A. and Mary R. Beard, *The Rise of American Civilization* (2v., New York, 1927) II, 54; the heart of Beard's discussion of the Civil War is in chapters XVII and XVIII.

classes, and in the accumulation and distribution of wealth."[11] The roots of this profound conflict between the "capitalists, laborers, and farmers of the North and West," on the one hand, and the "planting aristocracy of the South," on the other, Beard found in a complex series of factors—in "social groupings founded on differences in climate, soil, industries, and labor systems, in divergent social forces."[12] But attention was focused not upon this complex series of factors but upon what, in Beard's view, was the significant outcome of these forces—the creation of different economic systems in North and South with their attendant differing interests in politics (in the Beardian view political interests were almost entirely dependent upon economic interests). Thus, the basis of the Second American Revolution was essentially the struggle between two conflicting economies.

This rivalry of economic-political interests was described in considerable detail by Beard. He pointed out that the Southern planters sought to secure from the federal government protection for their slave labor system and the return of all runaway "property," and at the same time wished to prevent the government from doing anything to aid business enterprise (no protective tariffs, no national banking and currency systems, and no ship subsidies). The planters, with the help of the free farmers of the North and West, controlled the federal government in the 1850's and secured the adoption of the policies they favored. But in 1860, the free farmers outside the South had joined with the Northern "capitalists" in an economic-political program which reflected the interests of those two groups: a protective tariff, free homesteads, a Pacific railway, and opposition to slavery in the federal territories.

All other North-South differences (or similarities) were strictly subordinated, in Beard's pages, to this conflict over economic interests. The institution of slavery as a moral issue dividing the country received scant treatment. Beard discussed slavery, but primarily as an economic system: "the institution of slavery as a question of ethics was not the fundamental issue in the years preceding the bombardment of Fort Sumter."[13] In a similar fashion, he reduced ultimately to an economic basis the clash of rival sectional cultures and civilizations which Turner, Channing, and

[11] *ibid.*, ii, 53.　　　[12] *ibid.*, 51.　　　[13] *ibid.*, 40.

other historians in the "nationalist tradition" had described. The Second American Revolution, he insisted, had involved a struggle between rival social and economic classes, and only by the "accidents of climate, soil, and geography" was it a dispute between geographical sections. Channing's designation for the struggle, "The War for Southern Independence" (a phrase which expressed Channing's concept of conflicting nationalisms) Beard described as "fairly precise," but he added that it suffered "a little perhaps from abstraction."[14] (Although he had praise for Channing's emphasis upon economic factors, Beard censured him for not centering his explanation of the Civil War period even more completely around an economic thesis.)[15]

The conflict of economic interests which was at the heart of the Second American Revolution was in Beard's opinion an "irrepressible conflict," and he specifically used that phrase to describe it. Going beyond the concept of irreconcilable differences, he took the position that war itself was inevitable; in view of the irrepressible conflict, Beard wrote that

a transfer of the issues from the forum to the field, from the conciliation of diplomacy to the decision of arms was bound to come.[16]

But it should be noted that he repeatedly minimized the role of battle, and did not picture a "revolution" in which force and violence played a crucial role. Armed conflict, he wrote, had been only a "transitory phase" of the economic and social changes; the fighting was but a "fleeting incident" in the story; the physical combat "merely hastened the inevitable."[17]

The "core of the vortex" of the Second American Revolution lay not in the fighting during the Civil War but in the social and economic changes, in the

flowing substance of things limned by statistical reports on finance, commerce, capital, industry, railways, and agriculture, by provisions of constitutional law, and by the pages of statute books.[18]

The Second American Revolution, in summary, was basically eco-

[14] ibid., 53.
[15] See Beard's review of Channing, *History of the United States*, Vol. vi, in *The New Republic*, xliv, 310-311 (November 11, 1925).
[16] *Rise of American Civilization*, ii, 10.   [17] ibid., 54.
[18] ibid.

nomic in nature, marking the dividing line between the "agricultural era" and the "industrial era" in the United States.

Beard's emphasis upon economic factors, operating through social classes, to the virtual exclusion from serious consideration of all other factors, was enough to differentiate his interpretation from the "nationalist tradition"—even from those historians in that tradition (like Channing and Turner) who had put considerable stress upon economic forces. But what distinguished Beard's views even more sharply from the "nationalist tradition" was the pattern of sympathies and antipathies which proceeded from his progressive reformist position. The "nationalist tradition" had been explicitly or implicitly critical of the institution of slavery (as distinct from slaveholders) on ethical or ideological grounds, and critical also of the doctrine and practice of secession on the grounds that it would have involved the destruction of the nation. But in Beard's pages, both the moral issue involved in slavery and the question of the Union's preservation were minimized to the point of virtual denial that they were significant questions. This did not mean that Beard discussed the Civil War in an attitude of near-complete detachment, for his intense dislike of Northern business "capitalism" was evident throughout his discussion; the most striking display of this antipathy came in his description of the results of the Civil War.

Either by direct statement or by unmistakable implication, the "nationalist tradition" had viewed with favor the results of a struggle which, whatever its other consequences, had resulted in the preservation of the Union and the destruction of the institution of slavery. In Beard's pages, on the contrary, the most important result of the Second American Revolution, confirmed by the military defeat of the Southern planters, was the coming to power of the "northern capitalists and free farmers." Rule by that combination after 1865 had, in Beard's view, been essentially rule in the interest of the Northern capitalists, and the results of that rule drew some of Beard's sharpest and most pointed criticism. In chapter after chapter of *The Rise of American Civilization* he poured forth his dissatisfaction, the titles of some of the chapters indicating their critical tone, such as "The Politics of Acquisition and Enjoyment," or "The Gilded Age." His own deep disappointment at the results of the Civil War seemed to be expressed in the 1892 platform of the Populist Party, whose indictment of the post-Civil-War United States declared (as summarized and quoted at length by Beard)

that America was ruled by a plutocracy, that impoverished labor was laid low under the tyranny of a hireling army, that homes were covered with mortgages, that the press was the tool of wealth, that corruption dominated the ballot box, "that the fruits of the toil of millions are boldly stolen to build up colossal fortunes for a few unprecedented in the history of mankind; and the possessors of these in turn despise the republic and endanger liberty."[19]

So infused with hostility to Northern "capitalism" was Beard's interpretation of the Civil War era that its over-all implications (whether so intended or not) could be construed as pro-Confederate in several important respects. His view that the ethical issue involved in Negro slavery was not a fundamental factor in the irrepressible conflict, and his description of the aims of the North almost solely in terms of economic benefits, were positions that were squarely in agreement with the contentions of Confederate sympathizers beginning with Jefferson Davis. Beard's criticism of Northern "capitalism" was so unrelieved and this theme so dominated his pages that the Southern planters very nearly became the heroes of the narrative, and Beard very nearly became the ally of John C. Calhoun. From Beard's words, it was easy to gain the impression that the Southern planters, whatever else they had done, had at least opposed Northern "capitalism" and kept it from ruining the country before 1860. The planters, as Beard pointed out, specifically citing Calhoun, had predicted dire results if Northern capitalism got in control of the national government; in truth, Beard stated, the "triumph of business enterprise" in the Second American Revolution *was* accompanied by the

inevitable factors foreseen by southern statesmen—a growing army of wage workers haunted by poverty, an increasing solidarity among skilled craftsmen, and periodical uprisings of labor in industry and politics.[20]

The point is not that Beard was a Confederate sympathizer intent on attacking the "nationalist tradition" in order to defend

[19] *ibid.*, 210.   [20] *ibid.*, 211.

the South. His interpretation was presumably neither pro-Northern nor pro-Southern, but economic; it said in effect that all previous explanations of the causes and nature of the Civil War (pro-Northern or pro-Southern) were unrealistic since they did not recognize the crucial role of economic forces. But since the dominant interpretation at the time of Beard's writing was the "nationalist tradition," it was this explanation, as the current ruling one, which served primarily as the foil for Beard's point of view, the background upon which he sketched his own contrasting interpretation. Beard was not a defender of the Confederacy, but the implications of his viewpoint could be interpreted as pro-Confederate; and his interpretation, as it turned out, was to be used by some Southern-born historians to vindicate the Confederacy.

Where the historians in the "nationalist tradition" had pictured a conflict between rival section-nations rooted in social, economic, cultural, and ideological differences, Beard described what was essentially a struggle between two economies having its origins in divergent material interests. The historians in the "nationalist tradition" had maintained that this conflict and the war which grew out of it settled at least two basic questions which were supremely important for the United States—the integrity of the Union and the fate of the institution of human slavery—and that the settlement made was by and large a fortunate one for the United States. Beard insisted, by contrast, that the primary issues involved in the strife were the rival economic-political interests of the two competing economies; the ultimate outcome of the strife, in his view, had been the triumph of Northern "capitalism," and in his description this outcome had been unfortunate for the nation in many ways.

Beard's interpretation of the Civil War came at a time favorable for its reception by historians and by intellectuals in general. The way had been prepared for it in part by the conversion of many intellectuals to the cause of reform, and Beard provided the progressives with a point of view which they considered more "realistic" than any which had preceded it. The Beardian "realistic point of view" in history, as one reviewer of *The Rise of American Civilization* pointed out, had by 1927 been widely accepted "even in the most polite academic circles"; this reviewer predicted that in contrast to the criticism which had greeted Beard's earlier *Economic Interpretation of the Constitution* in some circles, Beard would now be praised, and "what was supposed to be the chief fault of his technique a dozen years ago will now be acclaimed its greatest strength."[21]

An additional appeal of Beard's views lay in the fact that they were fresh and sprightly and conveyed a general mood of pin-pricking balloons of ostentation. *The Rise of American Civilization*, as Carl Becker pointed out in the idiom of the 1920's, was "free from bunk"; it was a book in which the usual appearance of the muse of history was somewhat altered:

Her hair is bobbed, and you can see her bare knees if you care to look, for she rolls 'em too, and will in any company as like as not be seen tapping a cigarette or fumbling for a lip-stick.[22]

Beard, and this should be emphasized, was not a "debunker," and the group to which his viewpoint proved most attractive was not the debunkers but was, instead, the progressive reformers. Nevertheless, the general tenor of his "realistic point of view" also had a certain appeal to the debunking spirit common in the 1920's.

Whatever the varied sources of its appeal, *The Rise of American Civilization* was highly praised (with a few exceptions) by reviewers, both historians and nonhistorians alike. In many of the reviews, it is difficult to single out the opinion of the reviewer on Beard's interpretation of the Civil War as distinct from his portrait of American history as a whole, but (in the absence of specific reservations to the contrary) it is perhaps not unreasonable to conclude that the reviewers were in general equally favorable to both.

Beard's reformist economic interpretation received strong reinforcement with the publication, in the same year as *The Rise of American Civilization*, of the first two volumes of another major historical synthesis: Vernon L. Parrington's *Main Currents in American Thought*. Between the two syntheses and their two authors there were many points of similarity. Parrington came from

---

[21] Evans Clark in *The New York Times Book Review*, April 24, 1927, p. 6.

[22] Carl L. Becker, "Fresh Air in American History," *The Nation*, CXXIV, 560 (May 18, 1927). Blinkoff, "The Influence of Charles A. Beard," chapter IV, contains a discussion of the reception accorded Beard's interpretation of the Civil War, and lists reviews of the *Rise of American Civilization*.

a social and economic background similar to Beard's—he too was a middle-class Midwesterner, born in the 1870's and turned reformer and scholar. At several universities, particularly the University of Washington (his academic home from 1909 until his death in 1929), he had combined scholarship and reform in roughly the same proportions as had Beard.[23] The focus of Parrington's *Main Currents* differed somewhat from that of *The Rise of American Civilization*—it was concerned more with literary figures and currents and paid less detailed attention to developments in politics and economics. But Parrington's definition of "American Thought" was so broad, and he visualized such a close relationship between an individual's ideas and his social background, that the subject matter of *Main Currents* and that of *The Rise of American Civilization* were not really different. In *Main Currents*, the economic and political history of the United States was discussed in terms of the ideas of individual literary figures, while in *The Rise of American Civilization* the same subject was considered in terms of the sweep of economic forces and the currents of politics.

In Parrington's volumes as in Beard's, economic forces were not one set among many powerful sets of forces at work in history, but instead were dominant to the extent of practically excluding other factors as primary agents of causation. For Parrington, as for Beard, the economic interpretation was a weapon with which one castigated the foes of progressive reform. Parrington was much more concerned with personalities than was Beard, and his volumes were filled with heroes and villains. An ardent Jeffersonian, his sympathies throughout American history were with the individuals whom he identified as "agrarian democrats" and his sharp animosity was aroused by those whom he identified as their opponents—principally Eastern "capitalists" (critics were to point out that there was a tendency in Parrington's pages to explain the actions of individuals whom Parrington opposed in terms of economic self-interest, but to explain the actions of persons he favored in terms of the ideals of agrarian democracy).

[23] The personal and intellectual background of Parrington is discussed at greater length in Thomas J. Pressly, "Vernon L. Parrington and the History of American Literature" (MS, 1946) Widener Library, Harvard University.

Parrington's discussion of the Civil War was not as extensive or as direct as was Beard's, and he did not use the phrase "the Second American Revolution"; but his point of view was the same as Beard's in all essentials. He explained the origins of the war primarily in terms of an economic conflict between three "rival imperialisms"—"eastern capitalism," "southern slavery," and the western "inland empire." In the mid-nineteenth-century era of "fluid economics" and of "economic romanticism," he wrote, these imperialisms had driven "blindly to a collision."[24]

Parrington's sympathy in this struggle of rival imperialisms was clearly with the "agrarian democracy" of the West, and he described the outcome of the Civil War as a serious defeat for this group. His criticism of the post-Civil-War United States was every bit as sharp as Beard's. The Civil War, he maintained, substituted the "captain of industry" for the Southern planter as the "custodian of society." Although the war had eliminated slavery, it had also brought defeat to the "old ideal of decentralized democracies, of individual liberty"; in addition, Western agrarianism came under the control of Eastern capitalism, and the United States entered upon the era of "the great barbecue."[25] Parrington's progressive-reformist hostility to business ("eastern capitalism") gave his interpretation a tone that, like Beard's, came near to being pro-Southern. Whatever criticism he levied against the South of Calhoun and Jefferson Davis, Parrington also pointed out that Calhoun had erected a last barrier against those "middle class ideals" which triumphed after the Civil War: "consolidation in politics and standardization in society . . . a universal cash-register evaluation of life."[26]

It is a paradox that during the 1920's, when neither public opinion nor public policy supported political and economic progressivism, the two major studies of American history from the progressive point of view were published and were favorably received. Parrington's interpretation of the American past, including the Civil War, appealed in general to the same groups as did the viewpoint of Beard, and for the same basic reasons. *Main Currents* was

[24] Vernon L. Parrington, *Main Currents in American Thought* (3v., New York, 1927-1930) II, pp. iv ff.
[25] *ibid.*, II, 473-474; III, 4.　　　　　　[26] *ibid.*, II, 81-82.

hailed by reviewers with an even stronger degree of approval than had greeted *The Rise of American Civilization*, and was awarded the Pulitzer Prize in history.[27] And within two years after both books appeared, the crash of the stock market in 1929 heralded a major depression from which, in turn, a new reform movement emerged; this chain of developments had the effect of greatly enhancing the appeal of the Beard-Parrington reformist economic interpretation of history.

The New Deal reform movement was in many respects a continuation of the progressive movement of the early years of the century, and in the 1930's much of the intellectual atmosphere of the progressive movement was recreated. Social reform became the goal of a new generation of intellectuals, and the reform zeal of some of the older generation was revived. There was in the air probably a more widespread spirit of hostility to business than had characterized the progressive era, due primarily to the effects of the depression of 1929-1933. Large numbers of businesses failed, causing the loss of considerable sums of money to the general public and reducing the prestige of business; congressional investigations revealed malpractices in some businesses; businessmen whose confident words had filled the air in the days of "Coolidge prosperity" publicly admitted, during the depression years, their alarm at the state of the economy and asked for assistance from the federal government. The adulation of business and the businessman, exemplified in such best-selling volumes of the 1920's as Bruce Barton's *The Man Nobody Knows*, was replaced in the 1930's by a mood in which regulation and control of business by government seemed to many persons necessary and desirable.

In such a milieu, the Beard-Parrington interpretation of the Civil War, with its hostility to Eastern "capitalism," increased in favor. Symptomatic of the spirit of the times was the publication and favorable reception in 1934 of Matthew Josephson's volume, *The Robber Barons* (dedicated to the Beards), in which the business leaders of the post-Civil-War period were flayed. The volumes of Beard and Parrington became the acknowledged historical handbooks of progressives. Beard became one of the foremost in-

[27] The reception accorded *Main Currents in American Thought* is described at some length, with a list of reviews of the book, in Pressly, "Vernon L. Parrington."

tellectual leaders of progressivism, and in addition won the personal respect and admiration of many individual reformers with whom he came in contact; keen of intellect, gracious in manner, he was known affectionately as "Uncle Charley." When a group of progressives associated with *The New Republic* compiled a symposium at the end of the 1930's on *Books That Changed Our Minds*, they dedicated it to Beard, and he and his writings were given a prominent role in the symposium.

Beard himself began around 1935, in the opinion of some observers, to modify his economic interpretation of history, and his *Basic History of the United States*, published in 1944, made no mention of "the Second American Revolution" (in fact, it contained no explicit statement of the causes of the Civil War). By the 1950's, as will be indicated presently, the Beardian economic interpretation of the Civil War seemed to have lost some of its former popularity with historians. But, so long as the issue of domestic reform remained dominant in the United States of the 1930's, the Beardian viewpoint was, from all indications, quite widely accepted, and it seemed likely that the concept of "the Second American Revolution" (despite Beard's abandonment of the phrase) would have a lasting influence upon attitudes toward the Civil War.

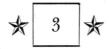

Marxists Interpret the Civil War

THE GROWTH of the movement for social reform in the United States after the Civil War was paralleled on a much smaller scale by the rise of Marxian socialism. The doctrines of Karl Marx had been known in the United States before the Civil War, and after the war organizations and political parties for their propagation were formed (*Das Kapital* was a "better seller" in the United States in 1889).[28] Like the non-Marxian reform movement, the Marxian movement experienced a flowering in the first decade and a half of the twentieth century. On the eve of the First World War, there was a vigorous Socialist press in the United States, and the Socialist Party under the leadership of Eugene Debs won a certain measure of success at the polls: Socialists held various municipal and state offices, there was a Socialist Congressman, and in 1912, Debs as presidential candidate of the Socialist Party received approximately 900,000 votes. The Socialist movement never gained anything like majority support (its peak vote in 1912 amounted roughly to only seven per cent of the total vote cast in that election), but it was an active and vocal minority by the time of the First World War.

Just as the turning of historians to the non-Marxian movement for social reform had stimulated a new outlook on the Civil War, so too did twentieth century Marxism provide the basis for a distinctive point of view which differed radically from the "nationalist tradition."[29] The original Marxian interpretation of the Civil War was formulated in the 1860's—by Marx himself and by Frederick Engels. In some ways, Marx and Engels explained the

[28] Mott, *Golden Multitudes*, 323. Mott's criterion for "best seller" in 1889 was a sale of 500,000 copies; "better sellers" in his classification are those books whose sales were large but are believed not to have reached the 500,000 figure. He lists one "best seller" published in 1889 (Guy de Maupassant, *Stories*), and five "better sellers" in addition to *Das Kapital*, including Rudyard Kipling, *Soldiers Three*, and Mark Twain, *A Connecticut Yankee in King Arthur's Court*.

[29] For a general discussion of the subject, see George O. Virtue, "Marxian Interpretation of the Civil War," *Nebraska History*, xxx, 19-49 (March 1949).

causes of the Civil War in a fashion quite similar to that of the most ardent abolitionists of the North. They placed the blame for the war squarely upon the South; they asserted that the secession movement had resulted from a conspiracy by Southerners; they insisted from the first outbreak of hostilities that the cause of the war was slavery.[30] (Marx specifically asserted that the war was not concerned merely with differences over the tariff question.)[31]

Yet, although the views of Marx and Engels on the Civil War were similar to those of the abolitionists, they were by no means identical (and this was to be true of all subsequent Marxist interpretations as well—they might be similar to interpretations by non-Marxists, but they were not identical). For, although Marx and Engels desired a victory for the Union armed forces in the Civil War, they could not accurately be called "supporters of the Union" without serious qualification. They repeatedly expressed their scorn for the Union states—the bourgeois democracy, the "model country of the democratic swindle," in the words of Marx, "where fraud has so long remained supreme."[32] Support for the Union was for Marx and Engels a means toward the goal of "the" social revolution predicted by Marx. The unimportance of the Union as compared to the ultimate goal of revolution was frankly stated by Engels in a letter to Marx in November 1862; at this time when the military outlook for the Union was dim indeed, Engels wrote that it was good

that even in America the bourgeois republic exposes itself in thoroughgoing fashion, so that in future it can never again be preached on its own merits, but solely as a means and a form of transition to the social revolution.[33]

Marx and Engels were critical of Lincoln and the Yankees for trying to wage war in a constitutional manner, and urged that it must be conducted on "revolutionary lines." In one of the last comments we have on the war by either of the two men, Marx was still

[30] Richard Enmale, ed., *The Civil War in the United States by Karl Marx and Frederick Engels* (New York, 1937) 4, 58ff., 71, 81, 164, 227ff. The views of Marx and Engels on the Civil War are found in a series of articles by Marx published in the New York *Daily Tribune* in 1861-1862, in a series of articles by Marx and Engels published in *Die Presse* (Vienna) in 1861-1862, and in letters between Marx and Engels dated 1861 to 1866. These sources are collected in the volume edited by Enmale.

[31] *ibid.*, 58ff.   [32] *ibid.*, 255, 258, 271.

[33] *ibid.*, 259.

searching for the revolutionary aspect of the struggle; he wrote Engels in April 1866 that after "the Civil War phase the United States are really only now entering the revolutionary phase."[34]

There is no evidence which indicates that the views of Marx and Engels on the Civil War had any appreciable influence on attitudes in the United States in the 1860's. But in the first decade and a half of the twentieth century, when Marxian Socialism was reaching the peak of its popular appeal in the United States, Marxists set forth interpretations of the Civil War which won more attention. The Marxist who in the early twentieth century wrote most extensively about the Civil War was Algie M. Simons, one of the leading publicists in the Socialist Party at the time.

The background of Simons was more similar to that of Eugene Debs (or Turner or Beard) than it was to that of many of the Eastern members of the Socialist Party. Born (in 1870) and raised in a primitive Wisconsin community of some two hundred inhabitants, he had attended the University of Wisconsin in the 1890's and there studied history under Turner (he was a frequent guest in the Turner home, and even fired the household furnace for a time).[35] Upon graduation from the university in 1895, he spent two years as a social service worker in Chicago; profoundly aroused by the Chicago slums, he reacted not only against the Republican Party views of his family but also against the capitalist system. He became in 1897 a member of the Marxian Socialist Labor Party and then, in 1900, joined the new Socialist Party; from this period until 1916 he was an editor of various Socialist publications.

Simons set forth his views on the Civil War at greatest length in a pamphlet published in 1903, *Class Struggles in America*, and in a book published in 1911, *Social Forces in American History*. As revealed in these two works, his interpretation of the Civil War rested upon a Marxian view of history centering around three main concepts: the importance of economic forces in history to the virtual exclusion of all other factors; the fundamental signifi-

[34] *ibid.*, 277.
[35] I am greatly indebted for information concerning Simons to a Princeton University senior thesis, deposited at the Princeton University Library, by John J. Harmon and entitled, "Algie Martin Simons, 1870—" (ms, 1947); this thesis is based in part upon personal interviews with Simons (who died in 1950).

cance of class struggles in history; and the inevitable and imminent decline of the capitalist system.

The economic basis of society, Simons asserted, determined social institutions and social classes; when the economic environment changed, new social classes with new economic interests were created, and these new classes struggled to gain control in society.[36] Applying this general interpretation to the history of the United States, he visualized the role of the Civil War as a crucial one.[37] For the Civil War, in his view, was essentially a class struggle growing out of the economic developments in the United States of the midnineteenth century. Because of these economic developments, a capitalist class had arisen in the North in the 1850's based upon "wage slavery," and this class sought to get control of the national government and to advance its economic interests through the Republican Party (an essentially "revolutionary" party, declared Simons, since it demanded that control of the government be transferred to a new social and economic class). But the economic desires of this class conflicted sharply with those of the Southern plantation owners, whose economy was based upon "chattel slavery," and when the capitalist class obtained control of the national government through the victory of the Republican Party in 1860, the Southern planters seceded.

Thus, whereas Marx and Engels in the 1860's had explained the coming of the Civil War in terms of a conflict over slavery, Simons emphasized a struggle over economic interests. The war, he insisted, was not caused by hostility to chattel slavery, nor was it caused by fervent love for the Union; the genesis of the war lay in the conflicting economic interests of the capitalist class in the North and the planter class in the South. Simons did not, apparently, use the phrase "irrepressible conflict," but his description left no doubt that the competing economic interests were, in his view, irreconcilable; moreover, he declared that once the capitalist

[36] Algie M. Simons, *Class Struggles in America* (Chicago, 1903) I, 29-31, and *Social Forces in American History* (New York, 1911) *vii-viii*, 317-318. In the historical writings of Simons there were occasional indications of a Turnerian emphasis upon the influence of the frontier and of the westward movement; even within the Socialist movement, Simons championed the influence of the West, maintaining that the frontier furnished the best material for the Socialist movement and the best labor unions (see Harmon, "Simons," 54-56, 62).

[37] *Class Struggles*, 12-18; *Social Forces*, 216-237, 254-284.

class came into power through the election of Lincoln, secession and Civil War were inevitable.[38]

The tremendous significance of the Civil War to Simons lay in the fact that it had confirmed the control of the government in the hands of the capitalist class which the economic revolution had brought to power in the North. Now capitalism, after a long period of dominance, Simons wrote in the early years of the twentieth century, was itself to be overthrown in turn. The "decadence" of capitalism had reached such a degree that, in the opinion of Simons, the "next step in social evolution" was clear: the collective ownership of the means of production by laborers. Labor, he wrote, was beginning to organize, to flock to the Socialist standard, and was "certain of victory" in what was to be the final class struggle in the history of the United States.[39] (Simons entitled the last chapter of his *Social Forces* "The Triumph and Decadence of Capitalism"; this phrase so aptly expressed the Marxist viewpoint that it might well be described as the theme of all Marxist accounts of the history of the United States since 1865.)

Simons' volume, *Social Forces*, was widely reviewed in periodicals in the United States; his views seem to have attracted considerable attention and they were received with enthusiasm in Socialist circles.[40] But the available evidence does not indicate that the writings of Simons were an important direct influence in spreading an economic interpretation of the Civil War among non-Marxist historians. The non-Marxist historians who would presumably have been most sympathetic to the point of view of Simons were those who were turning to the cause of social reform. But if Carl Becker was representative of this group, it would seem that while historians were becoming progressives, they, like the

[38] *Class Struggles*, 15-18; *Social Forces*, 261-263.

[39] *Class Struggles*, 29-31; *Social Forces*, 317-318. In 1913, another Marxian Socialist, Herman Schlueter, published a volume discussing those Civil War issues indicated in its title, *Lincoln, Labor, and Slavery*. Although this volume was not directly concerned with the causes and nature of the Civil War, enough was said on the subject to indicate that Schlueter's interpretation was in most respects identical with that of Simons; see in particular the "Preface" and chapter I.

[40] Harmon discusses in considerable detail the reaction to *Social Forces* in "Algie M. Simons," 127-139. For representative reviews of *Social Forces* by non-Marxist historians, see: Guy S. Callendar in *The American Historical Review*, XVII, 614-616 (April 1912); William E. Dodd in *The Dial* (Chicago), LII, 85-86 (February 1, 1912); William O. Scrogg in *The Mississippi Valley Historical Review*, I, 117 (June 1914).

country as a whole, were not turning to Marxist views of history. Simons' *Social Forces* called forth Becker's classic stricture—it was a book, he stated, written "without fear and without research."[41]

The prime significance of Simons' interpretation of the Civil War was its expression, before the First World War, of an economic point of view similar to that which was later to be expressed by Beard. This fact naturally leads to the question—did Simons specifically influence Beard? That Beard was acquainted with the historical writings of Simons is indicated by the citations in his *Economic Interpretation of the Constitution of the United States*; whether Beard's "Second American Revolution" interpretation was directly inspired by the views of Simons is, so far as the knowledge of the present writer is concerned, a matter of speculation. The general similarities between the interpretation of the causes and nature of the Civil War by Simons and by Beard is clear. It would seem worthwhile, however, to point out that there was a basically important difference between the interpretations of the two men: that of Simons was set in the framework of a Marxist view of history (including a forecast of the overthrow of capitalism) while that of Beard was cast in a profoundly different framework. The reformist economic interpretation of the Civil War which became widely popular among historians in the United States was not the Marxist version of Simons but the non-Marxist version of Beard. In the 1930's, when Marxists once again formulated explanations of the causes of the Civil War, even they took as their point of departure the writings of Beard rather than those of Simons.

The Socialist movement declined rapidly after the election of 1920, the Communist movement gained few adherents, and for a decade after 1920, Marxism seems to have had relatively little influence in the United States. But the economic depression in the years after 1929 sharpened and deepened the disillusionment of some intellectuals with the United States and its past; it served in particular to focus that discontent upon the economic system which had suffered such a severe shock, and "capitalism" was held by some to be on the verge of collapse. The Communist regime in

[41] Carl Becker, "The Reviewing of Historical Books," *Annual Report of the American Historical Association for the Year 1912* (Washington, 1914) 133.

Russia, in the eyes of some intellectuals in the United States, presaged a society organized on new and superior principles; in addition, Marxism-Communism seemed to some intellectuals to offer valuable opposition to the rising threat of fascism. Due apparently to such factors as these, Marxism in the 1930's again became a tangible force among some intellectuals in the United States.[42]

In such circumstances, a Marxian interpretation of the causes and nature of the Civil War was set forth in the writings of a few individuals in the 1930's, notably Louis M. Hacker, James S. Allen (the pen name used by Sol Auerbach), and whoever it was who wrote under the pseudonym, "Richard Enmale" (*EN*gels, *MA*rx, *LE*nin). Louis M. Hacker was the most widely known figure of this group; born in New York City in 1899, he graduated from Columbia University and spent several years in the 1920's and 1930's as an editor of various encyclopaedias and yearbooks. In the mid-1930's, he became associated with the department of economics at Columbia University, and at about that same time was described as "one of the best known of the younger American historians" (editors of *Harper's Magazine*) and as "the most intelligent post-Beardian historian in the country" (John Chamberlain).[43] He became president of the American Marxist Association and served as one of the editors of the *Marxist Quarterly* published by that association in 1937. Allen and Enmale were known primarily as authors whose writings were published

[42] Observers are not agreed in their estimates of the extent, the importance, and the significance of Marxism and/or Communism among intellectuals in the United States in the 1930's (there seems to be general agreement, outside the ranks of Marxists and Communists, that the influence of Marxism and/or Communism was confined largely to intellectuals). For discussions of the subject, see: Henry B. Parkes, *Marxism: An Autopsy* (Boston, 1939); Eugene Lyons, *The Red Decade* (New York, 1941); James Oneal and G. A. Werner, *American Communism* (New York, new and revised edition, 1947); Arthur M. Schlesinger, Jr., *The Vital Center* (Boston, 1949) chap. VI and *passim*; Bernard De Voto, "The Ex-Communists," *The Atlantic Monthly*, v. 187, pp. 61-65 (February 1951).

[43] *Harper's Magazine*, v. 170, 4th page (not numbered) following p. 512 (March 1935); John Chamberlain, as quoted by Dixon Ryan Fox in Louis M. Hacker, *A Short History of the New Deal* (New York, 1935) 7. For a discussion of Hacker's changing historical viewpoints, see John F. Gerstung, "Louis M. Hacker's Reappraisal of Recent American History," *The Historian* (Albuquerque, New Mexico) XII, 140-166 (Spring 1950); Hacker's Marxian interpretation of the Civil War was set forth primarily in writings from 1933 to 1937.

in Marxist periodicals and by the International Publishers Company, New York (the publication agency for the Communist Party in the United States).

Hacker, Enmale, and Allen explained the causes of the Civil War in a manner superficially similar to Beard.[44] They endorsed the Beardian concept of the Second American Revolution, and there were words of praise in their writings for Beard as the leader of the "liberal bourgeois" school of historians (Simons was seldom mentioned). Like Beard and Simons, the Marxists of the 1930's found the origins of the Civil War in the economic transformation which had brought the Northern "capitalist" class to power in the United States in the midnineteenth century; they too described the conflicting interests of the industrial North and the agricultural South—although they put more emphasis than had Beard or Simons upon the ideological difference between the free labor system of the North and the slave labor system of the South. Yet, upon close examination, the views of Hacker, Enmale, and Allen seemed to differ from the Beardian interpretation almost as much as from the "nationalist tradition."

The dissimilarities between the point of view of the Marxists and that of Beard centered around their contrasting concepts of the Second American Revolution. The Second American Revolution described by Beard had been simply one incident in the history of the United States, but to the Marxists here under discussion the Civil War was part of a revolutionary tradition which was at the heart of American history. The "only true and genuine tradition of American history," wrote Enmale, was "the revolutionary solution of deep-seated social antagonisms"; in a similar vein, Hacker published an article in 1935 devoted to the thesis that the "history of the United States is the history of revolution."[45] The Marxists found the tradition of revolution at the heart of the American past, and they also found it at the heart of the American future, for they held that the historical role of the Second Ameri-

[44] James S. Allen, *Reconstruction: the Battle for Democracy (1856-1876)* (New York, 1937) 17ff.; Enmale, ed., *Civil War, xviii*; Louis M. Hacker, "Revolutionary America: An Interpretation of Our History," *Harper's Magazine*, v. 170, pp. 437ff. (March 1935), and "The American Civil War: Economic Aspects," *Marxist Quarterly*, I, 201ff. (April-June 1937).

[45] Enmale, ed., *Civil War, xxv*; Hacker, "Revolutionary America," 431.

can Revolution had been to prepare the way for the inevitable proletarian revolution of the future. (Hacker was particularly critical of non-Marxist historians who diverted attention from the revolutionary tradition and destiny of the United States. He denounced Turner, for example, in scathing language on the ground that he had perverted the study of American history by "his insistence upon the uniqueness of American experience"; Turner, Hacker charged in 1933, had led American historians away from their proper study of "the origins and growth of American capitalism and imperialism" into the "futile hunt for a unique 'American spirit' "—thus, Turner and his followers were "the fabricators of a tradition which is not only fictitious but also to a very large extent positively harmful.")[46]

This predestined proletarian revolution was eagerly awaited by the Marxists, and Louis Hacker, writing in 1935, pictured it as a possibility of the immediate future. "We are living," Hacker declared, in the "last stage of capitalism now," and while he admitted that it was difficult to predict the precise manner in which the actual "capitalist collapse" would come about, he asserted that

unmistakably, the initial signs of a revolutionary situation are beginning to appear in the United States today. Who knows? It still may be the destiny of the present living American generation to watch and participate in the unfolding of great events . . . a turning of our backs on the past and a renewal of mankind's upward climb after the hampering restraints of an outworn system of production have been shaken off.[47]

Enmale and Allen did not write of the coming revolution with quite the tone of urgency used by Hacker (perhaps because they were writing two years later), but they clearly expressed their hope and their expectation of revolutionary changes in their own era.[48]

Beard had specifically minimized the role of fighting and force in the Second American Revolution; the Marxists, however, without explicitly stating that "revolutions," past and future, necessarily included the use of force and violence, implied this through-

[46] Louis M. Hacker, "Sections—or Classes?", *The Nation*, v. 137, 108-110 (July 26, 1933).
[47] Hacker, "Revolutionary America," 431-432, 443.
[48] Enmale, ed., *Civil War*, xxiv-xxv; Allen, *Reconstruction*, 215.

out their writings. Allen, for example, in discussing the Civil War era, contrasted Lincoln, who "shied away from the full historical tasks of the epoch" and wished to carry on a revolution by constitutional means, with Thaddeus Stevens, the "true leader" of the bourgeois revolution, who advocated unconstitutional, revolutionary methods and who was "the logical expression of the policy demanded by the revolutionary epoch."[49] In like manner, Hacker noted that in the Civil War force was first employed by the "counter-revolutionists" (the Southern planters), and he praised the North of 1861 for promptly meeting the use of force with force. The lesson of 1861 for his own day was spelled out clearly by Hacker: when the capitalist collapse came, he wrote, whether society should sink into chaos or emerge "revitalized" depended upon "the growth and discipline of a class—and politically-conscious revolutionary force" such as had appeared in 1776 and in 1861 to carry those revolutions to their "predestined goals."[50] (Characteristic of the Marxists of the 1930's was their language of historical determinism—"the policy demanded by the revolutionary epoch," or the "predestined goal" of revolutions.)

The evaluation of the results of the Civil War-revolution in the Marxist interpretation also distinguished it sharply both from the "nationalist tradition" and from the Beardian point of view. Beard had been unsympathetic to the results of the Second American Revolution and bitterly critical of what he described as the rule of the "Eastern capitalists" in the quarter-century after 1865. It might have been expected that the Marxists, in view of their opposition to capitalism, would have been even more scathing in their denunciation than was Beard—but this was not the case. For the Marxists viewed the Second American Revolution in the light of their deterministic philosophy of history; that revolution had been a bourgeois revolution, and although the bourgeoisie had betrayed "democracy" after the Civil War, the function of the revolution had been fulfilled and the way prepared for the proletarian revolution of their own day. The historical "mission" of the Second American Revolution, in this view, had been to assure the triumph of American capitalism; this revolution had served a de-

[49] Allen, *Reconstruction*, 19-23.
[50] Hacker, "Revolutionary America," 444.

sirable function, by and large, for the triumph of American capitalism was a necessary prelude to its decadence and downfall. Allen expressed most explicitly this evaluation of the Civil War as revolution:

the destruction of the slave power was the basis for real national unity and the further development of capitalism, which would produce conditions most favorable for the growth of the labor movement. . . . The stage was being cleared of outworn and hackneyed properties to make way for a new and contemporary drama in which the chief protagonists would be the bourgeoisie and the proletariat. . . . The bourgeois republic "as a means and a transition form to the social revolution"— this was the main historical import of the bourgeois revolution to the proletariat.[51]

Thus, the conviction that a proletarian revolution was inevitable and desirable led Marxists, if not to satisfaction with the results of the Second American Revolution, at least to an acceptance of that revolution as a necessary and preliminary step in the predetermined stream of history. It is unnecessary to point out that this Marxist "acceptance" of the Second American Revolution was vastly different from the satisfaction with the results of the Civil War which characterized the "nationalist tradition."

The Second American Revolution had been, in the view of the Marxists, a step forward in American history, and Enmale and Allen insisted that bourgeois historians (failing "to appreciate fully the class dynamics of historical development") had slighted the role taken in this praiseworthy revolution by two proletarian groups —the "American working class" and the Negroes. The Marxists advanced a dual explanation of the part played by the American working class in the Civil War. On the one hand, Hacker, Enmale, and Allen were apologetic for its lukewarm role in opposing slavery and upholding the Union, ascribing this to the "political immaturity" of American workers; on the other hand, Enmale and Allen also emphasized the strong stand for the Union and strong opposition to slavery of some American workers and asserted that despite its political immaturity, labor as a class had been one of the most influential factors in the victory of the North.[52]

[51] Allen, *Reconstruction*, 26-28. For a similar point of view, see: Enmale, "Editor's Foreword," in Allen, *Reconstruction*, 11; Hacker, "Revolutionary America," 441.
[52] Hacker, "Revolutionary America," 438ff., and "The American Civil War," *Marxist*

No such dualism characterized the discussion by most Marxists of the role of Negroes. Enmale and Allen insisted that Negroes had played an important part in winning the Civil War and that they had made a conscious and heroic struggle for democracy and civil rights in the period of Reconstruction (Negroes did not figure in Hacker's account of the war).[53] This point of view concerning Negroes in the Civil War era also received special emphasis in the 1930's and 1940's through the writings of two other Marxists, W.E.B. Du Bois, well-known Negro intellectual, and Herbert Aptheker. Du Bois and Aptheker presented some variations from the interpretation of the Civil War by Hacker, Enmale, and Allen. Du Bois in a volume devoted primarily to the Reconstruction era, explained the coming of the war much as did the abolitionists in the 1860's, ascribing it primarily to the institution of slavery and emphasizing repeatedly the moral issues involved in the slavery controversy; in accordance with this viewpoint, he sharply criticized the "sweeping mechanistic interpretation" of the Beards on the ground that it omitted from consideration the moral wrong of slavery, the "triumph of sheer moral courage and sacrifice in the abolition crusade," and the struggle of Negroes in their fight for freedom.[54]

But only the extreme abolitionists of the 1860's matched the bitter invective against the South and Southerners which characterized the numerous writings of Herbert Aptheker. Aptheker described the Old South as a "huge fortress in which prisoners were held, at hard labor, for life," a militaristic region ruled by the group of whites whom he referred to as the "slavocracy" or "slavocratic oligarchy."[55] The essence of the institution of slavery in the Old South, he asserted, was cruelty—slaves, since they were

---

Quarterly, I, 191-192; Enmale, ed., *Civil War*, xixff.; Allen, *Reconstruction*, 24ff., 176ff. Marxists have singled out for special praise Joseph Weydemeyer, German-American working-class leader, friend of Karl Marx, and officer in the Union Army; see Enmale, ed., *Civil War*, xx-xxi, and the recent biography by Karl Obermann, *Joseph Weydemeyer* (New York, 1947).

[53] Enmale, ed., *Civil War*, xxiiff.; Allen, *Reconstruction, passim*.

[54] The quotations are from W.E.B. Du Bois, *Black Reconstruction* (New York, 1935) 715; for representative statements in this volume of Du Bois's explanation of the coming of war, see pp. 15, 29, 48ff., 714-716, 722.

[55] Herbert Aptheker, *Essays in the History of the American Negro* (New York, 1945) 13, 62-63.

human beings, "*had* to be maltreated, had to be made to suffer physical cruelty, had to be chained and lashed and beaten into producing for another's profit."[56] The Civil War came, declared Aptheker, when the slaveholding planters rebelled against national control (and he, like some of the Unionists of the 1860's, referred to the struggle as the "slaveholders' rebellion"): a "bloodstained, militaristic oligarchy saw its national power ripped from it and its local, internal power seriously threatened by a revolution of its mudsill, its base. It rose in rebellion itself in a desperate attempt to stop the clock of history."[57] Running throughout Aptheker's writings was a glorification of the abolitionists and of the Negro people; the "desire for freedom," he insisted, was "the motivating force in the history of the American Negro people" which had "always determined their actions, policies, and efforts."[58] (Although Aptheker's criticism of the South and of Southerners was similar in its virulence to that of nineteenth century abolitionists, his historical materialism, including his insistence that the "Negro question" was basically a "material" one rather than a "moral" one, clearly distinguishes his philosophical position from that of most of the abolitionists.)[59]

Although the views of the Marxists differed, in the main, more drastically from the "nationalist tradition" of the Civil War than did those of Beard, they offered a much less severe threat of supplanting that tradition, for, in contrast to the wide popularity of the Beardian economic interpretation, the appeal of the Marxist viewpoints seems never to have been great in the United States. Even at the height of the vogue of Marxism among American intellectuals in the 1930's, only a few historians (judging from their published writings) accepted the interpretations of the Civil War advanced by Marxists. By the late 1940's, even the two historians who had been the best-known spokesmen for a Marxist interpretation of the Civil War no longer advocated this explanation, and were apparently not Marxists: almost two decades before

[56] Herbert Aptheker, *The Negro People in America* (pamphlet, New York, 1946) 45; for a similar statement, see *Essays in the History of the American Negro*, 7ff.

[57] *ibid.*, 204.

[58] *ibid.*, 73; see also: Herbert Aptheker, *The Negro in the Abolitionist Movement* (pamphlet, New York, 1941), and *American Negro Slave Revolts* (New York, 1943).

[59] Aptheker, *Negro People in America*, 34-35, 66.

his death in 1950, Algie M. Simons had become a member of the bureau of medical economics of the American Medical Association, while Louis M. Hacker, once a strident critic of American capitalism who wrote in the *Marxist Quarterly*, had now become a fervent eulogist who wrote in *Fortune* magazine.

CHAPTER SIX

"THE NEW VINDICATION OF THE SOUTH"

Ulrich B. Phillips

WHILE economic interpretations of the Civil War were winning favor in the twentieth century, important developments were under way both in historical scholarship in the South and in the relations between the South and the rest of the nation. These developments formed an important aspect of the background for the attitudes of many Southern historians toward the Civil War after 1900.

The Southerners who, beginning toward the end of the nineteenth century, journeyed to Johns Hopkins, Columbia, and other universities outside the South for graduate training inaugurated the modern era of historical scholarship in the South. Many of them returned to the South to teach, and many of them (whether or not they taught in the South) centered their teaching and research upon the history of the South. They pioneered in the collection of source materials for the study of Southern history, laying the foundations for the subsequent large archives in the South; they performed much of the basic research which provided the detailed scholarly basis for subsequent studies of Southern history. Their efforts and exploits, like those of pioneering groups in other fields, were in many ways heroic.

But the fact that now, for the first time, trained Southern historians using Southern source material were beginning to write the history of the South posed an important question—how would Southern historians relate the history of their section to that of the nation at large? It was to be expected that some of them, like native-son historians of other geographical sections, would feel (and not without some justification) that their section and its history had been misunderstood by "outsiders" who frequently had not made a detailed study of the section's own historical source materials. Yet, granting that the native-son historian, be he New Englander, Westerner, or Southerner, could study the materials for the history of his section much more thoroughly than most outsiders, what was to prevent the native-son's historical writing from deteriorating into sectional chauvinism in which the point of view of the nation would be lost sight of completely? How achieve a balance between the sectional viewpoint and that of the nation?

In a very real sense, this dilemma might be described as the central problem of Southern historical scholarship in the twentieth century—paralleling what could be described as the central problem in the history of the South itself (not only in the twentieth century, but ever since the 1820's): the relationship of the South to the nation as a whole. Just as the Civil War was the crux of the latter problem, so historical writing about the Civil War era has been the crux of the former.

The story of Southern historical scholarship and the Civil War in the twentieth century can, for the sake of convenience, be considered in two chronological phases, with the line of division falling in the early 1930's. The history of the first chronological period has already been partially told in the discussion of the "nationalist tradition," but there remains for consideration the commanding figure of Ulrich B. Phillips.

The first generation of Southern-born trained historians was not agreed in its approach to the problem of how to relate the South's history to that of the nation as a whole. As we have seen, many of the historians of this generation (including, among others, William E. Dodd, Woodrow Wilson, William P. Trent, and William G. Brown) combined admiration for the South of Thomas Jefferson, and for the individual Southerners of the Civil War generation, with criticism of the institution of slavery and of the secession movement. So far as the history of the Civil War and Reconstruction was concerned, they achieved the workable compromise integration of the South's viewpoint with that of the rest of the nation—an integration represented, by and large, in the "nationalist tradition."

This was not true, however, of all the historians of that generation, and in particular it was not true of some of the students of William A. Dunning at Columbia University. Dunning established what was virtually a center of Southern studies at Columbia around the turn of the century, and for two decades directed the research of a number of Southern-born students. Many of his students investigated Reconstruction in various Southern states, and their studies were, in general, sympathetic to the position of the white Southerners of the generation which had fought the Civil War and had lived through Reconstruction. Unlike Wilson and other "liberals" of the New South, many of the Southern-born Dunning students displayed sympathy in their writings not so much for the South of Thomas Jefferson as for the South of John C. Calhoun and Jefferson Davis; they showed a tendency not so much to criticize some aspects of Southern life and history as to defend nearly all its aspects. Ulrich B. Phillips was probably the most distinguished of all Dunning's students, and Phillips' researches were to be especially influential in spreading among historians a more sympathetic attitude toward the *ante-bellum* South.

Born in Georgia in 1877, Phillips had graduated from the University of Georgia before going to Columbia at the turn of the century.[1] Besides being one of the few students of Dunning who devoted his studies primarily to the *ante-bellum* South, he was a pioneer among all historians in that field. He unearthed and investigated new source materials, particularly the records of Southern plantations, and his thorough studies (which, beginning in 1902, were published over a span of more than three decades) provided by far the most authoritative picture of the Old South by a scholar up to that time.

Phillips' interpretation of the history of the South was characterized by its strong emphasis upon the factor of race. The presence of large numbers of Negroes in the South, the fact of physical differences between the white and the Negroes, and the wide differences in the over-all social and cultural levels of the two races —these were, in the opinion of Phillips, fundamental features which explained much of the South's history. Especially did they

[1] Descriptions of Phillips and discussions of his views of history are to be found in: Wood Gray, "Ulrich Bonnell Phillips," in William T. Hutchinson, ed., *The Marcus W. Jernegan Essays in American Historiography* (Chicago, 1937) 354-373; Fred Landon, "Ulrich Bonnell Phillips: Historian of the South," *The Journal of Southern History*, v, 364-371 (August 1939); Philip Charles Newman, "Ulrich Bonnell Phillips—the South's Foremost Historian," *The Georgia Historical Quarterly*, xxv, 244-261 (September 1941); Richard Hofstadter, "U.B. Phillips and the Plantation Legend," *The Journal of Negro History*, xxix, 109-124 (April 1944).

help to explain the plantation-slavery system, which was the focal point of his studies, for the key to his interpretation of that system was his insistence that its function had been primarily that of schooling and civilizing a dependent race.

Phillips described the economic aspects of plantation slavery, but they were not, in his opinion, its most important aspects. Rather, the plantation-slavery regime was essentially an instrument through which the whites had controlled, disciplined, and schooled the Negro slaves. Phillips did not express hatred for the slaves (on the contrary, he generally spoke of them in a tone in which sympathy and affection seemed to be mingled), but he considered them, by and large, an "inert and backward people." He insisted that the best interests of both whites and blacks had required the maintenance of a system of racial adjustment controlled by the whites. Through the plantation-slavery method of racial regulation, the planters had "developed a fairly efficient body of laborers out of a horde of savages," and had made the most efficient use of "ignorant and slothful labor"; but, even more important, this system had served as a school for the masses of blacks, training "a savage race to a certain degree of fitness for life in the Anglo-Saxon community."[2]

Although Phillips conceded that the plantation-slavery system had brought certain disadvantages both for society and for the individual, he emphasized that there were disadvantages for whites as well as blacks, and that the benefits of the system far outweighed its defects. That regime kept money scarce and population sparse in the Old South, and in its business aspects it had as many drawbacks as attractions; but, to Phillips, all this was more than compensated for by the fact that it "kept the main body of labor controlled, provisioned and mobile. Above all it maintained order and a notable degree of harmony in a community where confusion worse confounded would not have been far to seek."[3] In

2 The quotations in this paragraph (in order) are from the following writings by Phillips: *American Negro Slavery* (New York, 1918) 343; "The Plantation as A Civilizing Factor," *The Sewanee Review*, XII, 262 (July 1904); "Conservatism and Progress in the Cotton Belt," *The South Atlantic Quarterly*, III, 3 (January 1904); "Introduction," John R. Commons, *et al.*, eds., *A Documentary History of American Industrial Society* (10v., Cleveland, 1909) I, 71. Phillips referred to the "inherited inequality of the races and the unfitness of negroes to conduct white men's government" (*The American Historical Review*, X, 698 [April 1905]).

3 *American Negro Slavery*, 401.

a similar vein, Phillips granted that the plantation-slavery system had "wrought the initial and irreparable misfortune of causing the Negroes to be imported," that as a training school it contained no provision for the graduation of its "students," that it harbored cruelty and imposed especial injustice and hardship upon "the exceptional 'person of color.' "[4] But here again, the picture he drew had many more bright spots than dark: the relation of planter and slave, he stated, "was largely shaped by a sense of propriety, proportion and cooperation"; the rule of the planters was "benevolent in intent and on the whole beneficial in effect"; the plantation system at its best produced "considerate and cordial, courteous and charming men and women, white and black."[5] Perhaps the most accurate summary of Phillips' evaluation of the "plantation scheme of life" is the one with which he closed his best known book, *Life and Labor in the Old South*: that scheme of life had its imperfections, but "its face was on the whole so gracious that modifications might easily be lamented, and projects of revolution regarded with a shudder."[6]

This "plantation scheme of life" had been overthrown in the Civil War, but Phillips did not set forth systematically and in detail an interpretation of the causes of the war. There were, however, scattered references to the subject throughout his writings, and near the end of his life, in 1932, he delivered a series of lectures which he entitled "The Course of the South to Secession." From such sources one can form a picture of his explanation of the coming of war.

Expressing his disagreement with Rhodes' statement that slavery was the sole cause of the Civil War, Phillips asserted that the explanation was more complex, and that the "plantation system," "climatic conditions," and other such factors must all be taken into account without singling out any one as *the* cause.[7] But at the heart of these complex factors, just as at the heart of the plantation-slavery system, he found the question of race. The prime unifying force in the Old South (and the New South), the essence of

---

[4] The quotations (in order) are found in: *ibid.*, 343; Commons, *et al.*, eds., *Documentary History*, I, 100.

[5] The quotations (in order) are found in *American Negro Slavery*, 296, 328, 514.

[6] Ulrich B. Phillips, *Life and Labor in the Old South* (Boston, 1929) 366.

[7] *The American Historical Review*, XXXIV, 465 (April 1929).

Southernism and Southern nationalism, and the basis for the doctrine of Southern rights, was for Phillips the resolve on the part of Southern whites that the South should be and should remain a "white man's country." This, he declared, was the "central theme" of Southern history.[8]

One gets the clear impression that it was Phillips' opinion that the South would never have gone down the pathway to secession and war had it not been for the abolitionists of the North; their attacks forced Southerners against their inclination into an unyielding and rigid defense of the institution of slavery:

The abolitionists made certain false charges against the Southern system. In repelling these calumnies the Southern leaders thought it advisable to ignore all the bad features of slavery and deny their existence, to praise the institution as beneficial to all parties concerned, and to advocate its permanent maintenance instead of its gradual disestablishment. This change in the Southern attitude was to a large degree involuntary. . . . With the motive of preserving the lives and the welfare of both white and black, they [the Southern Whites] avoided and frowned upon criticisms of slavery.[9]

In particular, Phillips charged that the abolitionists were ultimately responsible for the failure of the South to get rid of slavery on its own initiative. Had it not been for the violent abolitionist agitation, he argued, "it is fairly probable that within the nineteenth century slavery would have been disestablished in some peaceable way in response to the demand of public opinion in the South."[10]

Not only had Northern abolitionists attacked the South, Northerners had also, Phillips charged, grasped the lion's share of federal appropriations after the 1830's and, by means of tariffs, had kept Southern markets in their hands. In view of the outcome of the election of 1860, the South faced the alternative, in his opinion, of submitting to the prospect of "early oppression" or of seceding

[8] See: "The Central Theme of Southern History," *The American Historical Review*, xxxiv, 30-43 (October 1928); E. Merton Coulter, ed., *The Course of the South to Secession* (New York, 1939) *passim*.

[9] *The South Atlantic Quarterly*, iii, 3-4 (January 1904). For a similar point of view, see *The Course of the South to Secession*, 110.

[10] *The South Atlantic Quarterly*, iii, 8. For the expression of a similar sentiment by Phillips, see his "Georgia and State Rights," The American Historical Association, *Annual Report for the Year 1901* (Washington, 1902) 158.

immediately. "The South alone," he declared, "stood in danger from a roughshod majority. The North could not possibly have had a reasonable fear of aggression by a crushing block of Southern votes."[11] In short, it would seem that Phillips held the North and Northerners primarily responsible for the Civil War.

The difference in emphasis in the writings of Phillips and in those of William E. Dodd or William P. Trent was striking. Instead of criticism of the institution of slavery on humanitarian grounds, Phillips presented what could be interpreted as a defense of the institution on the grounds of the social necessity for racial guidance and control; instead of disapproval of the theory and practice of secession, he placed blame for sectional conflict and war upon the North, especially the Northern abolitionists; instead of praise for the South of Thomas Jefferson, he expressed admiration for the white planters of the Civil War generation. Other Southern students of Dunning had demonstrated sympathy for the white planters in the Reconstruction era; Phillips broadened this sympathy to include the *ante-bellum* period as well. He even dedicated one of his volumes to the Southern planters as a group in words accurately portraying the spirit in which he interpreted the Old South:

To The Dominant Class of The South Who In The Piping Ante-Bellum Time Schooled Multitudes White And Black To The Acceptance Of Higher Standards Who In War Time Proved Staunch And Who In The Troublous Upheaval And Readjustment Which Followed Wrought More Sanely And More Wisely Than The World Yet Knows.[12]

Phillips occupies a significant place in the story of changing attitudes toward the Civil War. More than any other single historian, he was responsible for the revision of the picture of the plantation-slavery system presented in the pages of Rhodes and of such Southerners as William P. Trent. There may well have been, as recent critics have suggested, certain limitations in Phillips' research, but he could speak about the Old South with more authority than any other historian of his day because of his extensive

---

[11] *The South in the Building of the Nation*, IV, 395. See similar ideas in *ibid.*, IV, 421, and in Phillips' volume, *The Life of Robert Toombs* (New York, 1913) 195.

[12] Ulrich B. Phillips, *A History of Transportation in the Eastern Cotton Belt To 1860* (New York, 1908) *v*.

investigations of the sources. He was, by common consent, the outstanding historian of his generation of Southerners, and his influence, both as a writer and as a teacher at some of the leading universities of the country (primarily the University of Wisconsin, the University of Michigan, and Yale), was great. For his sympathetic portrait of the *ante-bellum* South, he won the acceptance of many historians, non-Southern as well as Southern.[18]

In terms of the problem of striking a balance between the point of view of the nation and that of the section, the role of Phillips' scholarship might be described as a "corrective." His picture of plantation slavery, based upon extensive research in Southern sources, served to "balance," one might conclude, the less sympathetic picture by Rhodes and other non-Southern historians. But at the time of Phillips' death in 1934, developments were under way which, in the opinion of many observers, were to carry some Southern historians well beyond the limits of "corrective" scholarship.

[18] Some of the clearest indications of the influence of Phillips' interpretation of the Old South is furnished by the reviews of his volumes; the reviews are listed in Everett E. Edwards' excellent bibliography, "A Bibliography of the Writings of Professor Ulrich Bonnell Phillips," *Agricultural History*, VIII, 196-218 (October 1934).

Some Southern Historians
since the Early 1930's

By the 1930's, both historical scholarship in the South and the writing of Southern history were entering upon a new phase which might be described as a coming-of-age. This new phase (part of a general quickening of intellectual endeavor in the South) was marked by the growth of graduate schools of history in the South; the University of North Carolina, Vanderbilt University, and other centers emerged where students could be given professional training as historians without leaving the South. Similarly, the history of the South became firmly established as a recognized field of study for scholars in American history; it was estimated that by 1940 nearly a hundred universities and colleges were offering courses in the history of the South (this compares with an estimate of six colleges and universities offering such courses in 1913).[14] The primary centers for the study of Southern history and for the training of Southern graduate students were, by the end of the 1930's, not at Johns Hopkins, Columbia, or the University of Chicago but in the South. The capstone to this coming-of-age was the formation in 1934 of the Southern Historical Association (with a membership made up almost entirely of trained historians), which began in the next year the publication of *The Journal of Southern History*. This organization and its journal soon became the principal focus for historical studies in the South and about the South. Historians of the generation to which Phillips belonged now saw the fruition of many of their pioneer efforts, and a younger generation of Southern historians continued to build upon the scholarly foundations previously laid.

And yet, promising as were these events for the future of his-

[14] Wendell H. Stephenson, "A Half Century of Southern Historical Scholarship," *The Journal of Southern History*, XI, 7 (February 1945), and "Herbert B. Adams and Southern Historical Scholarship at the Johns Hopkins University," *Maryland Historical Magazine*, XLII, 9-13 (March 1947).

torical studies in the South, they served to sharpen one horn of the dilemma facing native-son historians: they heightened the possibility that Southern-born historians, trained in the South, writing the history of the South at Southern universities, and using predominantly Southern sources might become as "biased" in their own way as were the "outsiders" against whom they complained. The precedent set in similar circumstances by some New England historians and by some Western historians who wrote the history of the United States as the history of their own particular sections did not offer much ground for optimism. And, by an irony of history, certain developments in the United States after the First World War made it all the more difficult for Southern historians to escape a narrowly sectional outlook—developments which resulted in an increase of tension between some Southerners and some non-Southerners.

By 1920, the South had traveled down the "road to reunion"— the road of sectional reconciliation and reintegration with the life of the nation. "Reunion," in this sense, did not imply that the South and the rest of the nation saw eye to eye—or should see eye to eye—on every disputed question. It did mean that the measure of agreement between Southerners and non-Southerners was great enough to permit the resolution of differences on issues affecting the section and the nation within the framework afforded by a common nationalism. But after the First World War, various currents and tensions in American life placed a strain upon the sentiments of sectional reconciliation and nationalism which Wilson, Trent, and other Southerners of their generation had displayed. Under the pressure of these tensions, some Southerners came to consider their problems in terms of the South *versus* the nation, and some non-Southerners came to consider their problems in terms of the nation *versus* the South.

These strains and tensions could be seen in several different areas. One area concerned the economic relations of the South with the nation. Much attention was focused on various aspects of this question in the years after the First World War: the agricultural depression of the 1920's as it affected Southern farmers; the problem of farm tenancy; the increasing industrialization of the South; the role of such programs of the federal government as the Tennessee Valley Authority; and the issues encompassed in the designation of the South by President Roosevelt as "the nation's number one economic problem." Out of the consideration of such issues as these, two dissimilar groups of Southern intellectuals raised their voices in protest against current economic trends.

One was the "Nashville Agrarian Movement," which took form around 1930 with the publication of the symposium, *I'll Take My Stand*.[15] Members of this group urged their fellow Southerners to resist the encroachment of the industrial economy and civilization which had swept over the rest of the nation, and to return to the agrarian civilization and to the agrarian subsistence type of economy which, they asserted, had characterized the Old South. The evidence seems to indicate that the Nashville movement was confined entirely to intellectuals, and that even among Southern intellectuals it was decidedly a minority movement composed primarily of individuals of quite conservative political and economic views. There was, however, a second group of protesters made up of the Beardian or Parringtonian type of "progressives" who were hostile to many of the practices of "big business." They claimed kinship not with the Nashville group but with the Populists of the 1890's. This second group of protesters did not form a separate "movement" nor did they specifically urge a return to the conditions prevailing in the Old South. Instead, they vigorously criticized the "New South" spirit and program and insisted that the South's economic difficulties were due primarily to its status as an exploited "colony" of Northeastern business interests.

In a second region of society embracing what might be called "folkways" or "culture," tensions also appeared. The contrasts in society and culture within the United States, between farm and city and between the various sections, formed one basis in the 1920's from which H.L. Mencken and his followers could satirize many ideas, many practices, and many persons; frequently the individuals or groups satirized lived outside the metropolitan centers of the East. The famous Scopes trial at Dayton, Tennessee, in 1925 brought down upon the people of Tennessee, and upon

---

[15] The history of this movement is recounted in Thomas J. Pressly, "Agrarianism: An Autopsy," *Sewanee Review*, XLIX, 145-163 (April-June 1941).

Southerners in general, the full torrent of the Mencken-inspired scorn. The Scopes trial was the most publicized of several such events which were interpreted by some Southerners as "attacks" upon Southern life; these Southerners reacted by extolling the virtues of the South and condemning outsiders (the twelve Southern intellectuals who contributed to *I'll Take My Stand*, for example, stated that it was the Scopes trial which made them include in their volume a condemnation of "science"—as an ally of industrialism).

Probably more important than either of the fields mentioned above as a source of tension between Southerners and non-Southerners was a new dispute over the role of the Negro in Southern life. It has been suggested, as we have seen, that one of the bases for the reunion of North and South was the widespread agreement by the 1890's that the attempt of the North to solve the "Negro question" in Reconstruction had been a failure and that henceforth the problem must be left primarily in the hands of white Southerners.[16] This *modus vivendi*, however, had been challenged before the First World War, and after 1920 there were signs that it was breaking down and that the "Negro question" was once more becoming a major issue which separated many white Southerners from many individuals in other sections of the country.

The *modus vivendi* collapsed presumably because the fundamental conditions upon which it rested were rapidly changing after the First World War. For one thing, the life of Negroes in the United States was changing in many respects. With the First World War, the migration of Negroes from the South reached a high peak; outside the South, Negroes could and did organize into such associations as the National Association for the Advancement of Colored People. Through this association and through their own normal voting strength concentrated in large urban areas, Negroes became a force in national and local politics. In addition, a "renaissance" was underway among Negro intellectuals (sometimes called the "Harlem Renaissance"), marked by outstanding achievements in many of the arts. In addition, at the same time that the life of Negroes was changing,

[16] See above, chapter four, note 3.

the attitudes of many whites toward the Negro were also shifting. This became especially marked in the 1930's when the New Deal reform movement was the dominant force in American political life, for one phase of this reform movement was the effort to better conditions for Negroes. Toward the end of the 1930's, the conflict of ideologies between democracy and totalitarianism (in which it was argued that a democratic society fosters the free development of the individual) gave impetus to this move for improvement of conditions.

By the 1930's, it was clear that although the white South was altering its attitudes toward the Negro (and altering them, from its own viewpoint, with considerable speed), it was not altering them as rapidly as a segment of public opinion outside the South was changing. The resulting differences of opinion between many Southerners and many non-Southerners were highlighted in a dramatic fashion in the Scottsboro case of the early 1930's. To some Southerners, Scottsboro seemed a deliberate inflammatory "crusade" against the South by irresponsible elements for their own selfish ends (including members of the Communist Party in the United States); to some non-Communist non-Southerners, Scottsboro seemed, whatever the personalities or organizations involved, an instance in which white Southerners were denying elementary justice to Negroes. Following Scottsboro, there was a succession of other incidents involving "chain gangs" and lynchings, and (with the advent of the Second World War) the question of a national Fair Employment Practices Commission was debated. Such incidents both revealed and added to the tension on the question of the role of the Negro in Southern life. From this question stemmed the most tangible evidence of the reviving South *versus* non-South hostility—the attempt to create a Southern political party in the presidential election campaign of 1948.

As a result of these various developments, there occurred in the South a season of reexamination of the relationship between the South and the nation and of reformulation of attitudes toward the nation. Such seasons had been periodic in the South since the 1820's, and just as in previous periods of this type, individual Southerners were not all agreed in the stand they took. But it was in such an atmosphere that some (not all) Southern-born historians expressed interpretations of the causes of the Civil War characterized chiefly by their ardent defense of the South and by their sharp criticism of non-Southerners. Such interpretations were voiced with particular emphasis by historians Charles W. Ramsdell and Frank L. Owsley.

Charles W. Ramsdell, born in Texas in 1877, had studied, like Ulrich B. Phillips, at Columbia under William A. Dunning; unlike Phillips, however, he spent his long teaching career, from 1906 until his death in 1942, in the South at the University of Texas. Whereas the placing of blame for the Civil War upon Northerners had occupied a fairly minor role in the voluminous writings of Phillips, this theme was prominent in the less extensive publications of Ramsdell.

Writing in 1937, Ramsdell located the responsibility for the Civil War, in the sense of the immediate outbreak of hostilities, specifically upon the shoulders of Abraham Lincoln. Developing in detail a thesis which had been expressed as far back as 1861, he charged that Lincoln had decided on war in the Fort Sumter crisis and had deliberately "maneuvered the Confederates into firing the first shot in order that they, rather than he, should take the blame of beginning bloodshed."[17] In Ramsdell's argument, the policy of Lincoln toward Fort Sumter left no alternative but war; to the objection that war might have been averted had the Confederates allowed Sumter to be provisioned, he replied that the "Confederate government could not, without yielding the principle of independence, abate its claims to the fort."[18] The parallel claim which a defender of Lincoln might have urged—that the federal government could not, without yielding the principle of nationality and/or constitutional rule, abate its claims to the fort —was not discussed.

Just as Lincoln could have prevented the outbreak of war had he followed a different policy, so too, in Ramsdell's opinion, Northerners could have greatly lessened the sectional conflict which preceded secession had they ceased their agitation of the slavery question. And that agitation was needless, he insisted, be-

[17] Charles W. Ramsdell, "Lincoln and Fort Sumter," *The Journal of Southern History*, III, 285 (August 1937).
[18] *ibid.*, III, 263.

cause slavery would have died out had it been left alone. Phillips had suggested that it was "fairly probable" that slavery would have been disestablished in the nineteenth century had it not been for the abolitionists. Ramsdell, in turn, worked out in great detail the argument that "slavery had about reached its zenith by 1860 and must shortly have begun to decline," whether or not the Civil War had occurred—basing his case primarily upon the contention that slavery had reached its limits both in profits and in available land which would support its products.[19] He admitted that the question of whether slavery would have disappeared without the Civil War was a matter of speculation and that such matters were, in his words, "dangerous ground for the historian." But at a later date, he restated his thesis and used language yet more uncompromising:

There can be little doubt that the institution of chattel slavery had reached its peak by 1860 and that within a comparatively short time it would have begun to decline and eventually have been abolished by the Southerners themselves.[20]

The Civil War was thus unnecessary, in Ramsdell's opinion, and he insisted that it was not worth what it had cost. Since he thought that slavery would inevitably have been abolished by Southerners themselves, the destruction of slavery as a result of the war was not for him a matter of great import. Similarly, he was not impressed with the claim that the preservation of the Union was tremendously important. Why was the Union so valuable, he asked, that it was worth the costs of the war? If the Union government had not "coerced" the seceded states, the most that could have been expected was

that two or three of the border slave states would have decided to join the cotton Confederacy, or that adjustments of boundary or customs lines might have given trouble for some years after 1861.[21]

Whereas historians in the "nationalist tradition" had maintained that the Civil War had solved certain problems, Ramsdell insisted that it had created a whole host of new problems; and, like

[19] Charles W. Ramsdell, "The Natural Limits of Slavery Expansion," *The Mississippi Valley Historical Review*, XVI, 171 (October 1929).

[20] Charles W. Ramsdell, "The Changing Interpretations of the Civil War," *The Journal of Southern History*, III, 23 (February 1937).

[21] *ibid.*, III, 22.

the Beardians, he ascribed most of those problems to the fact that the war had removed the planter opposition to industrialism. Was there not ground, he demanded, for "the tragic conclusion that it [the Civil War] accomplished little which was not otherwise obtainable?"[22]

Ramsdell became a leader in the rapidly growing historical profession in the South. One of the organizers, and one of the first presidents, of the Southern Historical Association (he had previously, in 1928, been president of the Mississippi Valley Historical Association), he was also one of the guiding spirits in planning the ten-volume cooperative *A History of the South* which began publication after the Second World War. His writings, compared to those of Phillips, were neither numerous nor lengthy, but he seems to have played an important role in spreading among some historians the assumption that slavery would inevitably have disappeared after 1860 even had there been no war, and the interpretation that Lincoln deliberately provoked war at Fort Sumter in 1861.

Ramsdell did not formulate an interpretation which was as extreme in placing upon the North the blame for causing the Civil War as were the views of Frank L. Owsley. Owsley was younger by more than a decade than Ramsdell, and his historical writings did not begin to appear until the 1920's. (Perhaps the fact that a younger historian was more drastically anti-North than Ramsdell was in itself an indication of the increasing sectional tension after 1920.) Born in Alabama in 1890, Owsley graduated from the Alabama Polytechnic Institute and then studied under William E. Dodd at the University of Chicago. Although not a student of Dunning's, he had words of praise for Dunning and his associates since under that group, in his words, "the Southern renascence began and the holiness of the Northern legend was first challenged."[23] In the South of the 1920's and 1930's, Owsley raised his voice against what he depicted as Northern injustice. He was one of the Nashville Agrarians and contributed an essay to *I'll Take My Stand*; reacting strongly against the role of North-

[22] *ibid.*, 27.
[23] Frank L. Owsley, "The Irrepressible Conflict," in Twelve Southerners, *I'll Take My Stand* (New York, 1930) 66.

erners in the Scottsboro case, he charged in an article in *The American Review* that this represented the North's third "crusade" against the South (the other two having been the abolitionist agitation and the Civil War itself). His writings on the causes of the Civil War expressed the most drastic pro-South and anti-North sentiments among Southern historians in the twentieth century.

Vindication of the South was Owsley's stated purpose in discussing the causes of the Civil War: to "point out the untruth of the self-righteous Northern legend which makes the South the war criminal."[24] In carrying out this purpose, his method was to fasten upon the North the guilt for causing the war (and for nearly every other aspect of American society which he disliked). His description of the "North" matched in villainy (although it is important to note that it did not surpass) the picture of the "slavepower" drawn by Herbert Aptheker. The North, Owsley charged,

defeated the South in war, crushed and humiliated it in peace, and waged against it a war of intellectual and spiritual conquest. In this conquest the North fixed upon the South the stigma of war guilt, of treason, and thereby shook the faith of its people in their way of living and in their philosophy of life.[25]

Owsley's interpretation of Northern war guilt was set in a framework of ideas which might be described as a synthesis of the views of the Confederates of the 1860's and the Beardian economic interpretation (and his ideas illustrated the ease with which the Beardian viewpoint could be used to support the Confederate viewpoint). Describing a conflict between an agrarian South and an industrial North, Owsley emphasized not so much the clash of economic systems in themselves as the competition between the two divergent ways of life which, in his view, grew out of the differing economies. There was an "irrepressible conflict," he maintained, between the agrarian way of life and that of an industrial society, and like the Confederates of the 1860's, he insisted that the moral issue of slavery was not a part of this conflict. Citing the views of Phillips, Owsley argued that slavery was primarily a question of race rather than of ethics—since Negroes of the Old South were "cannibals and barbarians," a system of racial dis-

[24] *ibid.*, 68.   [25] *ibid.*, 66.

cipline was necessary; the moral issue of slavery was branded by him as a "red herring" which had been drawn across the trail of the causes of the Civil War.[26] Not slavery but the different economic-political structure of the rival sections was involved in the irrepressible conflict; whereas the New England and Middle Atlantic states were by 1860 fast becoming an industrial "plutocracy," he declared that the Old South had a sound economic basis for free government.[27]

The cause of the Civil War, Owsley asserted, was the "egocentric sectionalism" of the industrial plutocratic North; failing to observe the "comity of sections," it had insisted upon forcing its way of life upon the South. Like Phillips, Ramsdell, and the Southerners of the 1860's, Owsley singled out the abolitionists for particular condemnation; their crusade was not just the work of a small number of fanatics, he argued, for many of the intellectual, moral, and political leaders of the North were their "political fellow travelers."[28] The philosophy of the North, he declared, was intolerant, crusading, and standardizing: "The South had to be crushed out; it was in the way; it impeded the progress of the machine; so Juggernaut drove his car across the South."[29]

The effort to vindicate the South through history seemed to enlist progressively more rather than less of the energies of Southern historians in the 1930's and the 1940's—and the themes emphasized in this effort were those which had been urged by Phillips, Ramsdell, and Owsley. Bitter condemnation of the abolitionists as a primary cause of the sectional conflict and the Civil War was the text of the volume, *The Slavery Controversy, 1831-1860*, published in 1939 by a young Southern historian, Arthur Lloyd Young. The vilification of Lincoln as the diabolically clever instigator of war in the Fort Sumter episode reached lengths that would apparently be difficult to surpass in John S. Tilley's *Lincoln Takes Command* published in 1941; while Tilley was a Southern lawyer rather than a trained historian, his volume carried a foreword in commendatory language by a Southern-born historian, Avery O. Craven.

[26] The two quotations in this sentence (in order) are taken from *ibid.*, 77 and 69.
[27] Frank L. Owsley, "The Fundamental Cause of the Civil War: Egocentric Sectionalism," *The Journal of Southern History*, VII, 4-6 (February 1941).
[28] *ibid.*, VII, 16-18.　　　　　　　[29] Twelve Southerners, *I'll Take My Stand*, 91.

Paralleling these volumes, defense of the South by attacking the North formed the theme of several of the addresses by the presidents of the Southern Historical Association in the 1930's and 1940's. The "Southernism" of these historians seemed to outweigh their obviously diverse views on other questions. The presidential address of the association in 1936 was delivered by Ramsdell, and in 1940 by Owsley; excerpts from both of these speeches which indicate their general anti-Northern tenor have already been cited above. In 1941, President Benjamin B. Kendrick (a former student of Dunning and born in Georgia) declared that if the South were the nation's number one economic problem, the reason lay in the fact that for three centuries it had been a "colony"; and Kendrick, in general a Beardian progressive in outlook, directed bitter criticism at Northern industrial interests for their part in forging a colonial status for the South.[30] This theme of the colonial status of the South was broadened in the presidential address of 1942 prepared by Albert B. Moore (born in Alabama and with graduate study at the University of Chicago). The South occupied a colonial position, asserted Moore, not only in the economic system but also in the "psychology, sentiment, culture, and politics" of the nation; for this situation, he too blamed the North, insisting that it had been engaged for the past one hundred years (and was still so engaged) in "reconstructing" the South.[31] The 1945 presidential address was devoted by Fletcher M. Green (born in Georgia, with graduate training at the University of North Carolina) to combating assertions of abolitionists and Northern historians that the Old South had been aristocratic in its political structure and practice.[32]

So pervasive was the attempt to defend the South in some of the addresses by the presidents of this association of historians that they were described as "polemics" by a member of the association, H.C. Nixon, who was himself an historian and a Southerner (and who had contributed an essay to I'll Take My Stand). Some of

[30] Benjamin B. Kendrick, "The Colonial Status of the South," The Journal of Southern History, VIII, 3-22 (February 1942).

[31] Albert B. Moore, "One Hundred Years of Reconstruction of the South," The Journal of Southern History, IX, 153-180 (May 1943).

[32] Fletcher M. Green, "Democracy in the Old South," The Journal of Southern History, XII, 3-23 (February 1946).

the presidential addresses, Nixon declared, fitted into the pattern of vindication of the South set by Southern historians shortly after the Civil War, making "point after point of a rebuttal or antithesis" and attacking "a Yankee thesis."[33] The contents of the files of *The Journal of Southern History*, he wrote in 1950, both reflected and supported "the interlinked doctrines of regional patriotism and conservatism. The Dixiecrats could find comfort in reading a number of them."[34]

It is not meant to suggest, and this should be emphasized, that all Southern-born historians teaching in the South shared the viewpoints of Ramsdell, Owsley, or the presidents of the Southern Historical Association here quoted. Just as Southerners were divided in their reaction to the vexed questions of sectionalism and nationalism after the First World War, so too were Southern-born historians divided in their attitudes toward the causes and character of the Civil War. As will be indicated presently, there were apparently a number of Southern-born historians who shared the "revisionist" viewpoints, and these viewpoints did not generally emphasize vindication of the South to the same degree as did Owsley's writings. In addition, there were some Southern historians whose scholarship seemed more or less completely free of any primary or overriding emphasis upon sectional vindication. In contrast to Ramsdell and Owsley, for example, Henry T. Shanks and Joseph Carlyle Sitterson (both born in the South and both teaching there) demonstrated in their respective studies of state secession published in the 1930's that they could write dispassionately of the crisis of 1861 and of the events leading up to it.[35] Neither Shanks nor Sitterson set forth a full and explicit state-

[33] H.C. Nixon, "Paths to the Past: the Presidential Addresses of the Southern Historical Association," *The Journal of Southern History*, XVI, 35 (February 1950).

[34] H.C. Nixon, "Southern Regionalism Limited," *The Virginia Quarterly Review*, XXVI, 164-165 (Spring 1950); see also p. 170. Another Southern-born historian teaching at Yale University, David M. Potter, expressed an opinion of the articles in *The Journal of Southern History* (other than presidential addresses) different from Nixon's; the articles appearing in the *Journal* from 1935 to 1949, Potter wrote, did not show perpetuation of old emotional attitudes nor were they concerned with sectional vindication (David M. Potter, "An Appraisal of Fifteen Years of the Journal of Southern History, 1935-1949," *The Journal of Southern History*, XVI, 28-29 [February 1950]).

[35] Henry T. Shanks, *The Secession Movement in Virginia 1847-1861* (Richmond, 1934); Joseph Carlyle Sitterson, *The Secession Movement in North Carolina* (Chapel Hill, N.C., 1939).

ment regarding the causes of the war, but at the least they apparently did not feel it necessary to place direct and exclusive blame upon the Yankees. In the same decade, Robert S. Cotterill (born in Kentucky and long a resident of Florida) in his history of *The Old South* discussed the coming of the Civil War in a spirit quite similar to that of Edward Channing and other historians in the "nationalist tradition."[36] Like Channing, Cotterill pictured the struggle of the 1860's as a "War for Southern Independence," and he found its causes in the development of "Southern nationalism" beginning around 1820; he did not seem to allocate guilt for this development upon any group of individuals, North or South.

One of the latest and most impressive demonstrations of the fact that some Southern-born historians could write the history of their section without being narrowly "sectional" in their viewpoint was made by Charles S. Sydnor (who was born in Georgia and had lived in the South for most of his life). In a volume published in 1948, Sydnor discussed *The Development of Southern Sectionalism, 1819-1848*—a topic which might be expected to tax the powers of the most objectively-minded historian. His declared purpose in this book was to seek the causes and to trace the development of Southern sectionalism without either defending or condemning its emergence.[37] That he was notably successful in this difficult task he had set for himself was apparently the general conclusion of both many Southern and many non-Southern historians. This achievement owed significance to the fact that some observers, Southern and non-Southern alike, considered Sydnor one of the most distinguished of present-day Southern historians.

Perhaps the state of historical scholarship in the South and the attitudes of Southern-born historians toward the Civil War by the 1950's were best symbolized in the cooperative *A History of the South* which was in process of publication in that decade (it was in reality *A History of the South* by Southerners since all the authors were Southern-born). From 1947 through 1951, five out of the proposed ten volumes had been published. A comparison of

[36] Robert S. Cotterill, *The Old South* (Glendale, Calif., 1936).
[37] Charles S. Sydnor, *The Development of Southern Sectionalism, 1819-1848* (*A History of the South*, v) (Baton Rouge, La., 1948) *xi*.

these five volumes with the only other comparable large-scale history of the South, *The South in the Building of the Nation* (13 v., Richmond, 1909-1913), furnished convincing evidence of the tremendous advance in historical scholarship in the South and about the South in the twentieth century.

At the same time, the volumes published so far seemed to reflect dissimilar attitudes concerning the history of the South and the Civil War crisis. Through 1951, three out of the four volumes which would cover the history of the South from 1819 to 1877 had been published, the three volumes being the work of two historians. One of the two historians, E. Merton Coulter of Georgia, whose two volumes embraced the years 1861 to 1877, seemed to share some of the viewpoints and general outlook which had characterized Ramsdell and Owsley. For example, he blamed the inauguration of war at Fort Sumter solely upon Lincoln (the question at issue, in Coulter's discussion, was simply whether Lincoln was a "bungler" or a "cunning villain"), and he insisted that had there been no Civil War, "What good the war produced would have come with time in an orderly way; the bad would not have come at all."[38] Coulter, particularly in the volume on Reconstruction, appeared to orient his historical scholarship around a defense of the actions of white Southerners against criticism by non-Southerners. The second of the two authors was Sydnor; although his volume, since it covered the years 1819 to 1848, did not deal directly with the causes of the Civil War, it seemed to reflect a decidedly different approach to the history of the South. In contrast to Coulter, Sydnor, as has been suggested, seemed to be concerned neither to defend the South nor to criticize it, but to understand both the Southern development and point of view and the national development and point of view.

Thus, at the middle of the twentieth century as at its beginning, Southern-born historians held diverse viewpoints toward the history of their section and toward the Civil War. Southern scholarship in the twentieth century made available to historians a large

[38] E. Merton Coulter, *The South During Reconstruction, 1865-1877* (*A History of the South*, VIII) (Baton Rouge, La., 1947) 1. For Coulter's discussion of Lincoln and Fort Sumter, see *The Confederate States of America, 1861-1865* (*A History of the South*, VII) (Baton Rouge, La., 1950) 37-38.

body of Southern source material, and this was undoubtedly a factor in the spread of interpretations of the causes of the Civil War more sympathetic to the South than had been the "nationalist tradition." In addition, Southern scholarship itself (like scholarship outside the South) was affected to some degree by the increasing tension between the South and the rest of the nation; and, matching the extreme anti-South views of some non-Southern historians, some Southern historians formulated explanations of the causes of the Civil War which harked back in spirit to the vindications of the South published in the 1860's.

CHAPTER SEVEN
"THE REPRESSIBLE CONFLICT"

The Beginnings of "Revisionism"

THE first half of the twentieth century, despite the optimistic expectations of many individuals in its early years, turned out to be an era of wars and rumors of wars. In such a period of international tensions, the opinions of some historians on war causation in general and on the causes of the Civil War in particular were to shift appreciably. Certain distinctive attitudes toward the causes of the Civil War became evident after 1920, and in the 1930's and 1940's these attitudes, known under the general name "revisionist," won wide support among historians. These "revisionist" viewpoints, like those of the Beardian progressives and of the twentieth century defenders of the South, were in part a conscious reaction against previous interpretations of the causes of the Civil War and, in particular, against the "nationalist tradition."

In the concluding paragraph of her doctoral dissertation published in 1921, Mary Scrugham suggested that a change was taking place in the attitude of the public toward war, and she predicted that this shift in outlook would have a pronounced effect upon the interpretation of the causes of the Civil War:

Public opinion is now turning against war—and especially against civil war, as a just and desirable method of settling disputes between civilized people. Because of this new trend of public opinion, the civilized world may yet reverse its present decision on the Civil War. It is entirely probable that the public of 1961 may hold that there need have been no appeal from the ballot to the bullet in 1861, had the American people of that day possessed sufficient political sagacity to distinguish between appearance and reality.[1]

Had Miss Scrugham used the date 1941 instead of 1961, and had she written "many historians" instead of "the public," her statement would stand as a remarkable prophecy of the rise of the "revisionist" interpretation. And she did more than simply predict

---

[1] Mary Scrugham, *The Peaceable Americans of 1860-1861: A Study in Public Opinion* (New York, 1921) 124-125.

that a new approach to the Civil War would be formulated; her volume was the first important statement in the twentieth century by an historian reflecting the distinctive outlook which was to characterize that "revisionist" approach.

This outlook was based upon the general opinion of war which Miss Scrugham herself displayed in the quotation just cited. On the one hand, she expressed a feeling of hostility to war, a feeling that war was not "a just and desirable method of settling disputes between civilized people" (this in contrast to the exaltation of war by Theodore Roosevelt or some other members of his generation). At the same time, complementing this feeling of hostility, she indicated her opinion that if men had only kept their eyes on "reality" in 1861, war could have been avoided. The implication here, and confirmed elsewhere in Miss Scrugham's book, was that "reality" in the universe made for peace, and there was a passing reference in the volume to the present era (i.e., *circa* 1921) as one which was "witnessing the dawn of universal peace."[2] Thus, war was not only undesirable, it was also unnecessary if human beings avoided "appearance" and faced facts.

This perspective on war provided Miss Scrugham with an approach to the Civil War different from that which had characterized most previous interpretations. She was primarily interested in, and sympathetic to, those individuals whom she described as "peaceable Americans" or "neutrals" in the crisis of 1860-1861. In her opinion, this group had been large, for she stated that four-fifths of the American people in 1860-1861 favored "compromise" rather than civil war or dissolution of the Union.[3] She minimized the alleged severity of the sectional conflict which, in most other interpretations of the Civil War, had formed the background for explaining the outbreak of hostilities (she wrote, for example, of "the basic lack of antagonism between the southern and the northern people," and denied that "there was basic antagonism between the northern and the southern people in regard to the slavery question in the southern states").[4]

The war, she declared, had not stemmed from a long-standing irrepressible sectional conflict nor had it been inevitable; instead,

[2] *ibid.*, 81.   [3] *ibid.*, 85.
[4] The two quotations (in order) are from *ibid.*, 60 and 58.

its causes were to be explained primarily in terms of the events of 1860-1861, and in terms of the actions of "extremists" and partisan politicians on each side, who had "willed" an irrepressible conflict (and she criticized Rhodes and other historians who had presented a different account of an irrepressible conflict).[5] The overwhelming majority of the American people had wanted peace in 1861, ran Miss Scrugham's account, but extremist politicians for their own selfish ends had aroused emotions, had cleverly obscured the "real" issues, and had manipulated events in such a fashion that war came.

This interpretation of the role of "extremists" in the events of 1860-1861 placed stress upon the importance of human emotions, and Miss Scrugham at times employed what she called "psychological explanations" of events, using such terms as the "instinct of counter-attack," a "suggestible state of mind," and the "law of the mental unity of crowds" (the citations in her volume contained references to such books as Graham Wallas, *Human Nature in Politics*, Gustave Le Bon, *The Crowd*, William McDougall, *Social Psychology*, and Edward L. Thorndike, *Educational Psychology*).[6] Underlying her discussion of the influence of emotions in the crisis of 1860-1861 was a predicated dichotomy between "emotions" and "war," on the one hand, and "realism" and "peace," on the other: the reality of that period, in her opinion, was the lack of differences worth fighting about between North and South, and the desire of the people for peace. Had emotions not carried the day, her discussion implied, "realistic" individuals would have favored compromise and would have been loath to fight—just as were the neutral "peaceable Americans."

The personal background of Miss Scrugham is interesting and significant, for she was born (1885) and lived in Kentucky, the border slaveholding state between North and South whose citizens in 1860-1861 were, as she noted, "the most peaceable [i.e., the most neutral, or the most ardent advocates of compromise] of all Americans."[7] In 1861, for example, after the firing on Fort Sumter, the Kentucky Legislature passed resolutions of neutrality, and

---

[5] *ibid.*, 11ff., 25ff., 64-66n2, 73ff., 99, 104.
[6] The quoted phrases are found in *ibid.*, 101-103.
[7] *ibid.*, 105.

the Governor proclaimed neutrality as the policy of Kentucky rather than support for either the Union or the Confederacy. Thus, Miss Scrugham's attitudes toward the Civil War had a general similarity to the views held by many of the citizens of her native state in the crisis of 1860-1861. (Some of her attitudes, too, in particular her hostility to the "nationalist tradition" as expressed by Rhodes, were presumably in the air in the seminar rooms at Columbia University, where she received her graduate training in history; for her mentor there, and the director of her dissertation from which the previous quotations have been drawn, was William A. Dunning, and some of the Southern-born graduates of Dunning's seminars, as we have seen, became outspoken critics of the Rhodesian "nationalist tradition.") The border slaveholding state background of Miss Scrugham has additional interest due to the fact that such an upper-South-lower-North geographical background (Kentucky, Tennessee, North Carolina, Indiana, Illinois, Pennsylvania) was characteristic of some of the historians who became the best-known spokesmen of the "revisionist" viewpoint —and in several cases this characteristic background was to include residence (whatever the state of birth) for a period of years in one of the former slaveholding states.

If Miss Scrugham's background was similar to that of some later "revisionist" historians, so too her opinions on the causes of the Civil War epitomized the later "revisionist" point of view. She herself did not become a widely-known historian, and her slender monograph seems to have attracted little attention when it was published in 1921. But in the following decade and a half there were signs that the attitudes of some historians were shifting, albeit slowly, in the direction which she had predicted and to which she had pointed. These shifting attitudes were not crystallized and set forth systematically as a comprehensive interpretation of the coming of the Civil War until the mid-1930's, and not until that later date did they attract widespread attention among historians. But one can clearly see in the 1920's and early 1930's indications of the trends of thought which flowered as the "revisionist" point of view—indications, as foretold by Miss Scrugham, of new attitudes toward the coming of the Civil War which were closely related to a new outlook on war in general.

One of the most important signs of these changing attitudes was the publication of a number of studies, all of which reflected interest in the efforts made in 1860-1861 to compromise the differences between North and South, and some of which reflected, in addition, sympathy for the proponents of compromise and hostility for the "extremists" of each side. In the "nationalist tradition," as in the Beardian progressive interpretation of the Civil War, the compromise efforts of 1860-1861 and the immedate outbreak of hostilities had not been the major focus of attention—for these interpretations had explained the causes of the Civil War primarily as an outgrowth of fundamental differences between the sections which had developed over several decades preceding 1861. Now, however, in the 1920's and early 1930's, W.E. Tilberg, Clinton E. Knox, and Gilbert G. Glover published investigations of the compromise efforts of 1860-1861, and Philip G. Auchampaugh and George Fort Milton published biographies of two of the foremost proponents of compromise in the 1860-1861 crisis, James Buchanan and Stephen A. Douglas.[8] Perhaps it was more than coincidence that in a period (the 1920's and 1930's) when the interest of many historians was focused on the ultimatums and mobilizations which had preceded the outbreak of war in 1914, students of the Civil War should have devoted more attention to the immediate origins of strife in 1861.

But more significant as an indication of changing attitudes of historians than the mere interest in the compromise efforts of 1860-1861 was the fact that some historians now championed the leaders who had advocated compromise between the sections in the 1850's and in the secession crisis. In most previous interpretations, with the exception of the views of the "peace advocates," the various proposed compromises had not seemed to furnish the basis for lasting peace between the sections, and such sponsors of compromise as James Buchanan and Stephen A. Douglas were pic-

[8] W.E. Tilberg, "The Responsibility for the Failure of Compromise in 1860," *The Historical Outlook*, xiv, 85-93 (March 1923); Clinton E. Knox, "The Possibilities of Compromise in the Senate Committee of Thirteen and the Responsibility for Its Failure," *The Journal of Negro History*, xvii, 437-465 (October 1932); Gilbert G. Glover, *Immediate Pre-Civil War Compromise Efforts* (Nashville, 1933); Philip G. Auchampaugh, *James Buchanan and His Cabinet on the Eve of Secession* (Lancaster, Pa., 1926); George Fort Milton, *The Eve of Conflict; Stephen A. Douglas and the Needless War* (New York, 1934).

tured in an unfavorable light. Now, however, Buchanan and Douglas (who had been bitter political enemies from 1857 on) found articulate champions among historians, and the basis of the championing lay in a concept of the Civil War similar to that of Miss Scrugham (and of the peace advocates of the 1860's)—the concept that the Civil War was "needless" and that it could have been averted had the advice and example of Buchanan or Douglas been followed.

The most important defense of Buchanan in this period was made by Philip G. Auchampaugh in his *James Buchanan and His Cabinet on the Eve of Secession*, a study published in 1926 (Auchampaugh was born at Brooklyn, New York, in 1897 and received his undergraduate and graduate training at New York State Teachers College, Syracuse University, and Clark University). Buchanan had been severely criticized by many supporters of the Union, as we have seen, and he had fared but little better at the hands of some other interpreters.[9] Auchampaugh, however, had high praise for Buchanan and for the policies he followed. The most significant feature of his volume, from our point of view, is the concept of the causes and character of the Civil War which served as a framework for his defense of Buchanan. Auchampaugh, like Miss Scrugham (whose volume on the "peaceable Americans" he cited), held that the Civil War had been unnecessary, "a needless and heartless 'Brothers' War.' "[10] The war was needless in the sense that it need never have occurred had not fanaticism and wild emotionalism held sway:

The fanaticism, the commercial greed, which wanted to use the wealth of the South by holding her in the Union, together with the foolish exaltation of slavery by Southern radicals, coupled with the pride and the hot temper of the South, brought about a wild insanity which, through the course of peculiar events, led to the overthrow of sane advice, and plunged the Union into destruction.[11]

It was needless, too, in the sense that its results were unfortunate and that it brought in its wake no needful consequences:

[9] The changing evaluations of Buchanan by writers of history are described in Frank Wysor Klingberg, "James Buchanan and the Crisis of the Union," *The Journal of Southern History*, IX, 455-474 (November 1943).

[10] Auchampaugh, *James Buchanan*, 201.

[11] *ibid.*, 200.

The Civil War was a great misfortune to the country. The finely balanced machine set up in 1789 was wrecked. . . . The marked legal gains to the negro race were in sharp contrast to the new chaining of both races to a new economic order that was still more destructive of Jeffersonian political liberty.[12]

This fundamental hypothesis that the Civil War was "needless" also provided the background against which George Fort Milton explained and defended the actions of Stephen A. Douglas in his biography published in 1934. Milton, a newspaper editor and historian, was born in the "border" state of Tennessee, was educated in Tennessee and Virginia, and lived until the end of the 1930's in Tennessee. His comprehensive and detailed biography was by far the most adequate and authoritative life of the Illinois Senator published up to that time (or since), and its importance was enhanced by the fact that it came as something of a capstone of over three decades of studies of Douglas and his times by several scholars.

Douglas, like Buchanan, had long been either neglected or portrayed in an unsympathetic fashion by many historians of the Civil War era. From 1866 until 1902, no biography of Douglas was published, and a common attitude toward him was reflected in omitting him from the *American Statesmen* biographical series, published in the 1880's under the editorship of John T. Morse, Jr., upon the ground (according to Professor Frank H. Hodder, one of the leading students of Douglas in the twentieth century) that his life was a "great failure."[13] While he had not been ignored in the general histories of the Civil War period, Douglas had generally been pictured in an unsympathetic light. Rhodes' estimate of Douglas, as we have seen, was particularly severe: Douglas, Rhodes stated, had introduced the Kansas-Nebraska Act of 1854 as "a bid for Southern support in the next Democratic convention"; in this fashion, his ambition had "wrecked himself and his party," and he had "hastened the struggle" and "precipitated the civil war."[14]

[12] *loc.cit.*
[13] Frank H. Hodder, review of William G. Brown, *Stephen Arnold Douglas*, in *The American Historical Review*, VIII, 390 (January 1903).
[14] The quotations in this sentence (in order) are from Rhodes, *History*, I, 429-430; III, 415; I, 494.

In the twentieth century, however, a new and more favorable evaluation of Douglas's ideas and actions had emerged from the researches of several historians, in particular Frank H. Hodder, P. Orman Ray, and Albert J. Beveridge.[15] Hodder (born in Illinois in 1860 and a long-time resident of Kansas) and Ray (born in Vermont in 1875 and a resident of Pennsylvania, Illinois, and California) were professors of history, while Beveridge (former United States Senator from Indiana) had turned to historical studies after a career in politics; of the three, Hodder was the most important figure in the twentieth century revival of interest in Douglas. While Hodder, Ray, and Beveridge were not in complete agreement in their interpretations of Douglas and his actions, they were all agreed that the evidence did not support Rhodes' severe criticism of Douglas's motives in sponsoring the Kansas-Nebraska Act of 1854; the origins of this act they found not in the presidential ambitions of Douglas but in conditions prevailing in the Western states and territories in the 1850's. Unlike Rhodes, Hodder and Beveridge appeared to be sympathetic, in varying degrees, to Douglas's position in the slavery controversy of the 1850's, and they pictured him not as a selfish politician who precipitated war but as a statesman who sought a just and practical solution to pressing and complicated problems. As early as 1907, Rhodes had noted (with regret, one suspects) that a reaction of sentiment in favor of Douglas was under way among some of the "younger" historians, and by the 1930's the ground was prepared for a sympathetic reinterpretation.[16] Building upon the foundations laid by Hodder, Ray, and Beveridge, and with access to a large body of Douglas manuscripts not used previously by scholars, George Fort Milton presented such a reinterpretation in his influential biography of the Illinois Senator.

---

[15] P. Orman Ray, *The Repeal of the Missouri Compromise* (Cleveland, 1909), and "The Genesis of the Kansas-Nebraska Act," The American Historical Association, *Annual Report for the Year 1914* (Washington, 1916) 261-280; Albert J. Beveridge, *Abraham Lincoln 1809-1858* (2v., New York, 1928), especially volume II; Hodder's numerous studies and book reviews pertaining to Douglas and his times (published from 1899 to 1936) are described in two articles by Professor James C. Malin, "Frank Heywood Hodder, 1860-1935," *The Kansas Historical Quarterly*, v, 115-121 (May 1936), and "F.H. Hodder's 'Stephen A. Douglas,'" *The Kansas Historical Quarterly*, VIII, 227-237 (August 1939).

[16] Howe, *Rhodes*, 158.

Milton was as sympathetic to Douglas as Auchampaugh was to Buchanan (although Milton was as severely critical of Buchanan as Douglas himself had been in the late 1850's) and, like Auchampaugh, Milton emphasized his conviction that the Civil War was "needless."[17] War, he asserted, had not been inevitable; it had been the work of men and of a special group of men:

in North and South alike, extremist minorities manipulated the machinery of the parties, seized the tools of government and committed the two sections to a brothers' war.[18]

These extremist minorities had been emotional, and Milton, like Miss Scrugham, contrasted "emotionalism" and "realism" in discussing the coming of war. The Civil War era, he wrote, was an age of emotional ferment exemplified by such crusades of the 1850's as those against liquor, against foreigners, and against slavery. But Douglas fought this "whole brood of emotion-born agitations" and was thus "a realist in an emotional age." His realism was demonstrated, in Milton's pages, by his solution for the vexed question of slavery in the territories—let the people of the territories themselves decide the matter under the principle of popular sovereignty; realism was further evidenced by his policy of "compromise and common sense" to preserve peace in the crisis of 1860-1861.[19] Had Douglas's proposal to extend the Missouri Compromise line to California been adopted, wrote Milton, "probably no Cotton State save South Carolina would have seceded"; but the Republicans, led by Lincoln, rejected this scheme and, therefore, upon them rests "the responsibility for the refusal of compromise and the soon ensuing outbreak of Civil War."[20]

The sympathetic reappraisals of Douglas and Buchanan involved a reconsideration of the role commonly ascribed to Lincoln by many of the historians in the "nationalist tradition." For, in that tradition, Lincoln's position in the Civil War era had gen-

[17] Although Milton repeatedly placed stress upon the needlessness of the Civil War (the subtitle of his biography of Douglas was "Stephen A. Douglas and the Needless War"), yet he stated in the opening pages of his biography the qualification that the war had been needless "at that time, at least." This reservation made Milton's fundamental position equivocal. See: *Eve of Conflict*, 2, and *passim*; "Stephen A. Douglas' Efforts for Peace," *The Journal of Southern History*, I, 261-275 (August 1935).

[18] Milton, *Eve of Conflict*, 370.

[19] *ibid.*, chaps. I, X, XI; "Stephen A. Douglas' Efforts for Peace," *passim*.

[20] The two quotations in this sentence are taken from *Eve of Conflict*, 526.

erally been sharply distinguished from that of either Douglas or Buchanan, and Lincoln had generally been pictured as a "nationalist" and as a practical realistic leader. In the writings of Miss Scrugham, Auchampaugh, Beveridge, and Milton, by contrast, it was Douglas or Buchanan rather than Lincoln who was described as the "nationalist" and the "realist."

Particularly striking was Milton's reappraisal of the relative positions of Lincoln and Douglas. The ideas and programs of these two leaders were not, in his pages, as far apart as usually pictured: Douglas, like Lincoln, was opposed both to slavery in the abstract and to the spread of that institution to the territories; like Lincoln also, Douglas desired to protect the states in their constitutional rights, wanted to preserve the Union, and was opposed to secession.[21] Thus, Milton's argument ran, their positions were similar on some of the most fundamental issues of the day. In those cases where substantial differences did exist between Lincoln and Douglas, it was Lincoln, Milton declared, rather than Douglas who was "sectional" and partisan in his approach. Lincoln and Douglas differed, for example, over what methods should be used to check the spread of slavery and to insure that it would eventually disappear. Lincoln's insistence that slavery be recognized as an evil and that national legislation be enacted to check its spread was, in the opinion of Milton, a "sectional" position; by contrast, he sketched the "national" position of Douglas, who, assuming that slavery would eventually die a natural death if left alone, urged that in the meantime the institution must not be publicly condemned—for the South's constitutional rights must be maintained and her honor must be respected.[22] Similarly, in describing the differences between Lincoln and Douglas in the crisis of 1860-1861, Milton pictured Douglas as the representative of reason (i.e., of compromise and, later, of peaceable separation in the hope of preventing war), and he praised Douglas's "economic realism," noting with approval "the lengths to which he would go to maintain peace."[23]

In the story of the coming of the Civil War as related by his-

[21] Milton, *Eve of Conflict*, 183-184, 519ff.
[22] *ibid.*, 183-184.
[23] *ibid.*, 519ff.; the quotations are taken from p. 541.

torians in the "nationalist tradition," Lincoln was the central personality and was in a sense the "hero" of the narrative. A similar key role was to be held, in the "revisionist" interpretation, by Stephen A. Douglas. Milton's biography provided the ablest and most complete full-length portrait of Douglas, and it provided a portrait eminently satisfying from the "revisionist" point of view. Published at a time when the attitudes of some historians were shifting in the direction it pointed, Milton's volume apparently gave added impetus to such a shift; it stands as a salient landmark in the development of "revisionist" attitudes, and it remains in the 1950's one of the major statements of those attitudes.

Praise for Douglas and/or Buchanan was in a sense *ipso facto* criticism of their "extremist" opponents of Civil War days. Hence, it was historically appropriate and was to be expected that the sympathetic reevaluation of Douglas, Buchanan, and other "moderates" should be accompanied in the pages of Scrugham, Auchampaugh, and Milton by an unsympathetic reexamination of the "extremists" of North and South. In particular were the Northern "extremists," the abolitionists, subjected to hostile scrutiny, and it was significant that in the 1920's and early 1930's denunciation of abolitionists (and blaming them for the coming of the war) was no longer confined to Southern-born historians. In fact, what was probably the most influential criticism of abolitionists in this period came from the pens of two historians who were not Southerners: Albert J. Beveridge and Gilbert H. Barnes.

Hostility to the abolitionists was a noteworthy characteristic of Albert J. Beveridge's two-volume (and unfinished) life of Lincoln published in 1928. Born in Indiana during the Civil War, Beveridge was the son of a veteran of the Union Army and, as we have seen, entered political life in the late nineteenth century as an opponent of the South and a waver of the "bloody shirt." One historian, Nathaniel W. Stephenson, has suggested that Beveridge was brought up in an atmosphere in which the abolitionist movement was glorified, but that he was shocked upon studying abolitionist literature as a man in his sixties and reacted against abolitionism in an extreme fashion.[24] Whatever may be the explanation,

[24] Nathaniel W. Stephenson, review of Beveridge, *Abraham Lincoln, 1809-1858*, in *The American Historical Review*, xxxiv, 619 (April 1929).

Beveridge was severely critical of abolitionists and assigned to them a not unimportant role in causing the Civil War. The extravagant vituperation of the Northern abolitionists, he declared, produced their counterpart, the Southern "fire-eaters," and he suggested (as had James Buchanan in the 1860's and some Southern-born historians in the twentieth century) that if there had been no abolitionists, slavery might have disappeared and war might have been avoided:

Had it not been for what they [the abolitionists] said and did and the fear and anger they aroused, it is not altogether impossible that there would have been no war and that slavery would in time have given way to the pressure of economic forces.[25]

Five years after the appearance of Beveridge's *Lincoln*, Gilbert H. Barnes' volume, *The Antislavery Impulse, 1830-1844*, was published. Barnes drew an unsympathetic portrait not only of the abolitionists but also of the antislavery movement as a whole, and his criticisms won more attention than did those of Beveridge. Born in Nebraska in 1889, Barnes studied at the University of Michigan as a graduate student under the direction of Ulrich B. Phillips; *The Antislavery Impulse* was dedicated to Phillips and in its opening pages Barnes acknowledged that his chief obligation was to Phillips. The *Antislavery Impulse* was an impressive book, a new study of the antislavery movement based upon previously unused source material, primarily the correspondence of Theodore Dwight Weld and other leaders of the movement in Ohio and other Midwestern states. The conclusions Barnes reached were provocative: that the antislavery impulse was primarily "moral," not "economic" in nature, and that the Midwest and its antislavery leaders (notably Theodore Dwight Weld) were more important in the movement than New England and its famed leader, William Lloyd Garrison.[26] The *Antislavery Impulse* attracted widespread notice among students of the Civil War era and was hailed

[25] Beveridge, *Abraham Lincoln*, II, 19. For a discussion of abolitionists by Beveridge, see *ibid.*, II, 18ff. J. Franklin Jameson, the distinguished leader among historians in the United States, criticized Beveridge's opinion that slavery would have disappeared by the action of slaveholders themselves had it not been for abolitionists. Elizabeth Donnan and Leo F. Stock, eds., "Senator Beveridge, J. Franklin Jameson, and Abraham Lincoln," *The Mississippi Valley Historical Review*, xxxv, 666-667 (March 1949).

[26] Gilbert Hobbs Barnes, *The Antislavery Impulse, 1830-1844* (New York, 1933) *vii-viii.*

as a study which broke new ground (although some of the characterizations of the volume as a pioneer work seem to have ignored an earlier study of political aspects of the antislavery movement in the "old Northwest"—i.e., the Midwest—Theodore Clarke Smith's *The Liberty and Free Soil Parties in the Northwest*, published in 1897).

The most significant feature of Barnes' volume from the standpoint of changing opinions on the Civil War was its unsympathetic attitude toward the antislavery movement. Previous accounts of organized opposition to slavery had been written by historians Albert Bushnell Hart (the son and grandson of abolitionists), Theodore Clarke Smith (long-time resident of Massachusetts and a graduate student of Hart's at Harvard in the 1890's), and Jesse Macy (a veteran of the Union Army whose family had actively supported the underground railroad in the 1840's and 1850's).[27] As was to be expected, Hart, Smith, and Macy were all sympathetic to the antislavery cause; typifying their point of view was the sentence with which Smith closed his volume (a volume written in its original form as a doctoral dissertation under Hart's direction): Smith praised the antislavery political organizations in the Midwest on the ground that they had accustomed men "to a steady adherence to a great principle, in the face of opposition, contempt, and abuse—to do right for right's sake."[28]

By contrast, the tone implicit throughout Barnes' book was hostile to the antislavery cause and to its leaders. The antislavery leaders were pictured as emotional, and at times irresponsible, propagandists who should rightly bear a considerable part of the blame for sectional conflict and civil war. The antislavery impulse eventually would "divide the nation," Barnes wrote; this impulse broadened into a sectional crusade against the South . . . it was a major factor in the rise of sectionalism and a prime cause of the final conflict.[29]

[27] Albert Bushnell Hart, *Slavery and Abolition, 1831-1841* (*The American Nation: A History*, XVI) (New York, 1906); Theodore Clarke Smith, *The Liberty and Free Soil Parties in the Northwest* (*Harvard Historical Studies*, VI) (New York, 1897); Jesse Macy, *The Anti-Slavery Crusade* (*The Chronicles of America Series*, v. 28) (New Haven, 1919).

[28] Smith, *Liberty and Free Soil Parties*, 307.

[29] Barnes, *The Antislavery Impulse, vii-viii.* The "divide the nation" quotation is from *ibid.*, 190.

Barnes' volume, like Milton's biography of Douglas, occupies a prominent place in the emergence of the "revisionist" viewpoints. Some idea of its specific influence can be gained from the comments of the two historians who became, in the late 1930's, the best-known champions of "revisionism," Avery O. Craven and James G. Randall. The crusade against slavery, Craven wrote in 1934, had been misunderstood (presumably by such historians as Hart, Smith, and Macy) as a story of devoted men fighting evil, but Barnes' study pointed the way to a sounder understanding; *The Antislavery Impulse,* Craven continued, was

basically sound and the story of the abolition movement has received its first fair corrections. Much will be done in days ahead. It will more nearly follow the path taken by Mr. Barnes than that taken by Hart or Macy.[30]

Barnes' book received similar praise from James G. Randall; the function of the book, declared Randall, might be described as "the revisionist interpretation of the antislavery crusade."[31]

Thus, by the mid-1930's, the writings of such historians as Miss Scrugham, Auchampaugh, Beveridge, Milton, and Barnes had revealed the existence of points of view about the men and the events of the Civil War era which were sharply at variance with many previous interpretations. Their studies provided much of the foundation necessary for a comprehensive reinterpretation of the causes and character of the war. And by the mid-1930's, not only were there indications that some historians were changing their attitudes toward the men and events of the Civil War era, there were also signs that the changed attitude toward war itself prophesied by Miss Scrugham had won acceptance from a sizeable portion of the American public.

For by the 1930's, a disillusioned attitude toward war was widespread in the United States. Hostility to war was preached in the 1920's and 1930's in a number of novels, plays, and poems in which some of the best-known writers of the day pictured its waste and brutality. Antipathy to war was rooted specifically in the reaction against American participation in the First World War—a re-

[30] Avery Craven, review of Barnes, *The Antislavery Impulse,* in *New York Herald Tribune Books,* April 22, 1934, p. 8.
[31] James G. Randall, review of Barnes, *The Antislavery Impulse,* in *The Journal of Southern History,* I, 96 (February 1935).

action which was both fed by, and exemplified by, the activities of the well-known "Nye Committee" of the United States Congress in the early 1930's. In some quarters it was vigorously asserted that the entrance of the United States into war in 1917 came not because of any justifiable concern over important issues but because certain "devils" ("munition makers," "Wall Street bankers," "British agents") had employed "propaganda" to stir up emotions and thereby induce people to fight. There was disillusionment, too, with the results of the war against Germany, and as wars and international tensions increased in the world of the 1930's, some individuals concluded that the First World War had settled nothing.

These various sentiments were reflected in the so-called "neutrality" ("keep-out-of-war") laws passed by the United States Congress from 1935 to 1937. And by 1937, the Gallup organization reported (whatever this evidence might be worth) that of the people it questioned in a poll of that year, sixty-four percent indicated a belief that the entrance of the United States into the First World War had been a mistake. The close interrelationship between these disillusioned attitudes of the 1930's toward the First World War and the "revisionist" explanations of the Civil War was pointed out in 1940 by the "revisionist" historian, James G. Randall:

Just as Americans beginning about 1935 executed something like an about-face in their interpretation of the World War . . . so the retelling of the Civil War is a matter of changed and changing viewpoints. In the present troubled age, it may be of more than academic interest to reexamine the human beings of that war generation with less thought of the "splendor of battle flags" and with more of the sophisticated and unsentimental searchlight of reality.[32]

If the studies of Miss Scrugham, Barnes, and other historians provided the foundation for a distinctive reinterpretation of the causes and character of the Civil War, the disillusioned attitudes toward war which were common in the United States by the 1930's furnished the general framework within which such a reinterpretation could rest. Moreover, these disillusioned attitudes,

---

[32] James G. Randall, "The Blundering Generation," *The Mississippi Valley Historical Review*, xxvii, 27-28 (June 1940).

to change the metaphor, supplied a climate of opinion in which this reinterpretation could win favor. By the mid-1930's, the times were ripe for a synthesis of the new points of view, and such a synthesis did appear and became popular among historians primarily through the writings of Avery O. Craven and James G. Randall.

Avery O. Craven and
James G. Randall

AVERY O. CRAVEN AND JAMES G. RANDALL, like Miss Scrugham, Beveridge, and Milton, were identified geographically with the upper-South-lower-North "border" states. Craven was a North Carolinian by birth (1886) and had attended college in his native state, completing his graduate training (after study at Harvard) at the University of Chicago in the 1920's; from the mid-1920's he lived in Illinois. Randall, born in Indianapolis (1881), attended college in Indiana and finished his graduate training at the University of Chicago before the outbreak of the First World War; after living and teaching in Virginia for eight years, he became, after 1920, a resident of Illinois. The published writings of both Craven and Randall dealt primarily with the Civil War era or related subjects, and from the mid-1930's onward contained many discussions of the causes of the Civil War. There were certain differences in point of view between the two historians, but their explanations of the causes and character of the Civil War fell, by and large, into a common pattern—a pattern which they themselves as well as their contemporaries distinguished from most previous interpretations.

The fundamental distinguishing feature of the point of view of Craven and Randall was their attitude toward war; for when they turned, in Randall's words, "the sophisticated and unsentimental searchlight of reality" upon the Civil War, this searchlight was focused through what might be called the "lens" of their own distinctive concept of war. When one seeks to define this "revisionist" attitude toward war, the word "disillusioned" seems to be the most accurate single adjective (for "disillusioned," the "revisionist" historians themselves would substitute "realistic"). This underlying disillusionment was expressed at greatest length and in the most explicit fashion in the writings of Randall, whose approach to war was similar to that displayed earlier by Miss Scrugham.

Randall expressed profound disgust for war, suggesting in 1940 that the "realist" should use, instead of the word "war," such words as "organized murder" or "human slaughter-house"; after the experience of a Second World War, he wrote in 1947 in a generally similar vein: "We still have not had a sufficient unmasking of war for the stupendous fraud that it is."[33] Supplementing his abhorrence of war was a world-outlook which, at least to non-"revisionists," seemed decidedly hopeful—an outlook in which peace appeared "normal" for human beings and war "abnormal":

In contrast to the normal and basically valid demand for peace, the desire for war, or the whipping up of hostile feeling by those who begin a war, is artificial, unnatural, and abnormal.[34]

From this point of view, "reality" and "rationality" were apparently equated with "peace." And, although Randall, writing after the Second World War, condemned those whom he called the "appeasers" of Adolph Hitler in the 1930's, neither he nor any other of the "revisionist" historians discussed the possibility that "rational" and "realistic" individuals might choose war in some situations as a last resort and as the lesser of evils.[35] One got the impression (it was not specifically stated, but most of the discussions seemed to point in that direction) that war was always useless, that war never settled any issue in a desirable manner, and that war was always the worst possible alternative in human relations.

From this general outlook on war, there followed a specific philosophy of war causation. Since war was equated with irrationality, abnormality, and unreality, it followed that the causes of war were to be explained not in terms of basic differences over important questions but in terms of "abnormal" and "artificial" emotions. This point was emphasized by Randall in 1940:

War-making is too much dignified if it is told in terms of broad na-

[33] The quotations in this sentence (in order) are from the following writings by Randall: "The Blundering Generation," 7; *Lincoln the Liberal Statesman* (New York, 1947) *xi*.

[34] Randall, *Lincoln the Liberal Statesman*, 88.

[35] Randall's criticism of the "appeasers" of Hitler is in his *Lincoln the Liberal Statesman*, 165.

tional urges. . . . When nations stumble into war, or when peoples rub their eyes and find they have been dragged into war, there is at some point a psychopathic case. Omit the element of abnormality, or of bogus leadership, or inordinate ambition for conquest, and diagnosis fails.

In 1945:

One of the most colossal of misconceptions is the theory that fundamental motives produce war. The glaring and obvious fact is the artificiality of war-making agitation.

In 1947:

There are writers who would have us believe that fundamental motives produce war . . . but a study of modern war-making reveals that such an idea is a fallacy.[36]

It would seem clear, in short, that Randall approached the study of the Civil War with a general philosophy of war and of war causation quite different from the ideas of most previous interpreters. This statement, in the opinion of the present author, is true of most of the "revisionist" historians, including Craven. An outlook on war similar to Randall's appears to be implicit throughout most of Craven's writings, although it is explicitly expressed only rarely; the following is one of the infrequent general statements on war by Craven and its tenor is in accord with the Randall position:

All wars in modern times are defensive wars, waged against foes so unrighteous that each struggle should, by all the rules of a just universe, be brief.[37]

When the causes of the Civil War were explained from the standpoint of this general philosophy of war and of war-causation, the principal conclusion which emerged was that the Civil War need not have occurred. Craven and Randall, like Miss Scrugham, Auchampaugh, and Milton, held that the Civil War was "needless," and it was this basic approach to the war which became the hallmark of the "revisionist" point of view and set it off most sharply from other interpretations. The Civil War, according to

---

[36] The quotations (in order) are from the following of Randall's writings: "The Blundering Generation," 11; *Lincoln the President: Springfield to Gettysburg* (2v., New York, 1945) I, 76; *Lincoln the Liberal Statesman*, 88.

[37] Avery Craven, *Edmund Ruffin, Southerner* (New York, 1932) 235.

the "revisionists," was "needless" in the dual sense suggested by Auchampaugh. It was needless, in the first place, from the standpoint that it need never have occurred. Most previous historians had commenced their explanation of the coming of the war from the basic historical fact that armed conflict had actually broken out in 1861. Craven and Randall began, by contrast, with the conviction that armed conflict need not have broken out. They maintained that other interpreters had proposed distorted and unconvincing explanations of the coming of war because they had been led by the fact that war did take place to the assumption that war was inevitable. One might find real merit in this suggestion and yet still conclude that the "revisionists" themselves seemed at times to approach almost to the other extreme—to the assumption that the outbreak of civil strife was itself unreal and "incredible":

That America [Randall declared] devoted to peace and busy with the affairs of a growing nation, should have become a snarling arena of internal conflict, however voluminously explained, is a matter whose "causes" seem unconvincing. It happened; otherwise it would seem incredible.[38]

The Civil War was needless to the "revisionists," in the second place, in the sense that it resulted in very few needful or beneficial consequences, and many harmful consequences. Running throughout the writings of Craven and Randall was the theme of disillusionment expressed also by the Beardian progressives and by the twentieth-century defenders of the South: the Civil War was not worth what it cost, and it brought in its wake much evil. Reinforcing this prominent theme was the expressed or implied assumption that conditions would have been much better had the war never occurred.

Craven, in particular, seemed to ascribe a heavy burden of ills to the war. Much in the manner of some of the Nashville agrarians, he drew an idyllic picture of an agrarian society (characterized, among other things, by decentralized government and a rich cultural life) which might have developed in the United States; contrasted to this picture was his description of conditions in the United States in the 1930's, conditions which he traced to the Civil War:

[38] Randall, *Lincoln the President*, I, 75.

Workers talking of "wage slavery," capitalists piling fortunes high while poverty and starvation stalk the streets; culture, a bought and borrowed thing, stored in museums, with intellectual sterility everywhere save in a few provincial corners! To such ends did three decades of quarreling and four years of bitter warfare make substantial contributions.[39]

Randall, too, expressed disillusionment with the results of the Civil War, although this theme was not as prominent in his writings as it was in Craven's.[40]

Neither Craven nor Randall was as explicit as Charles W. Ramsdell, E. Merton Coulter, or other twentieth-century defenders of the South in expressing the supposition that even had there been no Civil War, the institution of slavery would have disappeared and (in the words of Coulter, previously cited), "What good the war produced would have come with time in an orderly way; the bad would not have come at all." Yet, in the writings of both Craven and Randall, assumptions of this sort frequently seemed implicit, and, when such suppositions were questioned, Randall defended them on the ground that doubt on the subject was not "enlightened" (i.e., was not in accord with an optimistic view of the universe):

To suppose that the Union could not have been continued or slavery outmoded without the war and without the corrupt concomitants of the war is hardly an enlightened assumption.[41]

Just as the "revisionists" rejected the concept that the Civil War was inevitable, holding instead that it had been "needless," so too they rejected most previous explanations of the causes of the war. Craven and Randall (in accordance with the general philosophy of war and of war-causation set forth by Randall) specifically disavowed interpretations of the causes of the Civil War which

---

[39] Avery Craven, *The Repressible Conflict, 1830-1861* (University, La., 1939) 65-66. (For Craven's description of the agrarian way of life, see *ibid.*, 97.) Additional statements similar to the one cited are to be found in Craven's *Democracy in American Life* (Chicago, 1941) 68-69, 101-102. Craven described the reconstruction of the South by the "Radical" Republicans after the Civil War as a process which "in severity has never been matched in modern society by the terms that a victor has imposed upon a fallen foe" (Craven, *Edmund Ruffin*, 257).

[40] See Randall's *Civil War and Reconstruction* (New York, 1937) 687-688, and "The Civil War Restudied," *The Journal of Southern History*, VI, 448-451 (November 1940).

[41] Randall, "The Blundering Generation," 8.

placed primary emphasis upon underlying and fundamental differences between North and South.

Craven, for example, granted that there had been differences between North and South, and he stated (like the Beardian progressives) that the most fundamental differences were those arising from the fact that the South was rural and agricultural while the North was urban, commercial, and industrial.[42] But Craven insisted that the dissimilarities between North and South had been overemphasized, and he denied in particular that differences over the slavery question were as important as many historians had urged. Three-fourths of the Southerners in the Old South did not own slaves, he pointed out, nor did the Northern Republicans propose the abolition of slavery. Many North-South differences usually ascribed to the influence of the institution of slavery should be charged, he maintained, to the fact that the South was a rural society and a society faced with a race problem (the Negro "was far more important as a Negro in shaping life and giving peculiar quality to the South than he was as a slave").[43] The institution of slavery, he wrote in summarizing his views, "played a rather minor part in the life of the South and of the Negro."[44]

The differences which did exist between North and South, Craven declared, were merely part of the natural and normal pattern of sectional divergence in the United States and were "no greater than those existing at different times between East and West."[45] Such sectional dissimilarities did not in themselves explain the coming of the Civil War:

Differences—economic, social, and political—did not . . . portend an "irrepressible conflict" between North and South, to be settled only by bloodshed. The War Between the States in 1861-1865 did not come simply because one section was agricultural and the other industrial;

[42] Avery Craven, "The South in American History," *The Historical Outlook*, xxi, 107 (March 1930), and *Democracy in American Life*, 96-98.

[43] The quotation is from Craven, *The Repressible Conflict*, 24.

[44] Avery Craven, *The Coming of the Civil War* (New York, 1942) 93. For discussions of the role of the institution of slavery by Craven, see "Slavery and the Civil War," *The Southern Review*, iv, 243-255 (Autumn 1938), and *The Repressible Conflict*, chaps. i and ii.

[45] Craven, review of Arthur C. Cole, *The Irrepressible Conflict*, in *The American Historical Review*, xi, 355 (January 1935).

because one exploited free labor and the other slaves; or because a sectional majority refused to respect the constitutional rights of the minority![46]

In a similar vein, Randall asserted that the causes of the Civil War could not accurately be described in terms either of irreconcilable differences between North and South or of a struggle between diverse civilizations. Cultural, economic, and other types of differences had existed between North and South, and there had been sectional conflicts over such questions as slavery—but these factors were not sufficient to explain the coming of war.[47] They were not sufficient because particular grievances of North and South did not, in Randall's opinion, add up to serious harm of either section. He pointed out, for example, that the principal specific disputes over slavery concerned fugitive slaves and the extension of slavery to the federal territories. The census of 1860, however, listed only 803 escaped slaves and listed only two slaves in the hotly disputed Kansas territory; therefore, Randall concluded that the actual aspects of the slavery question in dispute were trivial and were greatly overemphasized:

What should be done about an almost non-existent slave population in the West, or about a small trickle of runaway bondsmen, was magnified into an issue altogether out of scale with its importance.[48]

(The standard employed by Randall in discussing this question should be noted: the important point, as he described it, was not whether the people of the 1860's considered the issues of their day important enough to quarrel over, but whether twentieth-century historians considered them that important. Critics were to charge that this approach—judging the past by the ideas of the present— was characteristic of the "revisionist" point of view and that it invalidated the "revisionist" understanding of history.)

Fundamental and irreconcilable differences did not bring on the Civil War; war had come, Craven and Randall maintained,

[46] Avery Craven, "Coming of the War Between the States: An Interpretation," *The Journal of Southern History*, II, 304 (August 1936). The Civil War, Craven emphasized in another place, was not the product of "natural factors inherent in the early sectionalism of either North or South" (*The Repressible Conflict*, 30).

[47] Randall, "The Blundering Generation," 15; *Lincoln the President*, I, 238; *Lincoln the Liberal Statesman*, 47.

[48] Randall, *Lincoln the President*, I, 86; see also *ibid.*, I, 238ff., and I, 78.

because normal sectional differences which were not basically serious had been magnified and emotionalized until the minds of men became dominated by "artificial" and "unreal" issues—and these issues led to war. The responsibility for this magnification and emotionalization of issues was firmly placed by the "revisionists" upon certain groups of individuals—the "extremists," primarily politicians and reformers who, it was charged, had stirred up emotions and produced the situation which resulted in war.

The problem of why the sections went to war, Craven asserted, was one of "emotions," "cultivated hostilities," and "hatred between sections."[49] These emotions, these hostilities, and this hatred were due, in his opinion, to the activities (in part, the deliberate activities) of extremist leaders. Because these leaders aroused and exploited emotions and because they created "unrealistic" pictures of the rival sections, they were important causal agents in bringing about the Civil War. The actual differences between the sections, he declared, would have been "insufficient" as a cause for war; but

the politician, North and South, sparring for advantage of person, party, or region, coined phrases and erected symbols, to the destruction of realities, which shifted the struggle from the values actually involved to one of words which stirred emotions by implying danger to "rights," to "honor," and even to "God's purposes."[50]

Thus, the conflict

was the work of politicians and pious cranks! The peoples knew little of each other as realities. They were both fighting mythical devils.[51]

The Civil War, he emphasized in 1942,

must, in large part, be charged to a generation of well-meaning Americans, who, busy with the task of getting ahead, permitted their shortsighted politicians, their over-zealous editors, and their pious reformers to emotionalize real and potential differences and to conjure up distorted impressions of those who dwelt in other parts of the nation. For more than two decades, these molders of public opinion steadily created the fiction of two distinct peoples contending for the right to preserve and expand their sacred cultures. . . . They turned the

---

[49] Craven, "Coming of the War Between the States," 304.
[50] Craven, *Edmund Ruffin*, 101.
[51] Craven, "Coming of the War Between the States," 305.

normal American conflicts between agriculture and industry, farmers and planters, section and section, into a struggle of civilizations.[52]

Displaying a similar point of view, Randall suggested that the causes of the war should be explained in terms of such words and phrases as "emotional unreason," "bogus leadership," "fanaticism," "misrepresentation," and "politics."[53] The issues of 1860-1861 were "forced and unnatural"; "artificial difficulties" had accumulated and made "real obstacles" out of "shadow objections"; and such large political groups as the Republican Party "produced quarrels out of things that would have settled themselves were it not for political agitation."[54] The Civil War generation, Randall suggested in summarizing his views, was a "blundering generation" which was "misled in its unctuous fury" and was "miserably hoodwinked by the demon of strife."[55]

Both Craven and Randall, in explaining the coming of the war, criticized the "extremists" and praised the "moderates" of the Civil War era much in the manner of Miss Scrugham, Auchampaugh, Beveridge, Milton, and Barnes. It was noticeable, too, that Craven and Randall tended to single out the abolitionists for a larger share of the blame of causing the war than any other "extremist" group. The abolitionists, Craven wrote, launched a drive against the South from the outside and "threatened to produce a race problem which had in large part been solved by the institution of slavery"; they thereby helped to pound the South into self-consciousness and to cause the movement for Southern independence.[56] Randall also criticized the abolitionists, writing that this "avenging force of puritanism in politics" was itself "a major cause of the conflict."[57]

Condemnation of the "extremists" was matched by acclaim for such "moderates" as Buchanan and Douglas who, it was said,

---

[52] Craven, The Coming of the Civil War, 2.

[53] The words and phrases are taken from Randall's "The Blundering Generation," 11, 15, and Lincoln the Liberal Statesman, 50.

[54] The quotations (in order) are from Randall, Lincoln the Liberal Statesman, 92; Lincoln the President, 1, 226-227; "The Civil War Restudied," 447.

[55] The quotations (in order) are from Randall, Lincoln the Liberal Statesman, 40; Lincoln the President, 1, 239.

[56] The quotation is from Craven, "The South in American History," 106. For another example of Craven's discussion of abolitionists, see The Repressible Conflict, especially chap. III.

[57] Randall, The Civil War and Reconstruction, 146.

had remained calm and had faced the issues of the 1850's and 1860's in a realistic manner. This sympathy for Buchanan and Douglas raised problems for Randall, who became the biographer of Lincoln, similar to those which had confronted his predecessor in that position, Albert J. Beveridge. Randall's discussion emphasized similarities in the policies of Douglas or Buchanan, on the one hand, and Lincoln, on the other. He placed particular stress, as had George Fort Milton, upon resemblances in the positions of Lincoln and Douglas; in fact, one could almost get the impression from the first two volumes of Randall's biography of Lincoln that Lincoln was essentially a Douglas Democrat (and at one point, Randall even urged the similarity between the policies of Lincoln and another Democrat, his opponent in the election of 1864, George B. McClellan).[58] J. Franklin Jameson, upon reading a portion of Beveridge's biography of Lincoln, had suggested to Beveridge that the ordinary reader would say that Douglas and not Lincoln was the hero of the work; one wonders if Jameson's comment would have been the same had he lived to read Randall's biography.[59]

The discussion by Craven and Randall of "moderates," "extremists," and the role of emotions illuminated, once more, distinctive features of the "revisionist" approach to the Civil War. Most previous interpretations had started with the fact that in the North-South dispute the "moderates" had not been able to carry out their policies, while the "extremists" came to have increasing influence as the dispute became more heated. But Craven and Randall seemed to begin with the conviction that the "moderates" *should* have been successful and that the "extremists" *should not* have become more influential. Many previous explanations of the coming of war had taken note of the intense emotionalism which had characterized the sectional struggles of the 1850's, but they had generally described the increasing emotionalism (and the increasing influence of "extremists") primarily as a result or an indication of the underlying historical situation, not as its cause;

[58] For examples of Randall's discussion of Douglas and Buchanan, see: "The Civil War Restudied," 451-454 (see pp. 451-452 for the comment on McClellan); *Lincoln the President*, I, 220-222; *Lincoln the Liberal Statesman*, 11-22.

[59] Elizabeth Donnan and Leo F. Stock, eds., "Senator Beveridge, J. Franklin Jameson, and Abraham Lincoln," *op.cit.*, 666-667.

the basic factor was the existence of a sectional conflict (over fundamental issues) which aroused emotions and spawned "extremists" who, in turn, exploited these emotions. Craven and Randall, by contrast, seemed to consider "emotions" and "extremists" almost as if they were independent of, and separate from, the historical situation in which they were found; the "emotions" and "extremists," it appeared, were more nearly the cause than the result of the state of affairs in the 1850's, and the important factor was not so much the existence of an historical situation which could be exploited by "extremists" playing upon "emotions" as the fact of exploitation itself.

Underlying the discussion of "moderates," "extremists," and "emotions" by Craven and Randall, there seemed to be the assumption that conditions in the 1850's were such, and the nature of human beings was such, that the individuals of that era should have remained calm and moderate. There seemed also to be the further assumption that had the people of each section acted without emotion, and had they learned the "truth" about the other section, the sectional disputes could have been solved without too much difficulty. Because of these assumptions, Craven's and Randall's explanation of the actions of the war generation frequently included a severe castigation of that generation: it should have remained unemotional and "realistic," it should have realized that its disagreements were not worth fighting about, and thus it should not have "blundered" into war. The spirit characteristic of the "nationalist tradition" was indicated, as we have seen, in the contention that both sides in the Civil War had been "right"; the spirit characteristic of "revisionism" was indicated in the contention that both sides in the Civil War had been "wrong."

The "revisionists" resented charges that their viewpoint was pro-Southern, insisting that they were critical of extremists without regard to section and were sympathetic to rational moderate men whatever their section. One could understand how the accusation of pro-Southernism could originate, for the "revisionists" apparently centered their criticisms upon the Northern abolitionists, and they seemed to detect instances of emotionalism and extremism more frequently in the North than in the South. But in reality, the "revisionist" line of historiographical ancestry ran not to the defenders of the Confederacy but to the "peace men" of the 1860's. There were some differences between the "revisionists" of the twentieth century and the discontented peace advocates of the 1860's, but by and large their viewpoints were remarkably similar: both groups based their thoughts upon the contention that war could have been and should have been avoided in 1861, and both groups insisted that the coming of war was to be explained not as the result of a sectional conflict over important issues but as the outgrowth of the agitations of "extremists." Reflecting the similar ideas of the two groups was the similar language they both employed; much like the words of modern "revisionist" historians, for example, were those written by H.S. Foote in the 1860's to explain the causes of the war—"incessant agitation of sectional factionists," and "unskillful and blundering management of men in power." Not the ideas of Jefferson Davis but those of Clement L. Vallandigham and H.S. Foote found their champions in twentieth century "revisionism."

The writings of Craven and Randall on the causes of the Civil War found a receptive audience, and the "revisionist" viewpoints apparently won wide acceptance among historians in the United States from the late 1930's onward. Diverse elements contributed to the popularity of these viewpoints: they appealed, as has been suggested, to the widespread dislike of war, they were supposedly founded upon the teachings of "modern psychology" concerning such subjects as "propaganda" and "emotions," and they seemed to furnish the comforting assurance that by ascribing the Civil War to the "extremists" of both North and South, twentieth century historians were acting in an "objective" or "scientific" fashion as befitted sophisticated observers of the past; in "recent years," as Craven expressed this opinion in 1942, "scholars have returned to a study of the Civil War as scientists and not as partisans. They have come to view the struggle as a national disaster."[60] Furthermore, although Craven and Randall were no more "debunkers" than was Beard, yet "revisionism," like Beard's writings, had some appeal for the debunking spirit. (In this connection, perhaps the posthumous publication in 1952 of William E. Woodward's history of the Civil War was of some significance. Woodward, born

[60] Craven, *The Coming of the Civil War*, vii.

in South Carolina in the 1870's, had introduced the word "debunk" into the English language with his novel *Bunk*, published in 1923, and he, more than any other single author, popularized the debunking technique in a series of iconoclastic biographies of historical figures. Woodward's interpretation of the causes of the Civil War was "revisionist" in approach, and he emphasized that the Civil War was needless. One of the clearest indications of Woodward's "revisionist" viewpoint was the title of his volume: after being tentatively named *The Civil War: A National Blunder* and *When We Went Crazy*, it finally appeared as *Years of Madness*.)[61]

Whatever were the grounds for its appeal, the Craven-Randall explanation of the causes of the Civil War did win the favor of many historians; by the mid-1940's this interpretation seemed to have as many adherents among historians as the Beardian economic interpretation.

[61] The tentative titles of *Years of Madness* are listed in *Who's Who in America*, xxvi (1950-1951) (Chicago, 1950) 3019, and in Woodward's obituary in *The New York Times*, September 30, 1950, p. 17.

"Revisionism" since the Second
World War

CRAVEN AND RANDALL continued to write on the causes of the Civil
War after 1945, but the major statements of the "revisionist" position after that date were made by two historians who were new-
comers to the ranks, Roy F. Nichols and Kenneth M. Stampp.[62]
Nichols was the older of the two historians, born (1896) and
educated in New Jersey and, from the mid 1920's onward, a member of the faculty of the University of Pennsylvania. He received
his graduate training in history at Columbia University and there
began his doctoral dissertation under the direction of William A.
Dunning, although Dunning died before any of the manuscript
was completed. This dissertation, published in 1923 with the
title, *The Democratic Machine 1850-1854*, was the first of a number of studies published by Nichols during the next quarter-century on various aspects of party politics in the 1850's; what might
be described in some respects as the culmination of these various
studies was his volume published in 1948, *The Disruption of
American Democracy*. This book discussed the causes of the Civil
War at length; its point of view was "revisionist," and it was
highly praised by such leading "revisionist" historians as Craven,
Randall, and George Fort Milton.[63] The volume attracted considerable attention; it was awarded the Pulitzer Prize in history,

[62] Some observers thought they detected a new emphasis in some of the writings of
Craven and Randall after 1945: Craven, for example, declared in 1950 that "great moral
issues" were certainly involved in the conflict between North and South, while Randall
suggested in 1947 that there were men of fine calibre among the abolitionists and that
"antislavery ideals had their noble aspects." See: Avery O. Craven, "The 1840's and
the Democratic Process," *The Journal of Southern History*, XVI, 162 (May 1950);
James G. Randall, *Lincoln the Liberal Statesman*, 25, 175-176. But, for Craven's views
since 1945, see also below, chapter eight, notes 26 and 44.

[63] See the following reviews of the volume: Avery O. Craven in the *New York Herald
Tribune Books*, April 25, 1948, p. 4; James G. Randall in *The Saturday Review of Literature*, XXXI, 17-18 (June 12, 1948); George Fort Milton in *The American Historical Review*, LIV, 161-163 (October 1948).

and, all in all, it constitutes an important recent statement of the "revisionist" position.

Nichols' book supplemented rather than altered previous "revisionist" explanations of the causes of the Civil War. Nichols, like Craven, Randall, and other "revisionists," found unconvincing former interpretations of the coming of the Civil War in terms of ideological, institutional, or other types of differences between the sections—such differences, he asserted, had existed in other times and places without leading to war.[64] He did not deny the existence of different and conflicting ideas in the United States of the 1850's; in fact he described at some length a number of what he called unlike and competing "emotional units or attitudes," singling out in particular "pervasive," "divisive," and "cohesive" attitudes.[65] But, like other "revisionists," he insisted that the conflict between these divergent "emotional units or attitudes" did not by itself offer a sufficient explanation of the coming of the Civil War.

His own interpretation of the causes of the war emphasized the role of "hyperemotionalism." "Hyperemotionalism" existed in the United States in 1861, Nichols explained, partly because of the dissimilar attitudes noted above and partly because of defects in the nation's political machinery. He cited, for example, the "baneful influence" of frequent elections, and declared that the "constant agitation" attendant upon these elections "certainly furnishes one of the primary clues to why the war came" (this was reminiscent of Confederate supporter James Williams who, as we have seen, suggested in 1863 that the ultimate cause of the Civil War was the system of frequent presidential elections).[66] This unsatisfactory political system and the "hyperemotionalism" it helped to create enabled "irresponsible and blind operators of local political machinery" to exploit "with little regard for the welfare of the general public" the existing divergent attitudes—and the result was war:

[64] Roy F. Nichols, *The Disruption of American Democracy* (New York, 1948) chap. XXVII.

[65] The quotations (in order) are from *ibid.*, 515, 21.

[66] The quotations are from *ibid.*, 515. See also James Williams, *The Rise and Fall of "the Model Republic"* (London, 1863) 11, 17-18, 400-419.

The constant heat generated in the frequent elections brought an explosion. The social, economic, and cultural differences had been so used by the political operators as to produce secession and civil war.[67]

Thus, in the pages of Nichols as in the pages of Craven and Randall, it appeared that blind and/or evil men had stirred up emotions and had thereby brought on war.

Nichols pushed the explanation of the coming of war one step back of irresponsible men and emotions—pushed it back to what he called the "processes of human behaviour." His interpretation of the ultimate cause of the war deserves quotation at length, for it illustrated some of the points of disagreement between the "revisionists" and their critics; this interpretation seemed to some "revisionist" historians sophisticated and realistic historical thought at a high level, while to some critics of the "revisionist" position, it seemed a collection of generalized truisms which were not focused on the most important questions:

The war came because of certain interests and activities characterized for convenience as the processes of human behavior, in which individual and general attitudes and emotional drives are constantly interacting—provoking and conditioning one another. At certain times and in certain circumstances, cooperative behavior predominates; but competitive behavior is seldom if ever absent, and when too vigorously aroused leads to a strife which ranges from argument to war. . . . The American Democracy sought from 1850 to 1860 to keep in power by encouraging cooperative behavior. But, deeply affected by the shocks of the collisions occurring within the society in which it operated and of which it was a part, the party failed to overcome the divisive attitudes and was shattered. The disruption of the American Democracy eventuated in defeat, secession, and civil war.[68]

Two years after the appearance of *The Disruption of American Democracy*, there was published Kenneth M. Stampp's volume, *And The War Came*, another discussion of the causes of the Civil War from the "revisionist" point of view. Professor Stampp was almost twenty years younger than any other of the "revisionist" historians discussed so far (and was thirty years younger than some of them). Born in Wisconsin in 1912, he had received his undergraduate and graduate training at the University of Wisconsin; he lived and taught briefly (1941-1946) in Arkansas and

[67] Nichols, *Disruption*, 516-517.   [68] *ibid.*, 517.

Maryland before going to the University of California in 1946. At first glance, Stampp's discussion of the causes of the Civil War seemed to differ on several important questions from the views of such earlier "revisionists" as Craven and Randall. Stampp, for example, stated that he was not concerned with proving or disproving that the Civil War was "inevitable"; he disposed of the matter with the common-sense observation (with which many critics of the "revisionists" would apparently have agreed) that the Civil War was no more necessary or inevitable than any other war. Neither was it any less so. Unfortunately, the issues were the sort that often produce hatreds that, in turn, drive men to mortal combat. Some wars have grown out of less serious causes.[69]

Stampp's view of the role of "propaganda" and of "extremists" in bringing on the war also seemed to connote an emphasis different from that of Craven and Randall. While he agreed that the "propaganda of northern and southern agitators" was "one of the prime causes" of the Civil War, he apparently placed stress upon a North-South conflict over important issues (slavery and "other economic differences") as a more basic cause: "Between North and South there did exist a profound and irrepressible clash of material interests."[70] The Civil War, he wrote, was "the product of deep and fundamental causes."[71] Finally, Stampp was not as ardent a champion as most previous "revisionists" of many of the various proposals for compromise in the crisis of 1860-1861. Certain basic sectional differences existed, in his opinion, which could not be compromised in view of the "tough realities of the 'irrepressible conflict,'" and he described most of the compromise proposals as "essentially superficial."[72]

Yet, on close examination it turned out that Stampp's point of view was fundamentally in accord with the "revisionist" tradition, and his volume was reviewed with high praise by such older "revisionist" historians as Craven and Nichols.[73] For there emerged

[69] Kenneth M. Stampp, *And the War Came: The North and the Secession Crisis 1860-1861* (Baton Rouge, La., 1950) 3.
[70] All the quotations in this sentence are from *ibid.*, 2.
[71] *ibid., vii.*
[72] The quotations in this sentence (in order) are from *ibid.*, 157, *vii.*
[73] See reviews of *And the War Came* by Avery O. Craven in *The Saturday Review of Literature*, xxxiii, 40 (December 2, 1950), and by Roy F. Nichols in *The American Historical Review*, lvi, 595-597 (April 1951).

from *And the War Came* the primary and strong implication that war could have been and should have been prevented in 1861 and that peace was the most desirable of all the various alternatives at that time. "Politicians," Stampp pointed out, did have an alternative to war in 1861: "They might have agreed that the price of war was too high, that a peaceful solution was worth any sacrifice."[74] Stampp himself appeared to agree, throughout the volume, that "a peaceful solution was worth any sacrifice," and this opinion made his outlook on the Civil War basically similar to that of previous "revisionists." The policy which, in Stampp's pages, offered the best chance of preserving the peace, the policy which seemed most logical and reasonable, was for the North to have acquiesced in "peaceful separation" in 1861—and this idea formed the principal basis for his study of the coming of war:

separation was the last hope for a peaceful settlement. Why the southern attempt to apply this solution did not produce peace between North and South will be the major theme of this book.[75]

Earlier "revisionists" had lauded efforts to compromise the sectional struggle, equating "compromise" and "peace"; Stampp instead favored a policy of separation and equated "separation" and "peace"; but the important fact was that Stampp and earlier "revisionists" both explained the coming of the war from the same basic philosophical position—that peace could have been and should have been preserved.

Stampp demonstrated in several different places throughout his volume an awareness that war could have been avoided had the South (instead of the North) acquiesced; "Southerners," he declared, "might have yielded to northern political supremacy and prepared to see their 'peculiar institution' go sooner or later."[76] Going even further, he wrote in 1952 that a "blunder that culminated in Civil War came in 1860 when Southerners refused to abide by the results of a democratic election."[77] Yet, in his volume

[74] Stampp, *And the War Came*, 3.   [75] *ibid., vii.*
[76] *ibid.,* 3.
[77] Kenneth M. Stampp, "What Caused the Civil War," in Richard W. Leopold and Arthur S. Link, eds., *Problems in American History* (New York, 1952) 424. Stampp's conclusion to this article, pp. 423-425, does not seem to the present author to express the same point of view as his book, *And the War Came*, or other volumes by "revisionists."

he formulated the problem of why the war came not in terms of why Southerners did not make fundamental concessions, not in terms of why Northerners and Southerners both did not make fundamental concessions, but rather in terms of "why Northerners were unwilling to acquiesce in disunion."[78] And he repeatedly demonstrated his perplexity over the fact that Northerners of the 1860's did not wish to let the Southern states go in peace (a solution which seemed so reasonable to this twentieth-century historian): "why Northerners believed that the formation of a Southern Confederacy would have been such a terrible disaster is not easily explained."[79]

The chief elements in Stampp's approach to the Civil War (the conviction that peace could and should have been preserved, and that the proper policy to this end was Northern acceptance of Southern separation) seemed to rest upon the same foundation as the thinking of earlier "revisionists": deep disillusionment with the results of the Civil War. And for Stampp, disillusionment with the results of the war (a war which ended with "the rich richer and the slaves only half free"), was apparently part of his more general disillusionment with nationalism and with what he called the "ideals of the nineteenth-century middle classes."[80] The sentences with which Stampp closed his volume well expressed the mood of disappointment which pervaded it:

Nationalists might rejoice that the Union was preserved. But what the Yankees achieved—for their generation at least—was a triumph not of middle-class ideals but of middle-class vices. The most striking products of their crusade were the shoddy aristocracy of the North and the ragged children of the South. Among the masses of Americans there were no victors, only the vanquished.[81]

If Stampp and his book be taken as an accurate indication, it would seem that the appeal of the "revisionist" viewpoints was not limited to historians who had reached maturity around the time of the First World War. How great would be the attraction of these viewpoints for a younger generation of historians was difficult to estimate. In the opinion of some observers, a favorable

[78] *ibid., vii.*　　　　　　　　[79] *ibid.*, 205.
[80] The quotations are taken from *ibid.*, 297-298. See also *ibid.*, 3, 239.
[81] *ibid.*, 298.

omen for the continued strong appeal of "revisionism" in the United States in the 1950's was the war-weariness and the sentiment of "neutralism" toward the international tensions of the day. "Revisionist" attitudes toward the Civil War, such observers argued, had originated (as the "peace interpretation") amidst the war-weariness and neutralist sentiments of the 1860's, had experienced their twentieth-century rebirth in the atmosphere of war-weariness and disillusionment following upon the First World War, and should thus, presumably, have a continued appeal in an atmosphere of war-weariness and neutralism following the Second World War. What the future held, no one of course could say, but from all appearances the "revisionist" interpretation of the causes and character of the Civil War was still widely held among historians in the United States in the early 1950's.

The major effect of the writings of the "revisionist" historians upon the interpretation of the causes of the Civil War was to shift the focus of attention from a long-developing sectional conflict to the immediate outbreak of hostilities in 1861. And in explaining the immediate outbreak of hostilities, "revisionists" called attention to the important role of emotions and to the agitation of extremists. There seemed to be considerable agreement among historians of differing viewpoints that the "revisionists," by shifting the focus of attention in this manner, had thrown some light on the causes of the war and had stimulated a healthy reexamination of other interpretations of the coming of war. Critics of the "revisionists" insisted that, granting the truth of the above statement, the "revisionists" had still confused the question of what caused the Civil War more than they had clarified it. On this last mentioned issue, needless to say, there was not agreement among historians.

CHAPTER EIGHT
"THE CONFUSION OF VOICES"

The Decline of the "Nationalist Tradition"

By the end of the 1930's, the attitudes toward the Civil War dominant among historians in the United States were considerably different from those which had generally prevailed from the 1890's to the First World War. Each of the interpretations of the Civil War which had emerged in the twentieth century (Beardian, Marxian, pro-Southern, and "revisionist") represented a challenge to the "nationalist tradition"; and the fact that some of these rival explanations, in particular those set forth by Beard and by the "revisionists," won wide support among historians signified a corresponding decline in the appeal of the "nationalist tradition."

As this tradition lost favor after the First World War, there was a corresponding decline in the reputation of the historian who had been the foremost exponent of that tradition—James Ford Rhodes. Just as, in the period around 1900, the new generation of trained historians had come to look upon the writers of Civil War histories in the 1860's and 1870's as biased and partisan, so in the 1920's and 1930's, in a somewhat similar fashion, historians turned a critical eye upon the scholarship of Rhodes. (Other historians who had been prominently associated with the "nationalist tradition" also received criticism. Channing's views on the Civil War, as we have seen, were rejected by Beard, while Turner in the 1930's and 1940's came in for a barrage of criticism from many different sources.)

Several factors help to explain this reevaluation of Rhodes. Later research necessitated a change in some statements of fact made by Rhodes, but criticism was directed more against the point of view of his *History* than against the facts it contained. His historical viewpoint had been somewhat "out-of-date" even in the 1890's, as has been suggested, in the sense that he did not place emphasis upon economic forces or upon the role of the West—an emphasis already to be found in that decade in the writings of Wilson, Channing, and Turner, among others. In addition,

Rhodes extended his *History*, in volumes published in 1919 and 1922, to cover the story of the United States from 1877 to 1909; even historians who sympathized with Rhodes' views on the Civil War and Reconstruction declared that he was writing in these latter two volumes of a period which he did not understand and in which he did not seem greatly interested. But a primary reason for the decline of Rhodes' reputation after the First World War was the fact that his views on the Civil War no longer had the widespread appeal which they possessed a quarter-century earlier. Rhodes had constructed the earliest and the most influential single expression of the "nationalist tradition," and at the same time the least complex and most pro-Northern expression; thus, when the reaction against that tradition set in, the writings of Rhodes came in for the most severe strictures.

Already by 1913, an anonymous reviewer observed in *The American Historical Review* that the views of Rhodes did not reflect the newer ideas on the causes of the Civil War (perhaps it was significant that a criticism of Rhodes in *The American Historical Review* in 1913 was made anonymously):

If he [Rhodes] has read the newer literature on the antecedents of the war, he has paid scant attention to its effect upon his earlier conclusions.[1]

Within the next decade, the storm burst in full force and continued on into the 1930's. Although their grounds for criticism differed, every separate group of historians, it seemed, was dissatisfied with Rhodes' *History*—and now there was no need for anonymity. On the one hand, the Beardians criticized Rhodes' emphasis upon the moral issue of slavery as the heart of the irrepressible conflict; they complained also of his businessman's conservatism in political and economic matters. It would seem, Beard wrote in 1919,

that Mr. Rhodes has seen America a part of the time through the windows of a counting house and the remainder of the time through the windows of the Centennial Club.[2]

On the other hand, the fact that Rhodes described an irrepressible

---

[1] *The American Historical Review*, xviii, 845 (July 1913).

[2] Charles A. Beard, "James Ford Rhodes," *The New Republic*, xxi, 82 (December 17, 1919); see also *The Rise of American Civilization*, ii, 36-37.

conflict over issues of fundamental importance in American life made him anathema to the "revisionists" of the Craven-Randall school. To the vindicators of the South, Rhodes seemed an apologist for the North, while a Marxist noted with disapproval his "tolerant attitude toward the South" and his "sympathy with the prevalent Northern disposition [in Rhodes' day] to let bygones be bygones."[3]

Illustrating the extent of the change in opinions, one historian now speculated whether Rhodes' hostile view of Stephen A. Douglas was not unconsciously colored as a result of a lawsuit brought by Douglas's sons against Rhodes' father.[4] Even writers sympathetic to Rhodes now acknowledged the criticism he was receiving and took pains to admit that he was "the last great workman of the school that did not distinguish between nationalism and Northernism" (N.W. Stephenson), or that his history was "written from the Northern point of view" (L.B. Shippee).[5] Rhodes became a straw man and a whipping boy for almost an entire generation of scholars; young historians, with the encouragement of their elders, in effect cut their professional teeth on him. It became almost standard procedure for a young scholar to begin his writing on the Civil War period with a quotation from Rhodes and then to devote his article or book to an elaborate proof that Rhodes was wrong. Seldom has an individual gained a reputation as a historian of the first rank as rapidly as did Rhodes in the 1890's, but seldom also has a historian lost such a reputation as rapidly as did Rhodes in the 1920's and 1930's.[6] (Perhaps the fact that so many scholars almost automatically began their

[3] The quotations are from Enmale, ed., *The Civil War in the United States,* xvii.

[4] F.H. Hodder, "Propaganda As A Source of American History," *The Mississippi Valley Historical Review,* IX, 10 (June 1922).

[5] N.W. Stephenson, "Mr. Rhodes as Historian," *The Yale Review,* x, 862 (July 1921); Lester Burrell Shippee, "Rhodes's History of the United States," *The Mississippi Valley Historical Review,* VIII, 136 (June-September 1921).

[6] For additional comments by historians on Rhodes and his viewpoints, see: Frederic L. Paxson's review of Rhodes, *The McKinley and Roosevelt Administrations, 1897-1909,* in *The American Historical Review,* XXVIII, 565-566 (April 1923); unsigned review of the same volume in *The Mississippi Valley Historical Review,* x, 200 (September 1923); Raymond Curtis Miller, "James Ford Rhodes: A Study in Historiography," *The Mississippi Valley Historical Review,* xv, 455-472 (March 1929). Various reviews of M.A. de Wolfe Howe's biography, *James Ford Rhodes: American Historian* (New York, 1929), also furnish indications of the changing evaluation of Rhodes.

studies of the Civil War era with a refutation of Rhodes constitutes one of the most impressive testimonies to the importance
of Rhodes as a historian and to the influence of the ideas he
expressed.)

The decline in the reputation of Rhodes was symptomatic of
the waning appeal of his point of view. The "nationalist tradition"
was not "dead" by 1940, and the attitudes associated with it still
had influence among historians. But it was evident that this tradition, after more than two decades of vigorous assault from all
quarters, had lost the commanding position it had once held, and
its supporters were now on the defensive. The question which naturally arises is: Why did this come about? Why was it that the
viewpoints of Rhodes, Wilson, Channing, Turner, and others of
that group lost favor and were supplanted, to a considerable extent, by rival interpretations of the Civil War?

One reason for change in historical attitudes has frequently been
the discovery of "new" evidence about the past (i.e., evidence
which up to that time has not figured prominently in the thoughts
of the particular group of individuals in question). To some extent, this cause for change was operative in this instance. To cite
one specific example, the investigations of Frank H. Hodder and
George Fort Milton, among others, led to a major reinterpretation
of the Kansas-Nebraska Act of 1854 and of the role of Stephen A.
Douglas in connection with that act. The major body of "new"
evidence made available to historians in the twentieth century was
that from Southern sources. The previously unexploited material
which Ulrich B. Phillips and other Southern historians unearthed
and used in their studies was an important factor in changing the
picture of the plantation-slavery system (and of the Old South in
general) painted by Rhodes and some other historians in the "nationalist tradition." In the twentieth century, for the first time,
scholarly writings portrayed in a sympathetic spirit the viewpoint
of the dominant groups of white Southerners in the sectional conflict. It seems reasonable to conclude that it was more than a coincidence that all the major new interpretations of the Civil War
advanced in the twentieth century (except those by the Marxists)
were explicitly or implicitly more sympathetic to the Confederate
cause than was the "nationalist tradition."

But, having said this much, the new interpretations of the Civil War still seem, by and large, to have been due not as much to new evidence about the past as to new experiences in the present. The experiences of historians in the twentieth century, and their reactions to their experiences, disposed many of them to see the previously known facts in a new light and to find some facts, both among those previously known and among those newly discovered, more significant than others. The Beardian and Marxian interpretations owed comparatively little to the discovery of new evidence about the Civil War era: these were not syntheses built upon a mass of research monographs—instead, as in the case of the Beardian explanation, the synthesis (*The Rise of American Civilization*) came first and was followed later by the special studies of other investigators embodying the same point of view. The "revisionist" explanation was undoubtedly constructed to some extent upon new evidence about the South; but the "revisionist" attitude toward war in general would seem to have been more important than new facts about the Civil War era in shaping that distinctive interpretation. Even the pro-Southern point of view would seem to have been due as much to the increasing sectional tension after the First World War as to the discovery of new facts about the South.

To many of the twentieth century historians, the new syntheses were appealing because they expressed a spirit toward the American past which, in the light of their own experiences and outlook, seemed to them more "realistic" than that of the "nationalist tradition." Rhodes, Wilson, Channing, Turner, and others in the "nationalist tradition," whatever their differences, had all studied the American past, as we have seen, in a spirit of sympathy and affection (to describe their viewpoint simply as "nationalistic" is inadequate, for it was both a broader and deeper emotion than that word normally indicates): although they studied the United States in its time of crisis—Civil War and Reconstruction—they found in its experience more cause for hope than for despair, more achievement for the common good than failures. By contrast, the common characteristic of the interpretations which challenged the "nationalist tradition" was their disillusionment with the Civil War era: the Beardians, the "revisionists," and the vindicators of the South were all dismayed at the long-run results of the war and Reconstruction; the "revisionists" and the Southern sympathizers were disappointed because the war had ever occurred; and several of the Marxists were scornful of all the history of the "bourgeois republic" except insofar as they interpreted it as necessary to prepare the way for the coming revolution.

The challengers of the "nationalist tradition" formulated their ideas in an intellectual environment in which (especially after the First World War) the spirit of nationalism was suspect and the spirit of sectional reconciliation between North and South which had characterized the "nationalist tradition" was being replaced by sectional antagonism. Moreover, in this environment there was a tendency to question all the values, standards, and viewpoints of the past generation. "There is nothing," James G. Randall declared in 1940, "that is not questioned. Revision has become popular and rightly so."[7] The historians who revised the "nationalist tradition" were not debunkers, but most of their revisions had the effect of showing the past in a less creditable light than it had previously been depicted. They were not really "pessimists" in their view of the Civil War era; they were bitterly disappointed idealists—disappointed, some of them, that the United States had not solved its problems short of war; disappointed, some of them, that the United States in becoming industrialized had not preserved all the virtues which they believed inhered in an agricultural society. But their bitterness stemmed not from a pessimistic philosophy (which presumably would have led them to expect little of mankind in the first place) but from an idealistic or optimistic outlook which expected much of human beings, and turned into disgust when those human beings, even when faced with difficult and complex problems, did not fulfill the high expectations of a later generation.

It is worthy of note that no one synthesis emerged from the various challenges to the "nationalist tradition." The one common

[7] James G. Randall, "The Civil War Restudied," *The Journal of Southern History*, VI, 443 (November 1940). The disillusioned attitude in which many historians approached the study of the Civil War in the two decades after 1920 is exemplified in a 1933 article by Richard H. Shryock (a Pennsylvanian, at that time a member of the faculty of Duke University): "The Nationalistic Tradition of the Civil War: A Southern Analysis," *The South Atlantic Quarterly*, XXXII, 294-305 (July 1933).

element in the rival interpretations was their disagreement with that tradition; they differed widely in their own explanations of the coming of the war, displaying almost as much disagreement with one another as with the tradition they criticized (the "revisionist" James G. Randall, for example, seemed every bit as critical of the Beardian viewpoint as he was of the interpretation of Rhodes; similarly, the Marxists, on the one hand, and the vindicators of the South, on the other, clearly represented two directly opposite poles of opinion). Much food for speculation was offered by the fact that the "nationalist tradition" was not replaced by any one synthesis and that there was sharp disagreement between its various challengers. Perhaps this was an indication of an increasing complexity and diversification of American intellectual life, including American historiography. Perhaps it was also symbolic of a period in American intellectual life in which there was considerably more agreement on the relatively easy (perhaps too easy) rejection of the standards and values of the past than on the more difficult task of formulating or clarifying standards and values for the present which would be more satisfactory than those rejected.

Some Signs of a New Outlook

IN HIS presidential address before the American Historical Association in December 1950, Samuel Eliot Morison described a shift in the attitudes of historians toward the American past and toward war. And in this address, Morison himself made a significant expression of the new and different attitudes which, in his opinion, were now finding favor among historians. Censuring the "debunkers and dialectical materialists" of the 1920's and 1930's, he stated his belief that their influence was now on the wane:

There is [today] a decided change of attitude toward our past, a friendly, almost affectionate attitude, as contrasted with the cynical, almost hateful one of young intellectuals twenty-five years ago.[8]

Morison also had words of criticism for those historians of the 1920's and 1930's who,

caught in the disillusion that followed World War I, ignored wars, belittled wars, taught that no war was necessary and no war did any good, even to the victor. All these antiwar historians were sincere, and few of them were doctrinaire pacifists, as their actions in the last few years prove; nevertheless, their zeal against war did nothing to preserve peace. It only rendered the generation of youth which came to maturity around 1940 spiritually unprepared for the war they had to fight.[9]

Instead of ignoring and belittling wars, Morison asserted, historians should have taken the lead in pointing out that "war does accomplish something, that war is better than servitude, that war has been an inescapable aspect of the human story."[10]

The climate of ideas which Morison described in 1950 was quite different from that of the 1920's or 1930's, and the dividing line between the two eras would seem to lie in the period around 1940-1941—that time of soul-searching and rapid reorientation on the

[8] Samuel Eliot Morison, "Faith of a Historian," *The American Historical Review*, LVI, 272 (January 1951).
[9] *ibid.*, 266-267. [10] *ibid.*, 267.

part of many American intellectuals (a process whose generally accepted symbol has become Archibald MacLeish's *The Irresponsibles*). The new attitudes alluded to by Morison had their counterparts, as always, in other countries within Western civilization; in the United States, these attitudes seemed to have stemmed primarily from the international tensions which absorbed the attention of many Americans from the late 1930's onward.

One aspect of these international tensions was the rise and strengthening of twentieth century totalitarianism abroad, creating, in the opinion of many individuals, a threat to the United States and to its way of life. The experience of seeing totalitarianism in practice greatly enhanced the appeal of the democratic constitutional system of the United States, whatever its imperfections (some historians, for example, now began to speak and write of "generalities that still glitter"). And the experience of war at first hand helped to produce a new outlook on war causation. Just as the First World War had its influence upon ideas of what caused wars, so too did the world wars of the 1930's to the 1950's— but, at least for some individuals, in a quite different direction. For it seemed to many Americans that the international conflicts from the 1930's to the 1950's had their origin, at least in part, in the antagonism of irreconcilable ideologies. It also seemed that these struggles, whatever else they involved, involved considerations of a moral or ethical nature.

Moreover, some individuals came to feel that the experiences of the twentieth century suggested a philosophy of the nature of man and of the nature of history different from what they called the modern "sentimental" and "excessively optimistic" point of view. This new outlook, as expressed in its most influential form by the theologian Reinhold Niebuhr, emphasized among other things the reality of evil in the universe, the complexity of the problems faced by human beings, and the tragedy inherent in existence; applied to history, this outlook led to criticism of what Niebuhr described as the confidence of modern idealism in "the possibility of an easy resolution of the tension between individual and community, or between classes, races and nations."[11] Histori-

[11] Reinhold Niebuhr, *The Children of Light and the Children of Darkness* (New York, 1944) 18.

ans who shared some or all of the ideas here described now found unsatisfactory previous explanations of the causes of wars which placed stress exclusively upon economic factors or which asserted that wars came because of "unreal issues" created by propaganda and emotionalism.

Observers were not agreed on how widespread among historians were the attitudes described by Morison, and there was obviously no way of knowing in the early 1950's whether such attitudes were a temporary phenomenon or whether they represented a long-range trend. But in a few scattered books, articles, and reviews appearing in the 1940's and 1950's, one could see indications of the effect of these attitudes on the viewpoints of some historians toward the Civil War. These indications were to be found primarily in criticism, based upon the ideas described above, of the two explanations of the Civil War which had won such favor in the 1920's and 1930's, the Beardian economic interpretation and that of the "revisionists."

Criticism of the economic interpretations of the Civil War, as has been suggested, was made in the 1930's by "revisionist" historians such as James G. Randall on the ground that no fundamental North-South differences, economic or other, had led to war in 1861. In the 1940's and 1950's, however, there appeared criticism of economic interpretations from the standpoint (unlike that of Randall) that basic dissimilarities between North and South had led to war, but that these dissimilarities were more ideological in nature than economic. Such a viewpoint was reflected by the literary historian Henry Seidel Canby in a volume published during the Second World War; Canby expressed agreement with those present-day students of the Civil War who, he stated, had "seen in their own time economic man and economic interpretations bombed into cellars by a war where ideologies have been more significant than potential profits."[12] Similarly, the economic historian George O. Virtue (born 1861), professor emeritus at the University of Nebraska, criticized economic interpretations of the Civil War in 1949 and expressed the opinion that the slavery issue had caused the struggle.[13] Probably the most widely-read

[12] Henry Seidel Canby, *Walt Whitman: An American* (Boston, 1943) 213.
[13] George O. Virtue, "Marxian Interpretation of the Civil War," *Nebraska History,*

criticism of economic interpretations of the Civil War was that made by Arthur M. Schlesinger, Jr. (born 1917), of Massachusetts and Harvard. In his best-selling book, *The Age of Jackson*, published in 1945, Schlesinger, although granting that the antislavery impulse had its economic aspects, declared that it was fundamentally a "moral impulse"; he insisted that the Civil War was primarily a sectional rather than a class war, and that it was "moral disgust" over the institution of slavery which had ultimately sent the North to battle.[14]

The expression of disapproval with the "revisionist" point of view was led by Bernard De Voto (born 1897), free-lance historian and long-time resident of Massachusetts, in two articles published in 1946. De Voto ascribed the general viewpoint of the "revisionists" to an "erroneous thesis" of the causes of the First World War. The "revisionist" interpretation of the Civil War, he charged, was based upon sentimentalism—upon the hopeful belief that if the South had just been left alone, slavery would have come to an end and all the unfortunate results of the Civil War and Reconstruction would have been avoided.[15] He argued that the "revisionists" evaded the basic facts of the historical situation they described: the fact of slavery (including the moral conflict over that institution) and the fact of secession (involving the breaking up of a free government by discontented individuals). Similar criticisms were expressed by Arthur M. Schlesinger, Jr., in 1949 when he charged that the "revisionist" position rested upon the optimistic and unwarranted assumption that evil in the world (the institution of slavery) would automatically be outmoded by "progress"; revisionism, he wrote, "at once evades the essential moral problems in the name of a superficial objectivity and asserts their unimportance in the name of an invincible progress."[16] Yet another critic of the "revisionists," Arthur M. Schlesinger (born

---

xxx, 19-49 (March 1949); Virtue criticized both Marxian and Beardian economic interpretations of the Civil War.

[14] Arthur M. Schlesinger, Jr., *The Age of Jackson* (Boston, 1945) 432-433, 505-506. Schlesinger was explicitly critical of Marxist views of the Civil War era: see *ibid.*, 432-433.

[15] Bernard De Voto, "The Easy Chair," *Harper's Magazine*, v. 192, pp. 123-126, 234-237 (February, March 1946).

[16] Arthur M. Schlesinger, Jr., "The Causes of the Civil War: A Note on Historical Sentimentalism," *Partisan Review*, xvi, 969-981 (October 1949); the quotation is taken from p. 976 of this article.

1888), professor of history at Harvard, suggested that while "other men, godlike in wisdom and operating in a political vacuum," might have acted differently in the sectional crisis, the fact remained that the extremists (whom the "revisionists" held largely responsible for the Civil War) were themselves part of the situation which the historian must explain.[17]

It is interesting to note that the critics of the "revisionists," like their predecessors in the "nationalist tradition," did not all speak with one voice on the question of the "irrepressible conflict." Arthur M. Schlesinger, Jr., seemed to insist that war itself was inevitable, but this was not true of De Voto, who, of all the critics of the "revisionists," seemed to be nearest to the spirit of Seward's "irrepressible conflict" speech and Lincoln's "house divided" speech of the 1850's. Without contending that armed hostilities had been inevitable, De Voto insisted that there had been fundamental conflicts between the sections which had to be confronted and put on the road to some acceptable solution if the sectional tension were to abate—and he asserted that these conflicts were neither accurately defined nor squarely faced by the "revisionist" historians.

In criticizing those interpretations which had won favor in the 1920's and 1930's, De Voto, Arthur M. Schlesinger, Jr., and other writers approached a position similar in many respects to the "nationalist tradition" of the Civil War. They emphasized the existence by 1860 of a deep-seated sectional cleavage over matters of fundamental importance, and they singled out as one of the primary factors causing this cleavage the institution of slavery and the differing sectional opinions on slavery; they insisted that historians must understand and explain this cleavage if they were to interpret the causes of the war; in describing this cleavage, their primary sympathies were with the type of society which had developed in the nonslaveholding sections, but they did not attempt to pin blame for the war exclusively upon Southerners; and

---

[17] Arthur M. Schlesinger, *The American as Reformer* (Cambridge, 1950) 43-44. The "revisionist" viewpoint was also criticized by the Dutch historian Pieter Geyl in his article, "The American Civil War and the Problem of Inevitability," *The New England Quarterly*, xxiv, 147-168 (June 1951); this article furnished a concrete example of the manner in which currents of ideas and of historical interpretation cut across national boundaries in Western civilization.

finally, without picturing all the results of the Civil War as beneficial or without claiming that all the nation's problems were solved by the war, these writers reflected the conviction that some basic national problems had been placed on the road to a desirable solution due to the outcome of the war. In contrast, for example, to what might be called the disillusioned "robber baron" evaluation of the results of the war, Arthur M. Schlesinger declared that the war had contributed, within certain limits, to "human betterment" (and Allan Nevins and Arthur M. Schlesinger, Jr., suggested that the "robber barons" themselves be reevaluated).[18] In a generally similar vein, Ralph Barton Perry asserted that the Civil War had meant, fortunately, the "triumph of the democratic creed" and the establishment of national unity.[19] This group of historians did not expect perfection from human beings or human societies; they saw in the outcome of the war not cause for despair and disillusionment due to the fact that perfection had not been achieved, but cause for hope and a measure of satisfaction due to important desirable consequences of the struggle.

If the views of De Voto, Schlesinger, Jr., and other writers discussed above represented in many respects a reassertion of some of the ideas and attitudes of the "nationalist tradition," they also represented something more than that—for the intellectual atmosphere in which De Voto and the others formulated their ideas was different in some important respects from that in which the "nationalist tradition" had taken shape. The intellectual climate of opinion in which the "nationalist tradition" emerged was characterized, as we have seen, by strong currents of nationalism and sectional reconciliation; the historians who expressed that tradition looked back with relief on the Civil War period as one in which the nation had been saved from internal disintegration and in which the cancer of slavery had been excised; most of these historians looked forward with a certain degree of confidence to continued peace, progress, and prosperity, for they wrote their histories, by and large, before the thinking of historians had been

[18] Schlesinger, *The American as Reformer*, 18; Allan Nevins, quoted in the *New York Times*, August 6, 1951; Arthur M. Schlesinger, Jr., *The Vital Center* (New York, 1949) 44.
[19] Ralph Barton Perry, *Puritanism and Democracy* (New York, 1944) 144.

deeply affected by doubts concerning the workings of the economic system which had emerged in the post-Civil-War United States, or deeply affected by disillusionment with war. The "nationalist tradition" thus reflected, in the main, the intellectual atmosphere of the turn of the century before twentieth century movements for social reform, before the twentieth century economic depression, before the twentieth century wars, and before Beard and the "revisionists."

By contrast, the ideas and attitudes expressed by De Voto and the other writers here under discussion reflected the intellectual atmosphere after the reform movements, the economic depression, and the wars of the first half of the twentieth century. De Voto and the others were "post-Beardians" and "post-revisionists" who had become convinced by the 1940's that the Beardian and "revisionist" approaches did not offer an adequate understanding of the Civil War. In their outlook, war and evil seemed to play an enduring role in the world, never becoming completely outmoded by historical "progress," and struggles stemming from irreconcilable ideological differences (involving considerations of an ethical or moral nature) seemed to be a recurring aspect of life. Such a struggle, it seemed from this standpoint, was involved in the Civil War, and therefore the viewpoints on the Civil War of Rhodes, Channing, and other historians who formulated the "nationalist tradition" now seemed "realistic" to some historians at the middle of the twentieth century, like De Voto, whose over-all philosophy was different from that of Rhodes and Channing. Thus the ideas and attitudes of De Voto and the others might be described not simply as a reassertion of the "nationalist tradition" but as the "new nationalist tradition."

Several of the individuals who expressed the "new nationalist tradition" were born in, or had been educated in, or had lived for a number of years in New England; none of them was born in or had lived in the one-time Confederate States—unlike the aggregation of historians who had formulated the "nationalist tradition" itself in the 1890's. Perhaps the fact that there were no Southerners in this group was merely a matter of chance, or perhaps it was one more sign of the reappearance in the twentieth century of a South *versus* non-South sectionalism in the United States.

The formulation of a "new nationalist tradition," it should be emphasized, was by the early 1950's only a tendency rather than a fully developed movement; it was confined with one exception to scattered and generally brief comments by writers who were not specialists in the history of the Civil War era. There was one major history of the Civil War period published after the Second World War which reflected a viewpoint similar to the "new nationalist tradition"—the large-scale history by Allan Nevins, *Ordeal of the Union*; but this work, as will be pointed out shortly, seemed also to reflect some other attitudes as well. The most that could be said, apparently, was that a trend was discernible in the 1940's and 1950's which might (but which also might not) foreshadow an important emphasis upon a "new nationalist tradition" by historians.

The appearance of this tendency toward a "new nationalist tradition" added to the mixture of viewpoints on the causes and character of the Civil War. By the early 1950's, economic interpretations had apparently lost some of the wide popularity with historians which they had possessed in the 1930's, but the Beardian viewpoint still had its adherents. Pro-Southern explanations of the war seemed to be losing none of their appeal among Southern historians, while the "revisionist" attitudes probably still had more support than any other single interpretation. Amidst such a confusion of divergent points of view, many historians probably sought in their own minds to make a synthesis of some or all of the various current interpretations. If such a synthesis were possible, the time seemed propitious for its reception—and historians were given the opportunity to evaluate one such attempted synthesis with the appearance, beginning in the late 1940's, of the opening volumes of what promised to be the most detailed history of the Civil War era yet undertaken by any single historian, *Ordeal of the Union* by Allan Nevins.

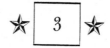

Allan Nevins and *Ordeal of the Union*

ALLAN NEVINS, the author of the latest large-scale history of the Civil War, was born in Illinois in 1890 and received his undergraduate and graduate training at the University of Illinois. His history, *Ordeal of the Union*, began with the end of the 1840's and, in the four volumes published by 1950, spanned the years through the inauguration of Lincoln; it was the first major detailed study of this era since the volumes of Rhodes (Channing and Cole had each covered the period from approximately 1850 to 1865 in one volume), and was, so far, on a larger scale than Rhodes' *History* (the first three volumes of which were devoted to the years from 1850 to 1862). Historians reviewing Nevins' volumes noted the wide research displayed in them as well as the felicitous style of writing; there were many predictions that these volumes would rank as a major work in American historiography. Rhodes' *History* had reflected many of the viewpoints on the Civil War dominant in the era in which it was published, and it had also helped to shape those viewpoints. The question arose: Would this also be the role of Nevins' *Ordeal of the Union*?

If Nevins' interpretation of the causes of the Civil War be described in terms of the attitudes so far discussed in this study, it was clearly not an economic interpretation, Marxian or Beardian (although economic forces were discussed at some length), nor was it similar to the Owsley type of vindication of the South. Instead, it seemed to represent a combination of some "revisionist" attitudes with some of the elements of the "new nationalist tradition"—a "combination" rather than a "synthesis," for those two sets of ideas were so different that it seemed impossible to assimilate them into one consistent and coherent pattern, and as a result several historians reviewing *Ordeal of the Union* suggested that there was a persistent dualism in Nevins' explanation of the coming of war.

Like the "revisionists," Nevins seemed at times to center his interpretation of the war's causes primarily upon the outbreak of hostilities in 1861 (rather than upon sectional conflict); war in 1861, he asserted, was easier than wisdom and courage, and he seemed to insist that war should have been averted and could have been averted. Like the Second World War, he wrote, the Civil War

should have been avoidable. Because the people and leaders of the United States did not act with determination and sagacity in solving the problems of slavery, sectional irritation, and a right adjustment of races, part of the country was half ruined for generations, and all of it set back by decades.[20]

The primary task of statesmanship in this era, in Nevins' opinion, was to provide a workable adjustment between North and South, and at the same time to persuade Southerners to modify and gradually abolish the institution of slavery while persuading Northerners to be helpful rather than critical during the process.[21] He seemed at times to imply that these objects could have been accomplished and war averted had it not been for the "errors" of political leaders, for the defects of the American political machinery, and for the baneful influences of emotionalism.

Writing of the "failure of American leadership" in the 1850's, Nevins singled out the Presidents for blame: "Zachary Taylor was stubbornly wrongheaded; Franklin Pierce was impulsively erratic; James Buchanan timidly fumbling."[22] In addition to the weaknesses of these individuals, the government which they headed, declared Nevins, did not have adequate planning agencies; the American political system was handicapped by its rigidity (in 1854 and 1858 the administration remained in office after being rebuffed at the polls) and political parties in the United States worked badly in the face of sectionalism.[23] In the atmosphere of such sectionalism in the 1850's, there were misunderstandings between North and South, and Nevins stated that the "unrealities of passion" were frequently dominant.[24] At times he seemed to approach the slavery question from this standpoint of emotional

---

[20] Allan Nevins, *Ordeal of the Union* (4v., New York, 1947-1950) I, *viii*.
[21] *ibid.*, II, 451.
[22] The quotations (in order) are from *ibid.*, IV, 463, and I, *x*.
[23] *ibid.*, IV, 469-470.
[24] The quotation is from *ibid.*, I, *ix*; see also I, 535.

unrealities, criticizing the abolitionists and implying that if men had just been "reasonable" about slavery, there would have been no cause for dispute:

Had both North and South sat down quietly, appraised the number and value of the fugitive slaves, got at the truth about all the reports of the kidnapping of free Negroes, and refrained from emotion and exaggeration, agreement might have been possible. Both sides were equally guilty of hysteria.[25]

If judged only from the passages so far cited, it might well be concluded that Nevins' interpretation of the causes of the Civil War, while not precisely the same as that of the "revisionists," was nevertheless quite close to their position. Yet, throughout Nevins' volumes there was, in the opinion of the present author, stronger emphasis upon attitudes which were more similar to the "new nationalist tradition" than to the "revisionist" viewpoint. For Nevins constantly placed stress upon the existence of a deep and fundamental cleavage between North and South—differences in ideas, ideals, aims, and outlook—which all added up to two divergent cultures by the 1850's.[26] He specifically stated (in contrast to the possible implication of some of the remarks noted above) that the historian must keep his eye focused upon that cleavage and the fundamental forces which produced it in order to explain the causes of the Civil War. That struggle, he declared,

was not a war created by politicians and publicists who fomented hysteric excitement; for while hysteria was important, we have always to ask what basic reasons made possible the propaganda which aroused it.[27]

Similarly, while Nevins noted the ill-fated decisions by American political leaders, he explicitly declared that there should be examination of more basic influences:

Obviously . . . it is the forces behind these decisions [by political leaders] which demand our study; the waters pouring down the gorge, not the rocks which threw their spray into the air.[28]

[25] ibid., I, 383.

[26] ibid., II, 520, 553-554. Nevins' concept of two differing societies, North and South, was severely criticized by the "revisionist" historian, Avery O. Craven—see Craven's review of Ordeal of the Union, Vols. III-IV, in The Yale Review, XL, 722-725 (Summer 1951).

[27] ibid., IV, 470.

[28] ibid., IV, 463.

As a matter of fact, Nevins' viewpoint, in many important respects, seemed most of all to represent the basic ideas of Rhodes brought up to date in terms of some of the findings of historical scholarship in the United States since the 1890's. Rhodes had more or less ignored the role of economic forces in his description of an irrepressible conflict; Nevins, while he discussed economic trends and factors at length, minimized their importance in producing a breach between North and South. Between the plantation-agriculture South and the Northeast with its developing manufactures there were economic differences, he stated, but the effect of economic forces worked more toward holding the sections together than in splitting them apart. He repeatedly emphasized his contention that the war was not one born primarily of economic grievances or of divisive economic forces:

One fact needs emphatic statement: of all the monistic explanations for the drift to war, that posited upon supposed economic causes is the flimsiest. . . . The war was caused primarily by social, moral, and political, not economic forces.[29]

The basic forces which, in the opinion of Nevins, were responsible for sectional conflict and war were not economic in nature but were concerned with the related questions of slavery and racial adjustment (like Ulrich B. Phillips, Nevins constantly emphasized the factor of race). When Nevins described these questions, he sounded much more like Rhodes than like the "revisionists":

The main root of the conflict (and there were minor roots) was the problem of slavery *with its complementary problem of race-adjustment*; the main source of the tragedy was the refusal of either section to face these conjoined problems squarely and pay the heavy costs of a peaceful settlement. . . . It was a war over slavery *and* the future position of the Negro race in North America. Was the Negro to be allowed, as a result of the shift of power signalized by Lincoln's election, to take the first step toward an ultimate position of general economic, political, and social equality with the white man? Or was he to be held immobile in a degraded, servile position, unchanging for the next

[29] The two parts of the quotation are from *ibid.*, IV, 465, and II, 244. For representative examples of Nevins' discussion of the role of economic forces, see: *ibid.*, I, 473, 535; II, 243-244, 266-267, 431n, 554; IV, 465-466, 470.

hundred years as it had remained essentially unchanged for the hundred years past?[30]

The basic differences between the sections centering around the related problems of slavery and racial adjustment seemed in the pages of Nevins, just as they had in the pages of Rhodes, to be irreconcilable. The slavery question, Nevins stated, was "in fact irrepressible"—"it could not be compromised; one section must yield its fundamental position."[31] (Nevins, like Phillips, placed much more stress than had Rhodes upon difference of race as the fundamental factor which made a solution of the slavery problem difficult; but, as we have seen, Rhodes, especially in his discussion of Reconstruction, had voiced his opinion of the importance of the "race question" and the "Negro question.")

Nevins did not shield the unsavory aspects of the institution of slavery from sight, and, unlike most of the "revisionists," he was forthright in his criticism of the institution—"the greatest wrong, the greatest misery, the greatest curse to white and black alike that America has ever known."[32] Yet, in a fashion similar to Rhodes, he took pains to point out his conviction that the evils of slavery belonged to the institution itself rather than to any special wickedness of the Southern people, and that both Northerners and Southerners were to "blame" for the perilous deadlock on the slavery question (Northerners, wrote Nevins, refused to "acknowledge that in equity they must share the heavy burdens of racial readjustment," while white Southerners refused to "treat slavery as a progressive and evolutionary system, leading by regular gradations to freedom").[33] Southerners, Rhodes had declared in 1893, deserved sympathy rather than censure on the question of slavery; the South, Nevins asserted in 1947, needed compassion and help rather than condemnation.[34]

Nevins insisted that some positive action toward solving the slavery question was necessary in the 1850's, and this aspect of his thought served once more to point up differences between his (and Rhodes') point of view, on the one hand, and that of the "revi-

[30] ibid., IV, 468-471.
[31] The two quotations (in order) are from: ibid., II, 78, and IV, 388.
[32] ibid., I, 461.
[33] The quotations are from ibid., I, 533; see also 458.
[34] ibid., I, 461.

sionists" on the other. The "revisionists" seemed to say and to imply that if the abolitionists had not attacked slavery, then the Southerners would not have defended it as a positive good, and it would eventually have withered away; similarly, they seemed to say and to imply that if the United States had just followed the lead of Stephen A. Douglas, and if the Republicans in 1860-1861 had just been willing to compromise on the issue of slavery in the territories, war could have been averted and all would have been well.

Nevins, by contrast, declared that drift was not enough to solve the problem of slavery and that this problem could not be shelved; he specifically disagreed with the supposition that slavery would have disappeared of its own accord had it been left alone, asserting that the *ante-bellum* South had been moving progressively further, not nearer, to emancipation and a "just solution" to the slavery problem.[35] While not as severe in his criticism of Stephen A. Douglas as Rhodes had been, Nevins was quite unsympathetic to Douglas in his sponsorship of the Kansas-Nebraska Act of 1854. Douglas, Nevins asserted, never understood the opposition of Lincoln on moral grounds to the Kansas-Nebraska Act, for he was a man of "dim moral perceptions" whose mind was "closed to the highest moral considerations as some ears are deaf to the finest harmonies of music"; Douglas through the Kansas-Nebraska Act, in the opinion of Nevins, converted more men to the free soil doctrine in two months than the militant abolitionists had converted to their position in twenty years.[36] Finally (and this was quite unlike most of the discussions of the subject by "revisionist" historians) Nevins upheld Lincoln's policy of refusal to compromise on the issue of slavery in the territories in the crisis of 1860-1861. A compromise course of "procrastination and appeasement" at that time, Nevins declared, would have brought only harm:

[35] *ibid.*, I, 411; IV, 468; see also I, 148-149.
[36] The two quotations (in order) are from *ibid.*, II, 108 and 341; see also 153-154. Nevins was decidedly more sympathetic in his discussion of the latter phase of Douglas's career—after Douglas had split from Buchanan and the extreme proslavery wing of the Democratic Party. But Nevins in nearly every case expressed agreement with the position of Lincoln rather than that of Douglas—and this was not true of the "revisionists." See: *ibid.*, III, pp. 24-26, chapters 10, 13-14; IV, chapters 10, 13, 15.

All hope of bringing Southern majority sentiment to a better attitude would have been lost if Lincoln and his party had flinched on the basic issue of the restriction of slavery.[37]

Perhaps the most accurate index of Nevins' interpretation of the causes of the Civil War was contained in his statement that the war "should have been avoidable." That this phrase was ambiguous in the sense that it was liable to different interpretations by competent historians was demonstrated, as will be indicated shortly, in the reviews of Nevins' volumes. To the present writer, however, these words of Nevins, when examined in the light of the first four volumes of his history, signify an explanation of the coming of the Civil War which was more in accord with the general pattern of the "new nationalist tradition" than with the "revisionist" position. The "revisionist" viewpoint could be expressed in the declaration that the Civil War "was avoidable"— and was avoidable because, in the opinion of the "revisionists," if the men of the 1850's and 1860's had only been unemotional and realistic, they would have realized that their differences were not great enough to warrant combat. By contrast, Nevins' position that the Civil War "should have been avoidable" implied that armed hostilities might have been evaded only if steps had been taken to end the irreconcilable differences between North and South; since, in the view of Nevins, the most important irreconcilable difference was that over slavery and racial adjustment, it followed that enduring peace between North and South depended upon some step which would have marked the beginning of the end of the institution of slavery.

[37] *ibid.*, IV, 469.

The Reaction to *Ordeal of the Union*

THE reaction to Rhodes' *History* among historians of that day (in the fifteen years after the publication of its first two volumes in 1893) had indicated at least two things: that there was a considerable measure of agreement in attitudes toward the causes and nature of the Civil War, and that many historians could write of the Civil War, only thirty years after it ended, dispassionately and without rancor. By contrast, the published reaction among historians to Nevins' *Ordeal of the Union* (in the four years after the publication of its first two volumes in 1947) demonstrated that almost the reverse was now true on both counts: the reviews of the volumes of Nevins revealed not only a sharp disagreement in interpretations of the causes of the Civil War but also that some historians in the 1940's and 1950's wrote of the Civil War with a greater emotional intensity than had their predecessors a half-century earlier.

Several historians (including Edward C. Kirkland, Oscar Handlin, and Arthur M. Schlesinger, Jr.) noted the above-mentioned dualism in Nevins' interpretation of the causes of the war and expressed the opinion that he had not made his viewpoint on this subject clear.[38] This alleged dualism might have been expected to elicit a certain diversity of opinions from reviewers, but by itself it could not have produced the widely different responses which greeted *Ordeal of the Union*.

Nevins' point of view was condemned by two Southern historians, Fletcher M. Green of the University of North Carolina and Robert H. Woody of Duke University—both of whom were born in the South, had received their undergraduate and graduate training at Southern universities, and had lived in the South all

---

[38] Edward C. Kirkland, review of *Ordeal of the Union*, Vols. I-II, in *The Journal of Economic History*, VIII, 190-192 (November 1948); Oscar Handlin, review of *Ordeal of the Union*, Vols. III-IV, in *The Nation*, v. 171, pp. 512-513 (December 2, 1950); Arthur M. Schlesinger, Jr., review of *Ordeal of the Union*, Vols. III-IV, in *The Christian Science Monitor*, October 14, 1950, p. 7.

their lives. Green and Woody censured Nevins on the ground that he was biased in favor of the North, and they charged that this partiality was due to his opposition to slavery on moral grounds. "Like the abolitionists of the period of which he writes," Green asserted, "Nevins seems to be blinded by his sense of moral values."[39] Woody also compared Nevins to the antislavery crusaders of the Civil War era, and declared that it "may all be very well to take one's stand with freedom as against slavery; it is worth suggesting, however, that it makes difficult an impartial account."[40]

But in a contrast about as pronounced as can be imagined, Nevins was criticized for almost precisely the opposite reasons by two other historians, Arthur M. Schlesinger, Jr., and Oscar Handlin—both of whom were born outside the South and had never lived there, both of whom had received their graduate training at Harvard and had remained there as members of the faculty. Whereas Nevins, in the opinion of Green and Woody, was too sympathetic to the abolitionists, he was, in the opinion of Handlin, too severe in his strictures against the abolitionists, making charges against them which Handlin stated were "not true."[41] Handlin and Schlesinger, Jr., were dissatisfied not because Nevins' moral judgments against slavery were too much in evidence in his interpretation of the causes of the Civil War but because such judgments were not enough in evidence. Nevins, Handlin asserted, classed together the extremists of North and South without making an ethical distinction between the two: "There is surely a difference between being a fanatic for freedom and being a fanatic for slavery."[42] In a similar vein, Schlesinger, Jr., charged that Nevins "never gives the moral factor full weight," and that he wrote "as if those who believed in human freedom and those who believed in human slavery were equally at fault" in the conflict between North and South.[43]

[39] Fletcher M. Green, review of *Ordeal of the Union*, Vols. I-II, in *The Mississippi Valley Historical Review*, XXXV, 128 (June 1948).

[40] Robert H. Woody, "Ordeal of the Union," *The South Atlantic Quarterly*, XLVII, 389 (July 1948).

[41] Oscar Handlin, review of *Ordeal of the Union*, Vols. III-IV, in *The Nation*, v. 171, p. 513 (December 2, 1950).

[42] *ibid.*

[43] Arthur M. Schlesinger, Jr., review of *Ordeal of the Union*, Vols. III-IV, in *The*

In between the positions represented by Green and Woody, on the one hand, and Handlin and Schlesinger, Jr., on the other, some historians expressed praise for the viewpoint of Nevins—but for quite different reasons. James G. Randall, the "revisionist," reviewed the four volumes with approval, singling out for special commendation their "appreciative treatment of things Southern" and hazarding the speculation that the South had "captured" Nevins; Randall's reviews left the reader with the impression that Nevins' outlook was quite similar to that of the "revisionists," although it was noted that Stephen A. Douglas was "given a surprisingly unfavorable treatment."[44] By contrast, John D. Hicks praised the *Ordeal of the Union* on grounds just the opposite from those cited by Randall; Hicks noted with approval that the institution of slavery got "no whitewash whatever" in the volumes, and voiced the suspicion that Nevins was "weary of appeasing the tender susceptibilities of over zealous defenders of the Old South."[45]

If the reviews of the volumes of Nevins accurately reflected the attitudes prevailing among historians, they seemed to indicate that in the 1940's—unlike the 1890's—it would be impossible to formulate a synthesis which could reconcile all the current widely divergent interpretations of the causes of the Civil War. Perhaps the reviews themselves furnished one clue as to why this was so—for in the reviews of *Ordeal of the Union* there was a recurrent theme which had not been present in the reviews of Rhodes' *History*: historians (including Ralph H. Gabriel, Richard

---

Christian Science Monitor, October 14, 1950, p. 7. Schlesinger, Jr.'s review of Vols. I-II is in *The Saturday Review of Literature*, XXX, 9-10 (October 18, 1947).

[44] James G. Randall, review of *Ordeal of the Union*, Vols. I-II, in *The New York Times Book Review*, October 12, 1947, pp. 1, 44-45 (the quotations, in order, are from pp. 44 and 45); Randall's review of Vols. III-IV is in *The Saturday Review of Literature*, XXXIII, 17-18 (October 14, 1950). Randall's fellow "revisionist" historian, Avery O. Craven, sharply criticized volumes III and IV of *Ordeal of the Union* as "shallow and biased"; Nevins' viewpoints, Craven wrote, "do not represent less of a bias or a better balance than is to be found in Rhodes or Von Holst" (*The Yale Review*, XL, 723 [Summer 1951]).

[45] John D. Hicks, review of *Ordeal of the Union*, Vols. I-II, in *The American Historical Review*, LIII, 846 (July 1948). Pieter Geyl, expressing approval of Nevins' viewpoint, stated that it did "not differ in essence from the traditional view" (i.e., the "nationalist tradition"), and specifically contrasted the viewpoint of Nevins, on the one hand, with that of Randall, on the other; *The New England Quarterly*, XXIV, 157-158*n*.3 (June 1951).

W. Leopold, Oscar Handlin, Arthur M. Schlesinger, Jr., and James G. Randall) now drew a parallel between the Civil War era and their own day, with its wars and threats of wars.[46] The experience of the United States in the 1850's, these historians declared, carried a message for the 1940's and 1950's, but they were not agreed as to the nature of that message.

The lack of agreement can be seen most clearly by comparing the statements of James G. Randall with those of Arthur M. Schlesinger, Jr. Randall, writing in 1947, made a direct comparison between the 1850's and his own day, the similarity resting in their "false agitation, proceeding downward in the direction of a needless war."[47] He seemed to imply that just as, in his opinion, war could have been averted in the 1860's had men remained reasonable, unemotional, and realistic in their outlook, so also by the same methods could present-day (i.e., 1947) problems be satisfactorily solved short of war.

Schlesinger, Jr., also writing in 1947, drew a parallel between the Civil War era and the present, and like Randall implied that that era held lessons valuable for his own day in its effort to avoid war. But quite unlike Randall, Schlesinger, Jr., defined the question of war or peace in terms of alternative policies of "appeasement or resistance." He seemed to equate the "revisionist" position with that of "appeasement" and to argue that, just as the policy of "appeasement" did not avert war in the 1930's, so it had not offered the best hope of preventing war in the 1850's and did not offer the best hope in 1947:

A future ["revisionist"] historian might say . . . that the primary task of statesmanship in the 1930's was to furnish a workable adjustment between the U.S.A. and Germany, while offering strong inducements to the German people to abandon the police state, and equal persuasion to the Americans to help the Nazis rather than scold them. In essence, this is Mr. Wallace's current thesis about the Russians. Comparisons with the issues of the Civil War may perhaps be extreme; yet one must face the hard fact that closed and authoritarian social systems tend to create a compulsive intransigence in their own ruling groups—and

---

[46] In addition to the reviews by Handlin, Schlesinger, Jr., and Randall previously cited, see Ralph H. Gabriel, review of *Ordeal of the Union*, Vols. I-II, in *The Yale Review*, XXXVII, 343-345 (Winter 1948), and Richard W. Leopold, review of the same, in *The Nation*, v. 165, pp. 684-685 (December 20, 1947).

[47] James G. Randall, in *The New York Times Book Review*, October 12, 1947, p. 45.

that these groups may respond much more to a firmness which wakens them to some sense of actuality than to a forbearance which is never great enough and always to be discounted.[48]

(In this analogy, presumably, the position of Stephen A. Douglas before he split with the pro-Southern wing of the Democratic Party in the late 1850's was comparable to that of Henry A. Wallace before he split with the Progressive Party in 1950.)

Disagreement in interpretations of the causes of the Civil War was intertwined, in the case of Randall and Schlesinger, Jr., with disagreement in analyses of the crisis of their own day. The fundamental question of how to secure peaceful settlement of intersectional and international disputes gave the Civil War experience, in the opinion of some historians, pertinence for the 1940's and 1950's; it also gave rise to differences of opinion held with intense emotions. Urgent feelings about the crisis of their own day reinforced the urgent feelings of historians about the crisis of the 1860's.

Thus, by the 1950's an anomalous situation prevailed: the further the Civil War receded into the past, the greater the disagreement among twentieth century historians over its causes, and the greater the strength of the emotions with which these divergent viewpoints were upheld. One could almost fancy himself back in the 1860's once again. Charges and countercharges of "abolitionist" and "defender of slavery" filled the air. Comparisons between contemporary figures and those of the Civil War era suggested themselves: Herbert Aptheker, writing of the South's "blood-stained, militaristic oligarchy," could be compared to the most extreme abolitionist; at the opposite pole, in a position analogous to the Southern "fire-eaters," was Frank L. Owsley writing of Yankee "crusades" against the South, and Yankee "egocentric sectionalism"; more moderate defenders of the South could be represented by Fletcher M. Green and Robert H. Woody, and more moderate supporters of the Union by Bernard De Voto and Arthur M. Schlesinger, Jr.; and, to make the parallel to the 1860's complete, Avery Craven and James G. Randall could oc-

[48] Arthur M. Schlesinger, Jr., in *The Saturday Review of Literature*, xxx, 10 (October 18, 1947).

cupy a place comparable to Vallandigham, Foote, and the other "discontented peace advocates." Here was material from which some twentieth century Swift could pen a new "Battle of the Books," not between the Ancients and the Moderns, but between the successors to the embattled Confederates, Unionists, and peace men of the nineteenth century.

The reason why this parallel could be drawn, be it repeated, was because historians in the middle of the twentieth century still found vital the issues involved in the struggle of the 1860's: the role of the Negro in American life; the interrelationship between majority will, as expressed through the national government, and the "minority rights" of geographical sections; and the question of how to secure peaceful settlement of intersectional and international disputes.

Historical interpretation seemed to have completed almost a full cycle. Some prominent twentieth century historians, like the men of the 1860's, were sharply disagreed over the causes and character of the Civil War. Once again, clashing viewpoints were upheld with ardor, and some historians now sought to assign personal and sectional "guilt" for the war. The words Oliver Wendell Holmes, Jr., had spoken back in the 1880's now seemed prophetic, now seemed to apply to a generation other than his own: Civil War issues, it appeared, could still draw fire from the hearts and minds of Americans.

They were drawing fire, too, in a fashion which suggested a comparison with the French and their most divisive national experience. The American Revolution, insofar as it was a movement which secured national independence and replaced a monarchical system of government with a constitutional republic, represented a settlement of certain fundamental questions; Americans, by and large, have been agreed that this settlement was wise and desirable. This area of agreement on issues of basic importance has spared the nation disruptive quarrels and has provided a framework within which solutions to problems could be sought by democratic and constitutional methods. One could have predicted, in the first decade of the twentieth century, that a similar pattern of interpretation would be characteristic of the Civil War. By the 1950's, however, a different parallel seemed perhaps more appropriate—the attitudes of the French toward their Revolution of 1789. The disagreement of the French people in evaluating their Revolution has been reflected in divisions of major proportions in many areas of their national life. The cleavages in the United States over Civil War questions by the 1950's was clearly not so deep nor so wide as that in France over the Revolution. But it was nevertheless true that the disagreement among historians over the meaning of the Civil War experience was matched, in the middle of the twentieth century, by sharp controversy in the arena of politics over issues related to those of Civil War days.

APPENDIXES

APPENDIXES

A

A LIST OF SELECTED COMMENTS ON JAMES FORD RHODES BY CONTEMPORARIES BEFORE THE FIRST WORLD WAR

Adams, Charles Francis, "Some Phases of the Civil War," *Studies Military and Diplomatic 1775-1865* (New York, 1911) 232-290.

Anonymous, review of Rhodes, *Lectures on the American Civil War*, in *The American Historical Review*, xviii, 844-845 (July 1913).

Anonymous, "Scientific History," *Publications of the Southern History Association*, xi, 308 (September-November 1907).

Bassett, John S., review of Rhodes, *History*, Vol. iv, in *Political Science Quarterly*, xv, 131-134 (March 1900).

Brown, William Garrott, review of Rhodes, *History*, Vols. v-vii, in *The American Historical Review*, xi, 181-186 (October 1905); xii, 680-684 (April 1907).

Burgess, John W., review of Rhodes, *History*, Vols. i-ii, in *Political Science Quarterly*, viii, 342-346 (June 1893).

Channing, Edward, and Hart, Albert Bushnell, *Guide to the Study of American History* (Boston, 1896) 46.

Channing, Edward, *The United States of America 1765-1865* (New York, 1896) *vii-viii*.

Dunning, William A., review of Rhodes, *History*, Vol. iv, in *The American Historical Review*, v, 371-374 (January 1900).
  "Rhodes's History of the United States," *Educational Review*, xxxiv, 109-115 (September 1907).

Fleming, Walter L., review of Rhodes, *History*, Vol. v, in *Political Science Quarterly*, xx, 535-539 (September 1905).

Hamilton, J. G. de Roulhac, review of Rhodes, *History*, Vols. vi-vii, in *The South Atlantic Quarterly*, vi, 87-91 (January 1907).

Julian, George W., review of Rhodes, *History*, Vol. iii, in *The Dial* (Chicago), xix, 68-70 (August 1, 1895).

McLaughlin, Andrew C., review of Rhodes, Vols. i-iii, in *The American Historical Review*, i, 366-370 (January 1896).

Paxon, Frederic L., *The Civil War* (New York, 1911) x, 251-252.

Reed, John C., *The Brothers' War* (Boston, 1905) 17.

Shepardson, Francis Wayland, review of Rhodes, *History*, Vol. iv, in *The Dial* (Chicago), xxvii, 312-314 (November 1, 1899).

Spencer, David E., review of Rhodes, *History*, Vols. i-ii, in *The Dial* (Chicago), xiv, 280-281 (May 1, 1893).

Stephens, H. Morse, "Some Living American Historians," *The World's Work* (New York), iv, 2316-2327 (July 1902).

Thomas, David Y., review of Rhodes, *History*, Vol. v, in *The Dial* (Chicago), xxxviii, 230-232 (April 1, 1905).

Turner, Frederick Jackson, "Recent Studies in American History," *The Atlantic Monthly*, lxxvii, 837-844 (June 1896).

Review of Rhodes, *History*, Vol. iii, in *Political Science Quarterly*, xi, 167-170 (March 1896).

Wilson, Woodrow, review of Rhodes, *History*, Vols. i-ii, in *The Atlantic Monthly*, lxxii, 272-274 (August 1893).

B

A NOTE ON THE SOURCES

A LIST of the possible and available written sources for a study of changing ideas and attitudes toward the causes and character of the American Civil War would be, as suggested in the preface, almost literally unlimited, since it would include all writings in which ideas of individuals about the past are expressed—newspapers, magazines, diaries, autobiographies, memoirs, letters, novels, poems, and plays, as well as more or less formal works of history (and in addition to written sources, one could also list other types of sources, as, for example, paintings or motion pictures). This situation precludes the compilation of a catalogue of writings on the subject covered in this volume which might be considered complete or definitive in a meaningful sense, and for this reason this note on the sources has the decidedly more modest aim of simply suggesting some bibliographical guides to the sources, some collections of sources, and some discussions of general historical problems of the type involved in this study which the present author has found useful.

Several bibliographies and collections of writings on the Civil War published from the 1860's to the 1880's are still of distinct value. One of the earliest Civil War bibliographies was that compiled by S. Hastings Grant and published in 1862: "Bibliography of the Civil War," *The Historical Magazine* (New York) VI, 113-115, 146-149, 186-187, 206-208, 245-247, 342-346 (April-November 1862). Four years later, a much longer bibliography appeared: John Russell Bartlett, *The Literature of the Rebellion* (Boston, 1866), listing several thousand items. In the same year, there was published James Kelly's *The American Catalogue of Books . . . Published in the United States From Jan., 1861, to Jan., 1866, . . . With Supplement Containing Pamphlets, Sermons, and Addresses on the Civil War in the United States, 1861-1866* (New York, 1866) (included in this volume, p. 303, is "A List of Books Published in the Southern States during the War"); a second volume compiled by Kelly which, like its predecessor, is a useful aid in ferreting out early histories of the war, was published in 1871: *The American Catalogue of Books (Original and Reprints) Published in the United States from Jan., 1866, to Jan., 1871* (New York, 1871).

The most extensive collection of writings on the war whose publication was completed or inaugurated during the three decades after 1860 was the well-known *The War of the Rebellion . . . Official Records of the Union and Confederate Armies* (128v., 1880-1901); this massive work, along with its sister publication, *Official Records of the Union and Confederate Navies in the War of the Rebellion* (30v., Washington, D.C., 1894-1922), contains some material illustrating attitudes toward the causes and character of the Civil War, but a much more useful source collection for this study, and a veritable mine of information about the Civil War, is Frank Moore, ed., *The Rebellion Record* (12v., New York, 1861-1871). Since many more Union sympathizers published histories of the war in the 1860's, the 1870's, and the 1880's than did supporters of the Confederacy, I attempted to supplement the published volumes with other writings in this period, and I found the following periodicals to be convenient repositories of writings on the war by Confederates and former Confederates (in effect, collections of sources): *The Index* (London, 1862-1865), *The Land We Love* (Charlotte, North Carolina, 1866-1869), *The Southern Review* (Baltimore, 1867-1879), and the *Southern Historical Society Papers* (Richmond, 1876-   ).

Beginning in the 1880's and 1890's, there appear bibliographies compiled by trained historians and archivists. Most of the standard bibliographies of American history published since the 1880's contain a wealth of material bearing on the subject discussed in this volume; of particular importance for my use were Charles K. Adams, *A Manual of Historical Literature* (3rd ed., New York, 1888), J.N. Larned, *The Literature of American History* (New York, 1902), Edward Channing and Albert Bushnell Hart, *Guide to the Study of American History* (Boston, 1896), Edward Channing, Albert Bushnell Hart, and Frederick Jackson Turner, *Guide to the Study and Reading of American History* (Boston, 1912), and Grace Griffin and others, *Writings on American History* (various cities, 1904-   ). In addition to these bibliographies of American history, the text, the citations, and the bibliographies contained in histories of the Civil War era form an excellent guide to published discussions of the causes of the war; this is particularly true of the volumes of Rhodes and Channing, of the pertinent volumes in *The American Nation, The South in the Building of the Nation*, and *A History of American Life*, and of two one-volume histories of the Civil War period published in the 1930's: James G. Randall, *Civil War and Reconstruction* (New York, 1937), and Carl R. Fish, *The American Civil War: An Interpretation* (New York, 1937) (on pp. 478 to 522 of this last named volume by Carl R. Fish, there is a bibliography compiled by William E. Smith which is one of the most helpful of all brief annotated lists of histories of the Civil War).

Specialized bibliographies published in the twentieth century list many writings on the causes of the Civil War. Among the most useful of these specialized bibliographies are the catalogues of library collections made up entirely or in part of items on the Civil War: Hugh Alexander Morrison, *The Leiter Library. A Catalogue of the Books, Manuscripts and Maps Relating Principally to America, Collected by*

the Late Levi Ziegler Leiter, with Collations and Bibliographical Notes
(Washington, D.C., 1907), has a long section devoted to Confederate
items in the collection; Douglas S. Freeman, *A Calendar of Confederate
Papers, with a Bibliography of Some Confederate Publications* ["now
in the Confederate Museum"] (Richmond, 1908), describes the items
suggested in its title, as does Charles N. Baxter and James M. Dear-
born, compilers, *Confederate Literature: A List of Books and Newspapers, Maps, Music and Miscellaneous Matter Printed in the South
during the Confederacy, now in the Boston Athenaeum* (Boston, 1917);
the "Catalogue of the Pierson Civil War Collection," *Princeton University Library Classed List, Volume VI, Special Collections* (Princeton, 1921) pp. 2985-3077, lists the writings in the Princeton University
Library's Pierson Civil War collection, a collection which is particularly
rich in volumes on the Civil War published in the nineteenth century;
Douglas S. Freeman, *The South to Posterity* (New York, 1939), is a
book-length essay discussing writings about the Confederacy, while
biographies and biographers of Lincoln are examined by Benjamin
P. Thomas in his *Portrait for Posterity* (New Brunswick, N.J., 1947);
Donald J. Berthong, *The Civil War Collection of the Illinois State Historical Library* (pamphlet, Springfield, Ill., 1949) describes another
important Civil War collection.

Other specialized bibliographies which have been useful in this study
are those cataloging the writings of individual historians and also listing, in some instances, reviews of the principal published writings of
the historian in question. A bibliography of writings by James Ford
Rhodes is printed in M.A. de Wolfe Howe, *James Ford Rhodes: American Historian* (New York, 1929), 353-359; the "public papers" of
Woodrow Wilson are listed and printed in Ray Stannard Baker and
William E. Dodd, eds., *The Public Papers of Woodrow Wilson* (6v.,
New York, 1925-1927); a list of writings by Frederick Jackson Turner
compiled by Everett E. Edwards is published in *The Early Writings
of Frederick Jackson Turner* (Madison, Wisconsin, 1938) pp. 233-268,
and on pp. 269-272 of this volume there is a convenient list of "References on the Life and Work of Frederick Jackson Turner," also compiled by Edwards; there is a "List of [John Bach] McMaster's Printed
Writings and Speeches" in Eric F. Goldman, *John Bach McMaster
American Historian* (Philadelphia, 1943) pp. 179-184; George W.
Robinson has published a *Bibliography of Edward Channing* (Cambridge, Massachusetts, 1932); and there are two bibliographies of the
writings of Ulrich B. Phillips—David M. Potter, Jr., "A Bibliography
of the Printed Writings of Ulrich Bonnell Phillips," *The Georgia Historical Quarterly*, XVIII, 270-282 (September 1934), and Everett A. Edwards, "A Bibliography of the Writings of Professor Ulrich Bonnell
Phillips," *Agricultural History*, VIII, 196-218 (October 1934) (Edwards' bibliography also includes a list of reviews of Phillips' vol-

umes); other helpful bibliographies of the writings of specific individuals are contained in the biographical sketches in Allen Johnson, Dumas Malone, and Harris E. Starr, eds., *Dictionary of American Biography* (21v. and Index, New York, 1928-1944).

If the period since the 1880's and 1890's has seen the appearance of bibliographies compiled by trained historians, it has also seen the publication of journals edited by and written by and for trained historians; these journals serve, through their review sections, as annotated bibliographies, and both their reviews and their articles make them repositories in which are expressed the ideas of historians on the causes of the Civil War. The journals are thus of great importance in the present study, and I have found the following ones to be of especial value for my purposes: *The American Historical Review* (1895-), *Publications of the Southern History Association* (Washington, D.C., 1897-1907), *The Mississippi Valley Historical Review* (1915-), *The Journal of Negro History* (1916-), *Agricultural History* (1927-), *The Journal of Southern History* (1935-).

As a final comment on bibliographical guides to published discussion of the causes of the Civil War, it should be stated that the single most extensive and most recent such guide is the essay (with bibliography) by Howard K. Beale mentioned in the preface: "What Historians Have Said about the Causes of the Civil War," Social Science Research Council Bulletin 54, *Theory and Practice in Historical Study* (New York, 1946) 53-102.

In seeking the identity and personal history of individuals who have written on the causes of the Civil War, I have found much of value in the following biographical dictionaries: James Grant Wilson and John Fiske, eds., *Appleton's Cyclopaedia of American Biography* (6v., New York, 1886-1889); *The National Cyclopaedia of American Biography* (14v., New York, 1891-1906); Allen Johnson, Dumas Malone, and Harris E. Starr, eds., *Dictionary of American Biography* (21v. and Index, New York, 1928-1944); *Who's Who in America, Volume I* (*1899-1900*) and later volumes (Chicago, 1899-); *Who Was Who in America, Volume I* (*1897-1942*) (Chicago, 1942), and *Volume II* (*1943-1950*) (Chicago, 1950); Jacques Cattell, ed., *Dictionary of American Scholars* (2nd edition, Lancaster, Pennsylvania, 1951). Biographical information concerning many historians and discussions of the development of historical thought and of the writing of history in the United States can be found in the articles listed above in Chapter four, note 62, and also in the following volumes: J. Franklin Jameson, *The History of Historical Writing in America* (Boston, 1891); John Spencer Bassett, *The Middle Group of American Historians* (New York, 1917); William T. Hutchinson, ed., *The Marcus W. Jernegan Essays in American Historiography* (Chicago, 1937); Michael Kraus, *A History of American History* (New York, 1937); Edward N. Saveth,

American Historians and European Immigrants 1875-1925 (New York, 1948).

The closely related problems of causation in history and of "relativism" and "objectivity" in the understanding of history have long been subjects for speculation and are discussed in what is now a large body of writings. One of the best recent guides to writings on these and other aspects of history and of historical understanding is Ronald Thompson's "Selective Reading List on Historiography and Philosophy of History," which is printed in Social Science Research Council Bulletin 54, *Theory and Practice in Historical Study* (New York, 1946) 141-163. In the United States, there has been a marked discussion in the twentieth century of causation and of "relativism" by such historians as Frederick Jackson Turner, Charles A. Beard, and Carl L. Becker, among others; from among the many well-known essays on these problems by twentieth century United States historians, I would like to single out three which seem to me particularly pertinent to this study of changing interpretations of the American Civil War: Frederick Jackson Turner, "Social Forces in American History," *The American Historical Review*, xvi, 217-233 (January 1911); William A. Dunning, "Truth in History," *The American Historical Review*, xix, 217-229 (January 1914); Carl L. Becker, "What is Historiography?" *The American Historical Review*, xliv, 20-28 (October 1938).

Since the Second World War, the general questions of "relativism" and "objectivity" in historical understanding have been reexamined by a number of individuals. The clearest and most important evidence of the renewed interest in these questions in the United States was the publication in 1946 of the previously-mentioned bulletin of the Social Science Research Council, *Theory and Practice in Historical Study*. This volume served as the focus for several discussions of historiography, and special sessions on that topic were held by such organizations as the American Historical Association, its Pacific Coast branch, and the Mississippi Valley Historical Association; some of the published papers resulting from these discussions are listed in Richard P. Cecil, "Objectivity and the Writing of History," *The Historian*, xii, 55-87 (Autumn 1949) note 3, and Cecil's article is itself an interesting discussion of the problem suggested in its title. Stemming from this same renewed interest in historiography and philosophy of history after the Second World War was a conference on "related problems in historical relativity" held at Reed College, Oregon, under the sponsorship of the Pacific Coast Committee for the Humanities, American Council of Learned Societies; the five papers read at this conference, including one by A. I. Melden on "Historical Objectivity, A 'Noble Dream'?" are mimeographed under the title *Conference on the Humanities* (1951).

Finally, there have been published in the past decade several studies of changing viewpoints toward historical events and personalities which offer the materials for illuminating comparisons with the changing interpretations of the American Civil War: R. B. Schlatter, "The Problem of Historical Causation in Some Recent Studies of the English Revolution," *Journal of the History of Ideas*, IV, 349-367 (June 1943); Paul Farmer, *France Reviews Its Revolutionary Origins* (New York, 1944); Alfred Cobban, *The Causes of the French Revolution: A Course of Readings* (pamphlet, London, 1946); Samuel Flagg Bemis, "First Gun of a Revisionist Historiography for the Second World War," *The Journal of Modern History*, XIX, 55-59 (March 1947); Pieter Geyl, *Napoleon: For and Against* (New Haven, 1949); Richard W. Leopold, "The Problem of American Intervention, 1917: An Historical Retrospect," *World Politics*, II, 405-425 (April 1950); Selig Adler, "The War-Guilt Question and American Disillusionment, 1918-1928," *The Journal of Modern History*, XXIII, 1-28 (March 1951); Dexter Perkins, "American Wars and Critical Historians," *The Yale Review*, XL, 682-695 (Summer 1951).

★ INDEX ★

INDEX

"corner-stone" speech of A. H. Stephens, 72; quoted, 24
Cotterill, Robert S., 251
Coulter, E. Merton, 277; quoted, x, 252
"Course of the South to Secession, The" (U. B. Phillips), 235
Cox, Samuel S., 103, 106, 108, 109, 111; described and quoted, 100-101
Coxey's army (Jacob Coxey), 136
Craven, Avery O., 248, 272, 286-289, 297, 321; quoted, 270, 319 n.44; described and quoted, 273-285; new emphasis in writings of after 1945, 286 n.62, 312 n.26, 319 n.44
Crittenden, John J., 7 n.13, 86, 144
croaker, 99
Cromwell, Oliver, 12
Crowd, The (G. LeBon), 259
Cuba, 199
cult of Lincoln and Lee, 188
Curry, J. L. M., 71 n.38
Curti, Merle, quoted, 165
Cuvier, Georges, baron, 182
Cyclopaedia (J. J. Lalor), 50

Dabney, Robert L., 87, 91; quoted, 73-74, 95
Daily Courier, see *Boston Daily Courier*
Daily Richmond Examiner, 64
Daniel, John W., quoted, 123
Darwinian thought, 167-168, 179
Das Kapital, 215
Davis, Jefferson, 4, 29, 56, 64, 65, 66, 67, 69, 70, 71, 72, 76, 78, 85, 87, 88, 91, 92, 95, 105, 113, 132, 133, 136, 155, 157, 208, 212, 233, 284; described, 60-61, 79-80; message to Confederate Congress quoted, 61-63, mentioned, 92; quoted, 74, 84, 89, 90; center of efforts to vindicate the South, 81ff.; blame for Civil War placed on him, 106, 142
Davis and Lee (B. J. Sage), 82
Dayton, Tennessee, 241
Debs, Eugene, 215, 217
debunker or debunking, 210, 284-285, 300, 302
Declaration of Independence (1776), 94
"Declaration of Independence" (Tennessee secession convention), quoted, 60 n.14
Deeds of Daring by Both Blue and Gray (D. M. Kelsey), 128
democratic faith of mid-nineteenth-century United States, 16
Democratic Machine 1850-1854, The (R. F. Nichols), 286

Democrat, or Democratic Party, or Democrats, 43-44, 46-47, 68, 70, 138ff., 198, 202, 282; S. A. Douglas and, 5-6; "war Democrats," 13, 110; party split in 1860, 19; and bloody shirt politicians, 43-47; Northern Democrats, 46-47, 109-110, 138ff.; pro-Southern Democrats, 69; "peace Democrats," 100ff., 106, 110; Douglas Democrats, 111, 138ff., 282; Cleveland Democrats, 140
De Pauw University, 198-199
depression of 1929-1933, 213, 220
Development of Southern Sectionalism, 1819-1848, The (C. S. Sydnor), 251
DeVoto, Bernard, 321; described and quoted, 305-308
discontented peace advocates, 99ff., 322
Disruption of American Democracy, The (R. L. Nichols), 286, 288
Division and Reunion (W. Wilson), 153
Dixiecrats, 250
Dodd, William E., 56 n.3, 135, 147, 154, 159, 232, 237, 246; quoted, 156 n.76
Dodge, Theodore A., 130; quoted, 128
"Mr. Dooley" (Finley Peter Dunne), quoted, 138
Douglas, Stephen A., 7, 9, 10, 13, 18, 19 n.33, 21, 86, 100, 111, 132, 138, 152; described and quoted, 5-6; described by J. F. Rhodes, 142 n.40, 263, 264, 297; interpreted sympathetically by "revisionists," 261-267, 281-282, 298, 315; described by A. Nevins, 315, 319; compared to H. A. Wallace, 321
Douglass, Frederick, 43, 154; described and quoted, 40-42
Draper, John W., described and quoted, 34-37
Dred Scott decision, 136
Du Bois, W. E. B., quoted, 226
Duke, Basil W., quoted, 137
Duke University, 317
Dumond, Dwight L., x
Dunne, Finley Peter ("Mr. Dooley"), quoted, 138
Dunning, William A., 135, 141, 142, 147, 148, 232-233, 237, 244, 246, 249, 260, 286; quoted, 148 n.59
Duyckinck, E. A., 24; quoted, 15, 30-31
Dye, John Smith, 26, 30 n.55; described and quoted, 19, 25

Early, Jubal A., 76-78, 87, 91, 137
East or Eastern United States, 136-137, 141-142, 165ff.

economic interpretation of causes of the
Civil War; affirmed, 23, 44, 48, 61, 65,
91-92, 116, 160 n.85 (Latané), 174ff.,
179ff., 206, 209, 247ff., 309, 310; denied, 313; *see also* Beardian interpretation of the causes of the Civil War,
Marxian interpretation of the causes of
the Civil War
Economic Interpretation of History, The
(E. R. A. Seligman), 200
*Economic Interpretation of the Constitu-
tion of the United States, An* (C. A.
Beard), 196, 197, 199, 200, 201, 210,
220
Edington, T. B., quoted, 122-123
Educational Psychology (E. L. Thorndike), 259
egocentric sectionalism, 248
election of 1860, 290; of 1896, 165; of
1948, 243
Eliot, Charles W., 37; quoted, 29-31
Emancipation Proclamation, 11, 22, 25, 37,
40, 67-68, 101-102n.4, 110, 139, 199
Emerson, Ralph Waldo, quoted, 12 n.21
emotions and emotionalism, 259ff., 280ff.,
287-288, 304
Engels, Frederick, 215, 217, 218; quoted,
216
England, 7, 143, 199
Enmale, Richard (pseudonym), described
and quoted, 221-226; quoted on J. F.
Rhodes, 297
Europe, 167-168, 195, 199
Everett, Edward, 9, 19 n.33, 22, 23, 57,
58, 107; described and quoted, 5-7;
quoted, 15 n.25
"extremists," 258ff., 265, 267ff., 280ff.,
289, 318; *see also* abolitionists, fire-
eaters

Fair Employment Practices Commission,
243
Farrar, C. C. S., 108; described and quot-
ed, 106-107
Federalist, 198, 202
Fenner, Charles, 130; quoted, 128
"fire-eaters," 56, 268, 321
"First American Revolution," the, 204
First World War, 140, 190, 201, 204, 215,
220, 240, 242, 250, 261, 273, 291, 295,
296, 299, 300, 303; reaction against
United States participation in, 270-272,
292; erroneous thesis of causes of, 305
Fish, Carl R., 153, 161 n.86
Fite, Emerson D., 135; quoted, 188

Fleming, Walter L., 147
Florida, 251
Foote, H. S., 107, 108, 109, 111, 114, 322;
described and quoted, 105-106; quoted,
284
Foraker, Joseph B., 138
Fort Sumter, 21, 25, 39, 63, 68, 72, 94,
110, 111, 121, 205, 259; reaction in
North to Confederate attack upon, 3ff.;
attack upon proof of Confederate war
guilt, 14ff.; reaction in Confederate
States to attack upon, 55ff.; cited as
evidence that Lincoln instigated war, 65,
92, 244ff., 248, 252
Fortune magazine, 228
Fowler, William C., 103, 106, 108, 114;
described and quoted, 100-101
Fox, Dixon R., 190, 191 n.141; quoted,
182, 221 n.43
Frank Leslie's magazine, 73
free-soilers, 37
French Revolution (1789), ix-x, 91, 115,
322-323
Freud, Sigmund, quoted, vii
Fugitive Slave Law of 1850, 25
funeral sermons on Lincoln, 30

Gabriel, Ralph H., 319
Galena, Illinois, 3
Gallup Organization, 271
Garfield, James A., 41
Garibaldi, Giuseppe, 113
Garland, Hamlin, 165
Garrett, William R., quoted, 133
Garrison, William Lloyd, 144, 268
Gay, Sydney, 38, 40
George, Henry, 198
Georgia, 70, 78, 80, 105, 249, 251
Germanic forests, 167
Germany, 320
Gettysburg address, quoted, 26
Geyl, Pieter, 306 n.17; quoted, 319 n.45
Giddings, Joshua R., 39; described and
quoted, 25-26
Gilman, Daniel C., 173
Glover, Gilbert G., 261
Godkin, E. L., 145 n.53
Gompers, Samuel, 124
Goodwin, Daniel R., quoted, 18
Goodwin, Thomas S., 15 n.25, 17 n.28
and n.29, 19 n.34, 22 n.41, 24 n.44,
25 n.46
graduate schools, 150ff.
graduate students, 150ff.

INDEX

Grady, Henry W., 156, 157, 166, 171; quoted, 155
"Granger" movement, 165
Grant, Ulysses S., 39, 41, 84, 85, 127, 136, 171
Gray, E. H., 30
Gray, John Chipman, 13 n.23
Gray, Wood, quoted, 100
Greeley, Horace, x, 39, 106, 115, 161; described, 25-26; quoted, 30; his *The American Conflict* described, 50
Green, Fletcher M., 249, 319, 321; described and quoted, 317-318
Guide to the Study of American History (E. Channing and A. B. Hart), quoted, 161

Hacker, Louis M., 228; described and quoted, 221-226
Hale, Edward Everett, quoted, 16
Hamilton, J. G. de R., 147
Hamilton, Peter J., 172
Hampton, Wade, quoted, 75-76
Handlin, Oscar, 317, 319, 320; described and quoted, 318
Hanna, Marcus Alonzo, 138-139, 198
"Harlem Renaissance," 242
Harmon, John J., cited, 217 n.35
Harper's Magazine, editors quoted, 221
Harper's Weekly, 73
Harrison, William Henry, 25, 30 n.55
Hart, Albert Bushnell, 135, 148, 152, 153; quoted, 161; as historian of the antislavery movement, 269-270
Harvard University, 150, 269, 273, 305, 306, 318
Haskins, Charles H., 151
Hay, John M., 62 n.18
Hayes, Rutherford B., 41, 121, 126
Hayne, Paul Y., 75 n.47
Headley, Joel Tyler, 33; described, 12-13; sale of his *The Great Rebellion*, 13 n.22; quoted, 15
Herring, Hubert, quoted, 199
Hicks, John D., quoted, 319
Higginson, Thomas Wentworth, 179
Hill, D. H., 76; quoted, 80, 89, 91-92, 95
historians; trained, 150ff., 190ff.; trained Southern historians, 154ff., 209, 231ff., 239ff.; trained Northern historians, 160ff.; and social reform, 195ff.
historical materialism, 199, 227
"Historical Revisions LIII" (D. W. Brogan), xi

histories of the Civil War, *see* Civil War, histories of
history, interpretation of, problems of "relativism" and "causation" discussed, vii-ix
History of American Life, A (A. M. Schlesinger and D. R. Fox), 190
History of England (T. B. Macaulay), 183
History of Negro Troops in the War of the Rebellion (G. W. Williams), 42
History of North America, 153
History of the American Civil War (J. W. Draper), described and quoted, 34-37; review of, in *The Nation*, quoted, 36
History of the American People (W. Wilson), 172
History of the Civil War in America, The (J. S. C. Abbott), sale of, 13 n.22
History of the Negro Race in America from 1619 to 1880 (G. W. Williams), 42
History of the People of the United States during Lincoln's Administration, A (J. B. McMaster), 183
History of the People of the United States from the Revolution to the Civil War, A (J. B. McMaster), 183, 184
History of the Rise and Fall of the Slave Power in America (H. Wilson), 39, 41, 50
History of the South, A, 246, 251
History of the United States (J. F. Rhodes), 161, 163, 295-296, 310, 317, 319; described and quoted, 140-146; reaction to by contemporaries, 146ff.
History of the United States (E. Channing), 182
History of the United States of America (J. Schouler), 129-130
Hitler, Adolf, 274
Hodder, Frank H., 263, 264, 298
Hodgson, Joseph, 76 n.48
Hofstadter, Richard, quoted, x
Holmes, Oliver Wendell, Jr., 322; quoted, x
Holst, Hermann Eduard Von, 131, 132, 161, 184, 319 n.44; described and quoted, 47-48; his popularity in 1870's and 1880's, 48; his *History* praised, 48-50
Holt, W. Stull, quoted, 173
Hotze, Henry, 66; quoted, 67-68
"house divided" speech of Lincoln, 22-23, 306
Houston, David F., 157; quoted, 158
Howells, William Dean, 124; quoted, 125
Hughes, Charles Evans, 140

· 340 ·

terpretation of S. A. Douglas, 142 n.40, 263, 264, 297; reaction to his views, 147ff., 259-260, 295-298, 317, 319; his views compared with those of U. B. Phillips, 235, 237, 238; his views criticized, 259-260; decline in reputation of, 295-298; his views compared with those of A. Nevins, 313-316; list of comments upon by contemporaries, 327-328
Richard "the Lion Hearted," 12
Rise of American Civilization, The (C. A. & M. R. Beard), 204, 207, 209, 210, 211, 213, 299
Rise of Silas Lapham, The (W. D. Howells), 124
Rise of the Dutch Republic (J. L. Motley), 7
"robber baron" evaluation of the results of the Civil War, 307
Robber Barons, The (M. Josephson), 213
Robinson, James Harvey, 196, 200, 201, 202; quoted, 197
Rockefeller, John D., 124, 151
Roman Catholics; and the slavery controversy, 101 n.4, 112-114; and Orestes Brownson, 112-114
Roman Empire, 74, 102
Roosevelt, Franklin D., 10, 15 n.25, 202, 241
Roosevelt, Theodore, 140, 258
Ropes, John Chipman, 13 n.23
Rowland, Dunbar, 160
Ruffin, Edmund, 56
Russians, 320

Sage, Bernard J., 88; described, 81-83
San Francisco, 68-69
Schlesinger, Arthur M., 190, 191 n.141; described and quoted, 305-307
Schlesinger, Arthur M., Jr., 317; described and quoted, 304-307, 318-321
Schlueter, Herman, 219 n.39
Schouler, James, 132, 133, 144, 149, 184; described and quoted, 129-131
Schurz, Carl, 3; quoted, 4
Scopes trial, 241-242
Scott, Dred, decision, 136
Scott, Sir Walter, viii
Scottsboro case, 243, 247
Scrugham, Mary, 262, 265, 266, 267, 270, 271, 273, 274, 275, 281; described and quoted, 257-260
"Second American Revolution" interpretation of the Civil War, 204ff., 212, 214, 220, 222ff.

Second World War, 243, 246, 274, 292, 304, 309, 311
sectional reconciliation, *see* reconciliation of North and South
sectionalism or sections, 174ff., 231ff., 250ff., 278ff.; "egocentric sectionalism," 248
Seligman, E. R. A., 200
Semmes, Raphael, 77
Sewanee Review, The, 156 n.76
Seward, William H., 29, 48, 63, 106, 142; his "irrepressible conflict" speech, 22-23, 306
Shanks, Henry T., 250
Shippee, L. B., quoted, 297
Simms, William Gilmore, 57 n.6
Simons, Algie M., 222, 228; and C. A. Beard, 204, 220; described and quoted, 217-219
Sitterson, Joseph Carlyle, 250
"slavepower," or "slavocracy," the, 37, 39-41, 48-49, 50, 130, 225, 226-227; "slavepower conspiracy," 24ff.
slavery, institution of, in United States, 205, 208, 212, 237, 266, 290, 296, 311ff., 317ff.; role in interpretations of causes of Civil War, ix, 163, 169; cause of Civil War, 6-7, 8, 11 n.19, 22ff., 36, 41, 42, 45, 48, 50, 51, 116, 129-130, 141ff., 159 n.81, 169ff., 175ff., 180-181, 189, 216, 226, 304ff., 313ff.; defense of, 24, 56, 58, 61, 65, 69-70, 89, 93, 101, 236ff.; not cause of Civil War, 61-62, 67-68, 72, 88-91, 93, 95, 235, 244ff., 247ff., 278ff.; various designations for, 89; criticism of, 133, 157ff., 166, 181, 207, 226-227, 232, 314; study of, 234ff., 298; disappearance of held likely had it been left alone, 236, 244ff., 268, 277, 315; *see also* Negro, slavepower
Smith, Benjamin G., 19 n.34, 21 n.39
Smith, Theodore Clarke, 135, 161 n.87; as historian of the anti-slavery movement, 269-270; quoted, 269
"Snow-Bound" (J. G. Whittier), quoted, 38
Social Forces in American History (A. M. Simons), 217, 219, 220
social history, 183ff.
Social Psychology (W. McDougall), 259
Socialist Labor Party, 217
Socialist Party, 215ff.
South, or Southern United States, ix, 136-137, 159, 166, 170, 204, 205; vindication of, by former Confederates, 74ff.;